Robert Anthony Bromley

A philosophical and critical history of the fine arts, painting, sculpture, and architecture:

With occasional observations on the progress of engraving, in it's several branches,

deduced from the earliest records - Vol. 1

Robert Anthony Bromley

A philosophical and critical history of the fine arts, painting, sculpture, and architecture:
With occasional observations on the progress of engraving, in it's several branches, deduced from the earliest records - Vol. 1

ISBN/EAN: 9783337730444

Printed in Europe, USA, Canada, Australia, Japan

Cover: Foto ©ninafisch / pixelio.de

More available books at **www.hansebooks.com**

A

PHILOSOPHICAL AND CRITICAL

HISTORY OF THE FINE ARTS,

PAINTING, SCULPTURE, and ARCHITECTURE:

WITH OCCASIONAL OBSERVATIONS ON

The Progrefs of ENGRAVING, in it's feveral Branches,

DEDUCED FROM THE EARLIEST RECORDS, THROUGH EVERY COUNTRY
IN WHICH THOSE ARTS HAVE BEEN CHERISHED, TO THEIR
PRESENT ESTABLISHMENT IN GREAT-BRITAIN,

UNDER THE AUSPICES OF

HIS MAJESTY KING GEORGE III.

IN FOUR PARTS.

VOLUME I.

By the Rev. ROBERT ANTHONY BROMLEY, B.D.
RECTOR OF ST. MILDRED'S IN THE POULTRY, AND MINISTER OF
FITZROY-CHAPEL, LONDON.

LONDON:
Printed at the PHILANTHROPIC-PRESS, St. George's Fields,
For THE AUTHOR; and fold by T. CADELL, in the Strand; J. ROBSON; and
HOOKHAM & Co. in Bond-Street; and C. DILLY, in the Poultry.
MDCCXCIII.

TO THE KING.

SIRE,

A HISTORY of the Fine Arts, making it's appearance in this age, can look up to no other character on the earth, at whofe feet it may throw itfelf fo properly and fo confidently for protection as before YOUR MAJESTY. In all the other fovereignties, and in all other countries, of the world, we only fee the relics of that patronage, of thofe fchools, and of thofe arts, which were once fo animated, and fo proudly brilliant.

Yet it is not merely by fucceffion that YOUR MAJESTY now ftands at the head of thefe. Their fame was never higher in the modern world than that which is now their claim in this country; and that fame is wholly the growth of your own reign. How old foever may have been the hiftory of thofe footfteps, by which they have been marked in Great Britain, the hiftory of their elegance and refined fpirit is comprized within the compafs of that period, which has given the generous and amiable influence of YOUR MAJESTY's exemplary mind to fpread it's general ornament over thefe kingdoms. It is a fact not to be queftioned, that in no æra of the arts, ancient or modern, they have been known to attain in any country, fo fpeedily as in this, thofe great and effential powers by which they are now diftinguifhed here. The emulations of genius will do wonders; but no emulation in the arts can rife to fo great fuccefs, without the concomitant encouragement of patronage iffuing from the fupreme influence in a country.

Yet that influence, SIRE, may prove equivocal in the ultimate value of thofe arts, if it does not fpring from a right foundation: the patronage, by which they are rightly elevated, muft not only be meafured by prudence, but muft be conducted on the pureft principles, or the meridian of thofe arts will be a fhort one, and inftead of aiding valuable knowledge, and perpetuating public or private honor, they may become debafed to the purpofes of legend, and falfehood, and perfonal adulation; their vigour may be fpent on thofe objects which are not worthy to be countenanced by wife and great minds.

How far fuch a genuine and principled patronage has gone along with the fine arts through the world, will appear in the progrefs of this work. The fhare which YOUR MAJESTY has in it, the character due to that protection, with which YOUR MAJESTY has taken up, and cherifhed, and reared, and eftablifhed thofe arts, and all that is elegant, in your empire, will not then ſtand on any ſuppoſed adulation, but on the uncontrovertible reſult of faƈts.

My utmoſt gratitude is, neverthelefs, due to YOUR MAJESTY for that generous permiſſion which you have given me to addreſs to your royal proteƈtion theſe humble endeavours to do juſtice to the intereſts of refined and elegant art.

That YOUR MAJESTY may long continue the bleſſing of a people univerfally ready to acknowledge their fenfe and eſtimation of it; and that you may long enjoy the pleaſure of ſeeing thoſe re-fined improvements both in arts and ſciences, which your reign has opened upon your dominions, more and more extended, is the ſincere prayer of

YOUR MAJESTY'S

MOST DUTIFUL,

AND MOST FAITHFUL SUBJECT,

FITZROY-CHAPEL,
Jan. 1, 1793.

Robert Anthony Bromley.

CONTENTS

OF VOLUME THE FIRST.

PART I.

THE GREAT AND LEADING PRINCIPLES, WHICH FORM THE HIGHER AND MORE IMPORTANT CHARACTERS OF PAINTING.

CHAP. V.

CHAP. VI.

CHAP. VII.

PART II.

THE PROGRESS AND PATRONAGE OF THE FINE ARTS IN THE ANCIENT WORLD.

BOOK I.

ASIA.

CHAP. I.

CHAP. II.

Fewer traces of the fine arts in Meſopotamia, becauſe it was the fate of

CHAP III.

CHAP IV.

BOOK II.

EGYPT.

CHAP. I.

CHAP. II.

CHAP. III.

BOOK III.

GREECE.

CHAP. I.

Preliminary obfervations on the general turn of mind, and fome national policy, of the Greeks, which were favourable to perfection in
the arts—the means by which they obtained the firft knowledge of thofe
arts from Afia and Egypt—the Greeks themfelves not improbably a
people of Afiatic defcent—the Pelafgi from Caucafus fettled in Greece
—the principles of Scythian theology introduced by the Pelafgi, and
not loft in Greece under all the variations of their own fubfequent mythologies, and the multiplicity of deities that fprang from thence—
thofe principles of Scythicifm the fource of the earlieft Grecian fculpture, which was all emblematic, and fo continued to the age of Dædalus—coins and other fculptures, and characters of writing too, capable
of being afcertained in Greece before the arrival of Cadmus—fculpture pufhed in thofe early ages by many circumftances not fo immediately felt by painting—the heroic ages, however, not favourable to great

CHAP. II.

CHAP. III.

CHAP. IV.

The general character of Grecian architecture, as fuperior to that
which had ever been feen before—the Greeks original in that fuperior
character—original alfo in the conftitution of an order, although
they might be led to it by obfervations of what had been done elfewhere—the antiquity of their firft order, the Doric—the procefs of the
orders on philofophic principles, according to which the Grecian mind
decided every thing—every poffible character proper for the variety of
architectural ftructure provided for in thofe orders, whofe principles
no caprice of fubfequent ages has been able to move or vary—the
eftablifhment of a diftinct character, founded on a ftrict attention
to the nature of things, the fixed object of the Greeks in each of
their orders—the extent with which that diftinct character was maintained by them in every part and portion of an edifice, fo as to form
a compleat whole, a very important and curious fpeculation—the
philofophy of engaging our moft rational fenfations aimed at and
accomplifhed in a moft ftriking manner by their architecture—that·
object greatly affifted by their ftudies and their powers to produce
harmony—how that harmony was effected—the affinity which has been
fuppofed by many to fubfift between the meafures of architecture and
mufic—the great caution with which any arbitrary invafions of the
Grecian examples, and efpecially of the principles of their orders,

CHAP. V.

A

PHILOSOPHICAL AND CRITICAL

HISTORY OF THE FINE ARTS, &c.

PART. I.

The great and leading principles, which form the higher and more important characters of painting.

CHAP. I.

Painting, considered as simple design, coeval with man, and the original writing of Nature.

THE history of painting is almost coeval with that of mankind. We would be understood to speak of it as simple design, which gives the proper foundation of the art. For doubtless the use of colours was a subsequent improvement, which has been growing at all times. This hinders not, however, but that the earliest drawings, or those which soon succeeded the earliest, might have the addition of those simple colourings, which common and early use might suggest to the untutored mind, and of which the savages in every part of the world have furnished to those who have first visited them a variety of specimens*. No contradiction can be given to the idea, that

---

* Mœurs des Sauvages, t. 2 p. 43, 44. Lettr. Edif. t. 17. p. 303, 304.

the firſt inhabitants of the earth knew the uſe of ſimple colours
for common purpoſes.   Coals, charcoal, chalk, &c. would ſerve
them very early.   And it would not be long before they would
come to the knowledge of other colours, the uſes of which
they would naturally extend.   Semiramis lived in very early days
after the flood, if we follow the uſual calculation of her age:
Diodorus Siculus ſpeaks of paintings done by her order in colours;
and what he has handed down on that ſubject the reader will
weigh with attention when he ſhall hereafter meet it.

It has been a common idea that painting was not in uſe
before the Trojan war.   If that be meant with reſpect to the
Greeks, and in the ampleſt ſenſe of the art as a combination
of colours, it may be true; but it can only be meant with reſpect to them: in any other relation, the idea muſt ariſe from
an extreme want of acquaintance with the arts of remote antiquity.   And with reſpect to the Greeks, it appears from the
authority of Homer, that in the time of that war they were
in the habit of painting other things*, if not the general repreſentation of objects, with colours of various kinds.   Nor is it
any proof to the contrary, that the word κυανος, moſt frequently
employed by Homer, ſpecifically expreſſes an azure colour,
which is a compoſition of mere white and black.

As the Greeks, therefore, in the drawings of their pencil
were in poſſeſſion of ſeveral colours, ſo we muſt ſuppoſe that
the early attempts, which Nature and neceſſity dictated to men, of
communicating their thoughts and recording circumſtances by

* Iliad, lib. 2. v. 144.   Lib. 11. v. 628.

drawings of fenfible objects, were not confined merely to lineal figures, but embraced fuch further aid of the few fimple colours which fcanty experience had put into their hands, as may juftify us in referring the origin of painting to a primitive period.

If, indeed, we were nicely to look into the origin of the art, as an expreffion of defign, it would feem in fome refpect to lofe it's name; for beyond all doubt it is innate in man. It is Nature herfelf in her firft rudiments; and Nature herfelf muft be forfworn, whenever this art is loft, or but retained with neglect. The talent of imitation is univerfal in man. It was neceffarily univerfal in the firft of the human race. Through long fucceffions of time man knew not how to write. He had no alternative but painting, by which he muft fpeak to the abfent. And the firft ufe of his fenfes taught him readily what to do. His own fhadow became the guide to his own image. Pliny*, the great interpreter of Nature, afferts that the firft picture was nothing elfe but the fhadow of a man drawn about with lines. He gives, indeed, the example in a girl of Sicyon, Corinthia by name. But Nature never waited till Corinthia's time for the firft exemplification of the principle. When once a man had thus obtained the image of himfelf, the next ftep of thought led him not only to his own image without his own fhadow, but by the eye alone to that of every other creature: and one, or a few fteps more, would give him the peculiar diftinction of one fpecies from another, or of one individual from another in the fame fpecies. From thofe fimple documents he

* Nat. Hift. lib. 35. c. 3.

would prefently take the range of univerfal Nature obvious to
his view.   He would naturally paint fmoke rifing in the air, if
he meant to write of a fire.   If an individual were killed, he
would reprefent one man lying on the ground, and another
ftanding over him with an inftrument of death in his hand.   If
a ftranger arrived in his country by fea, he would draw as
well as he could the reprefentation of a man fitting in a fhip.

Unqueftionably thofe firft effays of the art were very rude.
The human mind, though wonderfully ingenious when it has
caught firft principles, is as wonderfully flow in it's way to the
fimpleft operations, where thofe firft principles are themfelves
to be obtained.   Yet we cannot help thinking, that when
Ælian fays*, it was no uncommon thing in thofe earlier effays
of painting to fubfcribe under the figures, " this is an ox ;"
" this is a horfe ;" " this is a tree ;" he has rather overcharged
the faEt as a general one.   Let it have been fpoken of mankind
when and where it might, we may judge very fairly of what the
general rudenefs of Nature was likely to produce in this way
from what we know of the natives of South America, than whom
there was no part of the earth in it's remoter periods more fhut
out from foreign intercourfe, and confequently lefs benefited
by communication with ftrangers.   Thefe, till they were difcovered by the Spaniards, were doubtlefs felf-taught : Nature
was their only inftruEtor : and they are proved, even in Mexico,
to have been as rude in moft of the arts as almoft any people
that ever had Nature only for their guide.   In the art of which
we are fpeaking, fays a candid and able inquirer† into their

* Var. Hift. lib. 10. c. 10.   † Robertfon's Hift. of America, V. 3. p. 205.

hiftory, " their performances may be confidered as the earlieft
" and moft imperfect effay of men in their progrefs towards the
" difcovery of the art of writing." Yet thefe people knew how
to paint with a better effect than Ælian reprefents. The Mexicans, when invaded by the Spaniards, fent intelligence of the
event to Montezuma, their prince, by paintings, in which were
drawn the figures of every thing that attended their invaders*.
Thofe pictures were taken as the ordinary means of information, and they needed no key or explanation to the Mexican
monarch. They were taken too on cotton cloth, on which it
would be fomewhat neceffary, for the retention of defign, not
only to draw, but to colour too. Thefe methods of original
writing were fo effectual, that Cortes, having invaded the country, became afterwards indebted to their aid for the prefervation of his life. A confpiracy was formed to deftroy him, of
which being apprifed by a piece of cloth defcribing the portraits of the confpirators and their plans, he was enabled to
efcape the danger with which he was threatened. To fuch an
extent had thofe uncivilized Mexicans advanced in that way
of writing, that a book of figures, being in fact a book of their
letters, was given as a prefent to Cortes by Montezuma†.

To return to our purpofe. In thofe Mexican paintings we
have a moft fatisfactory proof that the talent of picture-writing
was original to mankind in a ftate of Nature, and neceffary
for their converfing with each other at a diftance. It was a
talent enjoyed alike by all. We find it not only where we
difcover the firft beginnings of the finer arts, but wherever we

* Robertfon's Hift. of America, V. 2 .p. 266. Acofta, lib. 7. c. 24. Raynal Hift.
Ind. V. 2. p. 370.　　　† Gomara's Hift. of the Indies.

obtain a hiſtory. Ancient ſtories are full of this talent as a
principle of writing. The claſſical reader will recollect the
beautiful fable of Philomela, who had no other reſource but
that *ſilent voice*, as Achilles Tatius elegantly calls it, conveyed
in a veſture which ſhe had woven for the purpoſe of deſcribing
on it what ſhe had ſuffered, and by which ſhe diſcovered to the
eyes of Progne, as effectually as any words would have related
to his ear, the ſituation in which ſhe was then placed*. It was
the firſt talent of writing employed by the Egyptians†. The
Phœnicians ſeem originally to have known no other method‡.
The old Ethiopians, whom Diodorus Siculus imagines to have
been the moſt ancient of all nations, wrote, he ſays, in the
ſame manner. The modern Chineſe characters are evidently
derived from this primitive practice§. And we may reaſonably
infer that the ſame practice originally prevailed among the
Greeks, becauſe in their language to paint and to write are
both expreſſed by one and the ſame word (γραφειν.)

Such an univerſal concurrence in the firſt ſtages of every
ſociety, when the want of communication with others muſt
have precluded the general means of imitation, ſhews indiſputa-
bly the force of Nature, and the attention with which ſhe impreſſed this talent on the human mind. But when we look forward to the comprehenſive powers which it has reached in the
progreſs of time, and conſider the ſplendor with which it ſhines
among the finer arts, the bounty of Nature in this ſingle inſtance ſuſpends for a while every other admiration of her

* Achilles Tatius, lib. 5.   Ovid's Metam. lib. 6.
† Tacit. Annal. lib. 11. c. 14.   Eſſai ſur les Hierogly. des Egyptiens, p. 28, 48, 114.
‡ Ibid. p. 26.   § Ibid. p. 35.

works. She has been liberal to man in the variety of neceſſary gifts: ſhe has adorned his mind with various portions of excellence: but when ſhe gave the talent, of which we are now ſpeaking, ſhe eſtabliſhed her claim to the never-ceaſing gratitude of the human race, which, without the introduction of ſo early and ſtrong a tuition, might hardly have hoped to attain an art that uſurps ſuch a compaſs of refinement, and calls for ſuch an infinity of ſkill;—from whoſe principles indeed has flowed whatever contributes to fill the name of the arts.

How the ruder traits of this *natural art*, if I may uſe the expreſſion, moved forward through the ſucceſſive gradations of ſubſtituting a part for the whole of a figure, then of putting one figure to ſignify many ideas, next of the ſymbolic or hieroglyphic character, afterwards of the ſyllabic by ſigns, till at laſt it reached the wonderful perfection of alphabetic writing, is not to our preſent purpoſe, which is content with ſhewing that it was the important voice of Nature ſpeaking in an uniform tone to the firſt capacities of mankind. And as it was Nature in it's origin, ſo ſhe has kindly watched over it's progreſs ever ſince, till in it's cultivation it has become the very ſummit of art. If it's firſt attempts have been degraded by the ſubſequent perfection of writing, it has triumphed in it's turn over it's rival, and by the improvements which it has acquired from time and from it's own infinite ſource of excellence, it has far outſtripped all writing in the magnitude of it's effect, in the ſcope, and force, and dignity, and univerſality of it's inſtruction. Theſe points are worthy of conſideration. We will endeavour to elucidate them.

PAINTING.

CHAP. II.

The advantages of painting, in an improved state, over all other modes of writing.

——————

SECT. I.

In the scope of instruction.

THE best composition of language can but display it's subject in progressive detail. It is not given to words to bring within the compass of their illustration more than one circumstance at one time. There must necessarily be an order of narration; and the mind must wait to receive from that order whatever events the narration supplies, let it be ever so impatient in it's expectations. Indeed the mind will be impatient, wherever the detail is interesting: it will anticipate what the tardiness of language has not been able to bring forward: it will often conceive more than it finds involved in the narrative: and it always feels a contrast to the quickness and comprehension of it's own ideas in the progressiveness which is inevitable to all ideas cloathed in words. Thus it is, whenever the mind is fed by the instrumentality of language.

But let the pencil give it's colouring to the subject, and the eye become the inlet to the instruction, and with one glance of the eye the mind seizes the whole; as with a single glance of it's own thought it can often take the largest range, and make itself commensurate to the most copious matter. Nor is this

with any difadvantage to thofe parts of the ftory, which language
would bring forward with it's beft colouring ; nor with any lofs
of thofe fecondary circumftances, to which the pen can give
their part in the general fcene, with all the variety and exactnefs
of expreffion. For while in a well-ordered picture, the mind
grafps the whole at once, it huddles together nothing : it difcriminates with perfect facility the bolder and the fainter fituations : and it feels in an inftant all thofe proportions of fenfibility which arife from the refpective fituation, and which in the
hands of the ableft penman, would employ the labour of pages
to illuftrate. A picture, fays Philoftratus*, pourtrays in one
forcible view what is already done, what is doing, and what is
yet to be done; not flightly paffing over each, but finifhing
what belongs to every circumftance, as if that alone were the
main object.

Let us take an example for our purpofe. The death of
Hector, and particularly in that moment when his body was
brought back into Troy, will give us one in every way circumftanced to do juftice to our fentiment. On the fide of
writing, it has every advantage that writing can have—the moft
mafterly difplay of the moft original and lofty poet, who was
equal not only to the firft attractions that could be given to real
incident, but to the livelieft and yet the correcteft fallies of
imagination—who knew human nature confummately well,
knew where and how to give the fineft touches to it's feelings,
and was perfectly poffeffed of that great touchftone of true
erudition, the art of coming by the fhorteft and choiceft ex-

* Iconum, lib. 1. in Bofporo.

preffions to the moft forcible ideas ; with a language too in his
hands, which by it's peculiar combinations was moft happily
calculated to facilitate this point.

Befides this, if ever there was a fubject that could call forth
the abilities of a Homer, that could make him collect himfelf,
and pour forth all the animation of his mind to meet with all
imaginable rapidity the ardent expectations of his readers, it
was that great event, fo fraught with every thing that could
ftrike a feeling mind, or fuggeft impatience to a curious one,
becaufe fo difaftrous to all that hero's family, fo fatal to the
city whofe gallant defender he had been, fo final to every hope,
and fo ruinous in it's whole complexion, that beyond it nothing farther was left for that exalted writer to extend his poem.

He has done as much as the pen in the hand of Genius could
do to croud that grand event into the fmalleft compafs. Scarcely
three common pages are employed, in which almoft every line,
and often words themfelves, are a fentence. He has beftowed
lefs upon embellifhment than ever poet or writer beftowed on
the like occafion ; for, in fact, every incident and expreffion
that Nature and fituation dictated, were themfelves the very
quinteffence of embellifhment. He has evidently haftened to
the principal group, in which was centered all the force and dignity and pathos of the fcene ; at the fame time that in touching
more lightly the introductory and furrounding images, language
could not give to each a more pointed felection of expreffion.

Yet what reader does not feel even the language and the
difpatch of Homer in this inftance, too flow for the anxiety

with which his mind fwells to anticipate all that is untold? We no fooner fee with Caffandra from the tower the aged father returning with his dear fon's remains, but we are eager to behold, before words can tell us, the afflicted throng that burfts in cries from the Trojan gates, to take their laft view of their loft protector; but, moft of all, to hear the heart-rending diftrefs of the widowed Andromache, with her defolate infant, and the maternal lamentations of the aged Hecuba. We are repaid indeed for waiting the progrefs of the narrative in the mingled tears of the generous, grateful, Helen, which give us more perhaps than the imagination could have ftretched itfelf to meet, but which form the fineft clofe to the character of the beloved hero, over whom it is natural indeed that a fond mother and a diftracted wife fhould hang in bitter lamentations : but when Helen weeps for the lofs of that amiable friend, whofe mild and kind deportment towards her, under circumftances which had fhaken the temper of almoft every one in Priam's houfe, was invariable to the laft ; this gives a finifh to the fcene, and endears to every reader the univerfally-lamented man, who now becomes not more the darling of his family, and of his country, than the darling of humanity.

But might not all this fcope of detail be embraced by the pencil with the fame effect, nay, with a more abundant one? forafmuch as the whole is caught at once upon the canvas, and abides upon the fenfes ; whereas in the poem it rifes only in fucceffion, wherein every fucceding gratification treads out in fome degree the impreffion of that which is gone by. Caffandra on the top of Pergamus, announcing the arrival of the body, and calling to the Trojans—the Trojan throng affembled below—

are circumftances which doubtlefs fpeak with more variety and glow of expreffion on the canvas than any language can give them. The weeping matrons and the infant around the body are beheld with no lefs ftriking effect. If there is any thing in which the poet may feem to have the advantage over the painter, it is perhaps in that great effort of pathetic, beyond which fobs muft choak all farther utterance of the heart-broken Andromache—" O! that thou hadft, in thy laft moments, " grafped my hand in thine, and faid fomething which I might " have remembered day and night, amidft my tears, for ever!" But why may not Andromache, hanging with ftreaming eyes over her loft hufband—his hand clafped in her's—her every feature marking affection mingled with agony—the hopelefs wifh juft ftarting from her lips—fpeak the fame fentiment with the fame eloquence? Even the ftiller grief of friendfhip in the Grecian Helen is capable of being expreffed by the pencil, and perhaps with a ftronger contraft to the more interefting and vehement diftrefs of the two Trojan matrons than the poet has given her; while her's and Hecuba's certainly contribute to form the grand climax of grief, which has it's completion in Andro-mache.

An anecdote of the two Carachi fhall clofe my obfervations here, and it will fpeak their purpofe more ftrongly than reafoning. One day, as they were in company, Auguftin took occafion to harangue on the excellencies of ancient fculpture, and in the courfe of his obfervations he was very earneft in praife of the Laocoon. Perceiving his brother Hannibal turned towards the wall, as if he paid no attention to the fubject, he ftopped a moment to rebuke him for his apparent indifference,

and then went on.   Prefently it was obferved that Hannibal had
been drawing on the wall, with a piece of coal, the whole group
of figures, on which his brother had fo long expatiated.   Not
only the reft of the company, but Auguftin himfelf, was fo
ftruck with the drawing, that he proceeded no further, de-
claring it was in vain to fay more, after what was before their
eyes.   Whereupon Hannibal, having finifhed his defign, turned
to the company, with this *bon mot*, " Poets paint with words,
" and painters fpeak with the pencil*.

SECT. II.

In the force of inftruction.

IF the painter can give a larger fcope to his fubject at one view,
he muft entertain and inftruct the mind with more force, than
the writer.   For where more caufes are combined and concentered together, the ftronger and more copious will be the effect.
Where the mind is affailed at once by the whole intereft of any
important fubject, it will certainly be captivated with the greateft power.   The fire which gathers in an inftant from many
quarters will be more intenfe than that which lingers in it's
progrefs.   What is it that moft forcibly excites genuine admiration in any cafe?   It is a great affemblage of admirable objects uniting in a whole, not the beft pofition of any fingle object or incident, nor of many given in detached views. It is true,
the pen can enter into all the minutiæ of language, and make
it's way by a thoufand little avenues to many of our feelings:
but it is from the ftronger and more marked affections, not from

* Bellori in vita Hannib.   Carachi, p. 31.   Felib. des Peintres, V. 3. p. 266, 7.

the niceft feleftion or colouring of words, that inftruftion rifes,
and the mind is impreffed with a moral. And there is no doubt
but every paffion that aftuates the human breaft is fully as much
in the power of the pencil, as of the pen, to delineate. Why
are we more affefted by a fpeech delivered immediately from the
lips of any great public fpeaker, than we fhould be by the fame
fpeech committed to writing, or than we are affefted by thofe
very orations of Tully or Demofthenes, which, we know, captivated whole affemblies, and carried them away as by a torrent? It is, becaufe the fcene itfelf is before us: we behold the
image and the animation of the fpeaker, and the images and
animation of the furrounding audience: from thence we catch
the fire ourfelves, and become involuntarily affefted. If it is
not the fame in faft, when thefe are fpread upon the canvas,
yet it is the fame in principle. And, in the opinion of Quintilian, it is the fame, in faft, upon the canvas, at leaft as to all
the effefts of oratory: " Piftura, tacens opus, et habitus femper
" ejufdem, fic intimos penetret affeftus, ut ipfam vim dicendi
" nonnunquam fuperare videatur *." The images do not indeed fpeak here, but they are alive to the fight, and they have
an eloquence peculiar to themfelves. Like thofe celeftial bodies, which the great Defigner of the univerfe has fpread to
our view upon the canopy of heaven, " there is (in the beau-
" tiful expreffion of holy writ) neither fpeech nor language in
" them, neverthelefs their voices are heard," as much to the
purpofe, and as audibly to the intelligent, as if they poffeffed
the moft articulate utterance. In the fpeaking and the filent
figure the medium is the fame; the eye informs the mind in

* Inft. Orat. 11. 3.

both—the eye, whofe fenfe conveys a far ftronger impreffion than that of the ear, as thofe will acknowledge who have had the misfortune to lofe the former, or any one who is fituated in a public auditory with the opportunity only of enjoying the latter. In the fpeaking figure the advantage indeed is pre-eminent, as it can gratify the fenfibility of the ear, as well as that of the eye; whereas the beft writing in the world can appeal in that way to neither.

Turn to the Acts of the Apoftles, and you find Paul preaching at Athens. Make allowance that you read his fpeech only in the abftract. You read in it the ftrong and fober reafoning of an enlightened mind, arguing to the profeffors of reafon, and from their own mifapplied principles overfetting idolatry, and confounding it's fupporters in the philofophic fchools. But go to the Vatican, and there behold that great apoftle, as the pencil of Raphael has given him, ftanding up in the Areopagus, firm, bold, and impaffioned, furrounded with his epicurean and ftoic opponents, in whom is marked all that variety of feelings which would characterize an affembly, of which " fome ftill " doubted," and others a little fhaken in their prejudices proffered " to hear him again :" then fay, in which of thofe reprefentations the apoftle's fpirit appears moft " ftirred within him," and by which of them the fpirit of your own mind is moft completely affected.

SECT. III.

In the dignity of instruction.

Nor is there less dignity, than force and scope, in the instruction which the pencil can give. Writing must cede the palm to it in this instance. What is it that gives dignity to language, and makes the sublime of expression completely full? Most certainly, it is action; that action, which lifts every scene to it's best moment, because it is the full and real exhibition of Nature, to which the artificial exhibition of her by words only holds a secondary place. To obtain this action, it is not necessary that words should be employed: for we all know, that if a man be perfectly silent, and in a striking attitude calculated to express any strong emotion of the soul, he shall give to those who behold him all the feeling that words could convey, and often infinitely more*. The dumb give proofs of this, and the deaf receive proofs of it, every day. Every pantomime speaks this truth: and the pantomimes of the ancients spoke it more strongly: " I understand you, your hands speak," exclaimed a philosopher of old to one of those mute actors. The entertainment, which of itself might be trifling enough, gains an importance from the earnestness of action, by which it is not beneath the attention of philosophy to be arrested.

If this is true of the silent figure, it is equally true of it, whether exhibited on the canvas, or standing on the ground. The criterion is, if the passion be preserved, and given in it's own energy; and if so, the effect is obtained, Nature is digni-

* Quint. Inst. Orat. 11. 3.

fied in the exhibition, and the inftruction is given as potent as it can come from Nature. Thus far the canvas claims, in common with real life, that action which lifts every fcene, and unaided by which the fineft writing in the world lofes many gradations of dignity.

But that action, powerful as it is to elevate, is only one among many circumftances which conftitute the variety of powers to be claimed by the pencil exclufively for it's own, as the fources of dignity to it's fcenes, which no writing whatever can emulate. The moft fuperficial obferver of paintings muft have marked the advantages they derive from the difpofition of the whole—the keeping of all the parts—the harmonious effects of colouring—the powers of light and fhade—fituation, attitude, and drefs—the power of contraft—and, not leaft of all, the power of combining, for the grandeur of effect, any circumftances which are connected with the fubject, or which are not unnatural, although they do not make a part of the fame moment, nor are connected in ftrictnefs with the fame incident.

In the laft of thefe powers the dignity of fubject finds a very important intereft; and it is employed with reafon, becaufe it is no more than a licence to fet forth the fubject in the beft poffible view. No circumftance can fhew more ftrongly than this the advantage which the pencil enjoys over the pen. For hardly ever did a fcene or incident arife, in which Nature or accident was kind enough to fhape every circumftance fo happily as to give a perfect difplay to the whole. But the painter breaks through thofe difadvantages and fetters. His narrative muft be finifhed, and his fcene muft be dignified. Heliodorus

in the hiftory*, having wickedly pillaged the temple of Jerufalem, is driven out of it by two young men miraculoufly fent
from God, who fcourge him feverely, ftanding on either fide of
him.   But when Raphael tells the ftory by his pencil, he gives
greater decorum and a nobler elevation to the fcene, reprefenting
the two figures as fufpended in the air, in a fwift motion towards
Heliodorus, but without wings, and therefore not decidedly
marked as angels, which might not have been warranted.
Again: when the fame great mafter defcribed the fire at Rome,
which approached the Vatican, and is faid (among the feries of
popifh miracles) to have been extinguifhed by Leo IV. on his
making the fign of the crofs; however devoted to the legend, the
painter thought fit to confult the greater dignity and animation of the piece, and perhaps, as he thought, of the miracle
too, by defcribing a high wind agitating the flames, and involving all things in hurry and confufion.

Thefe are powers, with which the canvas can fwell and exalt it's fubjects beyond any capacities of writing.   They are
powers, by which may be expreffed a multitude of ideas not
poffible to be communicated by any other means that are not
fupernatural.   And they are powers, in which there is no medium.   They either fpeak with dignity, or they have no effect.
They either exalt the reprefentation, or they become themfelves
degraded.   Every painting, to fpeak of it correctly, is either
divine or poor.   We are charmed by it, or we bear not to
look on it.   It is like mufic, which fills and lifts every paffion
it touches, or it is empty, and tires the ear.   And in either of
thefe fifter-arts we fo much expect this perfection, that if we do

* 2 Maccab. cap. 3.

not meet it, we endure nothing fhort of it; becaufe whatever is fhort of it, is not the art.

On the other hand, in writing, although poffeffing much merit, mediocrity is common, and all proportions of mediocrity. And this we bear in any of it's proportions, without being difgufted. Provided the compofition repays our inquiry by it's matter, although it be dreffed in no graces of diftion, we can read it, and repeat the reading of it, with confiderable fatisfaftion. The reafon is, we do not neceffarily look there for a dignity of ftyle. We do not confider that as indifpenfible either to our inftruftion or our pleafure. But will any man bear to bring his eyes repeatedly on a painting, whofe inftruftion is humbly and coarfely delivered?

When therefore the powers of the pencil are exerted with that force of which they are capable, we may fafely appeal to every man's feelings, whether the canvas or the hiftoric page has left upon his mind loftier and more exalted ideas of the fame fubjeft. We will mention one as loftily conceived, and as fublimely expreffed, in thofe writings wherein it is found, as any that can be felefted, becaufe it flows not from human thought, it is pure matter of divine revelation : I mean the general refurreftion, or the laft judgement. Let us not fuppofe that the pencil is inferior to the reach of this exalted fubjeft. It has already come from the hands of fome great mafters in prodigious grandeur. But we have no hefitation to affirm that it has never been embraced by the pencil in the beft manner of which it is capable, in that purenefs of enlightened impreffion with which we fhould expeft to fee it filled, after what has been revealed. This may feem a bold affertion, when two fuch mafters as Michael Angelo and Rubens look this affertion in the face. But the work of the former may more fitly be called the pagan, or at leaft the popifh, laft judgement, than the gofpel one : in point of *thought,* it is certainly faulty in many parts ; although in point of *defign* and *execution* through all it's parts, and as a great *whole,* it is the ftandard of art. The work of the latter, although wonderful in thought, and indeed every thing as far as it goes, yet is but partial in it's extent. It is therefore referved ftill for the pencil to fhew what can be done completely on that great fubject, which is fo peculiarly calculated for the affemblage of all it's powers. Thofe powers, we truft, will one day give that divine profpect to be contemplated by the human mind in all the fulnefs of it's own pure grandeur. Does the weight of fcriptural impreffion peculiarly forbid this? Try it by what has been done. Try it by the cartons of Raphael. Let any man read any of thofe fubjects in the facred book, and then take a view of the carton. Let him turn over the divine page ever fo often, and as often return to the carton: he will affuredly carry back from the picture not only nobler and more enlarged conceptions of the greateft part of thofe fubjects than the facred writer has left upon him, but nobler and more enlarged conceptions newly encreafing at every view. Thefe effects are not produced, becaufe the facred writers were defective, but becaufe they were writers, and becaufe words can never convey fuch ideas as may be brought to flow from fuch a pencil as Raphael's.

SECT. IV.

In the univerſality of inſtruction.

If the pen could equal the pencil in the ſcope, and force, and dignity of it's repreſentations, ſtill it can only communicate a partial inſtruction. It can only ſpeak to thoſe who have been taught it's language, and even to thoſe it is often involved in obſcurity and doubt. But were it ever to clear, ſince the ideas it conveys depend not for their preſervation on any actual forms or images brought home to the mind, but merely on ſounds or arbitrary marks, it muſt be tranſient in it's effects. The pencil, on the contrary, in it's improved ſtate, employs an univerſal language, intelligible to all in every country, and in every period of time—a language, which ſpeaks to multitudes at once, and to ſucceſſive generations ; and when once impreſſed on the mind, retains an abidance there, which time can rarely efface—a language, which needs no tedious ſtudy to acquire, but conveys it's ideas as it were by inſpiration. For Nature has given to the whole human race a common ſenſibility of the ordinary paſſions which move within them, the actions by which thoſe paſſions ſhew themſelves, and the general ſemblances of things ; ſo that every man, whether enlightened or not, can with much facility diſcern when any of thoſe paſſions or ſemblances are marked. Carry to any part of the world the " laſcivious women of Lewis Carachi," and although many perſons may not be able to explain the ſtory, which depends on a different kind of knowledge, you ſhall preſently be told that they were come to tempt that pious man in the garden. Let the Spartan boy, who ſo induſtriouſly hugs the fox which is eating into him, be ſeen where it may, it ſhall be declared to be the repreſentation of extroardinary pati-

ence in fome youth, or of fome rigid determination in him,
when he perfifts to conceal the animal at the rifque of his life.
What man in any fituation or ftage of fociety, who had ever
feen or heard of a battle, would fail to pronounce our " Wolfe"
to be the picture of fome great commander who died in the
moment of victory?

There are fubjects immediately growing out of this univerfality
of picture-language, in which words can give no affiftance ; fubjects, which form fome of the firft delights to the rational mind,
and often no inconfiderable inftruction.   Of this fort are all the
great fcenes of Nature, the fcenes of animal and vegetative life,
the beauties of perfpective and of local fituation, the improvements of manufactures and other arts, the treafures of productions which draw the laborious naturalift through inhofpitable
feas and climates.   Here the language of painting reigns not
only the fupreme, but the fole, arbitrefs ; and makes itfelf underftood alike by every individual through the earth.

Carry your view a little further, and you prefently find the
language of the world as much indebted to the pencil for it's
fuller elucidation of their own narratives, as ever the pencil
could be indebted to them.   Apelles proved this to his great
advantage, when he had been thrown by a tempeft into Egypt,
and was drawn by a falfe meffage delivered by fome ftranger to
go and fup with the king, who was known to have conceived by
fome means an invincible hatred againft him in Alexander's
court : what would have become of him under the indignation
of the monarch, who thought himfelf purpofely infulted, if the
art of the painter had not helped him more than his language
could do, by drawing on the wall with coal the picture of the

man who had betrayed him into that meafure*? When the hiftorian relates any of the great actions of old, or in any wife touches the fubject of antique, how fhall he make us rightly underftand him, where he fpeaks of arms and habiliments, of ornaments and fymbols? Here all muft be unintelligible, till the pencil affords it's defcription. So thought the heroes returning from the Trojan war, or fo thought the poets for them, when by fome fuch defcription they made familiar to Penelope the city of Troy, and all the operations of the fiege†: and fo thought Æneas, when by fome fuch defcription he illuftrated the fame fubjects to Calypfo‡. Vegetius§ therefore infifts, that painters, or thofe who could defign, fhould make a part of every legion in an army.

If we confult what we read, we fhould be apt to come into the opinion, that words at no time inform us perfectly, without reference to the painter's art. We fly of neceffity to his univer-fal affiftance. No man ever reads a fcene, or incident, or cha-racter, but he converts the words into an image, and fancies the fcene, or incident, or character to exift before him in fuch fhape as the writing has led him to conceive. The more animated the writing is, the more the mind haftens to fhape the image that rifes out of it: the ftronger and more perfpicuous that image is to the eye of the mind, the more perfect and accomplifhed is the writing, and the more are we affected by the reading. If writing fails to raife fuch an image within us, it is then poor and indifferent, or we are liftlefs towards it. Shall we hefitate then to pronounce, that of all the languages in the world that of the pencil is moft copious and univerfal?

---

* Plin. lib. 35. c. 10.   † Ovid's Epift. Heroid.
‡ Ovid de Arte, &c. lib. 2.   § De re Militari, lib. 2. c. 2.

CHAP. III.

*The display of moral subjects the purest office of painting, as a
mean of instruction.*

THE review we have given of painting, as taught and endowed
by Nature, is not merely a theoretical descant on it's excellence,
irrelevant to any uses that may be derived from it. We see it
to be an eminent gift of Nature for the purpose of instruction.
Whatever purpose, therefore, it may serve besides, if it does
not instruct, it is certainly lowered in it's exercise ; and the age
or country, whose taste shall be found to predominate in a departure from that superior purpose, is unquestionably debased
in it's taste, proportionably to the stages of that departure.

Pursuing that great feature of the art, we cannot resist the
conclusion, that moral painting, under which term we include
all that is historical or poetical, all that conveys a lesson, is it's
noblest display. Is there any other branch of it's exercise, to
which an equal measure of abilities is called ? Is there any other,
therefore, that conveys a higher idea of it's destination? The
moral painter must be strong in the resources of invention or
genius—in taste, which corrects and chastens these—in judgement, which adapts their ideas to the immediate spirit and object of the scene—in an intimate acquaintance with Nature,
which enables him to embellish, if not to follow, what is written
—in an accurate knowledge of the human frame, it's outward
organization, and it's inward affections—in the knowledge of
symmetry, perspective, and even general architecture. These, in

addition to an excellence in compofition and decorum, are indifpenfible to fill the mind, and guide the hand, of the man who
paints to inftruct. In other words, he muft participate to a
certain degree the gifts of the hiftorian, the poet, the philofopher, the anatomift, the geometrician, the naturalift, and the
architect. Like the bee, he muft extract the juices from various
flowers, before he can form that excellent compound of his art,
which gives to the mind, as honey does to the tongue, a delici-
oufnefs of tafte not to be gathered from a lefs excurfive range,
nor to be compaffed by any other fkill.

What a lofty idea does this give us of an art, which grafps fo
wide a compafs of talents, and calls for a portion of whatever re-
fines and enlarges the human mind? And how much below the
natural level, which this art is calculated to maintain, do they
reduce it, who make it fubfervient to fubjects in which hardly
any one of thofe liberal gifts is interefted, and from which therefore no liberal inftruction can flow? Little minds, which can
neither meet the comprehenfion of an enlarged fubject, nor hope
to rife to the difplay of it, will affect to depreciate and to damp
by every little infinuation this pre-eminent exercife of the art:
directly to traduce it as a fuperior exercife, would be idle,
becaufe it would be abfurd: they will affect to maintain it's
higher claims, while they endeavour to crufh it; they will lament it as at a ftand in the country, let it's progrefs be what it
may; they will defcry numerous imperfections in every perform-
ance of that kind, let it's merit be ever fo great; thus they will
have a poifon ready to be fpit upon every thing which opens to
the mediocrity of artifts, or to the habits of a country, a celebrity of pretenfion which either fhould be emulated by all, or
fhould be venerated by thofe who are neceffitated to move in a

fubordinate fphere. Yet fo it is, the empyric will calumniate
the phyfician's more accomplifhed fcience ; and the man, who
has learnt to manage but a fkiff on the fhallow ftream, will treat
as nothing the fkilful navigator who can brave the feas.

It is not, however, from it's pride of capacity, but from it's
utility, that we would eftimate the moft worthy application of this
art. We repeat it to be it's glory, that it is a mean of inftruct-
ing the world. Every fcience, of which our minds are poffeffed, either looks to that end, or it is a fcience falfely fo called.
Nay, every fcience, if it obtains not a pure and honourable
direction, will find one that debafes and corrupts. And this
has ever been the cafe with the art of painting. Wherever
there has been wanting a tafte for the higher application of it's
moral purpofes, that age or country has been diftinguifhed by
it's more trivial productions. It is the fame thing with learning
in general. When the more folid and improving writings of enlightened men ceafe to occupy the attention of a people, the
place of thefe is filled with thofe light and frothy productions
which diffipate or inflame the mind. It is therefore important
for every enlightened fociety to keep up this moft excellent art
in it's genuine deftination. Every great writer in every age of
the world, whether a lover of the fine arts or not, has ever
inculcated this leffon, when painting has been the fubject.
Ariftotle, whofe learning was too fcholaftic to fuffer him to be
an enthufiaft in the arts, was fo fenfible of this importance that
he gives it in charge, among other political inftructions, to the
governors of youth, " that they be allowed to fee no other pic-
" tures than fuch as have this moral and inftructive tendency.*"

* Arift. Polit. lib. 8. c. 5.

A moſt able and elegant writer, to whom the preſent age is indebted for much refinement in all the fine arts as well as for the
extenſion of it's learning, we mean the preſent Biſhop of Wor-
ceſter, has beſtowed ſome pages in his notes on Horace's Epiſtle
to Auguſtus, with a view of urging the importance of cultivating
the moral and inſtruﬅive deſtination of the pencil. The author
on whom he comments has given the true charaﬅer which dig-
nifies painting, in the following line,

Supendit piﬅa vultum mentemque tabella, v. 97.

It is when not only the eye, but the ſoul, hangs on the repreſentation, that painting riſes to it's proper ſtation, and produces
it's nobleſt effeﬅs. The eye may be pleaſed with various other
efforts of the art, which are worthy of pleaſing, but the ſoul can
never be fed by any thing which does not reach out to it an in-
tereſting affeﬅion. And ſince every affeﬅion may be reached
by the powers of the pencil, and the whole of the affeﬅions afford a moſt ample field for the contemplation of genius, it is
a misfortune when theſe in ſome of their branches do not engage
the firſt attention of every maſter; and in proportion as they
are negleﬅed, where there is no want of abilities to reach them,
the world has to lament the loſs of thoſe advantages, which it
might reaſonably expeﬅ from the natural ſubſerviency of ſo excellent an art to the intereſts of moral culture. This concluſion
is the very ſame which was ſo anxiouſly preſſed by Socrates
above two thouſand years ago in that celebrated converſation
with Parrhaſius recorded in the Memorabilia of Xenophon*.

If therefore we value ourſelves on the liberal arts, let us maintain them in that ſtrength and direﬅion wherein they beſt deſerve

* Lib. 3.

the name of liberal. If we prize the means of impreffing on the prefent and future generations thofe profitable leffons by which a people may become virtuous and enlightened, let us ftreng-then thofe means by every poffible encouragement. If it be the purpofe of fchools to inftruct, and to felect the inftruction which is moft valuable, let every influence be exerted that the fchools of art among ourfelves may not lofe this beft and primary feature of their inftitution, but that the emulation of inftruction may rife over every other emulation of the pencil, leading us to the contemplation of characters and manners, drawing out the affections of humanity, difcriminating the interefting fcenes of life, and affifting all the variety of improving views in their efficacy on the human heart.

It is thus that the ancients were ambitious to exercife the pencil. And among all the older and greater mafters of the modern fchools the fame ambition has been pre-eminent; the views of moral inftruction, in fome or other of it's branches, have generally guided every hand that held the pencil in the higheft fame. We can hardly make a queftion that thofe views would carry the preference of every great mafter in every coun-try and in every age, if there were not fomething peculiar to the age and the country, which turns the pencil another way. Every man of reflection and fentiment muft feel a pleafure re-fulting from every reprefentation which yields a fentiment; he muft be more highly gratified with the review of a noble moral growing from his own creation, than by any creation he may give to things incapable of exciting a refined fenfation, or of flattering the confcioufnefs of a fuperior talent. Every man, whofe ambition prompts him to take up the pencil, muft feel the influence of the fame ambition urging him to make it's highest attainments his own.

At the fame time, other caufes befides thofe which are local or temporary will often thwart and divert this natural ambition. And although it be right that it fhould be cherifhed in all, neither will the meafure or the turn of abilities fuffer it to fucceed in all, nor is the general culture of the pencil prejudiced, in faft, if many, who from thofe caufes do not fucceed in that way, fucceed in another. The bent of abilities is various, and without that variety of bent the various provinces of painting could no more be filled with effeft than the various provinces of human life, if all were fitted to move in the fame line of charafter. The lower departments of fociety are found to be accomplifhed beft by thofe, whofe meafure or turn of abilities would not figure equally in the higher. And fo it is precifely in the departments of painting. All cannot reach a hiftory, or an epic compofition : but thofe, who cannot, may fhine in the difplay of the fcenes of Nature much more than they who are unrivaled in the other : and thofe, again, whofe views or landfcapes would gain no admirers, fhall carry the world after them in a portrait. Amidft all this it often happens that the peculiarity of talent, by which Nature has marked individuals, is engaged in a difficult ftruggle with the general ambition, of which we have fpoken, to embrace the higheft ranks of the art. And nothing can fhew more ftrongly the natural pre-eminence of that higher charafter in painting, on which we have defcanted, than this general fenfe of it, and emulation to reach it, which have left fome capital mafters reftlefs and difcontented even under the confcioufnefs of diftinguifhed ftrength, and the acquifition of diftinguifhed fame, in another line of the art. Salvator Rofa, whofe landfcapes were his own, original, unborrowed, and fublime in their way, felt no joy in that character of painting, or at leaft in it's being confidered as the peculiar ftrength of his pencil; he wifhed to be looked upon as an hiftoric, or, however, as a poetic painter, and as fuch he conceived himfelf fuperior to all*. Van Dyke, difcontented with the fame which left him unrivaled in his portraits, would fain have given them up for the painting of hiftory, in which he certainly never appeared with equal advantage, if he had been encouraged by the court of France. And after him Sir Peter Lely, actuated by the fame reftlefs emulation, but without any reafon to fupport it, would have done the fame thing, if he had found that encouragement in England.

If the natural ambition of talents to gain the firft ftations of fame be that continual fpur to the mind of art, without which every fchool of art in the world muft languifh, Nature ftill keeps all right by that ftandard to which the ability of every man is brought, and which every man comes at length to know for the true meafure of his ftrength, and the decifion of his character. Thus every portion in this excellent art receives it's proper culture, every circumftance which contributes to it's perfection gains all that is due to it. For it muft be obferved, that no clafs of painting, how diftant foever from the higheft character of the art, if it be not impure in it's principle, ought to be accounted low or infignificant in it's fcience. Every portion of it is an ingredient in it's original conftitution as a writing, a feature in the general affemblage of it's character, and a conftituent part in the preparation of that inftruction, in which the art is

* Supplem. to De Piles, p. 16.

feen moft perfect. The artift, who embraces an hiftoric or poetic reprefentation, will rarely find a fcene which does not call for the talents that are diftinguifhed in all or moft of the particular claffes of painting. The local fituation will demand either rural views, or marine objects, or architectural order, perhaps all three: animal Nature makes a part of almoft every fcene : and even portraiture is found on many occafions to have it's importance in thefe fublimer exhibitions. Without that talent how would Panænus have perpetuated to pofterity, in the battle of Marathon, the perfonal figures of thofe Græcian generals who were fo defervedly dear to their country for the valour with which they had ferved it in that conflict ? We mean not, in this, to plead for the liberty of introducing living portraits into paft hiftoric fubjects. For the inftance we have adduced was not a paft, but a prefent, fubject, rifing in the fame period with the picture.

It is true, the general fenfe of the world has never confidered thofe particular claffes of the art as occupying it's fuperior pretenfions; and for a plain reafon, becaufe even landfcape, which is the moft refpectable of them, is rarely the vifion or ftudy of the mind in any portion, and the others are entirely the imitation of Nature, requiring only the eye and the hand to execute them, but nothing more of the mind than confifts in a few graces of difpofition. Yet independent of the degrees in which they are fubfervient to fublimer compofitions, they poffefs an eftimation of their own which is not to be overlooked. In all the various fcenery of rural nature, conducted through all the gradations of it's views, and cloathed with all it's appendages in the animal and vegetable world, we are led to admire the wonderful operations of the great Creator, and the various ftages of beauty which Nature has yielded to the influence and progress of society: the eye is not so much pleased with the prospect, as the mind is fixed in a serenity of enjoyment, and in a reverence of the wisdom in which the whole is formed. And are there not satisfactions of a most rational kind dependent on the talent which perpetuates the portraits of those who have distinguished themselves in their country or their family, or who have left their names precious by their friendships?

We are not therefore to discard the subordinate branches of the art, while we establish that which constitutes it's sublimity.

CHAP. IV.

The qualifications essential in the constitution of moral painting.

THE sublimity of moral instruction, which we have considered as the glory of the pencil, is to be pursued through it's qualifications.

In the first place, it is essential that it be directed to the inculcating of truth—unadulterated by legend, which imposes false principles on the mind, and unmixed with any partial system for the support of power. In this view it is painful to think what infinite labours of the pencil, whose execution have delighted the world, and will continue to delight it as long as they shall last, have been wasted and lost; if we may call that labour lost, which affecting to instruct gives every thing but

folid and approved inftruction. The moft divine pencil that
ever was guided by the hand of man will give us no inconfiderable regret under this reflection. It was fome misfortune to
Raphael, although to the art it was a feafonable happinefs, that
he was born in the age which brought him forth : but the art
itfelf has to lament that he was bred in that religion, which led
him to facrifice confiderably to a fyftem of fuperftition. The
patronages of Julius and Leo were noble patronages; they
were men of noble minds : and for once we will rejoice in the
Vatican, that they filled it's chair, and ftimulated a Raphael to
fill it's chambers. But they were the heads of a church; and
Raphael's harmony in faith left to his fenfe or his complaifance
lefs room for ftruggles. We fpeak not merely of a papal tincture marking many of his religious fubjects. Some of his moft
confiderable pieces were exprefs compliments to the papal
power, or exprefs records of papal miracles. We need not to
fpecify particulars; all who know his works will rightly apply
thefe obfervations. In the cartons indeed, which are now at
Windfor, and which are the lateft and beft of his works, he has
more happily preferved the purity of mind, and purity of inftruction, which fhould ever flow from the pencil. Thofe fubjects are taken from fcripture ; and if we except that which is
called *the keys*, and which unhappily ftands very forward in the
exception, and indeed hardly left him the power of fhunning it,
they involve nothing of human tradition or human fyftem. If
there be juftice in this criticifm on Raphael, whofe judgement
was as great as the ftrength of fuperftition will ever leave to
moft men, we cannot fuppofe that there has not been full as
much room for the fame criticifm on others. The fact is, that
the firft pencils of Italy have all had their fhare in it. The
religion of their country is confpicuous, wherever the fubject

of their paintings is religious. This has ufurped the moft confiderable portion of their time and their labours. Hence the
long catalogue of Romifh faints, which meet us in every place,
and to which we objeft only becaufe they are embraced as
faints, and with reference to circumftances or events which tradition or legend has reprefented as important to their faintfhip.
Hence too all the peculiarities of the Romifh communion, fuch
as the facraments, &c. which have either been made the fpecific
fubjefts of paintings, or have been occafionally introduced
where the fubjefts would permit, and indeed where the fubjefts
fhould never have permitted them. Even in the transfiguration
Raphael could not refrain from placing two monks on the
mountain.

It is indeed to be lamented that an art, whofe difplay is fo
powerful, and whofe inftruftion therefore comes fo home to our
feelings, fhould be clogged with any peculiarities of fentiment,
which may retard it's beneficial impreffion on any portion of
mankind. But it never can be otherwife, where the mind
fuftains a bias of fuperftitious faith fo ftrong and fo peculiar as
that of which we are fpeaking. No fyftem of religious belief
clings fo faft to the mind, and poffeffes it fo completely, as
that of the Romifh church, where it obtains at all. A man
muft be wedded to it entirely, or he muft defpife it. There is
no medium in it's influence. His full conviftion muft go with
it, or he is not of that communion. We mean not to be fevere
on any portion of mankind, let their religious faith be as different from our own as it may. All that we would imprefs by
thefe obfervations is, that no peculiarities of religious faith
whatever, no private fyftem of doftrines, ought to have place in
the inftruftion of the pencil. If the fubjeft be religious, let it

be the plain and broad truths contained in the pages of revelation, not the tenets of a particular communion. Thefe are fpots upon the canvas, which not all the embellifhments of the art can efface or hide. In no circumftance is the art fo much committed to neglect, and it's fuccefs to peril, as by the admiffion of fenti- ments which are not of an univerfal ftandard. We can bear with the thought that is low and puerile: we are not abfolutely offended by that which is fingular and unmeaning: but when we are met by that which would impofe on our underftandings, and beguile us with falfe principles, we look no further; we fee no beauties in the moft mafterly execution. In Michael Ange- lo's picture of God's creating the fun and moon—the work of a man who was the original of vaftnefs in defign—we only fmile to fee a little angel frightened at the moon, and flying for fhel- ter to the Creator. In the fame mafter's *Laft judgement* we feel no abfolute difpleafure to fee the bleffed virgin clinging clofe to her fon for fuccour; becaufe we prefently reflect that fhe might as well be fingled out for that thought, if the painter was deter- mined to indulge it, as any other perfon; although as he has not combined one fingle faint in her feeling, we muft leave to his own religious ideas, or to his fancy, to account for the thought as it ftands. But when in the fame laft-mentioned pic- ture, in a fubject of the moft awful nature rifing immediately out of divine revelation, we fee the profane, fabulous, falfe ftuff of Charon and his boat introduced—much more, when in the carton of *the keys* an apoftle, who had denied his mafter, is felected for a priority of confidence and for precedence not only over all the reft but over a beloved difciple, and in his prefence too, with the additional circumftance that this beloved difciple appears palpably mortified at the preference given to the other, and eager to convince his mafter of his own equality

of affection, not without fome previous remonftrance too which
we are led to fuppofe had taken place—further yet, when in
Raphael's *theology*, wrongly called by fome *the difpute on the
facrament* (although not an idea of difpute about it had then
entered his head, and if it had, neither would he have been fo
weak, nor would others have fuffered him, to wound his communion by recording fuch difpute) we fee the bleffed virgin fpecifically marked for the mediator, as much as Chrift is for the
regent of all things, while no regard feems to be paid to the
Almighty Father by angels, faints, or men ; and when we fee
the real prefence in the eucharift announced by the hoft in the
golden oftenforio on the altar ; were all the perfections that
have diftinguifhed all the pencils upon earth united in fuch
a picture, our admiration is choaked, and the only effect it
leaves upon our minds is a regret that fo much capacity of execution fhould be overthrown by fo much want of judgement.

In the next place, the dignity of moral inftruction is degraded,
whenever the pencil is employed on frivolous, whimfical, and
unmeaning fubjects. On this head, it is to be feared, there will
ever be too much caufe for complaint, becaufe there will ever
be perfons incapable of folidity, although very capable of executing this art with power. Strength of underftanding, and ability
in art or fcience, are very different things ; they are derived from
different fources ; and they are perfectly independent of each
other. The one can no more be inftrumental to the communication of the other, than either can communicate temper or
difpofition. The fineft art in the world may therefore be combined with the lighteft and moft fuperficial mind. Books are
written of a light and fantaftic nature by thofe who cannot
write otherwife, and yet will write fomething. And fo it is with

painting : the mind of the artift can but give fuch fubjefts as
are confentaneous to it's turn. The *night-mare, little red
riding hood, the fhepherd's dream,* or any dream that is not
marked in authentic hiftory as combined with the important
difpenfations of Providence, and many other pieces of a vifionary and fanciful nature, are fpeculations of as exalted a ftretch
in the contemplation of fuch a mind as the fineft leffons that
ever were drawn from religion, or morals, or ufeful hiftory.
And yet the painter, who fhould employ his time on fuch fubjefts, would certainly amufe the intelligent no more than the
man who fhould make thofe fubjefts the topics of a ferious
difcourfe. But what good has the world, or what honour has
the art, at any time derived from fuch light and fantaftic fpeculations ? If it be right to follow Nature, there is nothing of
her here, all that is prefented to us is a *reverie* of the brain.
If it be allowable to cultivate fancy; yet the fancy, which has
little or nothing of Nature in it's compofition, becomes ridiculous. A man may carry the flights of imagination, even within
the walks of the chafteft art or fcience, till they become mere
waking dreams, as wild as the conceits of a madman. The
author of obfervations on Frefnoy *de arte graphica** very properly calls thefe perfons " Libertines of painting": as there are
libertines of religion, who have no other law but the vehemence
of their own inclinations ; fo thefe have no other model, he fays,
but a rodomontado-genius, which fhews us a wild or favage nature that is not of our acquaintance, but of a new creation.

If not in fubjefts altogether, yet in manner, one of the firft examples of this kind, if not the very firft, appeared about the latter

* ¶ 176.

end of the fixteenth century in a Neapolitan, who is commonly
known by the name of Giofeppe d'Arpino, but whofe real
name was Jofeph Pin—the fame man, whofe contefts with Car-
ravagio for the fuccefs of their refpective novelties in manner
threw the arts and almoft Italy itfelf into convulfions. Of
Arpino only we fhall fpeak at prefent. He was not without
fome gifts. He had a florid invention, a ready hand, and confiderable fpirit. Yet having no fure foundation either in the
ftudy of Nature or in the rules of art, and building only on thofe
fantaftical ideas which he had formed in his own head, he run
into all the extravagancies which neceffarily attend thofe who
have no better guide than their own capricious fancy *. To the
wildnefs of manner introduced by this painter, and to the influence it obtained, Felibien attributes in a confiderable degree
that neglect and decay of tafte which took place in the Roman
fchool after the death of Raphael. For fo unaccountably does a
bad tafte, if it is but a new one, find numbers in the world to
befriend and protect it, that this artift was a favourite of Gre-
gory XIII. and his immediate fucceffor, and was fo well received
in France by Lewis XIII. that he was made by that monarch a
knight of the order of St. Michael.

When we are fpeaking of caprice and extravagance, muft we
not include under thofe terms the grotefque and ludicrous, or
can we admit thefe as contributing to inftruction ? In the broad-
eft view of ridicule as a fpecies of argument, the apology made
for it by the poet will not be allowed to give it a place in the
views of inftruction. What if it be true, that

ridiculum acri

Fortius ac melius magnas plerumque fecat res.

Hor. Sat. b. 1. fat. 10. v. 15.

* Graham's anc. and mod. Painters. Felib. 3 vol. p. 259. Monier, p. 161. 191.

the purpofes of inftruction are the laft at which it aims. It is much more concerned for the eftablifhment of it's own triumph than for the eftablifhment of what is true and right, againft which it is as often directed as to give them ftrength. Nor will the beft pretence it affumes be always found, notwithftanding the pains which have been taken by Mr. Hume to maintain it, that nothing ought to be embraced which is capable of ridicule.

In the works of the pencil far lefs concerned are it's objects or it's influence with the views of inftruction than where it is met as an argument of literary wit. In the former the burlefque and ludicrous affect no compromife with regular ideas, they are palpable departures from Nature, and abfolute diftortions of it, as fuch they can neither inftruct nor much amufe a reflecting mind. Shall it be faid that the defign, of which Richardfon fpeaks as coming from the Carachi's fchool, of a male and female fatyr fitting together in a fantaftic mood, although it was very probably meant as a piece of wit on the ftory of Corydon and Phillis, fhall pafs for an emblem of the folace which arifes from mutual love, or that it fhall teach us in any refpect upon that fubject? Shall the figures of Vefalius, in which he has humoroufly, but fomewhat beyond common feeling, given us to fee the fkin and flefh drawn off by degrees, and the figures in all the variety of contortions finking into death with extreme pain; fhall thefe be received as leffons of anatomical fcience? Yet we do not condemn them under the circumftances and the views which gave them birth. They were all the mere fports of an idle hour; nothing lefs than inftruction was intended to be conveyed. And let fuch *jeux d'efprits* keep their proper place, it is not our intention to reprefs

thofe efforts of art. There are fubjects, which will never ceafe
to pour themfelves on minds replete with livelinefs and pleaf-
antry ; fubjects, whether imaginary or real, whether tried or
untried by the pencil, in which genius may wifh to make a new
effort, though in the lighteft ftyle. Thefe are the mere recrea-
tions of genius. Thus the philofopher writes an ode or a fon-
net. And the fublimeft rules of art would no more endeavour
to reftrain thefe, than the profoundeft mind would think it fit to
be debarred from difporting itfelf occafionally with the lighteft
entertainment. In art, as in every other part of wifdom, *dulce
eft defipere in loco*. So Annibal Carach thought and acted ;
and we fhould rejoice to poffefs the volume of defigns in that
way, which was left by him, and came afterwards into the
hands of the Prince of Neroli*. Thofe defigns were meant
only as amufements, they neither affected inftruction, nor were
mixed with any fort of ferioufnefs. But Michael Angelo went
much further, and further than can be juftified, in that vein of
fpirit. With all his greatnefs he was as capable of being licentious in that refpect as any artift upon earth ; and the blame
only is, that he indulged his humour where he fhould have
repreffed it. We will not fpeak of the goatifh face, which he
has been cenfured by fome for having given to the great law-
giver and prophet of the Jews in the figure of Mofes fitting, becaufe we think that criticifm is rather carried too far; poffibly
the features may be a little more heightened than he would have
given them, if he had been cautious to avoid the fufpicion of caricature, but certainly they are the ftrong and fpeaking character of the Jew, let their approximation to any part of the ani-
mal-fpecies be what it may ; and it would be no eafy matter for

* Felib. 3. vol. p. 278, 9.

the moft difcerning mind to give that chara&er in all the dignity
of fituation and perfonal pretenfions, which were due to Mofes,
without calling forth thofe features, or by calling them forth in
much lefs ftrength than Michael Angelo has done. Had the
curious Lavatre been living when that figure was wrought, the
artift would have left, and might fafely have left, to all the principles affumed in Lavatre's theory the diffection of thofe features,
fatisfied with the choice he had made, and with the juftice he
had done to his art, but not accountable for any relationfhip of
qualities or ideas by which either ingenuity or the nature of things
might poffibly conne& the chara&er before him with any other
parts of creation. It is not therefore in that inftance that we
fhall cenfure that artift. In his "Laft judgement" he is more
reafonably open to that cenfure : there the ludicrous is certainly
fometimes improper and too ftrong to be perfe&ly approved in
that folemn compofition. The truth is, that the epic is loft
when the farce is fuffered to be mixed in it, and that equally
in the page and on the canvas. The Homer in poetry has fometimes flept here, as well as the Homer in painting. In his cha-
ra&er of Vulcan and Therfites, in his ftory of Mars and Venus,
in the behaviour of Irus, and in fome other paffages, he has
evidently lapfed into the burlefque, and has fo far prejudiced the
epic by departing from the gravity effential to it's magnificence *.
We cannot but lament that the vaft difplays of fuch exalted
genius in either of thofe kindred arts fhould be blotted by fo
negligent an inattention to the firft leffon of compofition, *quid
deceat, quid non.*

* Spe&ator, No. 279.

It may perhaps be faid that thefe obfervations, if ftrictly purfued and carried to their full length, would cramp too much the
force and fcope of genius in the art. Let us therefore weigh
that matter. For genius is a rare gift, which fhould not be
ftifled.

Genius is a creative imagination, which can not only embellifh
fcenes or incidents by the beft difpofition of concomitant circumftances, but give exiftence to new ones. It is a gift, by
which are poured into the mind with great copioufnefs the rareft
treafures of thought and idea. Confequently it is derived from
Nature, whofe ftores are as inexhauftible as they are infinitely varied; it is not acquired by labour, which can but give by it's own
fcantier meafure, and to which in it's beft progrefs Nature has
faid, " hitherto fhalt thou go, and no further." Genius is to the
human mind what the Nile is to Egypt, the prolific fource of
all that has ever embellifhed and enriched it in every way. By
that overflowing ftream that country became every thing, the
feat of all that was finifhed not only in natural but in intellectual
life, while it's independence enabled it to maintain thofe advantages. To manage it, art was called forth at firft; and when
managed, every art and elegance followed what was become fo
enriched. In the fame manner, the mind, fed by genius, makes
all the gifts of Nature her own, and improves upon them all. It
is every thing of which humanity is capable; it is ready in every
fubject to which it adverts; and while it is itfelf enriched, it
never ceafes to difpenfe that richnefs to every thing that
comes within it's reach. Art is it's firft offspring, and every art
and elegance prefently accumulates it's ftore. But then as the
Nile, along with every elegance, left alfo it's veftiges in much

redundancy of matter that was to be cleared before elegance was obtained ; fo genius has it's redundancy : it overflows not only in the finer and finifhed fentiments, but in much that requires to be dreffed : prolific in it's fource, it is impregnated with every variety of matter, which a competent fkill only can feparate, and muft feparate, to give it the beft application.

A further qualification of mind is therefore introduced here, indifpenfible to the moft valuable ufe of genius. And that is rightly called Tafte. Genius may fubfift in all it's vigour, without any portion of tafte. But the latter cannot be poffeffed in any eminent degree, without fome fhare, fome impreffion, of the former ; becaufe it is the province of tafte to drefs, refine, and cultivate the other, which it can never do, without feeling the fpirit of the other in fome degree. And if it did not feel that fpirit, it would be a gift beftowed in vain, without the capacity that is to call it into exercife. But then that capacity of genius which calls it forth will not neceffarily find the talent, which is to be fuperadded to itfelf, no more than Nature and art infepara-bly go together. And this is the very difference between the two. Genius is wholly beftowed by Nature : tafte, with fomething of Nature, is principally acquired. The one is an untutored ebul-lition of the imagination ; the other is a rectified judgement. The one is chiefly found in the mind, or in the country, where Nature is feen moft predominant ; the other, where fhe is chaf-tened and refined by the improvements of fociety and art. It has therefore been obferved that genius flourifhes moft in thofe cli-mates, where the tyranny of Nature has given the conftitution of government, and all the great fcenes and events which naturally fpring from thence, and where a hotter fun throws her forth in all her gigantic wildnefs, magnificence, and variety, which are

calculated to give an enthufiafm to the mind; while tafte is moft
eminently diftinguifhed under thofe lefs luxuriant appearances,
and that more temperate, regular, and civilized fyftem of things,
which naturally leads the mind to an habitual feleftion of what
is moft beautiful, the happieft, and the beft.

It is this feleftion which conftitutes tafte. It picks and culls
the flowers of Nature. It weeds her excrefcencies, it prunes her
luxuriance. It dreffes the harveft which genius has fown, and fepa-
rates the folid from the light. It is the effeft of reafon refined
and matured by time, by a freedom of thinking, and an improvement in knowledge, which uniting to enlarge the mind enable it
to difcern more perfeftly the various relations of things, and to
combine with happier art thofe mixed fenfations which give the
higheft entertainment to men of elegant minds.

Thus tafte becomes needful to be ingrafted upon genius, if
we would have the fruit of the latter mellowed into perfeftion.
And this is a leffon abfolutely needful for the painter to learn.
Tafte is a talent abfolutely needful for him to acquire. By this
he will be taught, that whatever terminates in whim, caprice, and
humour, can never give general pleafure; becaufe thofe difpofitions are fingular and perfonal in their nature, they arife from
no common principles or feelings, of which others, at leaft the
generality, can be fuppofed to participate—whatever is *outrée*
and extravagant can never be beautiful—whatever is caricature
can never exalt a fubjeft—whatever is empty or poor of fentiment can neither inftruft any perfons, nor pleafe the majority,
who will at leaft be fuppofed to have fome relifh for what is
excellent—whatever defeats the honourable and ufeful inftruftion

of a painting, robs it of that which all men look, or should look, to obtain from it.

CHAP. V.

Diſtinction between hiſtoric and poetic painting, and the reſpective provinces of each.

In the diſcuſſion of moral painting, an important diſtinction, for the ſurer force of it's inſtruction, is to be made between the reſpective provinces of hiſtoric and poetic painting—a diſtinction which has never yet been properly enforced, or attended to as it ought. We have all along conſidered the pencil as a noble ſpecies of writing: and if we keep that idea in our minds, the juſt bounds and proprieties of the art, in every branch of it, will be readily and correctly aſcertained.

What is the firſt eſſential of hiſtoric writing? Moſt certainly, perſpicuity. If poſſible, this is more indiſpenſible on the hiſtoric canvas than it is in the hiſtoric page, becauſe in the former our eyes alone muſt be our guide to the whole, and our guide at once; if theſe are not correctly poſſeſſed, the picture has no other comment, nor can furniſh any circumlocution to clear up the obſcurity; it is not by words, but by the preciſion of images, that we are inſtructed here. The hiſtoric painter muſt therefore lay down to himſelf this firſt duty, TO KEEP NEAR TO THE TRUTH OF THE HISTORY HE REPRESENTS.

This however is no flavish tie; it admits of fome latitude, reafonably reftrained. It is not neceffary that he confine himfelf to the precife *order* in which the event took place, the precife *fituation* of circumftances, or the precife *point of time*. In thefe feveral refpects he may exercife a difcretionary felection for the purpofe of giving the beft effect to the ftory: he may even indulge invention fo far as to introduce other circumftances which might well be fuppofed to have happened, although they did not, but which fhall all in their meafure contribute to give a more precife elucidation to the piece.

Within this fcope the flights of his invention muft be circum-fcribed here. For however painting may have been compared to poetry, it is dangerous to run the parallel too ftrictly with refpect to the hiftoric reprefentations of the pencil. Would the flights of poetry give greater perfpicuity to the truth of hiftory? Or would the hiftorian be pronounced more chafte and juft for the intermixture of his poetic talents? By no means. Equally im-proper therefore would be the indulgence of thefe by the hiftoric painter, beyond the degree in which they have a natural and known connection with the fubject, and give it a manifeft affif-tance. All arbitrary circumftances, vifionary allufions, and ex-trinfic adoptions, all intermixture of fable where the painting has affumed a known matter of fact, all perfonifications of ina-nimate nature, are illicit in his hands, becaufe as thefe do not affimilate with the hiftory, they tend to embarrafs and confound; they draw off the mind from the fimplicity of the narration to heterogeneous ideas which beget improbability. He fhall not therefore be at liberty, in the view of gratifying what may ap-pear to him higher embellifhment, to fhew his characters under any appearances which are not known to befit them, becaufe it is abfurd that he fhould be at liberty to difguife his ftory. He fhall not drefs them in any habits but thofe of the age and the country in which they lived, becaufe that would be to throw them into the moft complete difguife. He fhall be very much chaftened in his ufe of allegory, which is indeed inexpreffibly fine and precious and moft eloquent, where it is pure and chafte, that is, where it appears natural and artlefs, having a real exiftence in the place, and participating too (if poffible) in the event, reprefented; but it is abfolutely faulty and condemnable, where it is the mere creature of the brain, or of fabulous fyftem. He fhall not tranfport us by anachronifmal fictions beyond the period in which the fcene is laid; he fhall not bring together upon the fame fpot thofe who are known to have lived ages afunder; becaufe that would be to deftroy all the effect at once, by telling us we were impofed upon and deceived.

All thefe deductions, which in fact are fo many principles, will be found to arife from this fimple ground, that his ftory muft be brought to the eye of the informed mind as plainly as if it were related to his ear; and even to the uninformed, whofe eye it will perhaps more frequently meet in the great mafs of mankind, it muft carry fo much perfpicuity that he may readily catch the object aimed at, the main fact reprefented, or the great fentiment inculcated, with fome reference perhaps to the age or country from which it fprung, although he may want affiftance to difcover it's detail.

Let not the hiftoric painter imagine that his art is prejudiced by thefe limits. There is fcope fufficient here for the man of genius to place the fimpleft events in a moft interefting view, and to make thofe facts which are bare of themfelves moft fentimen-

tally expreffive. It is the dullnefs of genius that fuffers any
event, which has any natural importance in it, to become dull
in his hands.   The enriched underftanding will clothe with
richnefs every fubject that is not deftitute of matter: it will
fwell into importance thofe circumftances which to ordinary
minds would pafs for light ones; and it will elevate into grandeur thofe which have any capacity for elevation.   In writing,
all men are fenfible that there is a dignity of language, which
the fcholar knows how to employ, and by which he fhall lift
the humbleft themes into moft lofty conceptions; and this without one trope, without one figure, without one image that has
not it's reality combined with the fubject.   What we contend
for is, then, that the powers of the hiftoric pencil in the hands
of the fcholar, and conducted by the enlightened and enriched
mind, are equal to thofe of the pen in the felection of expreffion,
and in the communication of it's own life, and richnefs, and
elevation to the materials which are prefented to it's choice.   If
this narrows the operations, and increafes the difficulties, of the
hiftoric painter, it has thefe effects only to thofe who were never
gifted to fhine in this branch of the art, which never was and
never will be accomplifhed by the production of a vigorous and
attracting and regular inftruction but by the man of a ftrong and
brilliant mind; wherever it has been affected by emulation
without thefe gifts, it has never been able to rife beyond the
inefficacy of *inertia ftrenua*.

Yet it is this *inertia ftrenua*, it is this unfupported emulation
to produce an hiftoric painting, which has abufed the purity of
it's province, and baftardized too many of it's productions.
Sometimes artifts, who had gifts to excel in it, have been as
faulty as others in not knowing, or not attending to, the dif-

crimination between hiftoric and poetic fubjects. As if matters of fact were uniformly heavy and incapable of elegance,
they have conceived it neceffary to fly to extraneous fources for
aid, which their own independent fancies have fupplied, and
not the fubject before them. They have thought themfelves at
liberty, for the greater plenitude of the fcene, and (as they
hoped) of the effect, to collect from Nature at large whatever
might be adduced in alliance with their fubject, and oftentimes
from fable at large, however deftitute of fuch alliance it might
be. They have imagined it dependent on their own pleafure to
avail themfelves of the peculiarities of any one country, with
which they were moft fmitten, to deck the fcenes that belonged
to another. If the fubject were of valour, or of any high virtue,
fiction muft be called forth to complete the renown, which in
their opinions would be left too naked in the beft action or natural
fituation: a victory or a fame muft crown the hero with a wreath,
or fome divine character muft conduct him dead into glory: and
although he be a hero who never fet foot in Greece or Rome, it
has been thought impoffible that he can be accepted for a hero,
unlefs in the garb of an Alexander or a Scipio. If the hiftory
were grief, and of courfe a public grief as moft fit for the hiftoric
pencil, the very elements muft grieve too, all Nature muft come
forth in her fuit of mourning, and fhe muft iffue from her vifionary regions one of thofe divinities or fabulous talifmen of the
paffions, which fhall complete the characteriftic of woe, not to
be fpoken fufficiently by the accumulated affliction of a whole
multitude immediately concerned in the event. If any part of
Nature was to be defcribed, the heathen mythology was reforted
to for the emblem, as more forcible and fine than Nature herfelf
could fupply: a river-god fpouting forth a torrent, a Ceres covered with ears of corn, or a Bacchus with grapes, have been

taken in preference to a river, a harveſt, or a vineyard, where
thoſe have been the ſcenes of real events.   Thus the purity of
the hiſtoric line has been violated, and artiſts have produced a
mungrel-compoſition reducible to no certain ſpecies, an herma-
phrodite-attempt, half hiſtory and half poetry, conſequently
neither : they have become the very perſons, whoſe unſkilful-
neſs is ſo pointedly condemned by Horace for deſtroying the
grand and fundamental principle of unity in the piece.   He ſays
truly,

pictoribus atque poetis
Quid libet audendi ſemper fuit æqua poteſtas ;

but then he adds, for the prevention of ſo illicit a licence as that
we have now arraigned, both to painters and poets, and in all
the claſſes of their reſpective compoſitions,

Sidquidvis, ſimplex duntaxat et unum.

   Theſe tranſgreſſions of ſimplicity and unity in hiſtoric painting, theſe daſhes of the poetic and the fabulous in a compoſition of real events, have in a good meaſure been owing to the
unguarded ſtudy of the ancient baſs-reliefs.   Thoſe who have
ſtudied them ſhould have conſidered that a very conſiderable part of the knowledge which the ancients enjoyed was
involved in fiction, and conſequently that the works of their art
muſt deal conſiderably in fictitious allegory, which perhaps they
were the more tempted to embrace and cultivate, as it might
flatter their learning as well as their ſuperſtition.   But ſince their
days, and by means of more known truth, learning has little to
be flattered in theſe things, and ſuperſtition has ſtill leſs than
learning.   To men, however, who were endeavouring to produce
eſtabliſhed inſtruction from eſtabliſhed hiſtory, it ſhould have
occurred, that as the nature and the views of their art were varied

from thofe of the ancients, fo fhould their ufe of the ancient tafte have been conducted, at leaft, with more caution. Yet the impreffion derived from thofe ftudies has hardly ever been fhaken off. It has fixed itfelf on thofe who have only contemplated the fine arts as an elegant knowledge, no lefs than on thofe who have made them a profeffional practice. The Abbé Winckelman affords a ftrong confirmation of this affertion. He was a fenfible man, and deeply informed in the fine arts, yet his fuperftitious veneration of the Greeks never fuffered his judgement to paufe on the qualifications which fhould be put to the influence of their examples. Hence he urges upon the great artift the ufe of allegory without compromife: he confiders it as the grandeft difplay of tranfcendent abilities: he wants a fyftem of fymbology, by which all abftracted ideas might be couched under fenfible images: and thefe things he urges as the higheft atchievement of the hiftoric painter *. It may deferve to be confidered, whether he has not been much too extravagant in his notions of allegory, even where the painting may be more properly poetic; although the difference between that and the hiftoric province does not appear to have entered his thoughts.

With refpect to artifts themfelves, the impreffions of which we have fpoken, derived from thofe ftudies, have pervaded the beft abilities through every æra of the pencil. Raphael was by no means exempt from them. His painting of Attila is a proof how far a mind, which beyond doubt was moft competent to every exact meafure of the art, could be brought in the reprefentation of an hiftoric fact to the indulgence of a playful fancy, by combining fo much palpable fiction as the defcent of

* See his Reflections on the Painting and Sculpture of the Greeks, fec. 7.

two apoftles in the air.   If you fay that in this circumftance he
keeps near to the truth of the hiftory, (taking the legend for
fuch) only varying the two horfemen in the hiftory for the two
apoftles in the picture; yet we cannot allow the hiftoric painter
to take the fame liberties that a man does who writes a legend :
although that man, and many fuch, may impofe upon the world,
books will ftill be reforted to for hiftorical information; but here
both the utility and the exiftence of a fine art, in this branch of
it, is at ftake; if the pencil be permitted to mix palpable fictions
with it's hiftoric relations, there is an end of it's hiftoric ufe;
mankind will never look on it in this way, becaufe they will
always look with embarraffment, and confequently with difguft.
What we have faid of the Attila of Raphael, we are happy to obferve, is not equally to be applied to his Heliodorus, although fo
much a-kin both in the fubject and in it's manner; becaufe there
the variation affumed in the fituation of the two young men is
attended with no more fiction than the reft of the ftory, which
evidently leans on the affumption of a divine interpofition; thofe
young men defcend not from the air as apoftles; nor yet as angels,
for they have no wings; nor as any fpecifically marked characters; and confequently they induce no glaring impoffibility.   We
fhould alfo rightly obferve, in balance to any individual miftakes
which Raphael may have committed in this way, that he may
claim an apology which lies not in the power of every artift, who
has fo offended, to claim.   He was employed in the fervice of a
church which depends much on fiction.   And how could he refift,
if he had been difpofed, the injunctions laid upon him by the
head of that church, whofe fervice was certainly gratified moft
completely with the indulgence of fiction by his moft ferious
pencil?

If Raphael was thus thrown off his guard in that branch of the art which he might call his own, where shall we find others impeccable in it? Certainly, if any man after him could be expected faultlefs, it was Nicholas Pouffin. And he of all men living was leaft to be excufed for any tranfgreffions of that fort, becaufe he painted for no popes, or he was little conftrained to facrifice to the prejudices of his employers ; he was moreover a man of moft brilliant parts, and of moft juft and elegant conceptions. He knew very well, whenever wantonnefs was not fuperior to his judgement, how to maintain the pure, elegant, claffical delineation of hiftory. He was not only perfpicuous and ftrong in his ideas, but they were diftinguifhed with an elegance and a tafte which made them productive of a more copious and refined inftruction. In a word, his ftories were delivered as the gentleman and the fcholar would deliver them. And he was moft exact, in general, and correct in all the effentials of *coftume*, in the fimplicity and unity of defign. If the fcene was Greece, it was Græcian all : if Rome, nothing but what was Roman appeared : if Egypt, the eye was thwarted by no object that was not Egyptian. Yet he wanted not the imagery of poetry. No artift, fince the days of Michael Angelo, gave more proofs of poetic fpirit. But he fo chaftened that fpirit in his hiftoric compofitions, whenever he was cautious to be correct, he fo combined and interwove it with his matter, that it feemed to be more the natural iffue of incident than of abftracted genius ; it feemed to be rather the proper life and vigour of the fcene than the refource of a bold and independent imagination. Muft it not therefore be matter of inexpreffible regret, that Pouffin, the chafteft and moft claffical of hiftoric painters in the main, fhould be included in the number of thofe who have been inconfiftent in the hiftoric line, and have in fome degree contributed to derange it ? That he has occafionally fallen into thofe miftakes, his Pyrrhus, his Scipio, his Coriolanus, and a few others, when tried by the principles we have laid down, will give proofs which cannot efcape difcerning minds, and will illuftrate in their refpeſtive degrees, without a particular comment, the obfervations we have made.

What we have laft faid relates to the miftakes of the art. But the obfervations which have gone before, as principles for the due prefervation of it's hiftoric purpofe, will be feen in a more explicit view, if we exemplify them as they are warranted both in hiftoric writing and in hiftoric painting.

Firft, in hiftoric writing. When Livy puts into the mouths of his generals and other great charaſters thofe fpeeches, which may be confidered as fo many ftate-piſtures of the times, and on which the important events of the empire hung, do we think, or is it material to know, that he has written juft as they fpoke, or even the very matter which they fpoke? Turn to other hiftorians who have detailed the fame events, and you fhall find the fame cha-raſters in the fame moments delivering themfelves in a different manner, but producing ftill the fame effeſts. In faſt, the truth of hiftory is equally preferved by thefe writers in either way. The fame point is eftablifhed, the fame event is difplayed, though under a difference of afpeſt. The order of things, a reference to circumftances, the moments of aſtion, and perhaps the general view of the whole, are varied as each writer conceived the vari-ation might contribute to place the fcene in a better light. They have taken liberties in thefe refpeſts, but thofe liberties are within the bounds of the hiftory, or of thofe circumftances which, from the furrounding view of things, might well be fuppofed concurrent with the hiftory. They have indulged their invention : but that invention was merely a different drefs of the fame incidents, or the introduction of other incidents juft as natural. If thefe are poetic excurfions, they are excurfions within the compafs of facts ; for they combine nothing which the fpirit of the hiftory has not combined ;.they go for help to no part of nature, or of life, or of imagination, but that which is imme-diately affociated with the detail they reprefent. This extent of felection and invention not only is confiftent with the purity, but abfolutely conftitutes the elegance, of hiftoric writing. It is the fair and chafte drefs of facts, by which the mind is moft amply informed, and the feelings moft juftly approached : it gives the broad foundation not only for the fecuring of a moft inftructive impreffion, but for the carrying of that impreffion to as high a climax as the event will bear. Without thefe helps no climax of inftruction can ever be wrought, no impreffions of a higher, more polifhed, and more affecting kind can ever be attained. But then thofe who are moft pure and impreffive in this fpecies of writing do not take us into fairy ground for the accom-plifhing of thefe objects ; they do not tranfport us into regions of fancy for the inculcating of a leffon, which they wifh fhould be permanent in fociety, and which never can rife with a well-founded effect but from the juft, and folid, and confiftent repre-fentation of interefting events.

Let us now look for an exemplification of the fame principles in genuine hiftoric painting. And, abating for the exceptions we have already made, and for a few others which under another head will hereafter be noticed, the hiftoric paintings of Nicholas Pouffin are in general every thing we can defire on the queftion before us.

But to obtain a juft and clofe exemplification of the bound-aries of hiftoric painting, it will be neceffary to felect a compo-fition recording an event which is minutely known to us, and which therefore has happened within our memories. Happily, there is one, though only one, which comes within this pre-dicament, and which we embrace with greater fatisfaction, becaufe it is a compofition of the Britifh fchool fince the time when we may regularly fpeak of a fchool in Britain, and a com-pofition of that mafter who has introduced Britain to a tafte in the hiftoric line, which was very new to the acquaintance of her own artifts. In every part of it's compofition it is a moft happy illuftration of the genuine hiftoric fpirit, and of the art of working from a fingle event not only a lively and impreffive inftruction, but that dignity of fentiment which fwells in it's progrefs, and with it's own gradations enlarges the compafs of our feelings : and although in thefe refpects it is by no means an *unique* of it's author, yet as an exhibition which enables us from our own precife acquaintance with the fact to know exactly how far he has indulged himfelf in his management of the fubject, it becomes an *unique* to us. The painting, to which we allude, is " The death of Wolfe."

The firft glance of the eye is met and fatisfied by the greateft perfpicuity. We know it to be the out-fcene of a battle, in which the Britifh nation marked by the drefs of her army is concerned, and in the event of which, though victorious, as appears by the diftant exultation of one of her officers with the enemy's ftandard in his hands, the Britifh general falls in the moment of victory : a mortal wound forbids him to furvive. No fooner does the eye fix on the collateral circumftances, but we know that the fcene of action was foreign from Britain, for the

ships have conveyed thofe Britifh foldiers to the place; and that
this fcene muft be North America, for the favage warrior fhews
us that the country was his. In allegory, can any thing fpeak more
correctly than thefe? What language or refource of the art could
have told us fo much as thofe fhips have done, or told it fo well?
And is not that favage-warrior every way as juft as the crocodile
on the Nile? Without him no imagination would have found
it eafy to acquaint us by any other fymbol what was the country,
at leaft by no fymbol that could fpeak with fo much precifion,
and fo much in tone with the fubject, as that which has been
chofen. The female part of our fpecies has perhaps been taken
to mark the inhabitants of a country as often as the male: but
women can have nothing to do here; all is war; the allegory
therefore, if taken from our fpecies, muft be man, and that man
muft be a warrior.

Equally juft, but equally new to the hiftoric pencil, is the
character of drefs in which thofe victorious men are exhibited.
The pencil had never drawn a hero or a foldier in any country
but in thofe habits, which the heroic ages and nations of antiquity
had made in a manner peculiar to the field of battle. Had the
painter here been feduced by a kind of eftablifhed veneration, which in this cafe would have been moft abfurd, we might
have looked for ever without fuccefs for a Britifh army. This
obfervation expreffes in few words the good fenfe and the neceffity of what is called *coftumé*.

We come to the interior of the bufinefs, *in medias res*. The
general appears carried afide from the heat of the battle, and
attended, but in vain, by the anxious fkill of the furgeon to the
army. Near him is a group of Britifh officers, to whom the event

of victory has given a moment's time to survey their dying
general, and also to assist another officer who sickens under a
wound, but apparently not mortal, then just received. Think
not for a moment that this is a duplicate of impression, which
takes from the great effect that is to arise from the dying hero's
situation : you shall by and by be convinced of the contrary.
The news of victory is announced by it's acknowledged signal ;
a British officer at a distance waves triumphantly in the air the
enemy's standard which he has taken, and which shews us that
the enemy are French.

In every one of these circumstances there is a freedom, and a
most legitimate, judicious, and masterly, though abundant, freedom of variation from the real circumstances of the case. As
they stand before us, they are so natural that no one would hardly
expect them to be otherwise than they appear ; and they come
so near to the truth of the history, that they are almost true, and
yet not one of them is true in fact. But what was it to the
painter, or what is it to the feasted eye, or the feasted mind now,
if the great general who planned and executed that glorious
enterprise, which was crowned with victory, fell by a random-
shot presently after he had scaled those wonderful, and till then
inaccessible heights, on which his army formed before him to
battle just as they ascended ?   What if he died apart from the
battle, and in no respect attended as he is described, hearing only
as he died that the victory was gained ? What if no such group
of British officers discerned him dying, or gathered around the
sickening Monckton ? What if no soldier was actually perceived
to have seized the standard of the enemy ? ·What if no savage
warrior was either present in that afflicting scene, or present in
that battle, or carried a bow in that immediate service ? No

matter how far all or any of thofe incidents were true in fact. They are as fair in the fuppofition of the painter as if they had actually exifted, and infinitely finer and more effectually impref- five as he has thrown them together. Had he taken facts merely as they ftood, in vain would he have tried to reach any one paf- fion of the heart. But mark what a climax of moft interefting concern now rifes from the whole, gathering new feelings in it's gradations to confummate glory in the hero, and confummate ad- miration with diftrefs combined in the beholder.

That common foldier behind the dying general no fooner meets the eye than the heart catches the concern which has fo thoroughly appalled with horror a man not trained by ftation to the fineft feelings, but enured by habit to fcenes of death : his confternation is that which ordinary men feel and fpeak of, his head is chilled, and his hair is erect.—The favage-warrior in front gives a new tone to the feelings, a tone to which the human race is every where a ftranger, except among his tribes. It is not confternation on the view of death, it is not diftrefs for the lofs of a great leader; thefe he knows nothing of, for he is a fa- vage, and a favage-warrior. Thofe who fuftain that character in his country are known to feel an *unique* of compofure, of fettled fatisfaction, when a brother-warrior dies as he ought, although that warrior were the next in kindred and affection to themfelves: they will even ftimulate unneceffary pains and tortures to make the *exit* illuftrious and heroic. He therefore fits contem- plative over the event ; he fits, as if he watched the awful clofe, that it be great ; he fits, as one abforbed in the view of a warrior greater than himfelf. Looking back on this character in an alle- gorical light, is he not the perfection of allegory ? he participates in the fcene, he helps it, he gives a new lift to the fentiments

that poffefs us.—That lift is more exalted ftill, and acquires a
polifh, as the eye paffes to the wounded Monckton. What was
before the hardy admiration of uncultivated Nature becomes now
the fympathetic feeling of liberal manners, made more generous
by it's prevalence over the fufferings of the individual himfelf.
The fenfe he feels of pain or of danger is transferred, by
the expreffive language of his countenance, from himfelf to
the hero who is expiring before him. He himfelf becomes our
guide to the greater fenfibility which muft centre in the man, by
whom the laurels were prepared for every other brow, but never
more to be vifible on his own.—Thus reflected and turned back
again on the great centre of all, with fentiments thus progreffively
matured and heightened, we become fixed on the illuftrious hero
of the fcene. We are not difappointed; we are not brought to a
view which has been invaded or impaired by what we have feen
and felt before; no paffion has been rouzed to weaken the final
impreffion which awaits us, no paffion has been rouzed in vain.
We behold him a hero in death; not by ftruggling againft it, or
fhewing any contumacy of mind, but by that placid ferenity
which great minds only can poffefs, and which muft be infeparable from him whofe fenfe of duty and of fervice to his
country had found themfelves in that inftant fo glorioufly
accomplifhed; although that ferenity be inevitably fomewhat
infringed by that fenfe of pain, and that only, which muft be
infeparable from the human frame finking into immediate dif-
folution.

Thus has the judicious artift told this ftory on the canvas.
We have no hefitation to pronounce it one of the moft genuine
models of hiftoric painting in the world. If there be any
thing that may be called the intermixture of mere poetic, it is

only in the erected hair of the foldier behind. And yet furely the ideas, which proverbial fpeech has appropriated for the ex-emplification of certain paffions, may be gravely adopted without being confidered as the flights of mere poetic imagination. But if they are fo properly confidered, yet is the inftance before us combined in nature with fome degree of fact. Animals, almoft of every kind, will fhew it when furprized by ftrong affright-ment. And every man, on fuch occafions, feels fomething that approaches to fome portion of the fame effect. To heighten what Nature has given as a feeling, and on the occafion that is peculiar to it, is certainly within the province of the hifloric, as well as of the poetic, painter. We will only add, that among the ancients, who moft faithfully reprefented the genuine feelings of Nature, the erection of the hair is always mentioned by the graveft writers as the moft expreffive mark of dread and terror.

In thefe obfervations we fpeak to what may probably be the firft ideas of obfervers, at leaft of many. But we are fenfible that the effect here fpoken of was by no means the whole idea of the artift. The cap of that grenadier has fallen from his head, and lies befide him on the ground. The wind has evidently blown it off, and from the fame caufe his hair may be difturbed. But what a happy circumftance to the artift was that little guft of wind? how elegant, how compleat the idea? It gives us to fee the foldier's care and anxiety; he has neither time nor thought to mind the diforder of his own drefs; his whole attention is to the general; *totus in hoc eft.* If by fuch an incident as this the cap had not been carried from his head, all thefe touches of expreffion muft have been loft; it would have been next to impoffible for the artift to have given much character to this man, at leaft he could not have given to him the character in which he now ftands.

One remark more before we leave this picture. We have observed on a former occasion, that the introduction of portraits in historic subjects is a very condemnable licence : but we observed at the same time that this must be understood, where living characters are made a part of subjects long since passed. In such a case it is unworthy the dignity of the historic pencil, because it is done with a view either to flatter or to ridicule ; and it is a complete check upon the effect, inasmuch as we find something which we know at once not to be true. But in the display of events which have been transacted within our own days, far different is the introduction of the most exact portraits of those who have borne conspicuous parts in those events. Nay, we may be allowed, without prejudice to any of the principles by which that liberty is warranted in events so constituted, to employ it in those which have been somewhat previous to the existing generation, especially if they have arisen in our own country. For the same principles are common to both those cases, in which the paintings that are destitute of those personal likenesses are certainly deficient in what may be pronounced satisfactory, if not useful, information ; we should no more be content with fictitious countenances there, than we should endure the real countenances that are known to us in scenes of ancient date ; and this for the plainest reason, because we expect the historic painter to give us all the possible information he can. The picture on which we have commented is complete in this agreeable essential. It is a true delineation to posterity of those very persons by whom that very important enterprize was atchieved, so far as their return to their native country, or other possibilities, could obtain the delineation : ages to come may contemplate the features of those who so gloriously signalized themselves on the plains of Abram, and immortalized their names in the annals of

Britain. And is it not a pleafing advantage of the hiftoric pencil, that while it records events on which ages may feed with delight and improvement, it can keep alive to the acquaintance of thofe ages thofe illuftrious charaƈters, whom to know familiarly by the features of their countenance pofterity muft no lefs emulate than to know them by their deeds?

Poetic painting.

WE come now to the other part of the diftinƈtion which awaits our prefent enquiry, and fhall confider what belongs to poetic painting. In fome refpeƈts it participates of the fame effentials with the other branch of the art which we have already difcuffed. The foundation of it muft be laid in perfpicuity. If the fubjeƈt be Heƈtor, it muft not be miftaken for Æneas : if Rinaldo, it fhall not be poffible to fuppofe it Don Quixotte. Thofe incidents therefore, which lead more pointedly to the aƈtion reprefented, muft be attended to and marked with their own features, becaufe they are the moft immediate key to the defign, although in abundant parts of the management of thefe, and perhaps in every thing beyond thefe, the painter may be left very much to himfelf. To give an example of our meaning. Suppofe the fubjeƈt to be the concluding fcene of the Æneid— Turnus and Æneas in combat. What fhall prevent thefe from paffing for Heƈtor and Achilles, confidering the general fimilarity of circumftances, if we do not behold the adjoining city of the Latins befieged, fcaled, defolated, and in flames—perhaps the aged queen pendent from her own cord from a beam, if the idea be not thought too gothic—but moft certainly that ftriking and moft expreffive allegory of bad news and diftrefs, the meffenger with the arrow flicking in his face in full fpeed to Turnus, to urge him to the decifive and inevitable combat; although in the management of thefe the painter fhall be left to all the variety which his own genius may fuggeft. Again: if Dido be defcribed in all the diftraction of flighted love, when from the top of her tower fhe views the departing fleet of Æneas under fail, let us be certain that it is not Ariadne diftracted for the lofs of her Thefeus. The painter therefore muft at all events give us the pile prepared in the open court, and crowned with funeral greens and garlands, the Trojan arms, the robes, the picture, and more efpecially the fword, thrown together thereon; although his own judgement fhall be the guide to the difpofition of the whole.

Another effential, common to the poetic as well as the hiftoric painter, is the obfervance of *coftumé*. This is important for the prefervation of perfpicuity, as well as of good fenfe in general. Without this there would be no bounds to fancy, which would be apt to ftudy the entertainment of the eyes without regard to the underftanding. We fhould be carried at once into various parts of Nature and of life, and thrown into an affemblage of ideas which would make it difficult to fix on any precife one. But under this regulation the ftrongeft pufhes of the mind, like a fhip by her anchor, are pulled up and kept from launching beyond a prudential compafs. All would be wreck, if it were left to go it's full length. Whatever therefore be the fcene, the poetic artift, whofe field is Nature and art, muft find his graces within that part of Nature and art which is connected with the fcene before him; and thofe graces will always be not only confiftent, but fufficient for his purpofe. He fhall not therefore reprefent Alexander in a hat and wig, nor any other character in a coat of armour who never wore one. If architecture fill up his ground, it fhall be the architecture of the country and the age: the orders of Greece fhall not be feen in Egypt, nor fhall the huge and maffy piles of the latter be introduced into the land of tafte. If Arcadia be the fcene, although the objects thrown into it may excite pity and condolence, it fhall be all Arcadian, all ferenity, all frefhnefs, fragrancy, and life.

To thefe effentials muft be added a third, and not lefs important than either of the former; and that is, there muft be no inconfiftency, no contradiction of circumftances, no unnatural blendings. In every fpecies of poetic compofition, in the dramatic and the epic as well as in that of the canvas, this is a primary and indifpenfible principle. What Horace obferves of the former is equally true of the latter, in which the violation of this principle is found, *quodcunque oftendis mihi fic, incredulus odi**. It is in fact the " Cyprefs in the fea-piece," whatever it's fpecific inconfiftency may be.

Raphael was a great poet on the canvas, although he made the hiftoric profeffion of the art peculiarly his own. If Michael Angelo was the Homer of painting, as indeed he was, Raphael was the Virgil. And this parallel holds true not only in the graces he enjoyed, but in his being indebted for much of that enjoyment to the defigns of Michael Angelo. His " School of Athens" is ftrictly a poetic compofition, and we are forry to difcover in it the " Cyprefs in the fea." An affemblage of characters who are known by all never to have had exiftence together, and that affemblage brought into one and the fame group, on one and the fame fpot, moft certainly can never be juftified by poetic, any more than by hiftoric, licence. For although fiction

* Hor. Ars Poet. v. 188.

K

be the life and foul of poetry, it muſt not militate againſt common fenſe, nor combine impoſſibilities. And perhaps it is the
trueſt idea of poetic fiction, that it is more concerned in creating
the diſpoſitions and relations of things, which are known to have
exiſtence and a natural combination with the ſubject, than in
giving exiſtence to things which come not within one or the
other of thoſe predicaments.

Yet this muſt be underſtood with fome modification. It is not
meant to be aſſerted, that entities and non-entities, the living
and the long ſince dead, cannot be brought into the fame painting, although it be poetic. If heaven be combined with a fcene
on earth, they may take their place refpectively in each ſituation,
without any diſturbance of propriety, becauſe not only they do
not make a part of the fame maſs, but they form a diſtinct fcene
by themfelves : and if the fcene be entirely heaven, it is the nature of that fcene that they ſhould mix together in the fame groups,
whatever may be the diſtance of their ages, or the diſtinction of
their countries. If Raphael was fomewhat overfeen in his
" School of Athens," where he has brought together the living
and the dead in the fame earthly fpot, he has nevertheleſs been
more happy and fuccefsful in another poetic compoſition, his
School of Theology, or, as it is commonly called " The Diſpute
on the Sacrament," which afforded him the very ſituations in
which the living and the dead might be introduced with confiſt-
ency and correctneſs. We there fee both on the fame canvas,
but they are not brought together in the fame group, nor in fact
in the fame fpecific fcene. If apoſtles, prophets, and patriarchs are
brought before the eye in the fame canvas, and are made partici-
pators of the fame ſubject with divines and doctors of the church,
yet they are not on the earth at the fame time, they are judiciouſly

feated in the air, and fo they participate without any contradiction, and without any offence. It is no more inconfiftent with
good fenfe, or with enlightened doctrine, to fuppofe thofe departed characters hovering in the air over the interefts of theology
and the Chriftian church, than it is for Chriftian divines to teach
that there are fpirits above, and that thofe fpirits watch over
mankind, and minifter to their falvation. But it is an exalted
ftroke of poetry thus to reprefent the fublimity of theological
truths, by carrying their reach from earth to heaven; and it was
a mafter-piece of art to combine in the fame fubject things naturally diffociable, without appearing to combine them, without
any actual commixture, and with the prefervation of a real independent ground. Thus has Raphael taught his followers a leffon,
how the poetic genius may furmount what appears impoffible,
and how it may change the nature of things fo far as to embrace
with entire fatisfaction that which was improbable.

The leffon he gave in that work has not been loft upon
all that came after him. In a feries of pictures, produced
within thefe few years in our own country by a Britifh
artift, we fee the impreffions of that leffon finely illuftrated, not
only fo far as it was carried by Raphael, but to the full extent of
the principle; we fee too all the great properties which enter
into the difcriminated provinces of hiftoric and poetic painting
moft correctly and forcibly maintained. We are more happy
to felect this work as an exemplification of the principles we
have laid down, becaufe, as a defign, it is another triumph of the
Britifh fchool in a moft arduous line of the art, which does honour to it's prefent profeffor of painting *, from whofe hands it
came: the work we mean is "The Progrefs of Science and
" the general Cultivation of Society." We have felected this

* Mr. Barry.

feries of pictures more efpecially as an illuftration of poetic painting ; although the parts which claim to be confidered as hiftoric
are not lefs able and correct than thofe which are poetic ; but we
confider the greater portion of thefe pictures to be of the poetic
clafs, notwithftanding the artift himfelf has denominated three
of them only to be of that clafs, and the other three to be
hiftoric.   If he meant the firft picture, that of Orpheus, to be
confidered as hiftoric, which feems rather probable from the
greater reftraint which he has obferved in managing the circumftances of that fubject, yet the fubject itfelf, and more efpecially
as he has explained his ufe of it, muft certainly be fet down as
poetic.   We can only fpeak of the third and fifth pictures as
hiftoric.   Of thofe pictures, and particularly of the third the
grander of the two, we fhall take the prefent moment to fay at
once, that the hiftoric province is moft accurately maintained ;
there is the greateft perfpicuity throughout ; great exactnefs and
confiftency in the incidents and fituations ; the allegories are
beautifully imagined to mark the country in which the fcene
lay, and the images ingenioufly chofen to mark decidedly the
fcene itfelf; not a fingle anachronifm or unnatural blending is to
be found, all the characters introduced are of the fame age, and
they are not without an evident, or a reafonably fuppofed, intereft in the refpective fcenes.   One hefitation only hangs upon
our mind in this general fuffrage we give to their merit : we are
not quite fatisfied with the head of Chatham put upon the fhoulders
of Pericles.   If this be a blot on hiftoric purity, we cannot refrain
to obferve that the profeffor's art was faved from fome greater
blots more by chance than by deliberate judgement, if we are to
take his own words for it *.   He has reafon to be thankful that
he did not purfue his wifh of introducing general Paoli among

* See Barry's Account of thefe Pictures, p. 78. 90.

the Grecian victors in the third picture, and that in the fifth he had not room for thofe many illuftrious characters in England, to whom he would have given a place at the diftribution of the prizes. The firft would have been a fad miftake : and the laft thought, if indulged, would have funk all the dignity of the hiftoric, by making it a mere handmaid to portraits, whofe numbers would not have been more objectionable than their infipidity, as he himfelf gives us to underftand that they would not have had any vifible intereft in the fcene.

All the other pictures in that feries are poetic, and valuable exemplifications of the poetic province. The point of art in that province, on which we were engaged on Raphael's " Difpute on the Sacrament," and which primarily introduced the mention of that feries of pictures, is there managed in the fecond of that feries with the fame fuccefsful addrefs of which Raphael gave the precedent ; deities above participate in the fcene which is tranfacted to their fatisfaction below. But in the fixth and laft of that feries, which may claim to itfelf no lefs originality than grandeur and difficulty in it's compofition, the extent to which that point of art may be carried by the confiftency of it's principle is feen moft glorioufly exemplified, and moft critically juft. In the regions of Elyfium the Divine Prefence gives a natural fublimity to the fcene which is filled by men and angels : and we cannot avoid to obferve, that the method taken by this artift of leading the eye and the mind to the idea of God by his effects rather than by any perfonal form, is far more lofty, and productive of a more awful veneration, than any other mode which has been purfued by art : we are perfuaded that the Greeks would have done the fame thing, if they had obtained a true notion of him, if all their notions of the Divinity had not been corporeal.

In thofe regions, angels mixed among men, and men of all ages mixed among one another, and difcriminated only by the different groups which are formed by different ftudies and fervices to mankind, are the fcenes naturally to be expected. We fee with fatisfaction Defcartes affociated with Archimedes, Sir Ifaac Newton with Copernicus, Columbus and his chart of the weftern world with an angel uncovering a folar fyftem that had not been known before : Sir Thomas More fits naturally with Epaminondas, Socrates, Cato, and Brutus both the elder and the younger, as one of the great fextumvirate : John Lock properly makes part of a philofophic group with Zeno, Ariftotle, and Plato ; and all thefe naturally look up to a legiflative group, in which the great Alfred and William Penn are placed fide by fide, the latter of whom juftly offers his code of laws to the infpection of Lycurgus, Solon, Numa, and Zeleucus : great and good princes, who have heroically faved their country, and bleffed it by the wifdom and equity of their rule, are worthily affociated together here, how diftant foever they were from each other in their ages or their countries : and among the patrons of genius and the fine arts through the earth we behold with pleafure Lord Arundel of England and Lorenzo de Medicis affembled in the fame group with Alexander the Great.

But it is not in that particular point of art alone that we would call the attention of the reader to thofe poetic paintings. While every circumftance which conftitutes that province of the art is juftly maintained, and with fuperior beauties in fome of it's parts, particularly in the allegories, in the images felected and fuited to each fubject, and in the tranfition by which every fubject neatly conveys itfelf to the next, there is a merit in the aggregate of the work which is worthy of contemplation. The

great moral, which gave birth to the whole, and in which the
whole is wound up, is no puny thought, that " happiness pub-
" lic and private, prefent and future, depends on the cultivation
" of the human faculties for the benefit of fociety." To illuftrate this leffon by a courfe of energetic exemplifications calls
for no contracted compafs of knowledge, at leaft in the general
progrefs of literature and fcience. The difpofition neceffary to
the beft effect of fubjects fo enlarged in their fcope, and fo pregnant with bufinefs, as thofe which muft conftitute that courfe of
exemplification, is no lefs exquifite as an effort of art than the
felection of the fubjects themfelves is profound as an effort of
judgement. There is of neceffity therefore great profundity in
the whole plan; yet we do not find it confulted to fuch an extent as to defeat perfpicuity, although the artift himfelf has
declared * in favour of the former, and fomewhat contemptu-
oufly of the latter, which, happily for us, is not warranted by his
own works : he has afferted that a fubject in painting fhould
never be fo plain that it can be read at once. In that fentiment we do not concur with him, becaufe we do not find it in
any of the conftituent principles of painting, either as hiftorical,
or poetical, or as a writing, and we do not conceive that a painting fhould always become an allegory. Perhaps he meant that
fentiment as a kind of preliminary paffport to the depth which
he conceived to await our ftudy in that work, and which may
bear that fentiment as well as any other work, becaufe it is a
work of fcience, and fcience is never quite perfpicuous to thofe
who firft approach it. Neverthelefs we are contented to take
the effect which he has prepared for us, leaving the comment
with which he would introduce it. In the confideration of that
effect we enter into no circumftances of the art beyond the defign and the difpofition, the laft of which is pregnant with excel-

Ibid. p. 24.

lencies in the various incidents and groups both relatively to
each other and immediately to their own fpecific purpofes.   We
cannot forbear to mention what ftrikes us as beautiful inftances
of this in the fixth and laft picture of the feries—the difpofition
of the angels on the range of rocks which feparate Elyfium from
the infernal regions, and the different offices of thofe angels
bufied on the fates of men—the elevated fituation given to the
felicities of thofe who have cultivated peace and moderation upon
earth—and the ftill more elevated ftation, near the centre, afforded to the infpired bards of the world, who look up to the glory
that emanates above them, eager as it were to catch from it's
rays the fire with which their lips and their lyres were once
hallowed.

In the fketch which is given of the place of punifhment the
artift has fhewn, in the affemblage of his objects and in his manner
of treating them, that he has not ftudied Rubens in vain.   Expreffion fpeaks enough, and with an honourable variation on
the fpirit of that mafter, in the two hands which we are juft
permitted to fee amidft the clouds of fmoke that envelope the
the dark and deep gulph ; they are grapling at a group of infamous characters bound together by ferpents, and they pull down
by the hair two women who are a part of it.   It is next to impoffible not to fpeak in the very language of Rubens, when once
his principle has been imbibed.   Yet we give credit to our own
artift for the thought which has introduced an ambitious and
worldly pope, with a fiery globe on his fhoulders, making his
vice to become, in the full fpirit of Rubens, his everlafting
punifhment, while he ftill keeps up one part, and the only facred
one, of his character, by preaching in the flames like another
Phlegyas.

If the principles we have laid down in poetic painting have been happily maintained in that modern work, on which we have dwelt with pleasure, it is not always among others of the older masters, besides Raphael, that we find them preserved with equal chastity and care. We have already had occasion to observe, that Nicholas Pousfin was a great poetic genius, and a chaste painter in general ; and yet he has not always guarded, as much as he ought, against inconsistency and contradiction. Two of his poetic performances are particularly censurable on this ground. The violence of his fancy has there led him to combine things which are not only contrasts, but unnatural contrasts, sub-versive of each other. We allude to " the man flying from the serpent," and to " the death of Phocion." Are we to call these landscapes, or history-pieces? If the former, the eye is indeed delighted in each of them with a most gay and riant scene of Nature, but in each of them the scene below crushes in a moment every sense of rising pleasure by the mournfulness and dread which it awakens within us. If the latter, the lessons they would read are instantly lost by the gaiety with which we are attracted on the first lifting of the eyes. If we call them poetic pieces, which we ought to do rather than either of the others, yet the greater latitude of that class does not warrant the combination of scenes so contrary to each other. We must not however measure by the same reflection the Arcadia of the same artist, because Arcadia has a local scenery appropriated to it by a sort of universal consent ; that scenery was supposed never to be altered ; it can therefore never be disguised, and every attempt to describe Arcadia by any other scene would be out of charac-ter. It is that peculiar country, which is said to have been inha-bited by the happiest race of mortals, by men employed only on temperate pleasures, and who knew no other disquietudes than

thofe which befel the imaginary fhepherds in romance, whofe
condition has always been envied.   That country therefore can
never be painted otherwife than gay, although the eye be directed
to a melancholy object within it ; juft as Elyfium muft be Elyfium ftill, the happieft and moft verdant fcene that can be prefented to the fight, although it be replete with groups of ghaftly
departed fhades.

Such then are the qualifications, within which the poetic painter
has the whole range of Nature, and the whole fcope of imagination, to drefs his fcenes and give them force and attraction.   The
fact is, that the province of poetry in all it's branches is framed
to give pleafure, while the end of hiftory is to inform and inftruct.
The very mention of thefe two different objects in each is fufficient to account for the more abundant latitude to thofe inventive powers, which are to accomplifh the end of any poetic
reprefentation.   Lord Bacon defines poetry at large to be "hifto-
" riæ imitatio ad placitum;" that is, it is to be fo far like hiftory as
to elucidate the ftory, the object, or principle which it means to
imprefs, but conducted by a more enlarged freedom of invention
than hiftorical fidelity dare affert, and that for the purpofe of
giving pleafure.   In another place, but with allufion to the fame
diftinction, that great writer obferves *, that " poetry in general
" has the privilege of fhaping and adapting the reprefentations
" of things to the gratification and fatisfaction of the mind,
" while hiftory endeavours to bring our minds to be fatisfied
" with facts as they are."   With this diftinction admitted, we
would not think of going to the extent of Caftelvetro's affertion †,
that poetry has no bufinefs to inftruct.   For how wretched muft
be the poetic aim, which impreffes no fentiment, nor raifes the

* De Augment. Scient. lib. 2. c. 13.   † Comment. on Ariftot. Poetics, p. 29.

mind to any improving reflection ? On the canvas, or in the book, which with all the poffible ftrokes of poetic ability is fo frothy as to teach us nothing, we fhould certainly not bear to look long. We expect to learn fomething, efpecially in every work that makes pretenfion to importance. But then *pleafure* is certainly the vehicle of what we learn here : we depend on being amufed, and gratified in our fancy, at any rate : we look for all the imagery of embellifhment, by which a brilliant and correct invention amplifies it's fcenes, and exalts our conceptions. The only reftraint is, that the invention be correct as well as brilliant, and that the pleafure it raifes be not infringed by the introduction of any thing unnatural, foreign, and difcordant.

The field of pleafure is a large one ; and the means of adminiftering it are fufficiently large, even when they are fo reftrained. The poetic licence in the hands of the artift is fufficiently extenfive. Whatever is natural and of a piece is at his abfolute command. The vifionary has no exclufion. The emblematic fhall take the place of the real exiftence, which it is meant to figure. Embellifhment is natural drefs, and all Nature is it's fource. What a fund for the ftrong poetic genius ? In the production of the fublime and beautiful, what an infinite copioufnefs of materials is before him ?

There is a fublime of hiftory ; and the hiftorical difplay, which does not reach a portion of the fublime, is hardly worth our regard. But the fublime in the hands of the poetic artift is of a different caft ; it's means, it's fcope, it's execution, it's whole compofition is different. Look at "the laft judgement" of Michael Angelo : look at it as the whole of that awful event thrown together, not as a perfect and unexceptionable whole in point of felected thoughts and incidents, but as a whole that is managed by poetic abilities. What fublimity has it received from the pencil of that mafter? Not Homer himfelf could have lifted the fcene to more lofty conceptions. It is every thing that an univerfal convulfion of nature, an univerfal miracle of Omnipotence on created matter, can exhibit moft ftupendoufly fublime at the found of the laft awful trumpet. Earth and heaven contribute their portions to fill up this tremendous fcene, and prefent it with confternating grandeur to the beholding eye.

It is true that, in the view of confulting the advantages of art, the whole of that fubject as embraced by Michael Angelo was attended with fome embarraffments, becaufe one half of it was terror, and the other half was joy. And this circumftance feems to have difcouraged Rubens from purfuing the fame whole, if private tradition be right, and if we may infer fo much from the many portions of ftudies on that whole, which are ftill to be found, and were abandoned of courfe, as they were never brought to any actual defign. After various efforts it is plain that he determined on a divifion of the fubject, taking the terrific part by itfelf in " the fall of the damned," which he completed, and referving the happier fcene for the " refurrection of the bleffed," of which he left a fketch that unhappily was never carried into full execution. " The fall of the damned" had many ftudies before it obtained his final decifion in that painting which is now at Duffeldorff, where the fketch we have juft mentioned is alfo to be found. It is that particular work, diftinguifhed from any others by his hand that may be denominated " the fall of the damned," which we fhall felect here as another inftance of the grand and fublime in poetic painting; not lefs grand and fublime, although it be only a part of the laſt judgement, than the whole together appears, as wrought up by his great predeceſſor.

Perhaps " the fall of the damned" admits of being lifted by more various diſcrimination to a lofty and affecting moral than any other part of that extended ſubject. Even glory and happineſs, however they may be diverſified beyond our conceptions by the ſupreme Source of all effects, and in another world which we know not, are in their preſent impreſſions on us, with all their attractions, ſo much the ſame attraction, affecting one and the ſame ſenſe of fruition, that perhaps they do not rouze the ſame breadth of feelings, nor produce the ſame ſtimulating leſſons, that are excited by the proſpect of variegated miſery. All muſt feel them indeed, and be captivated by them, but in a very different way from that in which we are affected by their reverſe. For they captivate only in theory, and are capable only of being theoretically conceived, without affording the power of any ſpecific illuſtration. But there is nothing more ſurely known to us than pain and ſuffering, to whoſe moſt aggravated ſtages every ſenſe and experience can lead us by the cleareſt preconceptions.

This is the point which has enabled Rubens, with far leſs aſſiſtance than Michael Angelo derived from the conſpiring effects of convulſed Nature around, to reach our feelings by as high a ſublimity as can well be ſuppoſed to be accompliſhed by human genius on the ſubject he has choſen. In a general view of the laſt judgement the damned may be hurled into a deep and dark abyſs, without any other circumſtance than their being ſo hurled, and the thought ſhall neither be poor, nor common, nor unintereſting, becauſe there will be ſome effect in the contraſted

fate of the bleſſed to make this part of the ſcene diſtreſsful, there
will be dignity enough in the ſupreme ſeat of judgement to fill
it with an awful importance, and there will be terror enough in
the whole aſſemblage of events to make it dreadful.   But when
Rubens came to deſcribe the fate of the ſame objeɛts in a ſcene
contraɛted merely to what immediately concerned them, that
ſcene would certainly have been poor, and common, and unintereſting, if it had not been ſuſtained by ſome important moral,
which ſhould arreſt and fix the mind in awful contemplation of
the events that paſſed, ſhould make every incident big with
inſtruɛtion, and by a forcible impreſſion ſhould diſplay the divine
equity in thoſe meaſures of it's judgement and retribution.

And what moral can be brought more home to thoſe purpoſes, what better uſe can be drawn from thoſe meaſures of divine
judgement, than that on which Rubens has kept his eye through
the whole of that compoſition, and which he has conveyed in
every incident ?—that " every man's vice ſhall become his puniſhment." Is there a principle more likely to be juſt ? Is there a
ſentiment more likely to cure or reſtrain the habits of vice ? Is
there a ſentiment, whoſe detail to the eye and the mind, but eſpecially to the eye, can be exhibited with a more forcible and more
copious impreſſion? To be tormented by devils we ſuppoſe
to be at leaſt one puniſhment in hell. When this idea is caught
by the poet, whoſe ſpirit depiɛts by ſenſible images, he naturally
extends himſelf to all the views that can be drawn from it by the
perſonification of thoſe abſtraɛt turpitudes, which would engage
the diſcuſſion of the philoſopher or the Chriſtian. And this is
what Rubens has done. We muſt not blame him for the various,
and ſometimes ſtrange, forms in which his devils appear, nor for
the ſtrange manner in which they are buſied on the purpoſes of

torment, for he did not mean to preach to us as a strict
divine, but in his own way as a poet; and yet it will not be easy
for divines to overthrow the principles of his poetry, that devils
can assume any shape that suits their purpose. Bring the picture
to the eye of any vicious character who shall see it's parallel there,
and let it be supposed that the images given to the devils, and
their actions, are all poetic invention; what will be the conse-
quence, if there be any impression at all? Most certainly the
moral will take hold, although the dress be set at nought. The
consciousness that in some way or other the principle of converting vice into punishment will be made good, will not be avoided
by the capriciousness, if so we should call it, with which the poetic painter has imagined the scene: this imagination will only
excite another in ourselves, that if his be all fiction, that which
will be real cannot be less pungent and horrible to every sense.
When the prostitute sees that delicate hair, on which she has
bestowed so much time and pains, become the cord by which she
is dragged and bound to torture; and that delicate person, to
which she has given every attraction, become loathsome and
disgusting to devils themselves—when the pampered glutton sees
that he has been feeding his appetites only to provide a nicer
feast for devils to gnaw at continually—when the sodomite
perceives that his brutal and unnatural lust shall cling to him
longer than he may like, and shall be kept up whether he will
or no by the violence of devils in the shape which is said to
be next to man, when men themselves can no longer be the
instruments of feeding it—when the liar sees those malicious
fiends torturing his tongue in all the variety of practised agonies
—let all these, and all the rest who are there depicted, laugh as
they please at the humour, as they may call it, of the painter,
that humour shall lead them to another thought which will be

ferious, and that is, that in the end they are to be company for
devils, and to fuffer all, whatever it be, that the company of
devils can make them feel.   In this thought, whatever becomes
of the reft, Rubens is correctly and unanfwerably moral.   In
this thought he preaches as a divine, and not as a poet.   And
is the compofition then a moral one, or not?   If the thought,
that we are to be company with devils, cannot wean and deter
us from thofe vices which will make their company our doom,
nothing elfe can.   Affuredly this fingle thought, if properly
contemplated, for which however we are indebted to a higher
authority than that of Rubens, would go infinitely further in
morals than the philofopher's beauty of virtue, and would render unneceffary all the difputes of Chriftians about the fpecific
nature and degrees of future punifhments.   For is there a man,
whether inured at all to refined feelings, or in no refpect raifed
beyond coarfer ones, that is not ftaggered by the idea of being
configned to the company of devils?   We think it horrid
enough to be doomed upon earth to the company which ill
befits us ; but how much more horrid muft it be to be company
for devils in eternity ?

We have been led to preach upon the fubject, whether the
poetic painter be admitted to have preached upon it or not.
We wifh to do juftice to that excellent work, whofe principles
are folid, however they may be coloured by the fpirit of poetry
with afpects that are fanciful, and whofe views are honourable
and moral, as much as if they had been delivered with every
poffible gravity in every incident.   They are vindicable precifely on the fame ground which vindicates all that concerns
the fame fubject in the " Paradife loft" of our own immortal
Milton.   When Rubens took up this fubject poetically, he was

he was compelled to ſtrike out a field of his own, he was con-
ſtrained to draw from his own imagination. And the originality, which broke forth from his mind, is not more brilliant
to be beheld, than the effects of that originality on other great
minds beſides his own are curious to be followed. It has been
ſaid, and ſometimes truly, that great wits will jump together
into the ſame ſentiments on the ſame theme. But it is im-
poſſible for us to ſolve in that way the ſtriking ſimilarity which
appears in the great features given to the circumſtances of the
damned both by Milton and by Rubens. Many things too clear
to be overlooked conſpire to prove, that the fire and judgement of the former in all his views of hell were aſſiſted and fed
by this work of the latter. Milton was coming forward into the
world as a young man in the latter days of Rubens. It is a known
fact in his life, that he viſited Rome, and alſo the low countries.
And as the elegance of his mind carried him, in the former place,
through the Vatican, with the cloſeſt attention to every thing it
preſented, ſo there is no queſtion but he was equally attentive,
in the latter, to every celebrated work of ingenuity, and eſpecially to thoſe of a maſter whoſe fame was ſo recent, and ſo
univerſally eſtabliſhed, as that of Rubens. With theſe circumſtances adduced, his poem itſelf will decide the point. We
there ſee both the principles and the general images, which
diſtinguiſh this painting of Rubens, embraced by Milton, and
particularly in the ſecond book, whenever hell is deſcribed.

> " Thither by harpy-footed furies hail'd
> " The damned are brought."

Sin perſonified thus ſpeaks for herſelf, what the picture ſpeaks
for all the damned :

> " Theſe monſters, that with ceaſeleſs cry ſurround me,
> " Gnaw my bowels, their repaſt ; and then——

" Afresh with confcious terrors vex me round,
" That reft or intermiffion none I find."

Again:

" Here in perpetual agony and pain,
" With terrors and with clamours compafs'd round
" Of mine own brood, that on my bowels feed."

Of death it is faid,

" ——————— there he fhall be fed and fill'd
" Immeafurably, all things fhall be his prey."
" ——————— and pleas'd he was to hear
" His famine fhould be fill'd, and bleft his maw
" Deftin'd to that good hour."

It will prefently be feen how exactly alike the defcription of the great abyfs is given in the poem and in the picture. So far, therefore, the mode in which Rubens has conducted his fubject appears to have met the approbation, and even to have enriched the mind, of that great poet.

It was not in the power of Rubens to conduct that fubject in any other than a poetic manner. Had he tried to treat it hiftorically, a few moments would have fhewn the attempt to be impoffible, becaufe the traits afforded in fcripture are too few, and too figurative and indiftinct, to be made the groundwork of any reprefentation which looks fo clofely to points as the hiftoric. The truth is, thofe traits of fcripture are themfelves more nearly allied to the poetic, than to any other clafs of expreffion. And we conceive that with fome poetic licence they are not inaptly realized in every ftroke of Rubens's pencil here. " The worm " dieth not," if the confcioufnefs of vice, and the fufferings iffuing from it's fource, be a worm, whofe gnawings never leave a refpite to the mind and the body : and " the fire is not quenched," if the fufferings felt be a fire within, which keeps up a fever there, parching the bones, and confuming without ever deftroying; as Milton fays,

" Fed with ever-burning fulphur unconfum'd."

Yet Rubens was not inattentive to the popular notion, con-ftruing thofe images in a real fenfe. The vaft and fathomlefs abyfs, which at laft receives the damned, to complete the tortures which in their fall have been inflicted by devils in all fhapes hovering in mid-way, is filled with other fiends innumerable, which feem impatient for the prey that is defcending, and to grudge as it were both the morfels and the tortures that are fnatched by their fellow-fiends who drag them down : it is filled with fire, whofe fulphureous body emits not the flames which would exhauft it's ftrength, or fpread the gleams of light around, but which leave darknefs equally prevalent and more hideous ; with ferpents, and fcorpions, and all envenomed creatures, and monfters frightful to behold; it is an affemblage of every thing that is moft foul, and hateful, and ferocious in nature or in idea, even beyond what language has been able to mark in the reptile and bafer parts of creation as deftructive in their fpecies. But let Milton's defcription be taken ; and let the reader judge whe-ther the eye of that poet had not conveyed to his mind from this picture the ideas which accord fo clofely with what has been painted.

" A dungeon horrible on all fides round
" As one great furnace flam'd, yet from thofe flames
" No light, but rather darknefs vifible,
" Serv'd only to difcover fights of woe,
" Regions of forrow, doleful fhades, where peace
" And reft can never dwell, hope never comes
" That comes to all, but torture without end
" Still urges, and a fiery deluge fed

" With ever-burning fulphur unconfum'd.
" Such place eternal juftice had prepar'd
" For the rebellious."

BOOK I.

Again, more clofely:

" A univerfe of death, which God by curfe
" Created evil, for evil only good,
" Where all life dies, death lives, and nature breeds
" Perverfe all monfters, all prodigious things,
" Abominable, unutterable, and worfe
" Than fables yet have feign'd, or fear conceiv'd,
" Gorgons and hydras and chimeras dire."

BOOK II.

Further yet:

" ——————— Into this wild abyfs,
" The womb of nature, and perhaps her grave,
" Of neither fea, nor fhore, nor air, nor fire,
" But all thefe in their pregnant caufes mixt
" Confus'dly."

IBID.

And, laftly, in one comprehenfive expreffion by the prince of devils,

" Havoc and fpoil and ruin are my gain."

Such is the " fall of the damned" by Rubens, and fuch is the high fpirit of poetic talent through the whole, not only exhibiting by a fplendid proof the genuine principles of poetic painting, but in it's invention and in the whole train of it's images taking a path, for the exemplification of principles authoritatively underftood, which had never been trodden before. To higher and more fublime difplays of that talent on the canvafs, for the production of it's great objects, the pleafure, furprize, and elevation of the imagination, and a moral impreffion on the underftanding, it is impoffible to go.

Here, therefore, we shall close the inquiry which we have undertaken into the poetic and historic provinces of the pencil; hoping, that when Nature and principles have established so clear and so important a distinction as that which appears between those two great branches of painting, however that distinction may have been confounded by others, it will be more attentively and securely preserved in a British school. It is our duty to improve by the mistakes of others: and it should be our pride, that when science of every kind stands on such enlightened ground in our country, cleared from the errors of those who have gone before us, the finer arts which seem to have fled to us for preservation should be maintained on the chastest and purest principles. Perhaps this may be all the new excellence that is reserved for a British school, after those other excellencies to which the pencil has been carried in other ages and countries: but this purity of principle will be original in us, if it be completely and uniformly maintained; and in that maintenance of it we shall render a service to the arts, which will leave the British school by no means the least respectable and exemplary of those which have existed in the world.

CHAP. VI.

The cultivation of the fine arts a source of refined polish to the manners.

WE have considered the art of painting in it's superior and more enlarged character, as a mean of conveying and perpetuating solid and beneficial instruction. The observations we

have made have been felected much lefs to confult the theory
of this admirable art than to do juftice to that practical difplay
of it, which our own country has at length been fo happy as
to fee carried in the prefent æra to an excellence which forms
a new age in the hiftory of the pencil.   It were little to fay this,
if that particular excellence had not been followed by that
general excellence in the fine arts, which fets them and the patronage by which they have been reared in Britain upon a footing, that entitles both to a fame in many refpects equal to what
either has obtained in any age of the world.   What we have
hitherto faid, in order to illuftrate the fuperior interefts of this
art, and the principles on which thofe interefts ftand, will find
it's relation, as we proceed, to the future fubjects which await
our difcuffion, particularly in the laft part of this work, and will
enable us the better to do juftice to thofe fubjects.   In the mean
time, before we clofe the part on which we are engaged, we conceive that it will be no improper introduction to all that follows,
if we reflect on that amiable and refined polifh and improvement, which the cultivation of the fine arts never fails to introduce into the minds and manners of any people.

A people that have no arts can have no manners fit to be
fpoken of.   As they know not the proper value of each other,
for each other they have but little efteem and ftill lefs civility.
As they have not the temptations of ingenuity to fill their time,
their time is confequently difpofed in the ruder and more fullen
habits of indolent, if not of favage, life.   The neceffaries of
fubfiftence occupy their whole care; and not knowing how to
provide and preferve thefe in the greateft perfection, they are
bereft even of the loweft evidence of improved life in the
choice, and variety, and more exquifite preparation of food.

So much depends on arts in general; but much more on the finer arts. The human mind has been well compared to a piece of marble in the quarry, replete with veins which are invifible, and whofe beauties cannot be conceived until it is dreffed, but which come forth in multifarious ornament by the hand of the polifher. Learning and knowledge in general is that hand which gives the polifh to the mind, and elegant art beflows it not lefs eminently than any other branch of knowledge. By that the powers of the mind receive expanfion, and are led to new fcenes of perception, and new fubjects of enjoyment. For all our faculties are given by providence for good and beneficial ends, and the extenfion of the rational powers muft, in their natural confequence, be followed by rational enjoyment. In the arts of elegance this is true, if not exclufively, yet more eminently than in other parts of knowledge; becaufe all other knowledge may in it's confequences introduce direct vices, whereas it is hard to conceive how any thing but direct cultivation can be the iffue of the more elegant arts. The pleafure of ingenuity is the grand decoy, by which Nature leads us to improve ourfelves and others, and of which fhe has given fome fenfibility in every breaft. We are lifted by this pleafure from one ftage of it to another, and fo from one perception of honourable improvement to a greater. If the fource of this pleafure be lefs copious in ourfelves, we are attracted by the defire of it towards thofe who are able to difpenfe it : and this foundation of focial improvement being laid, every other generous affection foon follows, and a general melioration of our whole manners. We gain by degrees nobler and more comprehenfive views of human nature, and of it's capacities to honour us, and make us happy. The purpofes of human life rife up in a fuperior ftyle before us, and we are emulous to meet them.

As the finer feelings take place, the rougher parts of our make wear off, and we wifh to know them no more. There is an infinuation in tafte which is beyond conception. Every portion of it makes way for a greater, and every fenfibility of it will dwell with nothing that is groffer. It gives a tincture to the mind, which affimilates every thing to itfelf. It is like the varnifh we lay over paintings, which preferves all the tints of nature in their refinement, unblended and unfullied by coarfer particles. Art in general has it's foundation fo entirely in the melioration of fociety, and the politer arts efpecially enter fo far into the finer feelings of our nature, and intereft our beft affections fo confiderably in the compafs they take, that when we have been in the habit of tafting their improvements, it is impoffible we fhould be lefs than civilized in the general tenor of our manners, and almoft abfurd to fuppofe that we could relifh what was lefs than civilized. As individuals, or as a public, the face of order, decorum, elegance, fociability, and liberality of deportment muft fhew itfelf ftrongly in our general turn, and characterize a people fo trained and elevated by art.

Luxury, we grant, will follow, and ever has followed, where the arts have gained an eftablifhment. But it is not every luxury that is evil ; there is a luxury of tafte, which is perfectly legitimate, and highly to be emulated. The luxury we mean is not that enervating and wafting luxury, whofe fole object is profufion and wanton indulgence, whofe immediate confequence is vice, and whofe ultimate iffue is the ruin of a people. This luxury may have owed it's birth to the art of commerce, but it has more frequently flowed from wealth fuddenly acquired by foreign conqueft, in which commerce has had the leaft concern, although it may often have furnifhed the firſt pretence. Far different from that is the luxury which liberal art ſupplies—the luxury of living to intelleĉtual enjoyment; of contemplating Nature in her beſt attráĉtions; of gratifying the mind with univerſal excellence; of feeding the ſenſes with the beauties of order, ſymmetry, and every grace; of raiſing the affeĉtions by thoſe imitative ſcenes, which give the pureſt leſſons, or by thoſe harmonious chords which lend the fineſt touches to the ſoul; of converting with the greateſt caſe all the bounties of Nature to the beſt and moſt permanent enjoyment; of conſulting, if you will, the perfeĉtion of many animal ſatiſfaĉtions, but of cultivating even in theſe the perfeĉtion of the rational powers. If, after all, the age of arts has been marked for the age of ſenſual luxury in any country, the latter has followed the former as the tares grow up with the wheat; the richneſs and melioration of the ſoil cannot give the one, without provoking the other. But then the other, which is but as it were an excreſcence of high humour, peeps out only in individual ſpots, and in particular ſituations. Aſſuredly the general face of the whole ſhews order, decency, and health.

From thoſe countries, which have been the ſeat of the arts in any conſiderable degree, our preſent argument will derive it's faireſt illuſtration. Aſia, without queſtion, was civilized much earlier than any other part of the world. Why? Becauſe ſhe obtained all the arts before any other people. Soon after the deluge ſhe became poſſeſſed of many of thoſe arts, which have ever ſince been the portion of poliſhed nations. The ſame may be ſaid of Egypt, which was not much behind. Aſia in the advantages of civilization. If the arts, of which thoſe countries were in poſſeſſion, were not altogether the arts of taſte and elegance, or if that taſte and elegance was not known by them in it's higheſt degrees, yet the ſtate of their arts was ſuch as enabled them to become preceptors to the Greeks, who afterwards carried taſte and elegance to the higheſt pitch, and who derived from one or other of thoſe countries all the arts which made them ſo illuſtrious. The ſtate of their arts alſo was ſuch as became ſufficient to humanize them, and make them very poliſhed nations. No hiſtory indeed is ſo dark and imperfect as that of both thoſe countries in their earlier periods. But from what remains of ſacred and profane authority we may aver, that if in thoſe countries there was found much pomp, magnificence, and voluptuous luxury, the primitive and reigning habits of eaſtern nations, there was alſo great courteouſneſs of manners, liberality of ſentiment, decency and delicacy of demeanor, hoſpitality, and reciprocal friendſhip ; all thoſe habits in general, which ſweeten and cement ſociety. In latter ages, the loſs of liberty and independance has been the lot of the one, and of a great part of the other, which has fallen a prey to the avarice and ambition of other empires. With thoſe revolutions the arts took flight in both countries : and where, ſince thoſe periods, have been the traces of refinement in their manners ? It is hardly poſſible to conceive a people more degraded than either. Yet China, which maintained her ſtation and her power from the graſp of foreign hands, aſſumes to herſelf ſtill, as ſhe has ever done, the character of *polite* as peculiarly her own. With what juſtice ſhe goes ſo far is another matter. But the fact is, ſhe very ſoon got poſſeſſion of many arts, and ſhe has never loſt, but improved, thoſe which ſhe acquired.

Greece will enable us to put the preſent argument in a more forcible view. She was juſt as ancient as any other country,

and she was far more heroic. For many centuries her history is distinguished by the express name of the " heroic ages." Yet who has ever spoken of the arts or the manners of Greece during those ages? Of arts she had but one, the " military", if it could deserve the idea conveyed by that modern phrase ; we should better call it, " fighting" in the field : and of manners, except in the worst sense, she had none. * All was roughness and barbarity ; bravery at best. She had neither morals nor principles. Plutarch says †, " those times produced men of strong
" and indefatigable powers of body, but they applied those pow-
" ers to nothing just or useful : on the contrary, their genius,
" their dispositions, their pleasures tended only to insolence, to
" violence, and to rapine. As for modesty, justice, equity and
" humanity, these were qualities disregarded by those who had
" it in their power to add to their possessions ; they were praised
" only by those who were afraid of being injured ; and they
" were practised only by those who abstained from injuring
" others out of the same principle of fear." The law of the strongest was almost the only one which the people then acknowledged. They had not in their language a word to express *virtue* originally. Examine all the discourses of Homer's princes and heroes, and you will not find one sentiment which argues a virtuous principle, you will be shocked continually by their grossness and indecency, and there is not an action of which they speak with the highest esteem, which does not bear the impression of a savage barbarity. The sense of *virtue* given to ᾿αρετή, whose original import was confined to valour,

* Thucyd. lib. 1. p. 2, 3. Strabo, lib. 3. p. 238. Pausan. lib. 2. c. 29. p. 179. Feith. lib. 14. c. 7. p. 452.

† In vita Thesei.

bravery, and perfonal courage, was much later in time, when, by the melioration of their manners, virtuous moral and focial principles began to kindle in the breafts of the people. And when was that time? It will be found, when the arts of tafte and elegance had begun to obtain a footing in the country.

When we fpeak of Greece, we would be underftood more efpecially to fpeak of Athens. The only ftate that could divide fignificance with Athens, was Lacedæmon; which from the firft to the laft was * fo ftrait and confined, fo hardy and fevere, fo martial and warlike in all her policy, fo devoted to the difcipline of the body, fo fyftematically neglectful of all cultivation of the mind, and fo obligated to the exclufion of art in every fpecies beyond what refpected the plaineft domeftic cafes, that fhe can make no part of an enquiry into the celebrity of Grecian arts and manners. But then in Athens we muft not look for manners even in the time of Solon, becaufe in his time the arts had barely begun to open their bud. We cannot look for a refinement of manners in his days, who ftruck his ftick upon the ground, telling Thefpis in anger †, " that if he went on with " his mock-ftories on the ftage, they would foon make their way " into contracts, and all private concerns." We muft go near two centuries further till the time of Pericles, or perhaps till the reign of Alexander the great, before we fee the Grecian manners in their higheft refinement, becaufe till then the arts of Greece had not reached their full meridian.

In the view of thofe times the mind that is infpired with a love

* Xenoph. de repub. Laced. p. 395. Plut. vita Lycurgi. Arift. de Repub. lib. 8. c. 4.

† Plut. in vita Solonis.

of the fine arts expands itself in flights of rapture, while it contemplates that aftonifhing burft of genius and tafte united, with
which the matured talents of Grecian artifts then came forth,
gathering to themfelves, their age, and their country that immortality of which no time fhall rob them; and enriching the world
with treafures, which as far as they remain entitle us to pronounce on thofe which have been loft, as well as upon themfelves, that they are the everlafting ftandards of perfect art;
while they have carried the inventive powers of the human mind
to a fplendour, on which the lateft pofterity fhall gaze with
never-ceafing admiration. In thofe times alfo it is, that we fee
what the arts can accomplifh in the melioration and refinement
of human manners. * We behold all the elegance, both in life
and in addrefs, that could be expected from the moft enlightened
minds—an eafe and a freedom, which reached to every individual
—a politenefs on all occafions, which was kept up by the very
dregs of the people—a circumfpection and decorum in moft
circumftances where decency was concerned, which, if violated
in fome cafes, was fatal to any character—a mildnefs and humanity, which was perfectly characteriftic, even to their flaves,
even to their beafts—a fenfe of honour, which carried them to
as great deeds as the fenfe of difcipline ever produced in the
Spartans—a pleafantnefs of demeanor, which ran through all the
habits of life, and yet never forgot the improvement of the mind,
and the embellifhment of fociety, in the very midft of their
feafts—a zeal for commercial intercourfe, becaufe it extended
their acquaintance with men and things, and civilized them,
rather than becaufe it enriched them—an attention to the
bleffings of education, becaufe it perpetuated the bleffings they

* See Monf. Goguet's Orig. of Laws, &c. 8vo. vol. iii. b. VI. art. 2.

enjoyed :—if they were luxurious in their living, they fhould rather be called dainty and delicate, than voluptuous and excef-five ; for they were temperate and fober to the greateft degree : —if there were debaucheries among them, fuch things are every where, and perhaps they can by no regulations be prevented in populous cities ; they were hidden, however, with care by the men, and by all the modefty which the women could fhew in their drefs. Such a fyftem of civilized manners was never found among them before the times of which we are fpeaking ; and fince the country has been loft, with all the arts that embellifhed it, fuch manners have never more been feen within it.

In this abftract, which the learned reader knows to be con-firmed by their own writers of their hiftory, and which every reader, who is not converfant with thofe original authorities, may find collected with great juftice and ability by the very laborious Monfieur de Goguet in his " Origin of laws, arts, and " fciences," we have not meant to fet forth the Greeks in any of their fituations as a people perfect in manners. We have no thoughts of finding among them an Utopian fociety, any more than an Utopian country. Many and great faults may therefore be found in their manners by thofe who have ftudied them clofely, and fome faults which may feem to overthrow their claim to fome of the commendations which we have given them. But let thofe inftances be properly weighed, whenever they are adduced. For example : let the perfonal afperities have been ever fo common, which were thrown upon one another by the Greek orators in their harangues, and particularly by Æf-chines and Demofthenes : thefe muft be laid to the liberties of profeffion, or to the warmth of public debate in fupport of a client or of a national object ; they can never be taken to decide on the general politenefs of a people ; for the fame men, who may conceive themfelves fheltered in the ufe of thofe freedoms under thofe particular circumftances, would be very backward to carry them in their general addrefs as citizens at large, even under the toleration which the fpirit of republican equality might be fuppofed to afford to thofe freedoms. Let the obfcenities of the old comedy, efpecially under Ariftophanes, have been ever fo well received in the Athenian theatre : it has ever been open to remark, that thofe fallies will be relifhed, when every other indecency will be fhunned, and they will be permitted to pafs in public affemblies, perhaps on the idea that " defendit numerus," when no mouth would dare to utter them in more private fituations : they are not fufficient, however, to overthrow the general charaĉter of decorum, and regard to decency, in the Greeks, and efpecially in the Athenians, when it is recollecĉted that irrecoverable difhonour even to banifhment and death, in proportion to the fituations of life or office, attended the man who was feen to be drunk ; that women were never fuffered to be prefent at the public games in which the combatants were naked ; and that the letters from a wife to her hufband, when that hufband * was carrying on an inveterate war againft them, and a courier was feized with the difpatches, were returned by the fenate unopened, to mark the refpeĉt which they bore to decency in fo delicate a correfpondence. Let us grant and deteft the barbarity, with which that people put to death the heralds of Darius, fent to them under the faith of nations ; the barbarity with which they put to death ten of their own generals, becaufe purfuing their vicĉtory at fea they did not ftop to pick up the floating bodies of their foldiers ; and the no lefs infamous barbarity, as well as injuftice, with which they took

---

* Philip of Macedon.

away the life of Socrates: ſtill they were in character a mild and humane people, notwithſtanding theſe caſual violations of that character, which were the effects of faction, the ebullitions of intoxicated fury, to which they were carried by popular influence, and to which they were always open in the nature of their public proceedings.

There are alſo ſome corruptions to be found in their manners, which may be thought, if not to have actually flowed from the ſoftening influence of elegant arts, yet at leaſt to ſtand as an argument of the equivocal advantages derived from thoſe arts upon the general manners. But let it be remembered that the fine arts, with all the powers of general melioration that can be given to them, are not urged as capable of extinguiſhing the human paſſions, and of ſtopping thoſe vicious pores which the tide of Nature will ever open in the human character: they are not urged as the means of producing theſe effects even on thoſe profeſſors of their refinements, who might be conſidered as moſt ſenſible of their impreſſions, and moſt proximate to their reach ; and much leſs are they urged as the means of producing ſuch effects on others, who may have little or no ſenſibility of their refinements. Let it therefore be true, that Greece ſwarmed with courteſans : neither were their numbers encreaſed, becauſe the Greeks were paſſionately fond of the fine arts, nor would their numbers probably have been leſſened by any melioration drawn immediately from thoſe arts ; but the one happened becauſe the Greeks were men, and the other might have taken place, had they been ſuperior to men, or at leaſt a nation of perfectly moral characters. Let it even be true, that Greece was more corrupt in the ſenſual paſſions when the fine arts were at the higheſt than at any other period : the nature of things must decide, caufes and effects must fpeak, whether the ftudy of what is philofophically pure, and elegant, and fublime, can be the fource of national fenfuality ; or whether we fhould not look for that fource to other luxuries which were the caufes rather than the effects of the fine arts themfelves ; for we are affured that in Greece thofe arts owed their elevation to that profperity which at the fame time generated every luxury. We fhall not therefore calumniate thofe arts, becaufe Phryne, the miftrefs of Praxiteles and of many others, had the effrontery to undertake the rebuilding of Thebes, provided it were publicly infcribed that fhe had rebuilt it ; nor becaufe Zeuxis dreffed in purple and gold made a fool of himfelf, and infulted all good fenfe, at the Olympic games ; nor becaufe Parrhafius ftill more infolently ftrutted about with a crown of gold upon his head : we fhall not calumniate the fine arts for thefe or any other pampered extravagances that fpeak a debafed mind, although they were current at the time, or near it, when Socrates and Phocion were doomed to drink the hemlock. Perfonal vanities, and perfonal exceffes, will prevail in fpite of every meliorating influence ; and there will be diffolutenefs in fociety, when every liberal art has done it's beft to diffeminate what improvements it can. But it is not to the fuppreffion of fuch exceffes that the remedy is adequate and natural, which thofe arts can fupply ; neither can they feed in any refpect thofe vices : they foften the mind, but not to corrupt it ; they foften to produce decorum. They will certainly produce that decorum, but fubject to fome exceptions, wherever their fpirit has been fpread ; it has been fhewn that they did produce it in the general face of fociety among the Greeks, notwithftanding the prevalence of private debaucheries, or any individual inftances of more public infolence ; the polifh, which they gave to the manners, was therefore confiderable, although they

did not accomplifh thofe cures which lie beyond the province
of any polifh to reach.

Thus then ftands the faĉt in Greece.   And the evidence, which
our own country can adduce in fupport of the fame argument,
is not lefs ftrong.   Faĉts at home fway all mankind with the beft
fatisfaĉtion.   And we will not go far back for vouchers.   The
reign of King William III. is but juft beyond all memory.   That
of Queen Anne is hardly yet loft to the remembrance of all.
There are feveral, who can recolleĉt the times under George I.
And we all know what was the face of things under George II.
In any of thofe periods no man will fay but that the fine arts, if
any thing like them was enjoyed here, were at a low ebb indeed.
The faĉt is, the country was then poffeffed of nothing that de-
ferved the name of fuperior art.   In architeĉture more was done
than in any other way.   In a branch or two of painting the
age beheld fome poor and infipid attempts, with now and then
a ftart of better genius, which could only be confidered as
remnant evidences of talents, which fomewhere and fometime or
other had been found with more power upon the earth.   In
learning and general philofophy the country was replete, as it
had long been, with many illuftrious names.   But learning and
general philofophy, or, in other words, the theories of books,
never of themfelves accomplifhed the true polifh of a people.
Of this the politer arts have ever poffeffed the main fource.

And what were the manners of the country under the circumftances of thofe ages?   They were as narrow and confined as
the poor femblances of art which they were enabled to exhibit.
The beft information fhews to us a people, in whom if there
was any paffion more predominant, it was that which held them

devoted to their own country, and to every thing that arofe from it. In fact, they had no devotion to any thing elfe. They had a commerce encreafing with the times, but which they purfued with the moft contemptuous opinion of thofe, with whom they carried it on. The eaft, the weft, the north, and the fouth, with which they had intercourfe, were confidered as countries below the condition of Britain; and their inhabitants as a people whom Britons made happy by their trade; forgetting in a great degree, unlefs in the mere calculation of gain, the benefits that were returned to them, and forgetting ftill more to look for thofe further intellectual difcoveries, of which commerce is the happieft handmaid. They lived every man at home, unlefs when private or public affairs called them to the metropolis, or elfewhere; which habit if any have confidered as better for the country at large, affuredly it cannot be in the idea of refining the manners, which on fuch a fyftem of living can never be effected in any country, although it were replete with nobles, no more than in one that is filled with peafants. Such, however, was the plan then: they mixed in their various claffes with their neigh-bours around: they heard, and they knew, and they looked for, nothing but what was within their reach: they fat contented under their own vine, and their own fig-tree; yet not without mellowing their minds, in one refpect, pretty generally and freely with the juices expreffed from the fruits that were ripened for them by Ceres, if not by Bacchus. Some travelled abroad, from the neceffity which was confidered, and fo far very happily, as a relic of fafhion peculiar to high ftations: yet the reft of the country were not much prejudiced in favour of fuch a plan: foreign travel was the fubject of much cenfure from many pens; and on one account perhaps the philofopher would fay with fome reafon, becaufe the end of it was generally loft to our countrymen

—the Englifh fought, and affociated with, the Englifh even
abroad; and having gone there from vanity, they returned with
emptinefs of mind.   If foreigners came hither, they were received
with fome fhynefs and referve, and were gazed at by the multitude with filly impertinence : in the prefence of ftrangers a *mau-
vaife honte* would overfpread the Englifh countenance, which
was bold as a lion within it's own houfe, or in it's own fociety.
They gazed with equal confufion of thought, if accident brought
before them any thing beyond the common works of ingenuity :
indeed they felt not themfelves lifted by any peculiar defires
towards thofe pleafures, becaufe thofe defires had never been
ftrongly awakened : the model of a fhip was the greateft admiration even of thofe who faw fhips fwimming every day in their
harbours, or near their coafts ; and thoufands in the country had
never feen one in all their lives.   To fum up our view of thofe
times : if you call the people fober, you miftake them : if you
call them wife, it was more in theories, and perhaps fomewhat in
their own conceit : if you call them liberal, it was in a local
view : if you call them expenfive, it was in the duller gratifications : if you call them curious and inquifitive, it was in the
drier fpeculations : if you call them elegant and enlarged in
any fhape, it is the groffeft flattery, with the leaft foundation of
truth.

Do we mean then to flatter the prefent times by a perfe&
contraft to the national chara&er in thofe paft periods ?   We
wifh it were completely in our power to give that contraft
with truth.   Neverthelefs we are affured that we can go with
truth a confiderable way towards it.   With refpe& to one part
of that contraft, as it concerns the prefent growth of the fine
arts among us, we fhall not anticipate here what will come more

properly in another place, when the period of time fhall call us
to do juftice to thofe artifts, who have carried their refpective
arts to their prefent height in this country, and to that illuftrious
patronage which has taught the country to be elegant, and to
nourifh the works of ingenious elegance.   It is enough for us to
fay here in general, that the arts have taken a moft deep and
comprehenfive root, and in the fpace of the laft thirty years
have thriven, under the foftering hand that reared them, to a
ftrength and vigour which is abfolutely unexampled, within an
equal period of time, in any age of the world.   They have diffe-
minated their refining influence through every branch of our
manufactures, which no longer come forth from the workman in
a plain and humble ftyle, as if fubftance alone were calculated
without form, and ufe without ornament: every thing now carries a defign, and expreffes that defign in perfect elegance, while
it confults equal, if not greater, ufe, and a much lefs expence.
The folid and the brittle, the richer and the lighter, what iffues
from the loom, and what is wrought from the furnace, fhews that
the mind of tafte has planned it, and that the hand of tafte has
finifhed it.   Commerce has difcovered thefe improvements, and
has borrowed from them new wings and a new expanfion.
Hence Britain is become a new emporium to the whole earth,
the emporium of tafte and elegance. The fcene is now changed;
we no longer fly to other parts of the world for the elegancies
of art, all parts of the world fetch them from us. A northern
power *, who feems impatient to tread in our fteps, and to jump
into refinement from barbarifm itfelf, counts it effential to her
plan to obtain every year packages confifting only of fingle articles in every fort of our manufactures, down to the minuteft

* Ruffia.

trifle, as patterns by which fhe forms the tafte of her people, and
employs their imitation.

Shall we fail then, when we take up the other part of the
contraft, and fay, that the refinement, which has given a new
aftion to the loweft occupations of the country, has aftually extended itfelf to our minds and manners? that the fuperior
principles, by which the hand of art is direfted, have participated in the melioration which has been vifible in the ordinary
produftions of that hand? and that the polifh we have received has not centered merely in the gratification of the eye or
the fancy, but in the general conduft of life? We may fafely
make the appeal : common obfervation is able enough to judge
of it.   And we will not labour the contraft, to the prejudice of
times fo recently paffed, farther than to afk any man who
has lived fifty years, if there is not now more opennefs, can-
dour, and liberality of fentiment among all claffes of people than
he has once remembered in Great Britain? if referve and prejudice have not infenfibly worn off in habits of thinking, in modes
of afting, and towards thofe that breathe not our own air ?   Is
not fociety now formed on a broader bafis ; and is not every man,
who has any portion of education, more a citizen of the world
at large ?   Is there not more agreeablenefs in our addrefs, more
urbanity in our converfation, more polifh in the general ftyle of
life ?   Are we not more awake to the embellifhments of education, and more attentive through life to what is connefted with
the more elegant apprehenfions of the mind, let it come from
what quarter it may ?   Nor let it be faid, in balance of thefe
encomiums on the prefent time, that thefe refinements in our
general manners have greatly refined away our virtue, and left
us more fenfual and corrupt.   What if more adulteries have

taken place in higher ranks, and more wretches have been executed in the lower? Injudicious miftakes in the bringing of
females forward to fociety, the fortuitous intervention of unhappy
circumftances afterwards, and perhaps the blood that is now and
then found to run in certain veins, will always lay a foundation
for the firft, which will be more or lefs frequent as times or acci-
dents affect; and a thoufand external circumftances in a country,
independent of it's private or public manners, may furnifh the
caufes of multiplying the latter. Be thefe as they may, be the
prefent period as diffipated or corrupt in a variety of ways as
any one chufes to paint it, yet this muft be granted, that it is at
leaft more orderly, more attentive to decorum, more delicate in
it's procedure, and more decent in all things than any period
before it.

If the arts in general have this power to humanize and polifh
the mind, no fmall fhare of that polifh muft be the claim of the
pencil, which occupies the firft powers of art by which the mind
is impreffed. We have already touched on the capacities which
are needful to the fuperior ufe of the pencil; and we fhall only
add, that it is an epitome of all thofe intellectual acquifitions
which give the beft finifh to the mind, and muft employ them
all, as occafion calls, or it never can fucceed. It is the inftrument
of truth and virtue, exercifed with the happieft effect: it puts
what is odious in the moft forbidding fhape, and it gives to what
is virtuous it's moft winning attractions. If it be in Nature, or
in any leffons, to fix the affections on their beft objects, this muft
fix them. If the manners of a people muft derive embellifhment
from the habits of a meritorious tafte, this may claim the firft
influence, which, in it's progrefs to refine the mind and improve
the heart, catches the eye's external fenfe with a delight, which

obtains it's full fuffrage to work every other effect upon the mind, the heart, and the manners.

––––––––––––––

The patronage of fine arts a luftre to greatnefs.

THE addrefs, which the fine arts have to make, in confequence of their general polifh, to thofe who have the power of raifing and fuftaining them, is very natural and juft. Can any efforts of human fkill be more worthy to employ the patronage of thofe who are concerned, from the higher fituations which they fill, to fee their fociety as much embellifhed as poffible; and more efpecially of thofe, to whom it is a firft wifdom to give every brilliancy to their own fupreme power over a country? Sovereignty is a moft delicate poffeffion, the prefervation of which in it's genuine fpirit has no medium: it fades upon the eye, and it abfolutely perifhes in the memory, if it be not maintained in that confummate luftre, which is congenial with it's nature and it's purpofe. And that luftre is not altogether the amplitude of power, but the amplitude of fhining talents around it. It is itfelf a planet to this nether world, and it muft have it's fatellites in the arts, which, while they borrow their fplendor from it's luftre, do ftill reflect back upon it a portion of the fplendor they had borrowed. Other acquirements, other talents will not form this luftre; becaufe, however they may grace their poffeffors, and do honour to the prince that fofters them, they fpread but a partial glare around him, not the glare that is reflected from the general face of a whole people, to whom they can communicate no general caft or influence. What a beauteous and noble afpect does it give us of fovereign power, when we fee the rays of it's influence benignly fhed, like thofe of the fun, to warm, fertilize, and adorn the face of the earth; when we behold it cherifhing induftry and every honourable emulation, giving ardour to genius, bringing forward into juft eftimation the works of univerfal excellence; and thus fpreading over a people the bleffings of a rich and fruitful cultivation? Then indeed it is a portion of that power which is " ordained above *", and is exercifed above in univerfal goodnefs: then, in the elegant language of eaftern allegory, it " comes down as the rain, and diftils as the dew, as the fmall rain " on the tender herb, and as the fhowers upon the grafs †". The prince who thus watches over the growth of his people, and rears them up to that high and polifhed charaĉter in the arts, which moft exalts them among the nations, rears up at the fame time to himfelf a monument more honourable and more lafting than any other with which fovereignty would inmortalize it's poffeffors. Let others feed upon the power which allures only the more exceptionable paffions, and in it's exercife too often confounds the beft principles with the worft: let them felicitate themfelves on the glare of majefty, which to weak minds paffes for glory: or, let them reckon the illuftrioufnefs of their charac- ter from the extent of their dominions, and the infinity of their people. The power which is not converted, by the princely alchymy we have mentioned, into the fterling pre-eminence of a people, is but a milder tyranny; if it does not crufh, at leaft it does not fuffer them to rife. The glare, which is reflecﭏ from a throne, independent of the people's elevation in charaĉter, is at beft the glare of a meteor, foon fpent, and fcorching but not ge- nial while it lafts. And what is it to bear the fceptre over fub- jeĉts as numerous as the fand on the fea-fhore? All promifcu-

---

* Rom. cap. xiii. v. 1.　　　　† Deut. c. xxxii. v. 2.

ous, undiftinguifhed, multitudes are mob : and the empire, which
is not polifhed in arts, and refined in manners, is the empire of
a mob.

Not fo the people who are cherifhed to every liberal improvement, nor fuch the fortune of the prince who ftudies fo to cherifh
them.   Revered he muft be in a great degree, nay, he will be
beloved not a little, although prejudice or reafon may look
ever fo unfavourably on other parts of his charaƈter.   The lift
which he thus gives to his country will enfure to the virtuous
monarch the full affeƈtion of his own age, and the full admiration of ages to come ; and it will refcue the exceptionable charaƈter from many cenfures.   It is the charity in princely life,
which covers a multitude of fins.   Who that fees in Alexander the Great the illuftrious patron of liberal arts, does not
forget the deftruƈtive paffions that fwayed him, and lofe fight of
his wide-wafting fword ?   Adrian was little better than a monfter
in heart and principle : yet certainly the apellation is foftened
on every man's tongue, who refleƈts on the elegant improvements to which the Romans were carried in his days, and by the
fpirit of his patronage.   When we fpeak of the houfe of Medici,
the name founds fweetly to every ear ; admiration, delight, and
almoft homage follow that love of letters and of the arts in
that family, which gave fo brilliant a refurreƈtion to both, after
a long extinƈtion : and although we know that the reverfe of
letters, and of the arts, and of virtues difgraced fome of the laft
branches of that houfe, who funk in wretchednefs of mind by the
fame proportion in which their forefathers had rifen to glory,
yet cannot that extinguifh the reverence which in all enlightened minds will never ceafe to meet the name of Medici.

When we look to the perfonal fituation of princes, what is

there fo proper to engage their private attention, and to fill the
leifure of their time, as the arts of elegance ?   The lot of princes is peculiar.   They cannot, if they would, participate in thofe
purfuits, or thofe fatisfactions, which are the general portion of
their fubjects.   The cares of government are great on every
head that wears a diadem, and is united with a heart that feels
and regards it's truft.   And whether or no their own particular
fituation, as fovereigns, augments or diminifhes thofe cares in
their own perfons, ftill they muft feel as men the neceffity of
relaxation, and as high a fenfibility as any men of the pleafures by which the paffage through life may be fweetened.   But
then it is not every pleafure that will befit their ftation. It muft
be an elegant pleafure, it muft be a pleafure that has it's feat
in the mind.   Their characters will ftand the higher ftill, both
for the tafte of their minds and the rectitude of their hearts, if
it be a pleafure which incorporates with their truft ; if it be a
pleafure, which becomes a new fource of celebrity to their people ; making the very hours of inaction, which are wafte or
pregnant with mifchief to all other fituations, replete in their
hands with no lefs bleffings than the hours of their council.   In
the elegant arts they find this refource, and their people find
thefe bleffings.   What gives confummation to the human mind,
if it rifes into a pleafure, muft be a pleafure that fills with
competent dignity the moft exalted of human fituations : what
gives confummation to the human mind, if it rifes into a natural
tafte, muft be glory to any people.

How far the great ones of the earth have been happy enough
by a judicious direction of their tafte to lay this foundation
of fame to themfelves ; in other words, what has been the
progrefs of the fine arts, particularly in the fuperior purpofe

of perpetuating valuable inftruction to the world, from their firft records to their prefent eftablifhment in our own country ; and what has been the fpirit of thofe patronages by which they have been fupported from time to time, it will be our bufinefs to illuftrate in the fequel of this work.

PART II.

BOOK I.

ASIA.

CHAP. I.

Aſſyria, under Semiramis—the age in which ſhe lived—evidences of enamel—very probable that the fine arts might be under-ſtood in the age of Semiramis, on the uſual calculation that ſhe lived ſoon after the deluge—that probability reduced to certainty on the calculation of a greater antiquity in the world, which will admit the Scythian conqueſt of Aſia, and the evidences of arts during that period, to have intervened between the deluge and the age of Semiramis.

THE firſt ſtages of the arts will naturally be looked for in that eaſtern quarter of the world, which was firſt peopled and im-proved. But we muſt preſcribe conſiderable bounds to our expeſtations, when we look ſo far back. Independant of all other circumſtances affeſting the preſervation of records ſo early, rude muſt have been the early traits of deſign, although ſuggeſted by Nature, and ruder ſtill all early attempts at pain-ting, which has uniformily proved itſelf to arrive lateſt to per-feſtion of all the arts of deſign. Whether in the operation of ideas it were a previous effort to draw a figure, or to mould one of the plaftic earth, is quite immaterial. Certainly the former comprehends all the principles of knowledge which belong to the latter, and many more. And it is from every age that the pencil has been gaining fome of thofe numerous powers of execution, which give completion to it's works. In it's firft attempts therefore, or at leaft in thofe which are left to be confidered by us as fome of the firft, we muft not difpute about perfections. And yet, we doubt not, the enjoyment afforded by thofe attempts, whatever they were, was equal on all fides to what has ever been felt by the moft polifhed nation furveying the moft finifhed works ; for thofe attempts were competent to meet the tafte, which was then prepared to receive them.

We are now alluding to Affyria, in a very early age, under Semiramis, the head of that empire, and indeed the miftrefs of all Afia, if we except India, by the authority of Diodorus Siculus*. She reigned forty-two years after the death of her hufband Ninus, and, as we collect from Diodorus and Juftin, fhe died about 2050 years before the Chriftian æra—an early period, to exemplify the arts of defign, and to furnifh exemplifications fo remarkable as thofe which we fhall prefently mention.

But let us be fure that we do not tread on fairy ground ; at leaft, let us endeavour to clear our way from difficulties which may poffibly prefent themfelves to fome minds with refpect to the period before us.

The queftion is, on what principles of calculation we are to

* Hanov. Edit. p. 107.

proceed for the adjuſtment of that period, in which Semiramis and her huſband Ninus lived. It is true that hardly any inveſtigations are more perplexed and illuſory than thoſe which depend on ſacred chronology, or which ſeek their reſult from the reconciling of profane with ſacred authority. And that perplexity from both thoſe ſources preſents itſelf very ſtrongly in ſome views of the preſent queſtion. For if we follow Uſher and the chronology of the Hebrew text, which ſtates the creation of the world to have been 4004 years before the birth of Jeſus Chriſt, the period of Ninus, taking him for the ſon of Nimrod, and the great-great-grandſon of Noah, would fall ſomewhere above 2200 years before the Chriſtian æra, and about A. M. 1800. On the other hand, if we conſult profane hiſtory*, we hear of the conqueſt of Aſia by the Scythians under one known by the name of Brouma 1500 years before the Aſſyrian conqueſt of it by Ninus and Semiramis: we find the princes of the eaſt tributary to the Scythians for that length of time: and as we inveſtigate collateral evidences†, we find the names and the preciſe periods of princes, particularly in Perſia, whoſe reigns go ſo much farther back than Ninus, that they give room for the introduction of the Scythian power, beſides ſtrengthening the credibility of it in other ways:—Caiumarrath, under whom the firſt Perſian ſovereignty roſe up, reigned 3321 years before Jeſus Chriſt, and 1200 years before Ninus; and 112 years after him the acceſſion of Giamſchid is found in the year 3209 before our æra: but here the whole age of the world, as fixed by the Hebrew chronology, is almoſt abſorbed at once by either of thoſe facts, and

---

* Ibid. lib. 2. Juſtin, lib. 2. c. 3.

† Mirkhond. D'Herbelot. Bailly hiſt. de l'Aſtron. anc. p. 354, 355. Dancarville's reſearches, &c. vol. 3. p. 113—116. who has greatly confirmed thoſe profane authorities, and the relative periods of Caiumarrath and of Ninus.

at leaft we are carried by them vaftly beyond the deluge, although they leave the period of Ninus much the fame in it's
diftance from the birth of Chrift; for with the admiffion of
thofe facts, and calculating from them, Ninus muft have reigned
2121 years before the Chriftian æra. In order therefore to give
thofe facts the force they claim from their authorities, we muft
take another courfe of facred chronology. The common copies
of the feptuagint-verfion make the creation of the world to be
5270 years before the Chriftian æra. By that calculation we
fhall find ourfelves nearer to a reconciliation with thofe profane
authorities, and to a capacity of admitting the events they ftate,
without lofing the fame refult as to the particular period of
Ninus: for if we deduct 3321, the period of Caiumarrath, from
5270 the age of creation, it will leave A. M. 1949 for the period of the Scythian conqueft, 300 years after the common
reckoning of the deluge. Again: if taking our data from the
deluge in A. M. 1649, we add 1500 years for the length of
time from the Scythian to the Affyrian conqueft, not only the
period of Ninus falls exactly 2121 years before Chrift, but with
that addition to the other two numbers, the whole age of the
world to the Chriftian æra becomes precifely 5270 years, agreeable to the feptuagint chronology.

The authors of the Ancient Univerfal Hiftory are difpofed to
throw the period of Ninus to a very late date indeed, fo late as
747 years before Jefus Chrift, making Ninus the Nabonaffar of
facred hiftory. They follow chiefly the Samaritan calculation,
which gives 4305 years to the age of the world before the Chriftian æra. But in that idea they feem not to have been aware
of the evidences refpecting Caiumarrath and Giamfchid, no
more than they have regarded the relations of Diodorus and

Juftin; for if we deduct 3321, the period of Caiumarrath, from 4305 the age of creation before Chrift, it would bring the Scythian conqueft within the firft thoufand years of the world, and greatly prior to the deluge on any fuppofed reckoning.

There is no neceffity therefore to difplace that antiquity, which makes Ninus the fon of Nimrod, and fixes the Affyrian conquefts made by him and his queen Semiramis, who accomplifhed as great a portion of them as he himfelf did, to the period of about 2100 years before the Chriftian æra. If thofe Perfian facts may be depended on, the proof is completely made out to that age of Ninus : and that he prefently followed Nimrod, we are almoft warranted to conclude from the language of fcripture, which fpeaks exprefsly of Babylon as rifing in that very period, and moreover calls our notice to the Affyrian power as then forming, when it fays* that " his kingdom was then begin-" ning," and farther that "out of that land went forth Afhur and " builded Nineveh ;" which cannot be conftrued as expreffive of an event that happened 1500 years afterwards. And if it be faid, that the fcripture has made no other mention of the Affyrian power till thofe 1500 years were elapfed at the age of Nabonaffar ; the anfwer is eafy, that the fcripture does not meddle with the detail of any nation, but fo far as it becomes, by the conduct of it's rulers, involved with the hiftory of the Jews ; and Affyria firft became fo involved at the acceffion of Nabonaffar.

If, in the refult of this inveftigation, the length of time between Ninus and the deluge, or however between him and the creation, be greatly increafed, it produces no contradiction in the

* Genefis, c. 10. v. 10, 11.

profane authorities which have told us both of the Scythian and
Affyrian conquefts ; for Diodorus and Juftin had evidently no
apprehenfions arifing from any interfering fyftems of chronology, and the other authorities have ftrengthened the fame events
with a full knowledge of thofe fyftems in their minds. If, in
the fame refult, the antiquity of Ninus and Semiramis, as compared with the preceding age of the world, be confiderably lefs
than it would have appeared under the Hebrew chronology of
Ufher, and confequently that the antiquity of thofe evidences
which may concern the fine arts is reduced in the fame proportion ; we muft recollect that it only changes hands for that proportion of time, and that the fine arts may find under the Scythians the fame progrefs which was given to them by the Hebrew
chronology under the Affyrians : it is no little antiquity, however, to thofe arts that they were purfued 2100 years before the
Chriftian æra ; and it is enough for us to get poffeffion of truth,
if we can.

A French writer, and a very ufeful one, the Abbé Millot in
his Abridgment of Ancient Hiftory does not indeed encourage
the univerfal hiftorians in the length to which they have gone by
poftponing the age of Ninus ; yet he feems to offer it as a queftion, whether thofe immenfe and magnificent works, particularly
in building, which are related by Ctefias and Diodorus Siculus to
have been done in the age in which they have placed Ninus and
Semiramis, can reafonably be afcribed to an age fo early.
" Thefe," fays he, " are to be received in a great meafure as fic-
" tions." And why ? " Beeaufe," he fays, " the buildings of
" Babylon and Nineveh, with other works of magnificence, were
" ftupendous beyond example, and the fcite of thofe cities was
" beyond example extenfive."

As to the extenſiveneſs ſo their compaſs, and eſpecially of Ni-neveh, the larger of the two cities, if Diodorus and Cteſias have impoſed a fiction, the ſcripture has impoſed one too ; for they both agree in the ſame circumſtances, only in different words. Diodorus ſays,* " the city was 480 ſtadia or furlongs in circuit :" the ſcripture ſays,† " it was three days journey :" evidently meaning for a man to go round it. Now 480 furlongs make ſomewhat more than ſixty miles, and ſixty miles were three days journey, twenty miles a day being the common computation for a foot traveller. ‡ It is remarkable that the number of furlongs ſpecified by Diodorus rather exceed the three days journey men-tioned in ſcripture; and the comment of Jerom on the paſſage in Jonah is therefore rather curious for it's exactneſs : he ſays, " *vix* " trium dierum civitas poſſet itinere circumiri." Taking 150 ſtadia for twenty miles, as Herodotus and Bochart expreſsly do, there were juſt thirty ſtadia over the uſual computation of three days journey.

As to the ſtupendouſneſs of their public buildings, and parti-cularly of their walls, when we recollect that the famous wall of China was 1500 miles in length, 45 feet high, and 18 feet thick, it will appear leſs improbable that one or both of thoſe Meſopo-tamian cities might have walls an hundred feet high, ſufficiently thick for ſix chariots to go abreaſt, and that they might have 1500 towers whoſe height was 200 feet. And as to other circumſtan-ces of magnificence, any man who has been in the Eaſt in the preſent age might ſilence the ſcruples of an European mind on the ſubject of that ſplendor, which has not even now left the

---

* Lib. ii. p. 65.   † Jonah. c. iii. v. 3.

‡ Bocharti Phaleg. lib. iv. c. 20. col. 252.   Herodot. lib. v. cap. 53.

much-exhaufted princes of Afia, nor the proud manfions of their refidence, and which muft have been infinitely more within the power of fuch potent monarchs as thofe of Affyria to be exhibited and maintained.

No reafonable exception therefore, we conceive, can be taken to the authority under which we fpeak of Semiramis, and to the antiquity in which we have placed her. She was the firft amazon of the world in arms*; at the fame time fhe gave attention and encouragement to thofe arts, which by fubfequent improvements have come to be diftinguifhed by the name of the fineft. However fhe might have been led by the difcoveries of thofe who had gone before her, fhe feems in fome inftances, which at leaft appear firft in her hands, to have attained difcoveries which were the labour of after-ages in other countries to acquire. But let the reader judge of thefe for himfelf, when we have ftated the facts.

Having caufed a bridge to be thrown over the Euphrates, which ran through Babylon, in the narroweft part of the river, where it was about five furlongs over, and having erected at each end of the bridge a moft ftately caftle, one fronting the eaft, and the other the weft, which caftles were refpectively enclofed by three different walls of confiderable height, and built of † " burnt bricks," each of them forming a circle at fome diftance from the other, and diminifhing the fweep of their refpective circuits as they approached to the centre in which the caftle ftood; fhe then proceeded to decorate thofe walls; and firft of the caftle which fronted the weft, the larger and more fplendid

---

* Diod. Sic. lib. ii. p. 94.   † ἐξ ὀπτῆς πλίνθȣ. Diod. Sic. lib. ii. p. 97.

of the two.* We fhall give the account by an exact tranflation
of Diodorus. " On the middle wall of the three were repre-
" fented in colours, in imitation of life, all kinds of animals;
" and this painting was done on the bricks when they were
" yet green and unburnt."† " On the inmoft wall next the
" caftle, as well as on the towers which rofe from thence to a great
" height, were not only painted in colours animals of all kinds,
" refembling life; but there was a hunting-piece of confiderable
" length, grouped with a great variety of animals, which were
" taken in the fize of four cubits at leaft ; and among thefe Se-
" miramis was feen on horfeback throwing her dart at a panther;
" and near her was her hufband Ninus, ftriking to the earth with
" his fpear a lion which feemed to be clofe upon him."‡ It is
not exprefsly faid, that thefe laft paintings were done on the
bricks before they were burnt: the reader muft be left to judge
of that for himfelf.

On the outward wall of the other caftle, which feems to
have been folely or principally decorated, that wall being equal
only to the inmoft wall of the firft caftle, " inftead of the repre-
" fentation of animals, there were brazen § figures of Ninus,
" and Semiramis, and the chief officers of ftate, and of Jupiter
" himfelf whom the Babylonians call Belus : and alfo armies
" drawn up in array, and various hunting-pieces, affording a va-
" riety of pleafure to the beholders."‖ That the whole of thefe
pieces on the wall of this caftle are to be confidered as reprefentations in bronze, feems to be fully intended by the language,
which fets out with the mention of brazen figures, and appears

* Ibid.   † εν 'σμαῖς ἔτι ταῖς πλινθοις. Diod.   ‡ Diod. ibid.

§ χαλκᾶς εικόνας.   Diod. ibid.   ‖ Diod. ibid.

to fpeak of a different fpecies of work from the paintings on the walls of the oppofite caftle, when it fays, *inftead of the repre-fentation of animals*, for the fubjects on the feveral walls are not altogether different. The original word indeed, Φιλοτεχνια, which we have rendered *reprefentation*, decides nothing on the point, becaufe it relates indifcriminately to any exercife of inge-nious art.

Let the execution of thofe feveral works have been mixed with whatever portions of rudenefs it might, they are altogether in their age a moft extraordinary piece of hiftory to the contem-plation of the fine arts. And we wifh to paufe on them a mo-ment longer.

There can be no great peril in the giving of an opinion here. It is pofitively faid, with refpect to one of the walls at leaft, that the colours were laid on the bricks before they were burnt. Here then is enamel at once. And if the paintings on the other walls of the firft caftle were not done in the fame way, which we fhould regularly fuppofe that they were, then they were done in *frefco*.

We are not much furprifed to difcover fo early an attempt at enamel, when we know from other unqueftionable authorities that the Affyrians were expert in the knowledge, and long prac-tifed in the habit, of burning bricks to a remarkable hardnefs. It was but an eafy ftep of thought to conceive, that the colours which they might lay on thofe earthy fubftances would be fixed by fire. All their moft magnificent erections were built of bricks remarkably burnt. When Nimrod firft propofed the building of Babel on that very fpot, or however in that plain of Shinar

in which Babylon flood, the fcripture reprefents his people fay-
one to another, " let us make bricks, and burn them thoroughly,"
or, as it is exprefled in the margin of the bible, " let us burn them
" to a burning."* It has fo happened that fome fragments or
ruins of thofe ancient pieces of workmanfhip have remained to
be feen in later ages, and they have confirmed that reprefentation of fcripture, and alfo the relation of Diodorus, fo far as
concerns this point. In the year 1574, Rauwolf a German traveller, † endeavouring to find the vefliges of ancient Babylon, fays
that he found, among other antiquities of great beauty, but in
great defolation, " the old bridge which was laid over the Eu-
" phrates, and of which fome pieces of arches flill remained, *built*
" *of burnt brick*, and fo flrong that they were admirable."
Whether this was, in fact, the old bridge built by Semiramis, or,
as a modern writer‡ would fuppofe, a later bridge built at Seleucia which fucceeded to Babylon, is very immaterial to our
prefent object : we fhall only obferve, that if Rauwolf knew the
Euphrates when he faw it, and if Strabo§ knew what he wrote
when he tells us that Seleucia was built on the Tigris, and was
300 fladia or above forty miles diflant from Babylon, thofe ruins
feem very probably to have been part of the old bridge at Babylon, more efpecially as we do not recollect any mention in
hiflory of any other bridge that was built over the Euphrates.
But to return.

It may be afked, how thofe arts, of which we have fpoken
above, came to be underflood in the age of Semiramis, that is,
full 2000 years before the Chriftian æra ? In the anfwer to this

* Genefis, cap. 11.   † See Ray's Edit. of thofe Travels, part ii. cap. 7.
‡ Salmon's Mod. Hift. vol. 1.   § Lib. xvi. p. 738. Edit. Paris.

question we muſt proceed by two different ways, in order to ſa-
tisfy all, and to give the caſe it's full juſtice. Firſt, it muſt be
viewed on the calculation of the Hebrew chronology, ſuppoſing
only 2000 years to have elapſed from the creation to the age of
Nimrod, and conſequently to Ninus conſidered and taken as his
ſon. In the next place, it will demand to be viewed on the ſuppoſition of a greater antiquity in the world, and with the admiſ-
ſion of the Scythian conqueſt, and of the means which may
appear to have been furniſhed by the periods of that empire to
the ſubſequent age of Ninus and Semiramis, near 1500 years later
from the deluge.

We will, firſt, ſuppoſe them to have lived within three or four
hundred years after the deluge, and ſhall enquire from ſcripture
or other authorities what means appear to have been afforded
them, within that ſpace of time, by which they could attain a
knowledge of thoſe arts that have been given to them.

Very few are the traits of any circumſtances preceding the
flood to be found in ſcripture : but thoſe which are found may
perhaps help us to ſome uſeful conjecture in the preſent caſe ;
and it will be our buſineſs to ſhew their utility, by ſhewing the
probability of their not being loſt to the firſt generations in the
new world.

Among the firſt line of deſcendants from Adam by Cain we
find ingenious men, who very early ſtruck out uſeful diſcoveries,
and laid the foundation of arts : thoſe of building, and agriculture, and muſic, and the founding of metals are particularly
mentioned. And we cannot doubt that theſe had others in their
train, and of the more refined ſort too, when they ſo readily

found their way to one of the fineſt of all, that of muſic. If we go to the line of Seth, we find indeed nothing of this kind ſaid of his deſcendants in ſcripture; but it appears from Joſephus, if his authority may be leaned on, that there were not wanting artiſts among them, and men who were zealous for the preſervation of their arts. For, he ſays, the ſons of Seth, being aſſured of the deluge that would happen, were careful to erect two pillars, the one of brick, the other of ſtone, on which they left engraven the principles of aſtronomy, that the ſcience of it might not be loſt : and thoſe pillars, with the documents they contained, were ſtanding a long time after Noah.

There is ſomething here into which it is worth our while to look, and on which a reaſonable conjecture may be exerciſed without impertinence, eſpecially when it may tend to ſome illuſtration of the queſtion before us. That they made choice of a column for the records which they wiſhed to preſerve, was wiſe ; becauſe it was neceſſary that thoſe records ſhould be elevated at a conſiderable height above the natural ſurface of the ground, that they might not be buried in the great maſs of ſediment which muſt attend ſuch an inundation : and, beſides, no other conſtruction of walls could have reſiſted with equal ſtrength the preſſure of the waters, and leſs ſtill if they had been ſufficiently elevated for the purpoſe above-mentioned. But why were there two pillars? or, why was the one of brick ? That one of them was of ſtone, was moſt natural ; becauſe it will not be queſtioned that ſtone was fully as much calculated for duration as brick. And that which was of ſtone either was ſufficient to contain the elements of aſtronomy, if thoſe alone were in their contemplation to be preſerved, or if it were not ſufficient, and they meant only to record that ſcience to poſterity, they would have cho-

sen another also of stone. . We cannot help thinking it injurious
to their zeal to suppose that they meant to rescue from the deluge
the science of astronomy alone.   So generous a care for posterity
would certainly lead them to take the same means of handing
down every other science or art, which could by that means be
conveyed to the notice of future generations.   And the opportunity was a fair one. The pillars might be formed to shew their
notions of architecture.   Their sculpture, whatever they had of
it, would leave it's specimens on proper parts of the stone. And
their engraving would speak for itself.

Was the pillar of brick then intended merely as a duplicate
to the pillar of stone?   Certainly not, for the reason suggested
above, that if the latter should perish, they could not expect the
former to stand.   Why then, we ask again, was one of those pillars formed of bricks?   May it not be reasonably supposed that
it was for the recording of some art, which could not well be
committed to stone, and did not depend on engraving?   We are
aware that they engraved on bricks, as well as on stone, in early
ages after the deluge : the Babylonians wrote on bricks their
first astronomical observations.*   But we know of no instances
of that sort, unless this pillar be taken for one, before the flood.
And it should seem rather extraordinary that when the sons of
Seth had adopted an erection of stone, they should at the same
time have recourse to another whose surface was more broken by
joints, and therefore less convenient for engraving, if such was
merely their use of it. Is it too visionary to suppose, that this
pillar of brick might be employed to preserve, through the medium of burning, their progress in painting ; and through the medium of painting, their progress in those mechanical discoveries

* Pliny, lib. vii. p. 413.

which painting is the beft means of defcribing? Whatever knowledge was preferved on this pillar of bricks, and was not fixed by the graving-tool, muft have been fixed by fire in the raw material. This idea is, however, merely conjecture. If Paul Lomazzo had good authority for what he has faid, it is no longer conjecture as to what the fons of Seth knew of painting : for he afferts that they had found out the way of reprefenting both images and portraitures by that art.* And fo much can hardly be doubted, when we confider the importance of that art to an early correfpondence at a diftance. Their zeal therefore to preferve what they had fo attained, amidft their other endeavours to preferve what was valuable in fcience, will appear the more natural.

Noah then had immediate communication with thefe men, all of whom were his near relations, and fome of them were his immediate progenitors. The time which had elapfed from the days of Adam, on the fhorteft calculation more than 1650 years, had afforded a confiderable fpace for the acquirement of arts, and for fome progrefs in them too. Noah himfelf muft have been a geometrician, or he would not fo readily have apprehended and executed the orders which were given him in the formation of the ark : and geometry is one of thofe arts that depend on defign. An hundred years paffed from the time in which thofe orders were given him to his entrance into the ark. Shall it be fuppofed that during that time he was inattentive to every thing but what was to accompany him in it? that he was lefs zealous for the prefervation of thofe parts of knowledge in himfelf or in fome of his family, which were to ferve him and them and their pofterity, after they fhould come forth from their confinement, in a new and vacant world, than the fons of Seth were,

* Idea del tempo della pittura, p. 22.

who muſt at leaſt be apprehenſive, if not certain, that they ſhould never ſurvive the deluge? There is every reaſon therefore to conclude, that Noah and his family delivered to the age immediately following that event whatever was known of importance to thoſe that immediately preceded it.

But if that were not ſtrictly ſo, Noah lived 350 years after that event; which length of time, on the Hebrew calculation, brings us to the reign of Semiramis. With thoſe elements of the arts of deſign, whatever was their extent, derived from preceding ages, in the hands of the deſcendants of Noah, might they not have come in 350 years to that progreſs which was exhibited in the days of Semiramis? Without thoſe elements, are they to be ſuppoſed leſs capable than the deſcendants of Cain, whoſe original diſcoveries without any other elements than Nature, and accompliſhed in one generation, as it ſhould ſeem, are expreſsly atteſted in ſcripture? But to judge of this from ſimilar effects in later days, which the farther progreſs of our inquiry will bring more pointedly to our view; conſider what was done in Greece within a period not greater than has now been mentioned, from the firſt olympiad to the days of Apelles. It was not twice that length of time from the hour that Greece obtained the firſt traits of deſign to her perfection in it, indeed from the hour that Cadmus made his appearance in the country. Conſider what was done in Italy after days of darkneſs hardly leſs deſtructive than a deluge, within the ſame ſpace of time or leſs, from the appearance of Cimabue to the death of Raphael. The Mexicans and Peruvians ſhew us how quickly a people may arrive at conſiderable improvements. Their reſpective monarchies had not ſubſiſted above 350 years, when the Spaniards appeared among them: and they were found regular in their policy, they had good laws,

they were acquainted with many arts and fciences, and the courts
of their emperors were extremely magnificent. The fubjeɛts of
Semiramis may therefore naturally be left entitled to that progrefs of art which they appear to have made, on the fuppofition
that the Aſſyrian monarchy rofe up very foon after the deluge,
without the intervention of any other great power in Afia, which
might become the conveyance of additional means to their knowledge and improvements.

But we muſt now view them with the advantages afforded
by a greater length of time, and by the progrefs in arts which
had been made by thofe who were mafters of Afia, or of any
great parts of it, before the Aſſyrian empire.

In the way to this difcuſſion it may not be amifs to get rid of
a queſtion, which may perhaps be put by fome, upon the general
afpeɛt of the argument into which we are entering; and that is,
why we did not fet out at once with thofe evidences of the arts
which are afforded by others before the Aſſyrians, and give
thofe others their fituation in the order of time, rather than bring
them forward in a fide-view, and as collateral proofs to fettle the
antiquity of others. To which we anfwer, that we did not chufe
to cancel fo abruptly a fyſtem of chronology like the Hebrew,
which has fo long been refpeɛted by many in the learned world,
and which is become a kind of companion to our tranflation of
the Bible in every hand. We were the more averfe to proceed in
that manner, becaufe, whatever may be the iſſue in any man's
mind refpeɛting the antiquity of the world, the courfe which we
have taken in our argument is ſtill unaffeɛted by that iſſue; we
have employed no reafoning in vain; the conneɛtion between
the knowledge of the anti-diluvian world and thofe who next

followed the flood will be juft the fame, and the means by
which an advancement in the arts might be attained at any rate
in the compafs of three or four hundred years after the deluge
will be juft as probable, whether Ninus and the Affyrians or any
other people were thofe who prefently followed Noah or his
fons.   And it is precifely the fame thing to us, whether we firft
difcover thofe arts in the hands of the defcendants of Japhet, or
in thofe of the defcendants of Ham or Shem.

It is alfo neceffary to acknowledge the lights which have been
thrown on this particular difcuffion by a late work entitled,
" Recherches fur l'Origine, l'Efprit, et les Progres des Arts de la
" Grece."   Of that work the author M. D'Ancarville has devoted
a confiderable part to the elucidation of the Scythian conqueft
in Afia as a faft, the very early period in which it took place,
and it's immediate influences on that part of the world, in the introduction of arts, a peculiar inftitution of religion, and a general civilization conformable to thofe principles.   It is impoffible
for any man, without his profundity of refearch, founded on great
antiquarian learning, to have extricated this fubjeft from the
abyfs of antiquity in which it had lain : and we, who feel it our
duty to attend to fo important a circumftance in the origin of
the fine arts, cannot but be happy that we have confulted that
work, which we apprehend has yet reached but very few hands.
We confefs that the great ftrength of his views, added to the few
pofitive authorities left in ancient hiftory which declare the Scythian conqueft and it's duration, refts in the very extenfive
analogies by which he has illuminated the main faft : thofe
analogies are indeed of the ftrongeft kind, and demand to be
embraced as confirmations of thofe pofitive authorities, let the
confequence militate as it may with any habits of reckoning the

age of the world. It were to be wifhed that he had laid out his
matter in more order, that he had compreffed it as he might have
done in lefs compafs, and that he had ftripped it of thofe infinite
repetitions which only ferve to load, obfcure, and weaken it.
The purpofes, for which that hiftorical event becomes interefting to our enquiry, will be fatisfied without going, though ever
fo briefly, into all the matter which that author has marked out
for his readers. There are alfo collateral matters refpecting a
progrefs in the arts of Afia, in ages far more ancient than the Affyrian power, which, whether they grew out of the Scythian conqueft, or were at all referable to it, or not, or whether or no that
were in fact the very early power in Afia which it is reprefented
to be, will go a great way towards fatisfying the purpofes for
which the fine arts are interefted in this difcuffion.

Brouma, at the head of the Scythian nation, is faid to have
given that great extenfion to the Scythian dominion in Afia. His
defcent is afferted to have been from Japhet through the loins of
Magog, Japhet's fon, whofe name is given in fcripture to mark
the Scythians, and whofe character accords with that fiercenefs
which has always been fuftained by that people. In what particular degree of fucceffion Brouma ftood from Magog, does not
appear, nor is it very material to our immediate purpofe. The
period in which he reigned, affifted by other circumftances founded on aftronomical obfervations, appears to have been fomewhat more than 3600 years before the Chriftian æra. *

The footfteps of Brouma, and the influences of his principles
appear in all the parts of that immenfe continent. In India

* D'Ancarville, vol 1. p. 103—110.

thofe footfteps and influences have never been erafed to this hour ; they have given an everlafting creed to that country. That he was the firft civilizer and the firft legiflator of India ; that he gave it's people the firft knowledge of arts, and fciences, and agriculture ; that he wrote the four books of the Vedams, of which the two principal Shafters are commentaries, and which conftitute in a manner their bible ; is indelibly imprinted on their moft facred records, is avowed by the Bramins who call themfelves his defcendants as well as fucceffors, and is reported by all the moft refpectable hiftories of that country written by thofe moderns who have gained their intelligence on the fpot.* Many are the circumftances, in which the memory of Brouma as a Scythian ruler is retained by the Indians in the expreffion of their arts : † and innumerable are the circumftances, in which their veneration for his memory is ftill maintained, notwithftanding the prevalence of fubfequent religious factions which have fet up in different ftages of time the names of Chiven and Vichenou, but which could never obliterate that of Brouma, from whofe principles in fact they have fprung, and whofe principles they record in their own peculiarities. ‡ The diffufion of thofe principles through all the nations of the eaft without exception, through Egypt too, and afterwards through Greece, is manifeft in the wonderful fimilarity which prevailed in the primitive theology of them all, and which fhews them indifputably to have drawn from one common fource. That fource is found in all the features of Scythia, which the moft ancient authorities have re

* Voyage aux Indes Orient. tom. 1, p. 155. 214.   Voyage in Arabic, tom. 2, p. 14. Dow's Hift. Holwell. D'Ancarv. vol. 1. p. 101—125. vol. 3. p. 67—72.
† Ibid. vol. 1. p. 6, 7, 111, 112.   vol. 3. p. 93.
‡ Ibid. vol. 1. p. 112.   vol. 3. p. 73, 74. Voy. aux Indes Orient. tom. 1, p. 286.

corded, or which the fucceffions of time have ftill left in the fame tract of country *. It was fo eftablifhed as an original fpring of religion, that it obtained the name of Scythicifm, and was ranked the firft of all religions which affected any fyftem of principles ; it came next after Barbarifm itfelf, which had no principles ; it preceded long the religion of the Hellenes, fince called Greeks ; and longer ftill the religion of the Jews†.

If there be any difficulty in the evidences which have thus placed Brouma in India as a legiflator and father, and in Afia in general as a conqueror, it arifes from the miftakes by which in after-times his name became often loft in that of Bacchus. The compilers of the ancient hiftory of India, who were Greeks, have told us that the ancient Brachmans in their facred writings fpoke of Bacchus as the conqueror and legiflator of that country ‡; and Roman authors following that language have fometimes taken the fame ideas §. It muft appear altogether unaccountable how thofe ancient priefts of India, who were in fact the neareft fucceffors of that great legiflator, whatever was his name, in religious offices, and the depofitories of the Vedams, fhould fpeak of him by any other name than that by which he was known ; and if it could be fhewn that they fpoke of him by any term unequivocally defcriptive of Bacchus alone, the point muft be given up, and the whole argument which arifes from it. But the fact is, that thofe facred books of the brachmans are no

* D'Ancarv. vol. 3. p. 171, 2. et ubique.
† St. Epiph. adv. Hæres. lib 1. D'Ancarv. vol. 1. p. 42.
‡ Diod. Sic. Biblioth. lib. ii. Strabo Geog. lib. xiv. D'Ancarv. vol. 1. p. 37, 38, 95, 97, 102, 103, 108.
§ Plin. Nat. Hift. lib. vi. c. 31.

longer exifting : whether any of them may be in that confecrated vault at Benares, where the Vedams are faid to have been depofited, and whether thofe Vedams themfelves are now exifting, muft remain undetermined, unlefs we could penetrate that facred recefs*. That there muft, however, have been fome miftake in thofe reports of the Greeks is unqueftionable, becaufe the Brachmans could not fpeak of a character whom the world did not fee for near 2000 years after Brouma. But how then could fo ftrange a miftake be made? Very eafily, whether thofe Greek compilers had ever drawn any vouchers from books of the Brachmans, or had been guided by any thing which they or others had heard or feen in India. It muft be obferved that the name of Brouma became the diftinction of that Scythian character, of whom we have been fpeaking, after his apotheofis and deification by the Indians ; how he was called before, we know not, unlefs it was as M. D'Ancarville fays†, by the name of Ruder, which was ftill an expreffion by which they conceived the Supreme Being‡. Brouma came from Nyfus, a town in the higheft part of Scythia, and he built in Afia a town by the fame name, the boundary of his conquefts there to the eaft, Nyfus of the Oxydrachi. Thofe Greek hiftorians drawing their documents from the eaft, or any others going there, found that great conqueror and legiflator defcribed and fpoken of by the name of *Dionyfius*, "the god of Nyfus," as often as by that of Brouma § : for we muft recollect that he had been deified. It was natural for the Greeks, and quite in their character, to feize upon any circumftances which might be brought to flatter the antiquity or the heroifm of their own country ; and as the name of *Dionyfius*

---

* Voy. aux Indes Orient. tom. 1, p. 214. D'Ancarv. vol. 1. p. 95, 110. vol. 3. p. 95, 96.

† Vol. 1. p. 116.   ‡ Ibid. vol. 1. p. 106.   § Ibid. vol. 1. p. 116.

was one among a multitude of titles which they gave to their Bacchus, whom they fo called as "the god of Nyfus," in allu-fion to one of the tops of Parnaffus which was facred to him *, as Cirrha the other top was facred to Apollo, fo they haftily con-cluded that all the great deeds and honours afcribed in India to Dionyfius were intended for the deified hero of Greece. They might be the more induced to make that conclufion from other circumftances. The rites kept up by the Indians in the celebration of their feaft to the powerful principle of all things ; the emblem of the ox, under which that powerful principle was revered ; and the Indian dances then exhibited, called *devedaffi*, which feem to have come into that country with the wildnefs of the Scythian fe-males †, were fo exactly fimilar to the rites, the emblem, and the orgies employed in the Grecian feafts of Bacchus, which the Greeks had derived in fact from the Scythian fource in the eaft without knowing it or it's original purpofe, that they could not conceive how it was poffible for fo ftriking a fimilarity of circumftances to have any other object than that to which they were directed among themfelves‡. It is neverthelefs remarkable that one of the names given by the Greeks to their Bacchus was Βρημος and Βρομιος§; and fo the Romans fometimes called him *Bromius*‖; the feafts which were confecrated to him were called *Brumalia* **, εορτη των Βρημων; and the commencement of the new year was called *Bruma*††. How came this ? Lexicographers may imagine that the Greeks, and the Romans after them, derived Βρημος or Βρομιος, and *Bromius*, απο τη Βρεμειν, *à fremendo*, from the roaring noife

* Juven. 7, 64. Lucan's Phars. lib. v.
† Onefiсrat. ap. Calep. in Bactr.   ‡ D'Ancarv. vol. 1. p. 40, 41, 68—84, 98, 100.   § Proclus in comment. Hefiod, περι εργα και ημερας. D'Ancarv. vol. 1. p. 126, 7.   ‖ Luc. Phars. lib. v.   Ovid. Metam. 4. 11.   ** Cœlius Rodiginus. Conftant. in Geoponic.   †† Ovid. Faft. lib. 1. v. 163.

kept up in the rites of Bacchus. But may not a more natural and eafy reafon be given, becaufe they found in the eaft the deified character, which appeared to them to be their Bacchus, called *Brouma* as well as *Dionyfius?* and they naturally proceeded to give the fame name to the commencement of the new year, becaufe they found him reprefented by the Indians holding a chaplet, to fhew that he prefided over the year *.

With Brouma then came forward not only the firft principles of religion, and inftitutions of worfhip, which the Afiatics obtained, and which actually took the fame caft all over Afia, but alfo the firft knowledge of arts. Some of the finer arts became immediately neceffary to their religion. It is perhaps an effort naturally fpringing at firft from ruder knowledge to grafp the emblematic figure, as the moft expreffive mode of fixing both principles and practice in the fubjects of reverence. The firft ages, however, betook themfelves at once to this method of addreffing every public inftruction to the eye; they were fond of allegory as the moft fenfible, and perhaps to them the only practicable, illuftration of abftract fentiments; thus we may fay, without meaning any direct eulogy on allegory, that they were poets at fetting out, for they took up that which poetry has never left, and without which poetry muft probably leave the world. But by means of the emblematic figure they gave eftablifhment to every point of inftruction. And fculpture no lefs than painting affifted the accomplifhment of this. If it's aids, with which they made it their firft endeavours to become acquainted, were moft welcome to them, thofe aids have entailed obligations no lefs welcome to all fubfequent generations for the duration with which they can

* D'Ancarv. vol. 1. p. 128, 9.

perpetuate, if they be fuffered fo to do, the records of the earlieft times, and for the affurance with which they can deliver to us, by the fame means through which they taught the firft ages, all the principles which were cultivated by thofe firft ages themfelves. To that duration of fculptural monuments, happily preferved to this hour in two or three parts of the earth, we owe it that we can now fpeak both of the ftate of fculpture as an art, and if the myftical theories hidden under it as an allegory, in very early times which can be afcertained with confiderable correctnefs.

The cavern, or, as it is called in the country, the pagoda in the ifland of Elephanta near Bombay, if we could be affured of it's date, would probably anfwer our prefent views by the moft decided proofs. In that cavern we have a full example, and probably one of the moft ancient, unlefs Scythia had led the way by older ones*, of the choice which was made by the firft of mankind, after any inftitutions of religion had been formed, to excavate the bofom of the earth for the places of their worfhip, rather than conftruct them in open view. In that choice they were gratified by the emblematic ftudy throughout; for while the fides were filled with figures often hewn out of the rock, and announcing to their minds the various powers of the fupreme Being, the generator of all things, the vaulted roof gave the

* It is faid that in Scythia there was fuch a cave dedicated to her who was called the mother of the Scythians, and whom we alfo find to be called the wife of Japhet. D'Ancarv. vol. 1. p. 213, 214, 234. in the note; vol. 3. p. 36, 154. There are the like caverns or pagodas in Canara, Ambola, Illoura, and Salcette; whether all of thefe were older than that of Elephanta, may be uncertain.

figure of the world, and the figure of that chaotic egg from which they fuppofed the world to have been produced *.

M. D'Ancarville† is inclined to think that the fculptural monuments in the pagoda of Elephanta are not to be fet down as much older than the time in which the Affyrian monarchy may be fixed, that is, about 2100 years before our æra. And his principal reafon for that opinion is this, that a fword or large dagger is in one of the hands of a principal figure which has fix arms, and is alfo obfervable in many other figures in bafs-relief; and therefore he conceives that they muft have been executed later than the age of the Indian Chiven, who came to be deified and worfhipped in fome ages after Brouma, and who is alfo call- ed Hercules ‡, becaufe Hercules was armed with a club and a lion's fkin, which fhews that fwords were not then in ufe: and yet he thinks that they muft have been executed before the attri- butes afcribed to Brouma had been tranflated to Chiven, becaufe that principal figure, he is perfuaded, was not intended for Chi- ven but for Brouma.

In that opinion two things are taken for granted; that Hercu- les was Chiven, and that inftruments of iron were not in ufe in the time of the former, becaufe he took a club for his armour.

With refpect to the firft point, it is certainly to be fufpected that all the mention of Hercules which may have crept into In- dia, and gathered to itfelf the name of Chiven, is juft as fabu- lous, and as much the relic of Grecian vanity, as the application of the name of Bacchus to the character of Brouma. We are

---

* Ibid. vol. 3. p. 154, 155.   † Ibid. vol. 1. p. 122, 3.   ‡ Ibid. vol. 1. p. 105.

not told by this author what was the age of Chiven, unlefs we are left to find it in that of Hercules: and in that reference Chiven would be found later in time than Viçhenou the third legiflator of India, inftead of being the fecond, and next after Brouma; for the deified Hercules, (unlefs you mean him* who was the common anceftor of all the Scythians, which cannot be intended, becaufe he was long before the Scythian conqueft itfelf,) muft on every fyftem of chronology have been pofterior to the Affyrian conqueft.

With refpect to the latter point, there is nothing in the hiftory of metallurgy fo undecided as the firft ufe of iron after the flood. We are certain that it was found out before that epoch†. Fair reafoning would lead us to conclude, that it would ftand one of the beft chances, among the arts of every kind, to be preferved in the family of Noah, and to be communicated by them to their immediate defcendants. If we were to attend to the claims of various people on the antiquity of this knowledge, we fhould hear the Egyptians‡, the Phœnicians §, the Cretans, the inhabitants of Mount Ida ‖, the Cyclops**, the Chalibes††, and the Noropes‡‡, carrying their feveral pretenfions to the remoteft periods of time. It is fufficient, however, to remark, that in fome of the ancient monuments of Perfia, and particularly in the ruins of Perfepolis, whofe age can be afcertained beyond 3000 years before our æra, within 400 years after the reign of Brouma, and nearly 1100 years before Ninus, a dagger is feen in the hands of

---

* D'Ancarv. vol. 1. p. 208, 256—264.   † Genefis, chap. iv. v. 22.
‡ Chron. Pafcal, p. 45. C. Cedrenus, fo. 19. D.   § Sanchon. apud Eufeb.
p. 35. C.   ‖ Diod. lib. 17. p. 726. Strabo, lib. 10. p. 726.
** Pliny, lib. 7. fec. 57.   †† Ammian. Marcel. l. 22. c. 8.
‡‡ Strom. l. 1. p. 365.

the Mithriatic and other figures*. It is therefore assuming too much to say, that the use of a sword or dagger can decide for or against any particular period of antiquity : nor less assuming still is the conclusion, that such weapons were not known in the age of Hercules, let him have lived when he might, because that hero did not employ them. If another observation which that author has made be right, and it seems extremely intelligent, we must see the works of that pagoda to have been formed in an earlier age. He says that the use of the tamara-leaf on the monuments of India came from Scythia, and was peculiarly applied to the figures of Brouma, or the genii attending him, to shew that he was of Scythian origin; and that the use of that leaf on sculptural monuments ceased, when the worship of Brouma gave place to that of others†. This remark is fully justified in the pagoda of Elephanta. Consequently those monuments must have been executed before the influence of Chiven was known in India. They must have been executed in the zenith, as one may say, of Brouma's memory, and before any competitions arose to invade his worship. The execution of them, for the most part colossal, and cut out of the rock, and filling a space of 120 feet long by almost as many broad‡, must have taken up a great length of time, and have been interrupted by none of those divisions which arose from the pretensions of another legislator, and which actually subverted those of Brouma§. The works of that pagoda cannot be explained but upon the principles of that very ancient theology which was introduced by Brouma‖, and which became afterwards by the veneration of the people absorbed in himself. To secure that theology,

* D'Anc. vol. 3. p. 158.   † D'Anc. vol. 1. p. 5, 111, 112, 132. Vol. 3. p. 93.
‡ Ibid. vol. 1. p. 78. note.   § Ibid. vol. 3. p. 53, 73, 74.
‖ Ibid. vol. 1. p. 95.

and the immortality of Brouma, feems to have furnifhed a leading object to all thofe monuments; and therefore, although we cannot precifely afcertain their age, it feems reafonable to conclude that they were done when the intereft of Brouma was ftrongly eftablifhed in the country, but by no means at fo late a period as towards the approach of Ninus, when not only the Scythian power was vanifhing, but the worfhip of Brouma had long been extinct. There feems to be in thofe monuments a great fimilarity of execution in fome inftances, and in others a great inferiority of defign, to the fculptures which are now very well known in the ruins of Perfepolis: neither of thofe circumftances fhould incline us to think that the monuments of Elephanta were later in time than thofe of Perfia, for all artifts with equal ftimulations improve by time: the fubterraneous cavern fhould not appear a later idea than the proud edifice for a houfe of idols in countries fo near together, where the fame principles of theology are embraced, the fame fervour is alive in thofe that embrace them, and equal wealth is at hand to give them perpetuity. Why then may not the pagoda of Elephanta be equal in antiquity to the monuments of Perfepolis?

But if the fculptures in that pagoda fhould not be fufficiently ancient for our purpofe, others in the pagoda of Canara are allowed to be old enough. The bafs-reliefs, being cut in the rock itfelf, are an affurance that they are the fame figures which were originally formed there. And they exhibit not the Indian, but the old Scythian, character and features which are ftill difcernable in the Tartars, the defcendants of the Scythians—a great robuftnefs of frame, and ftrength of mufcles; the face large and full; the nofe flatted; the lips very thick; the whole countenance dull and heavy; the whole character fuch as is now a ftranger to

India.   Hence it has been conceived that thofe monuments were wrought by the Scythians themfelves, who took their own national charaĉter before it became fo blended with India as to have left it's original traits lefs fimple and diftinĉt.   A hardy people they were, and very ingenious too they muft have been, to go through fuch an immenfe work, which is fuppofed to have employed all the efforts that a whole nation could exert in the fculptural art for fome ages *.

It was not in India that the Scythians obtained thofe arts ; for the Indians were quite barbarous and without civil fociety, they lived difperfed in fields, when the Scythians came among them : thefe laft muft therefore have been poffeffed of ingenious arts in their own country, before ever they fet their feet in India.   The antiquity, to which we now refer, goes fo very clofe towards the flood, that it will hardly be expeĉted that we fhould be able to produce many proofs of what appears fo reafonable to be fuppofed ; but one will ftand for many, and for that one we are indebted to the antiquarian fpirit of Herodotus.   He tells us† that when *Scythes*, who was the third fon of the Scythian Hercules, and from whom the nation afterwards obtained the name of Scythians, received from his father the bow which was to become his portion, and which fell to him as the only one of his brothers that could draw it, he received at the fame time " a belt, the clafp of which was ornamented " with a vafe of gold;" and further, that " all the Scythians " invariably retained that vafe upon the clafps of their belts " from that period to the very hour in which he wrote that " account."   They retained it through all their branches as

* D'Ancarv. vol. 3. p. 50, 51.
† Lib. iv. cap. 10. p. 228.   D'Ancarv. vol. 1. p. 199, 260—280.

a mark of their common origin, and as it were the efcutcheon
of their nation. This little hiftorical anecdote is pregnant with
deep information. The execution of that vafe, doubtlefs as a
bafs-relief, prefuppofes and carries with it a knowledge of other
arts, without which it could not be fatisfied: a knowledge of
modelling and of cafting, which are involved with fome knowledge
of defign, were indifpenfible. If they could execute that vafe,
they doubtlefs executed by the fame art, and probably in fome
other branches of art, other articles of ingenious ornament or
ufe for perfonal or domeftic fervice. We fhould not do them
juftice, if we thought that they looked no further than to the
ornament afforded by that vafe; they muft have had a fymbolic
intent in the feleftion of it, although we may not clearly fee
that intent, nor can be fully affured of the precife form of the
vafe itfelf: it may have given the fecret origin to all the vafes of
the earth; and there is no reafon to be alledged, why it might not
be as much a fymbol of religion with the Scythians as the *patera*
was held to be among the Greeks and Romans. Thefe pieces
of workmanfhip they were able to execute in gold; and it is plain
that they were arrived at the ability to do them before the time
of that Hercules, the common father of the Scythian nation, to
whofe period we know not how to advance, and much lefs to
go beyond it by any affured chronology, but from whom muft
have prefently defcended the Brouma of India, if he were not
either that Scythes, or that Hercules himfelf. And perhaps one
of thefe fuppofitions would be the fhorteft to reconcile all, with
the admiffion of fome lofs of names in fo remote antiquity,
and fome anachronifms both of names and events.

Moft certainly there is no trace of art more old than that
which we have now mentioned from Herodotus, nor has there

probably been a people befides the Scythians, who could have furnifhed us with any traditions of art more early fince the flood. The tradition now before us derives collateral confirmation from the reports of modern travellers, who have difcovered in thofe mountainous parts of ancient Scythia various inftruments of metal, and evident marks of gold mines which have been worked with great labour in ages extremely remote*. In the coinage of Scythia, it is upon record, according to Hyginus†, that filver money owed it's invention to a king of the country named Indus, long before the Scythians paffed into India.

If the view we have taken of thofe very ancient works of art, which appear to have originated from Scythian genius or Scythian power in Scythia itfelf or in India, ftill leaves us uncertain in their refpective epochs, the ruins of Perfepolis will carry us out of every difficulty of that kind, and will give us antiquity enough on which our argument may rely : at the fame time they will not carry us from the original opening of this difcuffion, inafmuch as they demonftrate no lefs completely than the monuments of India the influences of the Scythian theology, while other evidences prove the influences of the Scythian dominion in the tributes paid to it by the fovereigns of Perfia‡.   .

By an aftronomical epoch we are affured that the dedication of Eftekhar, called by the Greeks Perfepolis, took place under the Sovereign Giamfchid at the commencement of the year 3209 before the Chriftian æra§. The reader will recollect that this

* Pallas's Voyage, tom. 2. p. 399, et feq.   † Fab. 274.   D'Ancarv. vol.
1. p. 23, 43, 151.   ‡ D'Ancarv. vol. 1. p. 36, 43.   § Hift. of anc.
Aftronomy, p. 130.   Bailly, p. 354. fec. 2.   D'Ancarv. vol. 1. p. 124.   Vol. 3.
p. 115, 137.

was only 400 years after the period affigned to Brouma's entrance into India. Befides the fculptural monuments at Perfepolis, the buildings of which are now feen in ruins, but thofe monuments themfelves are moftly preferved in their original ftate, there are a few others no lefs ancient at Nakfki-Ruftan, about two or three leagues from Perfepolis ; others, again, of equal antiquity are cut in the body of a mountain called But-cane, about fixteen leagues from Perfepolis ; and there is another remarkable piece of fculpture near Chiras, in the fame ftyle with the bafs-reliefs at Perfepolis. Thefe conftitute the undoubted monuments of the ancient Perfians, which may be carried back with affurance to the age of Giamfchid, if fome of thofe which we have laft mentioned may not have feen every hour that has paffed from the reign of Caiumarrath. In thofe periods fo very remote there appear the fulleft proofs, independent of thofe grander ones which are exhibited in the places we have juft mentioned, of a confiderable progrefs made in other parts of fculpture and engraving. Two pieces of golden money newly coined, and bearing the impreffion of the head of *Aries*, and on the reverfe his figure repofing on the ground, were offered to Giamfchid on the firft new-year's day of his reign, as a cuftomary congratulation which has been always kept up*. Mirkhond, inftructed by the ancient hiftory of the Perfians, records it of Giamfchid, that he had feals engraved for the purpofe of an impreffion on writings†. The fymbols of worfhip in his time were taken on a medal, which may be feen in D'Ancarville's Recherches ‡. Thefe abilities in coins, and feals, and medals, will furely carry along with them the general powers of executing figures in fculptural relief, and may

* Recueil des Peuples et Villes, tom. 3. pl. 122. No. 1. D'Anc. vol. 3. p. 115.
† Biblioth. Orient. p. 368. Giamfchid. D'Ancarv. vol. 1. p. 125. vol. 3. p. 116.
‡ Ibid. vol. 3. p. 172. pl. 21. No. 1.

fatisfactorily account for the workmanſhip of all thoſe monuments which are to be ſeen at Perſepolis and it's environs. Without queſtion there was ſufficient ability in Perſia to execute them
in the age of Giamſchid *.

We ſhall leave to thoſe, whoſe ſtudies of myſtic antiquity may
carry them to the inveſtigation of thoſe ſculptural monuments
both in Perſia and India, the abundant lights which they will
certainly obtain in that emblematical theology, which for ſuch a
length of ages became rooted in almoſt all the nations of the
earth. The principal uſe we have to make of thoſe monuments
is, their antiquity and their execution as works of art. The firſt
of theſe has been ſtated : we ſhall now offer a ſhort reflection on
the latter.

We muſt not look for deſign. The emblematic figure, loaded
with ſymbols, disfigured by dreſs, divided often between various ſpecies, and often multiplied in parts for theological theories,
ſometimes monſtrous and unnatural by it's ſize or it's conjunctions,
was ſubverſive of all power of deſign, if that power had been
poſſeſſed. It was equally ſubverſive of all expreſſion of character, if that had been aimed at, or if it could have been reached.
And yet in ſome inſtances, where the ſymbolic figure was not ſo
crouded, or where the emblematic principles were thrown into
ſurrounding figures, we find a degree of capacity in attitude that
is by no means contemptible in itſelf, but rather ſurpriſing in
ages ſo extremely remote. It may appear more ſurpriſing, but
it is undeniable, that they were not inſenſible of forefhortening,
and that ſome of their attempts in that way beſpeak much truth.

* D'Ancarv. vol. 3. p. 116, 137.

These obfervations are confirmed by fome inftances in the pago-. da of Elephanta, but by a much more ftriking example in the two figures bending in worfhip at the foot of the ox in the tem-ple of Meaco in Japan *. The figure of that ox butting againft the egg is worthy of obfervation ; and in general the animal-creation, with allowance for occafional emblematic disfigure-ments in parts, is exhibited with fuch an approach to juftice not only in the whole figure, but in the expreffion of the coun-tenance, that with all the opportunities of hitting that truth by the living figures before them, we cannot but fometimes wonder at what they have done. They feem on the whole to have been more able in the animal-figures than in the human, as it is natural to fuppofe that they would be. We take it for granted that the drawings we have received from thofe fculp-tures are juft ; they evidently do not flatter. And in the ruins of Perfepolis, more abundantly perhaps than in any other fitu-ation, will be found fufficient confirmations of all the remarks which we have now made.

One obfervation more we muft add, which is excited by one of the bafs-reliefs cut in the rocks of Nakfki-ruftan. The defign is now very common, and the reader may fee it from the beft au-thority in D'Ancarville, vol. 1. and 3. pl. 15. It exhibits *Mihir* or the Divine Spirit, in the form of a winged child, feated on a

---

* See ibid. vol. 1. p. 65. plate 8. we have not mentioned this Japanefe work before, not having fufficient data to afcertain it's epoch : but as the people of Japan defcended from the Scythians, and participated in a particular manner of the theology communicated by Brouma, and as the figure here referred to is the fimple and primitive emblem of the fupreme Being in the exercife of creation, which ftood at the head of the Scythian religion, there can be no doubt of it's deferving a place in very early antiquity. It fhould be obferved further, that this figure of the ox is in gold.

rainbow, and worfhipped by a Perfian kneeling on the top of a high flight of fteps : around the altars below are ranges of human figures, the produ&ions of *Mihir* ; their arms are interlaced, to fhew their common bond and common origin ; and they ftand one over the head of another, to mark their fucceffive generations *.   There are various other obje&s or forms, which contribute with thofe we have juft mentioned to make that piece of fculpture the moft extraordinary for it's myftic inftru&ion of all that are left by the ancient Perfians, and the moft worthy to be contemplated by minds enlightened by divine revelation.   But our bufinefs is with it's art.   And the attitude given to all the figures in their refpe&ive fun&ions is really no mean execution. It may admit of a queftion, whether that fculpture was not done before the reign of Giamfchid, and fo early as that of Caiumarrath.   Something fimilar to it in the arrangement of the figures interlaced is difcoverable on a pilafter in the ruins of Perfepolis.

The ftate of thinking, at which thofe ancients were arrived in the ufe of the arts, is a very important circumftance.   To us perhaps they may appear ftupid, that in India they gave to fome of their figures three heads, and to fome four ; or four arms, and fometimes fix ; that in Perfia they joined a human head to the body of an ox, or coupled portions of different animals together ; that not only in thofe places, but in many others, they gave to the obje&t of their worfhip two fexes, often conjoined under one frame, and fometimes forming two figures for that obje&t ; and that in Japan they made a great point of dire&ing the whole ftrength of an ox againft an egg.   If we fuppofe, as fome have done, that by thefe methods they meant to exprefs

* Ibid. vol. 1. p. 190.   Vol. 3. p. 118.

extraordinary ſtrength, extraordinary wiſdom, or extraordinary
fecundity ; that they meant to deſcribe an uncommon character;
or that thoſe were the mere expreſſions of whim ; the ſuppoſition
is ſhallow enough.   We muſt find their meaning in much deeper
emblematic combinations.   And for theſe, as they would lead us
too far from our purpoſe, we ſhall refer the reader to the firſt
and third volumes of D'Ancarville's work, where they will
be found minutely and ſatisfactorily explained.   It muſt be
obſerved, that allegory has generally moved in all ages pretty
much in the ſame way ; although it's flock of ideas be almoſt infinite, the manner in which they have been employed has ſeldom obtained much variety.   We mean not in this to defend the
merit of thoſe eaſtern emblems on which we have touched : moſt
certainly they will be accounted poor by thoſe ages which have
carried thoſe ſtudies to greater refinement, and more eſpecially
becauſe they were generally ſubverſive of all elegance in deſign.   But we do not ſeek refinement in times ſo remote : and
yet in thoſe eaſtern works there are numerous emblems, which
have been embraced by the lovers of allegory ever ſince, and
may be pronounced to have furniſhed the firſt hints, and given
the foundation, to all that profundity of ſyſtem.

Before we quit the monuments of Perſia, let us ſee what obſervations it's architecture in thoſe remote ages has left us to make.
Thoſe ages were long, very long, before any ideas of regular
order in architecture had taken poſſeſſion of the human mind.
We ſhall conſequently find the Perſians acting on thoſe notions
for the obtaining of ſtrength, and duration, and conveniency in
buildings, which common ſenſe with ſome further aſſiſtances from
ſtudious individuals muſt ſupply. It muſt be remembered that the
buildings, which are now ſeen in ruins at Perſepolis, were not in-

tended to be inhabited, but were formed for a temple. The idea that they were conftructed for a palace is contradicted in every way. * They were built entirely of marble in the moft maffy blocks, and it is evident that they never had a covering. But in both thofe circumftances they differ entirely from the palace of which Quintus Curtius† has fpoken, and which he fays was built of cedar, fo that it took fire throughout in an inftant. There has not been found, however, in thofe ruins by the moft attentive obferver a fingle ftone calcined by fire, nor do we know any inftances of buildings deftroyed by fire which were entirely conftructed of marble. The ruins which now appear muft have exifted either as buildings or as ruins when Quintus Curtius wrote his book 400 years after the deftruction of Perfepolis; and he fays, that the people dwelling in the neighbourhood could not point out the fpot on which either the town of Perfepolis or it's palace ftood: thofe ruins therefore were known to them to be no part either of the palace or of the town, or they could not have been at a lofs to point out the one or the other; we muft conclude them to have been at fome little diftance from both, moft likely in a folitary fituation, which was generally chofen by the ancient world for the exercife of religion. To thefe obfervations let it be added, that out of the great multitude of fculptures, amounting to 1300 in thofe ruins, as they have been counted by Le Brun, there is not one which has not an evident relation to religion and to the ceremonies of a worfhip far older than the time of Cyrus.

If thofe buildings then were intended for a temple, they muft have been conftructed before the time of Zoroafter, whofe epoch is fixed by aftronomical obfervation in the book of the Magus

* Ibid. vol. 3. p. 124, 126, 135.   † Lib. 5. p. 98.

Giamaſb, which was tranſlated into Arabic A. D. 1220, to have been 2450 years before the Chriſtian æra*, and 759 years after the acceſſion of Giamſchid. Subſequent to the eſtabliſhment of Magiſm by that great reformer thoſe edifices could not have been raiſed, nor could any part of their ſculptural works have been performed, becauſe he aboliſhed the uſe of temples, altars, figures and emblems of the divinity, except fire and the ſun, not one of which were afterwards ſuffered to be executed anew in Perſia†. To the ſeverity of his reform upon Scythiciſm perhaps thoſe ſtructures owe the greateſt part of their devaſtation ; ſome attempts to deface their monuments appear to have been viſible‡: altho' neither he nor his Magi are charged with having deſtroyed all the ancient religious figures of the country ; but in all probability thoſe of which we are now ſpeaking are indebted to their own immenſe ſtrength of conſtruction in marble, defying equally fire and the hammer, that their ruins have not been more complete.

Theſe ruins have been conſidered as the palace that was built by Cambyſes or his ſucceſſor. But for that idea there cannot be the leaſt foundation, unleſs theſe ruins ſhall be found to manifeſt the ſtyle and taſte that has ever been known in Egypt. For the prohibition of all religious ſtructures and ſculptures by Zoroaſter became an abſolute extermination of artiſts at leaſt, and of architects too in ſome degree, from Perſia; inſomuch that when the palace at Perſepolis was going to be built, both architects and artiſts were brought from Egypt to finiſh it, with many ornaments of which Cambyſes had ſpoiled the city

---

* Biblioth. Orient. p. 367. Hiſt. anc. Aſtron. p. 349.　　† Herod. lib. 1. c. 131. p. 56. Strabo, lib. 15. p. 732. D'Ancarv. vol. 3. p. 116.

‡ Ibid. vol. 3. p. 130, 135.

of Thebes*. Were thefe ruins then the works of Egyptian hands? Is the ftyle and diftribution of their ftructure, are their ornaments, fuch as have ever appeared in Egypt? The direct reverfe is the fact. And this will bring us at once to the point, what their architecture was.

It was as foreign in all it's component parts from the Egyptian, as both it's parts and the whole were foreign from any thing that ever appeared in the fubfequent ages of Greece or Rome. In huge and clumfy ftrength alone it approached to the Egyptian; but that was the rudenefs of fuch early ages, which knew not how to give ftrength without clumfinefs. And in all probability Egypt derived from thofe ages in Perfia it's huge and maffy notions of building, although the variation of ideas and habits in the two countries kept their architecture in other refpects afunder. †In that Perfian edifice we find all the columns infulated and independant, contrary to the univerfal practice of the Egyptians. It was evidently conftructed without roof or covering, it was every where open, it was full of windows, and in fact it was a window throughout: in all thefe circumftances nothing was ever feen like it in Egypt. All it's fculptures are in ftrong relief, whereas the Egyptian manner fcooped them in a hollow: there nothing is more common than to find an obelifk or a pyramidal form ftanding alone; not one of which is feen here. A kind of entablement, or rather a crowning, rifes over fome of the openings, which may appear fimilar in fome of it's members to what are feen in Egyptian architecture; but that may reafonably be confidered as a common thought, which neither might borrow from the other. In

---

* Diod. Sec. Biblioth. lib. i. p. 55.   † D'Ancarv. vol. 3. p. 129. note.

the forms and pofition of many of the figures the fame difference in the tafte of the two countries is no lefs ftrongly marked.
In thofe Perfian ruins all the figures ftand upon their feet;
whereas in Egypt they lie down like the fphinx: at Perfepolis
one of the figures in that motley clafs is feen with wings, which
were never given by the Egyptians to their figures of that kind.

Such are the circumftances which decide thofe Perfian monuments to have been the productions of an age, in which Perfia
muft help herfelf to the accomplifhment of them, and in which
fhe was directed by ideas of religion clearly appropriated to the
turn of her own country, and diftinct from thofe of every other
nation, but fo far as they flowed from the common fource of
Scythicifm itfelf. On the principles of that fyftem we muft
account for the ftriking fingularity of thofe infulated columns
and univerfal openings on all fides, which diftinguifh the formation of that Perfian ftructure from every other that has been
known in the world. The whole of it plainly derives it's conftruction from modes and habits of religious fervice that were
peculiar to Perfia. The provifion made in it, as it were, for an
univerfal vifta, leads us to fuppofe that it was calculated for
fome grand religious proceffion: and the fheets of bafs-reliefs
difplayed on the walls of the great ftair-cafe leading to the temple explains that proceffion to be the grand ceremony of ufher-
ing in the new year, which lafted for fix days, and was inftituted
by Giamfchid*.

Analyfing the particular parts of thofe ruins, we fee that altho'
the days were early in which that ftructure was raifed, they had

* See the plate of thofe bafs-reliefs, Chardin's Voy. vol. 2. pl. 58. D'Ancarv.
vol. 3. p. 138, 146.

gained the ideas both of columns and pilafters. The latter were fingular enough : they were fufficiently broad to contain whole fheets of bafs-reliefs in independant emblematical fubjects : they have obtained the name of pilafters*, and they have a crowning to their termination above, as the fides of the walls in general have ; but they are, in fact, a facing given to the end of the walls, which being extremely thick have of courfe drawn into greater breadth thofe facings or pilafters. Whether they had obtained the idea of a pilafter as a half-column, and in any way that came towards proportions, thofe ruins do not inform us, nor fhould we apprehend that they had obtained fo much.

Their columns were no lefs fingular in fome refpects, although they are not to be charged equally on the fcore of proportion, for indeed they do not appear to want that general proportion which leaves the eye pretty well fatisfied. In that extent the attainment of proportion in fimple ftructures is, in fact, no more than what may be reached by the early efforts of the human mind with a moderate degree of confideration, and without examples or fyftematic principles : to carry that proportion to all the nicety of perfection, which makes every part among many to bear it's fpecific relation with harmonious exactnefs to the whole, muft be the refult of mature ftudy referved for fucceffive generations. It is, however, beyond doubt a merit in thofe, by whom thefe early works were raifed, that they were capable of fetting out (if indeed there were no confiderable examples of architecture before them, and we know of none) with fuch portions of fcience, and of grafping ideas which all the ages that might follow them fhould ftudy and improve, but never abandon. The

* Ibid. vol. 3. p. 138, 149.

columns which are now feen in thofe ruins are much lefs to be reproached in the fimplicity, or in the untutored eccentricity of their make, than thofe which were found 3700 years afterwards in the licentious affectation of the eaftern empire at Conftantinople. In thofe Perfian columns we meet with every component part which has been eftablifhed for fuch a ftructure, although in no regularity which to improved ideas can conftitute the femblance of an order. Every column has it's bafe and it's capital, as well as it's fhaft. The bafes feem to be all of one kind, the refult of a fimple idea to give the column a firmer bed; yet it is not a fhapelefs block, nor a fingle block without members; thofe members which form the upper and the lower circles are alfo kept diftinct by a higher block between, which is very humbly fcored as it were for ornament; and fome of thofe members have ever been known by the name of a Torus. The fhafts appear fometimes fcored, if not a little fluted. But the capitals are moft remarkable of all, and indicate an epoch greatly prior to every other known diftribution of a capital, an epoch in which thefe muft have been the original fcheme of artlefs nature, either in thofe Perfians or in fome others not long before them. Thofe capitals fwell out in a kind of furbelow, or what fome would call a turban-cap, rifing in two or three fucceffions, and diftinguifhed at certain diftances by a fort of fillet tied clofe round; they terminate in an uncouth manner amounting to no given fhape, nor eafily defcribable, fometimes round, fometimes fquare, fometimes neither the one nor the other, and fometimes tapering. It is ftill more remarkable, that on many of thofe columns a huge animal repofes, with whofe figure of courfe it terminates; and nothing can decide more clearly than this circumftance as well as the irregular termination of the capitals in general, that thofe columns were never intended to bear a covering, and confequently that they never conftituted the part of a palace, but of an open temple.

Thofe architects had evidently a notion of an entablature, or at leaft of a cornice, which went not only over all the openings of doors or windows, but along the fummit of the fides of the building*.   In all their altars, and in every other conftruction, they finifhed their walls with a cornice at top†.   It appears to be diftributed in three parts : the lower member we fhould call an architrave, and that feems to have been cut out in the form of eggs, as an ornament : the middle one is evidently a frize, cut in rows of fimple indents ; and the uppermoft member is a corona or coping, which does not feem to project in front, but ftarts out at the angles with a degree of tafte, and the frize being drawn by an eafy curve at the angles to receive that projection of the corona, a very agreeable effect is produced.   There appears too very plainly an intention to reprefent a kind of moulding round all the doors and windows.   But we muft not fail to remark, that there is not feen one arch throughout the whole edifice.   All the openings are either cut out of a ftone, where their fize would admit that to be done, or they are covered with a large flat ftone at the top.   If any thing looks like Egyptian workmanfhip, it is this; and yet this muft be allowed to be the only refource of all thofe who knew not the fcheme of an arch.

We have only to obferve further, that in the infcriptions which are found in all the parts of thofe Perfian ruins, ‡the remains of gilding have been plainly perceived on many of the letters, which

---

* D'Ancarv. vol. 3. p. 126, 127. pl. 7.   † Ibid. vol. 3. pl. 19.

‡ Chardin's Voyage.   D'Ancarv. vol. 3. p. 147.

wherever they were cut in black marble neceffarily required
fome means of that fort to make them more plainly legible.
This circumftance, coupled with the age which we have given to
thofe ruins, fhews very clearly that the arts had made a very confiderable progrefs in that time. And if this circumftance fhould
be confidered by any perfons as too much for the arts to have
then reached, and confequently fhould be thought to turn the
evidence another way, it muft be remarked that the characters
employed in thofe infcriptions have hardly any refemblance whatever to thofe which appear on the medals that were ftruck under
the fucceffors of Cyrus. The buildings therefore on which thofe
infcriptions appear can have no relation to an age fo late as Cyrus, and much lefs to the ages below him. We can hardly make a
doubt that the language of thofe ancient infcriptions was that in
which the books of the firft Zoroafter were written, whofe books
might well be loft, when the language itfelf was forgotten ; and
therefore it is no wonder that thofe infcriptions have been abfolutely unintelligible to all the ages that have fince paffed. Nothing
of their language appears in the writings attributed to the fecond
Zoroafter. If therefore the fact be, as M. Nieburh has obferved*,
that there are three different forts of alphabets in thofe infcriptions
at Perfepolis, they only fhew that the buildings on which thofe
varying infcriptions are found were not all erected at the fame
time, but they do not prove that they were not all erected before
the æra of the fecond Zoroafter ; on the contrary, there having
been nothing like thofe alphabets known fince that æra, all thofe
changes of character, and the buildings on which they are found,
muft have taken place during the 759 years which followed Giamfchid and preceded that Zoroafter.

* Nieburh's Voyage, vol. 2. p. 130.

In this difcuffion, which we have difpatched with all the brevity we could ufe, we fee what advancements in the arts were
brought down to the age of Ninus and Semiramis, although they
lived fo early as 2100 years before our æra, and how little reafon
we can have to wonder that the proofs of thofe arts, which are
attributed to them by the writers of antiquity, fhould have been
eafily accomplifhed in their age.   As to the means by which the
original foundation of the arts was laid in thofe primitive cha-
ra&ers, under whom the Scythian nation was formed, they
were juft as eafily within the reach of him, who was diftinguifhed by the name of Brouma, as we have fuppofed them in the
firft ftate of our argument to be within the reach of Ninus.   If
the reader will carry his recolle&ion back to what has been
urged on that head in the former part of this chapter, he will find
the reafoning applicable in every ftep to Brouma, confidered as
neareft to the firft fources of information, if fo it fhall appear to
him, on all the documents we have produced, that the Scythian
leader muft be confidered as the neareft.

Let him have lived in what part of remote antiquity he might, if
we allow the uniform and uncontroverted tradition of the Indians
to be true, that he wrote the Vedams, he had clearly fome
confiderable improvements to communicate, for he had the
precious knowledge of letters, without which thofe books could
not have been written and delivered to others.   As the firft
difpenfer of letters to their country, the Indians have uniformly
recorded him*; perhaps in fables, when they affert and believe
that he came into India attended by the Mufes†; and that he
married the goddefs of fciences, called by them *Saraffouadi*,

---

* D'Ancarv. vol. 1. p. 125, 126.   † Diod. Sic. Biblioth. lib. 4. p. 249, 55.

and by the Greeks *Mnemofine**, in reference to the power and advantages of remembrance afforded by writing; but certainly in the moſt ſerious manner, when they exhibited his figure in a coloſſal ſculpture yet remaining, wherein they have placed him in the act of writing on a kind of olive-leaf, of which Indian books are made, with a bamboo-cane†.

That Brouma, conſidered as the author of the Vedams, did actually derive from the deſcendants of Japhet, or from ſome ſuch early ſource after the flood, the intelligence contained in thoſe writings, is demonſtrable by one plain circumſtance which they afford. The firſt book of the Vedams is ſo ſimilar in it's matter to the book of Geneſis, with the preſervation of names but little and rarely varied, and with only ſome few differences of circumſtances, as, for inſtance, that two were generally pro-duced at a birth in the firſt ages, that if there be any thing to be depended on in the evidences of India with reſpect to the anti-quity of thoſe Vedams, there can be no doubt the author of them received his information from the deſcendants of Japhet. For they are underſtood to have been written above 2000 years be-fore the Pentateuch of Moſes, which is calculated to have been publiſhed about the year 1491 before the Chriſtian æra‡; and Moſes received his information from the poſterity of Shem. We have ſpoken of that eaſtern Bible with greater confidence, relying on what we have read, more than on the authorities of others‖, which may nevertheleſs be depended on in that reſpect: for we have ſeen a tranſlation of a great many chapters which

* Ibid. lib. 5. p. 384-5. Sonnerat's Voyage, vol. 1. p. 155.　　† See the place of it in Sonnerat's Voyages, vol. 1. pl. 33. D'Ancarv. vol. 3. pl. 3. and vol. 1. p. 109.　　‡ D'Ancarv. vol. 1. p. 110. Vol. 3. p. 95.
‖ Ibid. vol. 3. p. 94, 95.

are faid to form that firſt book of the Vedams, and which were taken from thofe compilations that are treafured up in the archives of India as facred, and containing the principal matters of the Vedams themfelves. The tranſlation was made by a diligent and ſtudious young man, who tranſmitted them hither, and they are now to be feen in the hands of his father, my friend. The fame fource of information may be confulted with equal eafe by thofe who fhall be in India, with the fame advantages of language, and the fame difpofition to penetrate into all the fources of oriental knowledge.

CHAP. II.

Fewer traces of the fine arts in Mefopotamia, becaufe it was the fate of it's firſt empires to be obliterated from all traces of record—fome emblematic paintings in the temple of Belus—emulation fuppofed to be greateſt in ſculpture—nothing improbable in any of their coloffal works of that kind—their knowledge of ſcultural proportion—no inference from thence to their knowledge of ſcultural expreffion—their maturity in arts not to be confidered on the common principles of progrefs in other countries—painting the leaſt probable of all the fine arts to have been carried to perfeEtion in Afia.

Whether Mefopotamia was the cradle of arts, and the cradle of imperial power, or not, we have feen that fhe had fufficient means, on every calculation of time, to carry her as far in the arts as they have been carried in Afia. But the faEt is, that our view of them is rendered extremely confined and abrupt by the fingular fate which attended all the oldeft empires formed in that part of the eaft. Long as their refpective duration might have been, they are but to us the view of a moment : we no fooner look into them, but we lofe fight of them for ever. Thofe of Scythia, of Babylon, and Affyria, if the two laft were more than one empire, have been fo completely extinguifhed, that out of all the hiftories which muft have been employed by their do-minion and magnificence, a few fragments only are left, by which we know that they ever exifted. We muft not wonder indeed at this, when two fuch cities as thofe which were the heads of the Affyrian empire were made the objects of divine difpleafure, ter-minating in a defolation beyond all example, for the tyrannic ftrides with which their princes rode over God's creation, and efpecially over his chofen pofterity of Abraham. In this view the pride of Nabonaffar, who is faid to have deftroyed all the hif-tories of Affyria, that he might be confidered as it's firft monarch, was but an inftrument of the divine purpofe, and the forerun-ner of it's difpleafure. Nabonaffar indeed gained his object with pofterity, fo far as the authors of the Univerfal Hiftory have gain-ed profelytes to their opinion on the age of the Affyrian empire.

But if all thofe records, and all the memoirs of Afia, had re-mained, they would probably have afforded lefs to gratify the lovers of the pencil than any other lovers of art. We are not to conclude from hence, that painting wanted encouragement and cultivation in Affyria. An ambitious princefs like Semiramis, who was defirous of marking her age to pofterity, would natu-rally call forth every art in her country to immortalize her name. And fo we muft conclude when we review the traces which are left to us of the paintings in the temple of Belus, which is faid to have been founded by her. Thofe paintings may perhaps appear whimfical at firft view, and efpecially in a temple ; but they will fhew at leaft the peculiar turn or tafte of that age, and they will certainly ftrengthen the authorities which have handed them down to our knowledge *. In that temple then, we are told, that the pencil had difplayed fubjects in which the confufion of fexes and fpecies was ftrongly pourtrayed; not only the fexes of the human race, which being blended in one figure formed what is called *androgynes* or *hermaphrodites ;* but the two fpecies of human and brutal creation, which being confounded together formed what has fince been called *centaurs.* The folution of thofe fubjects is in fome degree hinted by the authority which has mentioned them, and it appears to have been handed down from the priefts of Chaldæa. It will be thought very natural by thofe who wait to confider the age, the country, and the princi- ples of theology which then prevailed: but it requires to be fome- what more explicitly opened ; after which we fhall not be incli- ned to think thofe fubjects very extravagant in an Aſſyrian temple.

We muft recollect that although Ninus had fhaken off the tri- butes† which had long been paid to the Scythians by the princes of Afia, yet the principles of Scythian theology were the ruling principles of the caft, and by no means leaft predominant in Chal- dæa, from which the fcripture tells us that Abraham, living in this very age of Semiramis‡, was caft out, becaufe he laboured to reform the idolatries of the country, which were the mytho- logies engrafted on the original principles of Scythicifm, and

---

* See Diod. Sic. lib. 2. p. 123. † Juftin, lib. 2. fec. 3. D'Ancarv. vol. 1. p. 25, 28, 37. ‡ D'Ancarv. vol. 1. p. 44. Semiramis was co- temporary with Terah, Abraham's father.

terminating in infinite deifications. The Affyrians then were deeply implicated in the emblematic theology, of courfe. And the paintings before us were a ftrong proof of it. They were intended to difplay a part of the great fubjeƐt of Cofmogony, which had then obtained the creed of the country. That creed was this; that in the firft hurry of creation fexes and natures contrariant to each other became ftrangely jumbled together, producing a race of indeterminate creatures, until the agents of generation, direƐted by the fupreme Being the fource of all things, recovered from that heterogenous race a new creation of proper beings in regular harmony and order. In the for-mation of fuch a creed we fhall not wonder to find mythology fettling itfelf on *Pan* and all his company. PAN, the ALL, had been revered as the fupreme generator of all things in every country in which Scythian feet had trodden, or to which Scy-thian principles had reached. He came prefently to be charac-terized under the name, and nearly in the form, of *Silenus**; and then the whole body of fatyrs became his agents—his agents for the produƐion of that harmonious regeneration, of which they were fuitable and willing agents from the lafcivioufnefs of their nature. With this clue we fhall reach at once the meaning of all thofe ancient paintings, fculptures, or engravings, in which fatyrs are furrounding *Pan*, very often with the emblem of *love* over their heads, fometimes purfuing thofe hermaphrodites to enjoy them, and in various other fituations and affemblages, which have all flowed from the eaftern cofmogony that made the fubjeƐ of thofe paintings in the temple of Belus. And that they were in-troduced particularly into that temple, we fhall not wonder when we refleƐ, that by attributing to Belus the divinity of Pan, all the

---

* D'Ancarv. vol. 1. p. 387.

other parts of the subject did but accumulate the reverence which they meant to direct to him. It then became Belus, from whom issued that wonderful harmony and regularity and fairness of generation in a new race upon the earth, which had got rid of the old deformities; and the Assyrians conceived that they were justified in the language which has been transmitted down to us as avowed by them, that the world in it's harmonious creation, and Assyria more especially as a part of it, flowed from the purest blood of Belus*.

We must be content to view those paintings as emblematic designs. In what manner they were executed as works of art, it is impossible to say, nor indeed how broad the subject of that cosmogony was taken. At any rate there was enterprize in them; they bespoke no creeping mind; they aimed at the highest character of the art, it's display of what was considered as religious history. If they were not done without rudeness, they seem nevertheless to have been executed durably, especially if they were remaining in the age of Berosus, from whose writings Diodorus Siculus derived his authority, and in whose time 300 years before Diodorus we do not see any reason why they might not have remained. Undoubtedly they were done in *fresco*.

Those paintings will force upon us the conclusion that the pencil was in very considerable exercise under Semiramis. And yet the Assyrians seem on the whole to have been more studious of sculpture than of painting. There is more in sculpture to meet the ideas of a people, who look to what is vast, and enterprizing, and striking, than in the stiller productions of the pen-

---

* Banier, vol. 1. p. 140. See D'Ancarv. vol. 1. p. 384—406.

cil. And perhaps a theology, which had become extremely multiplied in it's principles and objects, might find itself more completely gratified, and it's purpofes of devotion more effectually anfwered, at leaft in fimpler reprefentations, by the powers of the former than by thofe of the latter. We fhould not wonder, therefore, that fculpture was moft ardently purfued, or that it obtained a preference over painting; nor fhall we be at a lofs to account for every thing, however extraordinary, which meets us in the fculptural monuments of fuch an age and fuch a princefs. The immenfity of the ftatue given to Belus in his temple will appear to be natural. We read of ftatues in maffy gold forty feet high, weighing a thoufand Babylonian talents, and reprefenting their deities in both fexes on thrones of pure filver, with all that is moft formidable and ferocious in animal nature lying tame at their feet, and wrought alfo in gold*. However thofe inftances may fhake our ideas at firft, we fee them on cooler reflection to be very probable, as the ftudied means of overwhelming the idolatrous mind, and making it abfolutely captive. The procefs of fculpture too had encouragements of it's own, which the pencil could not always be fure of enjoying. It was not eafily interrupted by any circumftances or habits of war: it could be carried on, although the thunder of armies poured it's fury on the gates within which the artift was at work; nor did it need that perfect repofe and tranquility which muft invite the genius, and fteady the hand, that conducts the pencil.

Does it feem incredible that they were able to work thofe maffes of gold? Let it be underftood that they are afferted to have been wrought by the hammer†, σφυρηλατα, *malleo ductæ;*

---

* Diod. Sic. lib. 2. p. 98. Edit. Rhodom.   † Diod. Sic. ibid.

although we are not warranted by this or any other circumstance to think that the Asiatics did not then understand the fusion of metals in general ; nor shall we think so when we are told by Valerius Maximus that there was a colossal brazen statue of Semiramis, and by others that there were several brazen gates around Babylon, and by the scriptures that the art of metallurgy was in great practice both in Asia and Egypt in the time of Abraham*. But in those colossal statues of gold the hammer was the instrument, without encreasing the difficulty, nay, lessening it considerably.   For there is express authority, that in early ages gold was found in some parts of the east so pure that it needed only to be washed, and without any other preparation it became malleable and ductile.   Diodorus† calls that gold απυρος χρυσος, *apyrum aurum*, "gold that needed not the fire."   Strabo‡ and Pliny § speak of the same gold.   Modern history informs us of other countries in which that gold is found, and may be worked with the same facility ‖.

Does the largeness then of those statues render their reality less credible ?   We must recollect that in the ideas of those early ages, both in Asia and in Egypt, the perfection of every work as well in architecture as in sculpture was conceived to depend on the hugeness of it's size.   When in after-ages, which had been furnished with the means of better taste, Nero caused his statue of brass to be made by Zenodorus 110 feet high**, shall it be thought incredible that an enterprizing princess, who had gold and silver at her command, the almost vulgar ores of the country, and sup-

---

* Gen. c. 13. v. 2. c. 23. v. 15. c. 24. v. 22, 53.   † Diod. Sic. lib. 2. p. 133.   ‡ Lib. 3. p. 216. lib. 4. p. 290, 319.   § Lib. 33. sec. 20, 21.

‖ Alonzo Barba, vol. 1. p. 99. Voyage de Frezier, p. 76, 101, 102. Acad. des Sciences, 1718. M. p. 87.   ** Plin. lib. 34. c. 7. Rom. Antiq. du Nardini.

plied and worked with the greateſt facility, ſhould accompliſh a ſtatue of 40 feet in height ?

But there were other examples of ſtatuary in that age, which, as we read them ſpoken of by Diodorus Siculus*, muſt appear more extraordinary ſtill than any which have been mentioned. We now refer to the monuments which are ſaid to have been cut by her order in the rock of Baghiſtan, a mountain of Media; that mountain is reported to have been wrought by ſculptural labour into the ſhape of the ſtatue of Semiramis ſurrounded by the ſtatues of an hundred other perſons offering her preſents. If we take that account as it ſtands, we may obſerve in ſupport of it, that mount Baghiſtan was not the laſt mountain, if it was the firſt, which as we are told, the hand of man has brought into the form of a human or brutal figure. Travellers tell us that there are three mountains in China, which have afforded the like ſubjeⱶts for illuſtrious ſculpture†. And it is well known that Dinocratus would have done the ſame thing on the mountain Athos, to immortalize the figure of Alexander the Great, if that hero would have ſuffered him.

Perhaps with ſome variation of circumſtances we may find other authorities in modern times ſpeaking with more minuteneſs of the ſame works which were intended by Diodorus. M. D'Ancarville thinks that the ſculptures found in ſome grottos of a mountain now called " Biſutoun-koh" in ancient Media ‡, whoſe ſituation ſeems to agree with that of which Diodorus has ſpoken, are the monuments intended by that author. Of theſe ſculptures

---

* Lib. 2. p. 126, 127.   † Atlas Sin. p. 69.   China illuſtrat. lib. 4. c. 4.
‡ See Mem. de l'Acad. des Inſcrip. tom. 27. p. 166.   D'Ancarv. vol. 1. p. 123.

Ifidore of Charax has made mention : we are affured that they exifted in the time of Cyrus, and they are fpoken of in the accounts
of Alexander's expeditions.   As we find thefe fculptures defcribed by thofe who have viewed them, there appears indeed fome difference between the fcene they offer and that which we fhould
conceive from the fhort account of Diodorus ; and yet it is poffible that he might mean thefe, and that he was not fo fortunate
as to obtain a precife information concerning them.   They are
neverthelefs very worthy of attention, more efpecially as by the
manner of their workmanfhip, refembling very ftrongly the ftyle
of thofe ancient monuments which we have noticed in India,
they evidently carry themfelves back to an antiquity, which cannot be lefs remote than the age of Semiramis.   The defcription
given of thofe fculptures is this.   In the rock of that mountain
is cut a vault thirty feet high, as many in length, and half as
many in breadth.   At the further end of the vault a cornice that
is formed there fupports three figures in relief: that in the middle, having a turban on his head, is taken for a king; one of
the others, being a female figure, feems to be his queen ; and the
third figure appears to be an officer in their train.   Beneath the
cornice is a man on horfeback, bearing a weapon on his fhoulder, two of his horfe's legs are detached from the rock, and the
other two adhere to it ; this figure is coloffal, while all the others
in that vault are in bafs-relief.   On entering into it you fee alfo
in relief two fames, and a kind of crown or garland.   The whole
of the rock in that vault or grotto is fmooth and polifhed.   At
the diftance of fome fteps from it there are two other vaults or
grottos, in which are many infcriptions in characters long ago
loft to the knowledge of all Afia.   In one of thefe laft grottos
there are figures reprefented in a bath.

It is a misfortune that of the very few who have vifited thofe receffes there has not been one who had the power of defigning thofe fubjects, or who fufficiently confidered the gratification, and perhaps the ufe, that would be afforded to the ftudious in antiquity by the difperfion of fuch drawings as would lead us to a knowledge of the capacity with which thofe fculptures were done.

Till that opportunity is afforded, and the conclufion can be made with certainty that thofe monuments belonged to the age of Semiramis or near it, we muft refrain from fpeaking too clofely of the capacities of Affyrian artifts. If thofe capacities were in any degree equal to the fubjects they attempted, that empire and thofe who governed it muft have flood on high ground indeed for the fuccefs with which they had nourifhed ingenuity. But we are inclined to believe that the arts of Afia flood for ages upon ages pretty much upon a par, whatever might be the fpecific meafure of capacity which they had reached at their height. Of this we fhall prefently fay more. There is one obfervation, however, which we conceive may be offered without miftake on their general knowledge in fculptural proportion. We have no decided authorities to give them the credit of that knowledge in the age of Semiramis, but we imagine the argument to be fuch that in the iffue it cannot be denied them.

In the latter days of Nebuchadnezzar it appears unqueftionable that the Babylonians were accurate in the knowledge of fculptural proportion. That monarch fet up a golden image, fixty cubits high, and fix cubits broad*—the exact proportion which geometrical fymmetry has ever purfued in the reprefentation

* Daniel, cap. 3. v. 1.

of the human frame. It is enough to fay that it is the fame proportion which is obferved in the Laocoon, whofe height is thirty
parts, and it's diameter three. The principle eftablifhed in both is
to multiply the diameter by ten, and the produce gives the height.
How then came the artifts of Nebuchadnezzar by that knowledge ?   The conftruction of the ark by Noah proves it to have
exifted as the fettled principle of geometrical fcience familiar to
the earlieft ages of the world. That ark was 300 cubits in length,
30 in depth or thicknefs, and 50 in breadth.   We do not mean
to fay with Paul Lomazzo*, that it was meant to be fquared according to the fymmetry of the human body ; for the difference of
it's pofition from that of a man ftanding upright either introduces
a third meafure of breadth to be added, becaufe it was to contain
much, and would otherwife overfet, or it reverfes the relative fituations of breadth and depth in the human frame : if the diameter
be taken, on account of that difference, in the depth or thicknefs
inftead of the breadth, it will yield the fame proportion to the
length, which is properly it's height, as is found in the human
flature ; and taking it's pofition as it is, the fame proportion is
maintained comparatively between the breadth and the depth or
thicknefs of the ark, which appears between the breadth and
thicknefs of the human body.   Thefe proportions therefore were
among the earlieft acquirements of fcientific knowledge : Noah,
without the fuppofition of a divine command, might naturally
have derived them from the fons of Seth ; and we cannot fuppofe
a generation afterwards, that was not ftrangely deftitute of attention, to whom they were not equally plain. The age of Semiramis had the advantage, if there was any in this circumftance, of
thofe that went before it, as it could work upon their knowledge ;

* Idea del tempo della pittura, lib. 1. p. 95.

and therefore we can make no queſtion that the general truth of proportions was purſued in the ſculptures of that age. In all the works, on which we have touched, in India, and Perſia, and Japan, we ſee no cauſe to reproach them with the want of this general outline of proportion, whatever advantages they may want beſides. We have already obſerved that in the columns of Perſepolis, which drew their proportions very much from the ſame principles, and alſo ſhew us that the architects of thoſe early ſtructures had ſtudied thoſe principles, the eye is well ſatisfied with the attention which has been paid to this part of ſcience. And therefore when we are told, and probably with great truth, that the firſt ſculptures in Aſia, in Egypt, in Greece, and in every part of the earth, were little better than ſhapeleſs blocks[*], we know the proper diſtinction to be made; that they might be little better than ſhapeleſs in their action and ſpirit, but the days muſt have been early indeed when they were found ſhapeleſs in general proportion. That general proportion may be well known, and truly kept; and yet the attitude and expreſſion, which is the ſoul of the work, may be rudeneſs itſelf. On this laſt circumſtance we muſt be ſilent with reſpect to the age of Semiramis, having no clue to lead us but that which is put into our hands by the Aſiatic monuments now remaining, and which is no ſure one to guide us to the age of that princeſs : judging however from thoſe monuments, we conceive ourſelves warranted to ſay, that the artiſts of Aſia, although very humble, were neither inſenſible of attitude and expreſſion, nor at all times unſucceſsful in it. With theſe allowances given to them there is ſufficient ground, on the one hand, to reſtrain that kind of opinion which depreciates without reſerve all the works of thoſe ancient ages, as

* Goguet's Orig. of Laws, &c. vol. 1. p. 166.

abſolutely deſtitute of pretenſions to art, and on the other hand
to account for eulogies which are found in ancient authors on
the merit of many of their productions, although we may think
it reaſonable not to go the whole length of thoſe eulogies themſelves.

In Aſia more than in any other part of the world, and contrary
to what has been found every where elſe but in Egypt, becauſe
ſhe moved very much alike to Aſia in her nature and policy, any
one aſſemblage of the works of art, after the country came to be
in the habits and in the power of exerciſing it, might be taken as
no unfair criterion of the merit of any other aſſemblage, in any
other period of time, in the ſame branches. And this is the cauſe
why we ſo often find the works of ſculpture in one part of Aſia
pronounced by modern inquirers to be ſimilar in their execution
to thoſe which appear in another part. That ſimilarity has frequently been conſidered as a ground of reference to the age which
might be due to ſome of thoſe works, according to their reſpective ſituations: but we may properly obſerve, that on that ground
all judgement is ſupplanted, for ſimilarity would bring every
thing into one age ; miſtakes muſt therefore be made in the application of that reference, although the ſimilarity on which
it is grounded be right, for want of conſidering how that ſimilarity comes, and to what reflections it may fitly be carried.

The fact is, that the works of Aſiatic art are not to be ſcanned
on the common principles of progreſs in other countries, which
by length of time, and length of practice, advances regularly
to improvement and perfection. Such is not the principle
of Aſia in any part of it's nature or acquirements. In
this peculiar view it exhibits the moſt ſingular contraſt

to every other people on the earth, except the Egyptians. The Afiatics reached in the arts very foon almoft as much as they ever reached. They fhot up rapidly to the point of maturity, which by fome circumftances or other attending them they were deftined to attain, and there they ftopped. If we could view their finer arts from generation to generation, and could be affured of following their feveral epochs, we are warranted by what are ftill left of thofe arts in various parts of Afia, which cannot be all of one age, and by what we equally learn from their mechanical works, to conclude that the gradations of improvement would be found extremely few. The fame obfervations befit them as men. They ever fhot forth, and they ftill fhoot forth, quickly into mature life, where their natural and rational growth ends : they are men very foon, and foon capable of all the powers of which they are ever capable. Will it fhew too much of religious propenfity to fay, that fo the Almighty meant it to be with them in all things ? Having renovated the world, and the Afiatics as the firft fruits of that renovation, he threw them prefently into manhood, that little time might be loft for action. And all their generations fince have inherited and carried forward the gift. In the fame manner he feems to have thrown them as early into a kind of manhood in the ingenious arts, that little time might be loft by uncertain inveftigation to thofe who foon began, and foon came to the extent of, their capacities. The latter of thefe circumftances grew from the former by a law of Nature. But the Afiatics entailed it on themfelves by the laws of their own policy, and by their own fyftem of thinking and acting ; in confequence of which, all things have ever remained in the fame ftate with that people, and they never made any advantage of the duration of their empires to acquire new lights, and to bring firft difcoveries to perfection. It was a first principle in the inftitutions of many of their governments, to admit no novelty*; therefore they never travelled +, unlefs it were thofe who were navigators by fituation and habit; and therefore it is very true that all which we find of their principles in other countries were neither fetched nor derived by them from thofe countries, but were fetched by thofe that travelled from thofe countries to them ‡. In profeffions every man was to follow that of his family. In thofe of the arts, the meaneft of all profeffions in their eftimation, neither rewards nor fame were to be looked for. So that emulation was at an end, and every improvement from father to fon was hopelefs.

Yet they went on in the fame way without intermiffion. We do not find that their purfuits in fculpture flackened in any generations, of which we have records. In thofe which followed Semiramis at the diftance of fome hundred years, fculptures were common not only in temples but in private houfes. As far as they partook of religion, they were ftill kept up by Scythicifm; and it was the idolatrous images of Scythicifm which Rachel near 400 years afterwards carried off from the houfe of her father Laban, when fhe and Jacob departed from him §.

Let things have ftood in the country as they might with refpect to fculpture, we conceive that painting was the laft of the fine arts which could have furnifhed many proofs of advancement in Afia. It has been faid that the pencil can never be handled with power but under the enjoyment of liberty. Be that as it may, it feems unqueftionable, that it can hever be handled with

---

* Plato de Leg. lib. 2. p. 789.   † Plin. nat. Hift. lib. 6. p. 182.
‡ D'Ancarv. vol. 1. p. 136, 177.   § Gen. cap. 31. v. 19.

power in a climate, whofe exceffive and unremitting heat exhaufts
the finking inhabitant, relaxes every nerve, and leaves him liftlefs to every exertion, emulous only of the indulgence which oft-
returning fleep adminifters only to roufe him for a moment, and
then to receive him back into it's quietude. If tranquility be favourable to the genius of the painter, it is not that foftening,
finking tranquility; it is the tranquility which fprings from a mind
ftrong and braced, in the full enjoyment of it's powers, but in the
free enjoyment of them too, unruffled and unhurried. There
muft be life and fpirit, and a firmnefs in both, not only to elicite
the invention, and carry it up to degrees of enterprize, but to
fteady the hand, while it marks all it's purpofe with effect. Thefe
powers can no more be had where the vertical beams of the fun
leave the tawny inhabitants with fome difficulty to refpire, than
where in horizontal fainter vifits, fhorn of his beams, he fees
mankind benumbed and torpid, not more inert in body than in
mind. We do not fay that in the former fituation the genius and
the hand will not fhew themfelves in fome performances worthy
to be admired : but there can be no progrefs of art, no extenfion
to it's enterprize, no continued aims at perfection, which were
never feen but in milder and more temperate fituations.

CHAP. III.

Phœnicia, although a part of the Aſſyrian empire, to be viewed
diſtinctly in ſome reſpects as to the fine arts—the principles of
Scythian theology prevalent here—the ſpirit of Phœnician arts
firſt directed by thoſe principles—afterwards made ſubſervient
to the habits of commerce—ſcuplture much cultivated as a
commercial article—few traces of painting but what were in a
low taſte—improved and poliſhed ſentiment not diſtinguiſhed
in the Phœnician character—architecture much attended to,
and in great eſtimation—no proofs of the fine arts worthy
of particular conſideration in Carthage, although it was an
emanation from Tyre.

Pнœniciа, as a part of Syria, may be looked upon as a component member of the Aſſyrian empire. As ſuch, it might be
conſidered as bearing a part in thoſe views which have been given
of Aſſyria. But the fact is, that it did not go along with thoſe
views altogether, for it had views of it's own, which put the fine
arts upon a different footing within it from that which we have
hitherto found them to obtain in Aſia. The peculiarity of thoſe
views, whether they were more or leſs beneficial to thoſe arts,
may juſtify us in giving them a diſtinct conſideration, although
they ſhould be found to add but little materially new in the
progreſs of thoſe arts themſelves.

We do not mean to aſſert that Phœnicia did not participate
with the reſt of that continent in the diffuſion of thoſe Scythian
principles, which gave the firſt direction to all the arts that were

cultivated upon it. In that view it became a ftrong evidence of
the extent to which that Scythian influence was carried on that
fide of the Afiatic continent. The borders of Phœnicia afforded
the fpot, on which the Scythian conquerors erected a town as the
boundary of their progrefs to the weft, which town bore it's manifeft relation to them in the name of Scythopolis, and alfo in
that of Nyfus*, which became the general name of every boundary of their progrefs, as it was the name of the place from
whence they originally came. In that Phœnician or Arabian
Nyfus was kept up the worfhip of the Scythian divinity with the
fame ceremonies which were obferved in the Nyfus of India†.
The ox was there introduced, the original Scythian emblem of the
generator of all things‡ ; which from thence became the principal
divinity of the Arabians, hardly ever to be erafed afterwards from
their minds§, or to be difpoffeffed of it's fanctity as the object by
which they fwore‖. . The ferpent was no lefs revered in Phœnicia, where it was beheld as the emblem of a good genius, and was
made the fubject of very ferious writings by Hermes, whom Por-
phyry calls a Phœnician**. That ferpent appeared on their
coins twifted round the egg of creation, and fometimes twifted
round an olive-tree, as it was reprefented in Japan††: at other
times the ferpent was exhibited with the flower or leaf of the tamara, the Scythian emblem of divinifation, placed over his head‡‡.
They had in common with the Affyrians, and with the Perfians
too, the figure of *Tau*, and from them the Egyptians took it,
as they alfo took their *Kneph :* the Phœnicians employed that

* Stephan. Byzant.   D'Ancarv. vol. 1. p. 26, 28.   † Ibid. p. 38, 40.
‡ Ibid. p. 139. Diod. Sic. lib. 1. p. 19.   § D'Ancarv. vol. 1. p. 46, 72.
‖ Herod. lib. 2. c. 8. p. 162.   ** Porphyr. ap. Eufeb. præp.
Evang. lib. 3. D'Ancarv. vol. 1 p. 468, 476, and Pref. p. 13.   †† Ibid. p.
470, 504.   ‡‡ Ibid. p. 469.

figure of *Tau* on their medals in the form of a crofs, the union of whofe parts at the top was intended to mark the alliance of the fupreme generator with love, or the mihir, or the fpirit, as it was employed for the fame purpofe by the Perfians on their mithras*. In different fituations, although nearly connected together, the fame original principles will be feen to branch out into different afpects, and to produce various mythologies. And fo it was with the cofmogony of the Phœnicians, whether that was a variation peculiar to themfelves on the cofmogony which has already been mentioned as entertained by the Affyrians, or whether they embraced both the one and the other, for they were nearly allied. The notion, however, which prevailed in Phœnicia, as Sanchoniatho informs us, was this; " that in the com- " mencement of creation there were animals devoid of fenfe, " from whom were afterwards produced intelligent animals call- " ed *Saphafemin, beings that could look up to heaven*, who were " formed in the manner that eggs were hatched†". But the Phœnicians went ftill nearer to the cofmogony of the Affyrians, for they fuppofed " the firft created beings, who were both male " and female, in the bofom of the fea as well as on the earth, to " be faft afleep till they were awakened into life and action by " the noife of thunder‡".

We fhall go no farther than this to fhew in Phœnicia the pre-valence of thofe common principles of Scythicifm, which might be of lefs confequence here to be remarked, after what we have faid of Affyria, if they did not lay a foundation for further views in thofe who fucceeded the Phœnicians. Thofe principles, howe-

---

* D'Ancarv. vol. 3. p. 163, 164.   † Sanchon. ap. Eufeb. præp. Evang.
D'Ancarv. vol. 1. p. 470, 471.   ‡ Ibid. note.

ver, firſt brought the arts from the hands of theſe people, and directed their ſpirit. That ſpirit appeared very early on their coins
and medals. Beſides thoſe which have been mentioned as retaining the root of thoſe principles in the emblem of the ſerpent under various forms and combinations, it is remarkable that in the
adjoining Arabia, and therefore probably in Phœnicia too, the
primitive ſimplicity of obeliſcal monies, which grew from the firſt
impreſſions of religious rites, was employed in very early ages,
long before they found their way into Greece, and has never ſince
loſt it's obolary character in that country, whatever may have
been the change of it's name, or the variation in the ſhape of the
monies themſelves *.

From the firſt principles of their theology the Phœnicians
would naturally extend their arts to the perpetuation of objects more diſtantly connected with that theology, or more
immediately connected with themſelves and their own ſituation. Hence in the medals of Tyre they figured thoſe ambroſial
ſtones, which were found on the ſea-coaſt, and to which they paid
worſhip, as to an emblem of the divinity, long before the foundation of original Tyre, although the new city of that name was
fabulouſly ſaid, by a fiction engrafted on that worſhip, to have
been founded on thoſe emblematic ſtones: of theſe they made
ſuch account, that models of them, executed by their artiſts in the
moſt precious materials, were depoſited in the temple of Hercules at Tyre†. In that buſineſs indeed they came round to the
mythology of the egg, which when divided into two parts became the model of thoſe ambroſial ſtones on the Phœnician medals. They had their deity of the ſea, repreſented on other me-

* D'Ancarv. vol. i. p. 21, 29.   † Ibid. p. 502, 504.

dals as a female figure, but in the armour, and drefs, and action
of a man; which was plainly following the eaftern idea of the
two fexes in the divinity, only applied to their own peculiar circumftances as a maritime people; and that figure unqueftionably
gave occafion to the Minerva of the Greeks.   This deity of the
fea was diftinguifhed on their medals by the name of *Euplæene*,
which meant *a good navigation ;* and fhe was defcribed either as
ftanding on the prow of a veffel, or as holding the figure of it in
her hand : and from thence came the Venus of the Greeks, and
the notion that fhe was born in the fea, as well as that fhe prefided over maritime expeditions *.   But that female deity drew
the arts of Phœnicia ftill further.   †She was reprefented on the
medals of Sidon in the figure of one of thofe obelifcal ftones ‡,
to which worfhip was paid before men had devifed ftatues of the
divinity, and one of which was long preferved at Emefus in Syria.   That ftone was placed on a car §, which feems to have given
the hint to the ufe of thofe machines in religious ceremonies, and
to the reprefentation of deities feated upon them.   Prefently they
advanced further.   She obtained at Sidon, whofe protectrefs fhe
was, the name of Aftarte, and it is to her divinity that the allufion
is made, when we read of the Syrian goddefs ||.   They drew her
in the coins of that town as a buft, feated on a car, with the *mo-*
dius or *bufhel* on her head, as the fymbol of abundance ; from
whence it was undoubtedly carried to Diana of Ephefus : and
that Diana derived alfo from the Phœnician Aftarte the figure of
the crefcent put over her head, which had been given to the lat-

---

* D'Ancarv. vol. 2. p. 417, 418, note.   † Ibid. p. 420, 423.

‡ Herodian in Macrin. lib. 7. p. 436. D'Ancarv. vol. 1. p. 45. Vol. 2. p. 420, 421.

§ See a plate of it, D'Ancarv. vol. 2. No. 29. pl. 1.

|| Selden de diis Syr. Syntagm. 2. c. 2. p. 181.

ter in many medals of Sidon, in confequence of her being confidered, as Lucian fays*, to be the moon, and not unnaturally
when fhe was allowed to prefide over the fea. But in that buft of
Aftarte an important epoch was opened. We fee the firft traces
of thofe operations, by which fculpture came to fubftitute that
term of a human head in the place of thofe fhapelefs ftones ; while
it was not yet able in that buft to feparate the arms, and to diftinguifh other parts of the figure, for which reafon it was left as a
buft, and was cut off below the cheft†. Thefe works of Sidon,
which was the mother of Tyre, muft have been very ancient ;
they muft have been anterior by many ages to the days of Laban, when idols in fculpture growing from Scythian theology
were common in every houfe throughout Syria, as well as in Laban's. Thofe idols received the human figure ; they were called
" Teraphim ;" and we can make no doubt that long before the
days of Laban that figure had become regular, and that it was
executed in all proportions, fmaller as well as greater, fince
Rachel could carry away fome of thofe idols from her father,
and hide them under her ‡ ; and it would be longer before thofe
fmaller proportions would either come into common ufe, or be
regularly executed, than the larger. It was one of the fame idols,
but of a larger fize, which Michal fo long afterwards put into
David's bed, in order to deceive Saul §. We fee from hence the
deep root which thofe principles of theology had taken in that
country, and the continual exercife which they furnifhed to fculptural fkill.

Thus were the arts of Phœnicia put in motion by the principles of theology which had been eftablifhed there. And thus the

* Lucian de Dea Syria.　　　† See a plate of it, D'Ancarv. vol. 2. No. 29.
plate 2.　　　‡ Genefis, c. 31. v. 19, 30.　　　§ 1 Sam. c. 19. v. 13.

Phœnicians moved in common with others, to whom the fame principles had arrived, although in fome refpects they may be faid perhaps to have moved on a more enlarged fcale. But that which difcriminates their views from thofe of others in the exercife of the arts, was the influence of their commercial fpirit, which fucceeding next to the influence of their religious ideas, took up thofe arts as means of commerce, and confined them wholly to the ends of it. They were a commercial and fea-faring people from their very fituation. Inhabiting the coafts of Syria, with the ocean in their front, and mount Libanus on their back for fhip-timber, they naturally embraced navigation for their employment, and they were the firft navigators of antiquity. Every thing that was rare or valuable in Afia, and in Egypt, and in Greece, if that country had any thing valuable then, went through their hands. So enured to the habits of trade, it was impoffible for them to fhake off the influence of thofe habits in any circumftance by which they were affected; it was impoffi-ble for them to feel any other motives in the encouragement of ingenious fkill equally ftrong and dear to their minds with the profpect of gain. The fine arts were valuable in them-felves, they were fought for their great ufefulnefs to the pre-vailing theology, and they were precious to thofe who had any notions of tafte. They were therefore a moft important branch of commerce. Thofe, who had every market in their hands, could not be inattentive to the value of that ingenuity which had devolved in a manner upon themfelves, if not as it's only poffef-fors, yet as the only people through whofe hands others could obtain it at a diftance. Gold, and filver, and ivory, and pre-cious metals were in the greateft abundance among them : thefe became highly enriched in their value by the ingenuity and tafte of the fculptor's hand. We muft not wonder, therefore, to fee

thofe powers of art moft feduloufly cherifhed by the Phœnicians :
we muft not wonder to fee them, although they were traders, artifts too, attentively engaged in thofe works of ingenious fkill.
Perhaps it was to exprefs how much thofe works were in vogue,
and to what extent the paffion for them was carried in that country, that poetical fable has reprefented a Pygmalion as abfolutely
in love with an ivory ftatue which he had made *.

Whatever were his motives for a partiality to fculpture, thofe
of his countrymen were the hopes of commercial advantage.
And therefore it was fculpture which engaged their primary attention.   We have no evidences of their emulation in painting.
Sculpture was a marketable art. The precious materials, on which
it was employed, were every where intrinfic in their value, and
thofe of a humbler kind became precious by it's aid.   It was
therefore an intrinfic article in itfelf, and it's value was more certain, bceaufe it was not eafily apt to perifh.   If any other arts of
tafte were added to that, it was thofe which were employed on general manufactures, for the purpofe of commanding a market, and
of enfuring a price. But paintings had no ftaple value : they could
not be carried from one man or one place to another through
the earth, with the affurance of obtaining a fpecific value for
the art by which they were compofed. In after-times indeed they
came to be made articles of traffic by other people, but that ufe of
them was not difcovered in Phœnicia, or circumftances were not
ripe for the practice ; and the Phœnicians were not adventurers
enough to trade, and much lefs to employ their labour at home,
in thofe articles which were precarious in their price.   Painting
therefore made no figure among the other arts of that people ; it

* Ovid's Metam. lib. 10. v. 276.

was rather left in neglect. If we are to take our account of it's
general employment from the words of Comes, who fpeaks exprefsly of the cuftomary ufe to which the pencil was there devoted, we fhall think it low enough : he fays, "non folum in nu-
" mifmatibus, fed in picturis demefticis, .et in navigiis jumento-
" rum imagines pingere confueverunt".

With this trait all their encouragement of the pencil, and all the
eminence it reached among them, is clofed to pofterity. What
muft we think of all their patronage of art, if the whole force of
their pencil centered in "beafts of burthen"? But as they themfelves were the carriers of the world, perhaps they thought that
what partook of their employment was moft worthy of being
diftinguifhed.

It was therefore the fpirit of commerce, more than the fpirit of
tafte, which gave any of the arts of elegance, except architecture, a cultivation in Phœnicia. Thofe arts of elegance depended for their cultivation on the previous value annexed to their
ingenuity. Where that idea was out of fight, we find not a fingle production below the loweft and coarfeft fubjects.

Perhaps that felection of ideas fpoken of by Comes, and which
we may call the *burthen* of their tafte in domeftic pictures, was as
high as they could go. We muft not confider their character as
marked by polifhed and improved fentiment. When we have
made all proper allowances for fuperftition, the human mind was
probably never lower in ignorance than with them, when they were
out of their trade, or out of their particular profeffion. A fingle
fact will be fufficient to illuftrate this, efpecially when it is taken
not from their earlier, but their later, days. When Alexander

the Great was befieging Tyre, there ftood in the city an immenfe brazen ftatue of Apollo*, which had once belonged to the city of Gela in Sicily, till it was taken from thence by the Carthaginians, and given as a prefent to their mother-city of Tyre. In confequence of a dream by one of the citizens it was generally imagined by the Tyrians, that Apollo was determined to leave them, and go over to Alexander; to prevent which, they actually faftened his ftatue to the altar of Hercules with a golden chain. They were filly enough to believe that Hercules, the tutelar god of their city, would prevent the other, when faftened in that manner, from making his efcape†.

In architecture, neverthelefs, they became diftinguifhed; and they were moving towards that diftinction at all times. In every country, where there is wealth, that branch of art has been fought, for the beft reafon in the world, becaufe it is moft wanted. The Phœnicians have been confidered as the firft people who formed and inftituted an order. The Tyrian order has been fpoken of as prior to every other. We are not enabled to fpeak of the conftitution of that which has been fo called an order, unlefs we may confider it as exhibited, a great many ages fubfequent to thefe remoter times, in the pillars fet up by Phœnician architects in the porch of the temple at Jerufalem ‡. We confefs there is no evidence fufficiently clear to demonftrate their poffeffion of a regularly conftituted order before any others in the world. The reader will recollect that he has had before him the columns which are now left in the ruins of Perfepolis, and which were originally conftructed there 3209 years before our æra. Thofe co-

* Diod. Sic. lib. 13. p. 226.   † Rollin's anc. Hift. vol. 6. p. 188, 189.
‡ 1 Kings, cap. 7. v. 15—22.

lumns came near in fome refpects to the regularity of an order, yet certainly they cannot be fpoken of as formed in any decided fpirit of proportional conftruction. Neverthelefs, in all probability they are the oldeft in the world : and it may have arifen from the want of a right acquaintance with their age, and with the nature of the ftructure to which they appertained, and which being miftaken would naturally lead to a miftake in their age, that the architecture of Phœnicia has feemed to be the firft which came forward in any regularity, and therefore has obtained the character of an order. We fhould be apt to conclude that, fituated as the Phœnicians were to profit by the ingenuity to which any part of Afia had advanced, and open as Egypt was to their vifits, they could hardly avoid to act upon fome of thofe examples around them, which had antiquity enough to lead their purfuit; although it may be true, and it is at leaft very probable, that as their views of commerce fpirited up their genius in fome branches, and as their more enlarged acquaintance with the world refcued them greatly from thofe confined ideas with which the arts were generally profecuted in Afia, they would improve upon the approaches to a regularity in architecture which others had made before them. That they did advance very greatly in the courfe of time, we have the fureft teftimony in their employment under Solomon at Jerufalem. That circumftance muft induce the conclufion, that they had long obtained a celebrity in architectural profeffion, and in fculpture too. The employment, to which they were there called, winds up their character in both thofe branches of art. That character will ftand the higher, when it is recollected that at that very period the correfpondence between Judæa and Egypt was fo amicable, that a marriage had juft taken place between Solomon and the daughter of Pharoah. And does not that circumftance fhew, that the Phœnicians were confidered as more capable of a progreffive improvement in the arts than either the Egyptians or the reft of the Afiatics? It is true indeed that, as to Egypt, thofe were the days of that fad reverfe to the arts, which had come on after Sefoftris, and which not all the five following centuries had been able to terminate. Egypt therefore was going down in the world: Affyria was gone down in that obfcurity which covered the long interval from Ninias the fon of Semiramis to Phul the laft of it's kings but one: and the eftablifhment of magifm in Perfia forbad all thoughts of finding architects and artifts there. Yet both of them were found in Egypt fome ages afterwards by Cambyfes, to execute the defigns of his palaces in Perfia.

Let thofe circumftances have been as they might; let neceffity have been greater or lefs than choice in the call which was made by Solomon on the architects and artifts of Phœnicia, their talents were undoubtedly then of the firft rate. Defigns of fuch extent and magnificence as thofe of the temple and the palaces at Jerufalem, which were completed by Phœnician hands, or at leaft under the direction of a Phœnician architect, did never comport with moderate capacities. That man, and any others of his countrymen who acted with him, were certainly unlike the generation which rofe up afterwards when Alexander came before Tyre. Had he or they been then living, they would not have faftened Apollo to the altar of Hercules; or it muft be true that the moft enlarged conceptions may be combined with the groffeft weaknefs. The immenfe fcale of that architecture at Jerufalem, and it's innumerable ornaments; the fplendid throne prepared for Solomon, and formed of gold and ivory enriched with lions and other figures engraved upon it; the cherubims; the veffels

of gold; the altar; the pillars; and the great fea of brafs fupported by twelve brazen oxen, demonftrate thofe architects and
artifts to have been capable of the moft lofty ideas, whatever
might have been the proportion of merit in the execution of
thofe works. They demonftrate alfo that the arts in their hands
were aged, and that it was not fo late as about 1000 years before
the Chriftian æra that thofe arts became firft fo advanced in Phœnicia. What works of architecture or fculpture had been executed by thofe men, or by other Phœnicians, at home, the defolation which awaited and overwhelmed Tyre has forbidden us to
know; but there can be no doubt that the abilities, which could
do fo much at Jerufalem, had given confiderable proofs of themfelves at Tyre.

Such then were the Phœnicians, from whom the Carthaginians
immediately iffued. Thefe inherited from their original ftock
the fame predilection for commerce; but they did not inherit an
equal fpirit of enterprize in the arts. There is nothing therefore
in their hiftory but their clofe connection with the Phœnicians,
which can attach the mention of them to our inquiry, efpecially
while we are engaged in Afia, and on the ages of remote antiquity. We fhall juft obferve that Carthage did indeed become
ftored with immenfe treafures of painting and fculpture: but
not one of thofe treafures was the work of their own hands, or
the production of their own emulation. They were all the fpoils
of their conquefts, augmenting the loffes and fufferings of Sicily,
and deftined to become again the fpoils of a foldiery, or to be
carried by Scipio to Rome, or to be reftored by that conqueror
to their firft owners*. But we are told that the temple of Apollo

---

* Cicero, lib. 4. in Verrem, cap. 33. Appian de Bell. pun. p. 83, 84.

in Carthage was fingularly rich and fuperb, and that the ftatue of that god placed in that temple, when it was broken to
pieces by Scipio's foldiers, amounted to a thoufand talents of
gold*. It might be fo. Idolatry and fuperftion, or, if you will,
religion will lay under contribution even the calculations of mer-
cantile gain : no calculation is fo clofe or fordid, but it has fome
vanity or oftentation to be gratified. If that ftatue of gold were
their own workmanfhip, there was nothing in the age or in their
fituation, any more than in that of the Phœnicians, to hinder their
capacity for fuch a work, or for the magnificent building that
contained it. And the buckler of Afdrubal, which was ordered
to be laid up in the capitol at Rome as a choice fpoil, not only
becaufe it was his buckler, but becaufe it was excellently engraved, may as naturally be fuppofed to come from the trading Carthaginians, as any of the engravings on precious metals came
from the trading Phœnicians.

CHAP. IV.

*The fine arts not to be expected, but in a very confined view,
among the Hebrews or Ifraelites—the influence of Scythian
theology no where more prevalent than with them, and for a
long time—the arts that were connected with that theology retained much longer than for any other purpofes—fome of the
leading emblems of that theology retained by God himfelf in
his divine revelation—the retention of thofe emblems no argument againft the divine wifdom.*

THE Phœnicians were fo called by the Greeks†: originally they
were known by the name of Canaanites. As they were mer-

* Appian, lib. 14.   † Calmet, vol. 1. p. 272. Vol. 3. p. 131. Marfh. p. 290.

chants, at leaft fuch of them as lived near the fea-coaft, it has
caufed fome to be fo ingenious as to find the fenfe of merchant in
the definition of Canaanite *; which is evidently converting a
remote confequence into an original caufe, and arguing *à priori*
indeed for the deftinations of life, as it fuppofes an invincible neceffity on the mind of Canaan, the anceftor of thefe people, to
make his pofterity merchants. Part of their country became afterwards poffeffed by the Hebrews under the name of Paleftine.
We cannot therefore fpeak of that people in a more proper
place. Their concern in the fine arts was not indeed extenfive;
in it's objects it was entirely confined to religion, and was purpofely narrowed in it's exercife by the firft principles of Judaifm;
in it's origin it was entirely derived from Egypt; and in it's influence it went no farther than themfelves, becaufe it was a great
principle of their fyftem to have no communication with others.
All that is left therefore to be faid concerning them, if we adhere
to the immediate progrefs of the arts, is very confined. But
there is a connection with thofe arts fomewhat more remote, and
arifing from the view of the firft habits, and indeed of the
continued prejudices of that people, which may not be thought
irrelevant to the purpofe of our inquiry. If this fhould be
confidered in any refpect as a digreffion from that purpofe, it will
prefently lofe that name as it comes round to a moft impreffive
confirmation of the exiftence and diffufion of that Scythicifm,
which gave the firft fpring and direction to all the more elegant
arts. That confirmation will be made good, when we have fhewn
how faft and how long the minds of the Hebrews or Ifraelites,
by whatever name they came progreffively to be called, were poffeffed by thofe principles of Scythian theology, and with what

---

* Braun. de Veftitu. facerd. Hebr. p. 251.

policy (if we may ufe the phrafe) the Almighty conducted the procefs of that revelation, by which he meant to wean them from thofe principles.

We have feen already how common the idols growing out of that theology were in Syria, when Jacob left Laban; and they were not lefs common at the fame time in Canaan, when Jacob removed them all from his houfe*. When we come to take our review of Egypt, we fhall find that the Hebrews, while they were multiplying their numbers there, were inevitably encreafing the influence of mythological Scythicifm, which their long fojourning there did but imprefs the deeper on every generation. When they left that country, they fhewed very clearly the religious tuition which they had received in common with every other mortal that drew his breath in Egypt. They carried from thence the moft profound veneration for the ox and the ferpent, the one the emblem of the fupreme generator of animal life, the other the emblem of the great fource of intelligent Nature; thefe were the two common points of union in all the firft religions of the earth; to thefe it is hard to fay when they ceafed to be attached; and it is equally difficult to fay which of the theological or mythological emblems of the Scythians they did not embrace with a full belief that they were embracing a folid principle of religion†. Thefe were the idolatries to which they were fo prone; "the fin of Ifrael," as they were called; from which not all the prohibitions of God himfelf, the remonftrances of the prophets, and the punifhments which they felt from time to time were able for many ages completely to reftrain them. Hardly had their feet refted in the wildernefs, after the ftupendous proofs

* Genefis, cap. 35. v. 2.
† D'Ancarv. Pref. p. 12, 14. Vol. 1. p. 48, 323, 468, note.

which the Almighty had given of his protection and deliverance
of them from the power of the Egyptians, when, feeling the re-
turns of idolatrous attachments in the short abfence of Mofes,
they called upon Aaron "to make them gods which should go
" before them ;" and Aaron himfelf, inftead of remonftrating and
refifting, aftonifhingly fell in with their prejudice *. The idea
fuggefted to Aaron of having an idol to go before them was completely Scythian; for fo the Scythians acted in all their progrefs through Afia, with this difference that their idol was a living animal †, and that idol they brought with them into India under the name of *Bofwa*, which name the fpecies of it retains there
ftill‡. When the wifh of the Hebrews was completed in the
golden calf, it fhewed more plainly the origin from whence their
thought had fprung, although they had gathered it in Egypt;
for that *Bofwa* of the Scythians was an ox. The ancient Cimbri,
tutored by the fame example, carried an ox of bronze before
them in all their expeditions §. The Ifraelites, having gained
their favourite god, came next to dance around that emblematic figure on a fpecial feftival appointed; and every circumftance in that tranfaction correfponded with the feftivals which
were held in adoration of the emblematic "Urotal," or ox, in
that very part of Arabia near mount Sinai, where this event
took place‖. So that they were ready to embrace the idolatrous practices of any people, although they had never feen
them before. That was not the only inftance. When they
were become a little more fettled, they fell into all the habits of
necromancy **, which were peculiar to Chaldæa, and which
were carried on by means of the emblematic python or ferpent;

---

* Exod. c. 32.   † D'Ancarv. vol. 1. p. 140, note.   ‡ Sonnerat's
Voy. vol. 1. p. 184 pl. 59. D'Ancarv. vol. 1. p. 72.   § Ibd. p. 72.
225, note.   ‖ Ibid. p. 46.   ** Deut. c. 18. v. 11, 14. 1 Sam. c. 28. v. 7.

yet thofe practices were unknown in Egypt, from the reverence which that people paid to the repofe of the dead * : and this fpecies, if not of idolatry, yet of fuperftition, which had evidently grown out of the ruling emblematic theology, continued very ftrong among the Ifraelites above nine hundred years after the death of Mofes, when Jofiah abolifhed the pythons in the tribe of Judah and in the territory of Jerufalem†. Almoft to the end of their commonwealth they were as ready, as when Jeroboam fet up his golden calves in Bethel and in Dan, to follow thofe idols, wherever they were prefented to their eyes, and to defert for them the magnificent temple in Jerufalem‡. They never could forbear to liften to the tongues that faid, " behold, in thefe, thy gods O Ifrael, which brought " thee up out of the land of Egypt." Their idolatrous prejudices went ftill further, and fhewed them to be ready for every mythology which engrafted itfelf on thofe prejudices, fulfilling the words of Mofes, by facrificing even "to new gods " that came newly up, whom their fathers did not fear"§. But thofe gods, how varioufly featured foever, feem indeed to have had, in their minds, but one ultimate reference to a fupreme Being, although they intercepted all his homage, and therefore darkened his exiftence and his providence: and that fupreme Being they confidered only as one, *Jehovah;* they never were brought by the emblematic habits of Egypt and of Afia to view him in both fexes, although a predilection for an emblematic religion was no where ftronger than in their minds‖.

It is evident that thofe habits of emblematic devotion were not gratified without affiftance from the arts. And fo far as

---

* D'Ancarv. vol. 1. p. 468.   † Ibid.   ‡ 1 Kings, c. 12. v. 28, 30.
§ Dute. c. 32. v. 17.   ‖ D'Ancarv. vol. 1. p. 236, note.

thofe gratifications were concerned we may be fure that the Ifraelites never loft the means which thofe arts fupplied. But they felt
no impulfe to carry the cultivation of them farther. A very confined compafs of art, when once they were in the habit of it,
and efpecially when that art confifted chiefly in molten images,
was fufficient to fatisfy their old attachments; and as they were
not in the way of being fpirited up by examples from the genius
of others, fo their own ingenuity became more languid to general
exertions. They were much more able in the arts when they
firft came out of Egypt, than they appear to have ever been
afterwards. They had juft left a country where every ingenuity
was alive before them, where there was a call for ingenuous
fkill from every hand, and where the policy of government, however ftrict to them in other refpects, impofed no difficulties on
their endeavours to become as able and ufeful as they could in
thofe ingenious works which were the pride of the Egyptians. We
therefore view them in the beft advantages of their arts, when they
were come into the wildernefs. Bezaleel and Aholiab then gave
a character to their nation, which not all the fucceffion of fubfequent ages enabled them to equal or approach. It was not thofe
men alone, although they were fpecially felected as leading
artifts, who were diftinguifhed as fuch among that people;
the language of fcripture plainly bids us to underftand that
there were a great many others, " who knew how to execute
" all manner of work", and who were accordingly fummoned
by Mofes to the fervice of the fanctuary*. Neither was it the
molten image alone, or the works of ftatuary, to which they
were then competent. The engraving of precious ftones, and the
fetting of thofe ftones in plates of gold, were marked performances in their hands†. They were then alfo in the habits of coin-

---

* Exod. c. 36. v. 1, 2.   † Ibid. c. 39.

age, for it was settled by Mofes in what pieces of money every individual fhould make a contribution to the fanctuary*; and it is faid by good authority, that the merit of their coins was then much more advanced than thofe which the Greeks firft received from Ericthonius†; although the period of which we now fpeak was near a century earlier than Ericthonius, and a period very early in itfelf, for the Hebrews left Egypt 1597 years before our æra, and the tabernacle was fet up by Mofes precifely two years after‡. There muft have been a prodigious decline in the talents, or a very great alteration in the purfuits, of that people in the courfe of the next 500 years, by which time moft countries were improving faft in every knowledge, when Solomon could not find among his own fubjects proper workmen for the building of the temple and his palaces, but was conftrained to feek them from the neighbouring king of Tyre. The caufe, neverthelefs, was clear. It was not the purpofe of the Almighty to fee the Ifraelites improved in arts. To them the arts were dangerous things, and had either produced or helped on the corruptions which had been fo mifchievous to their minds and to their welfare. He meant them to be improved in that theology, which fo far from requiring to be helped by the arts, exprefsly forbad the image or reprefentation of any thing that was made upon the earth, or that was feen in the creation.

It is true, in the Mofaic difpenfation the Almighty did not commiffion that lawgiver and minifter of his purpofe to wipe away the influence of all emblematic ideas from the minds of his people. Nine hundred years before that difpenfation was given, the fecond Zoroafter had attempted, but with much imperfec-

---

* Exod. c. 30. v. 13.   † D'Ancarv. vol. 1. p. 49, 50.   ‡ Ibid.

tion, to effectuate in Perfia a melioration of that very theology, from whofe corruptions Mofes was called forth to lay the foundation of weaning the world. Yet that Perfian lawgiver, whofe firft feature looked with feverity on every image or emblematic figure of the fupreme Being, and even on every temple prepared for his worfhip, left the Perfians to behold his attributes in the contemplation of light and fire. The revelation to the Jews with more fuccefs, but with the delays of ages, effectuated it's reform on the very fame theology. It ftarted pretty nearly from the fame point in which the main principles of Zoroafter centered, when it faid, "thou fhalt not make to thee any graven image, nor any " likenefs of any thing that is in heaven, or in earth, or in the " waters ; thou fhalt not bow down thyfelf to them *." Yet it left it's countenance to fome of thofe very emblems which had been conftantly interpofed between the human mind and the fupreme fource of all things by every people that had participated of that theology, from the Scythians to the Jews. This is a curious fpeculation : and what other avenues foever it may open to reflection, one argument becomes decided by it, that fuch a primitive theology as that which we have ftated, and which the hiftory of the world will only fuffer us to find as an emanation from the Scythians, emanating themfelves from Japhet, was generally prevalent through the earth : and that however corrupt it might have been rendered by the mythologies of nations, or however unfortunate it might have been in it's firft affociation with emblems, it was founded in much ftrength of principle, and perhaps in a vindicable ufe of thofe emblems in their firft fimplicity, and to firft ages, could they have been fecured from all the corrupt confequences that flowed from them.

* Deut. c. 5. v. 8, 9.

When God directed the tabernacle to be made, two cherubims of beaten gold were ordered to be placed on the mercy-feat over the ark, with their faces turned towards each other, and their wings extended fo as to cover the whole mercy-feat*. If the authority of Mr. Stevens† may decide the interpretation of their name, it means *mafter* and *multiplier;* and fo they became a fign, which met the firft and leading idea of all others by which men had been accuftomed from the remoteft ages to conceive the fupreme Being as the *generating power* which multiplies all the beings of the earth. But farther: if the figure of cherubim were a conftant and uniform figure, and if thofe cherubims which Ezechiel faw in a vifion near the river Chobar‡ may be confidered as defcriptive of the two cherubims over the ark, then the latter had a face of the ox. It has been already mentioned that the ox, which was revered in Arabia was called *Adonai.* And accordingly Aaron, announcing the feaft to the golden calf, fpeaks thus, *Chag Ladonai Machar*§; that is, " feftum Adonai cras ;" " to-morrow is a feaft to Adonai," in our tranflation of the Bible it is faid, "to the Lord‖", adopting the thing fignified inftead of the type, and therefore ftrengthening the intended relation between them. Now "Adonai," according to the fame authority of Stevens**, means "the bafe of the Lord"; fo that the ox Adonai of Arabia was a fymbol of the throne of God. And how ftrongly was this idea met by the difpofition of thofe cherubims, in whofe faces the countenance of the ox was difcerned, and in whofe extended wings a kind of platform was effected over the whole mercy-feat? efpecially when the Ifraelites knew

---

* Exod. c. 25. v. 18, 20. † Interp. vocal. Hebr. Chald. Bibl.
‡ Ezech. c. 1 v. 7, 10. § Seld. de diis Syr. Syntag. 1. c. 14.
‖ Exod. c. 32. v. 5. ** Ubi fupra.

that on thofe wings the divine majefty meant to be feated, whenever it pleafed God to come down to his people, according to
thofe exprefs declarations, "and there I will meet with thee, and
" I will commune with thee from above the mercy-feat, from be-
" tween the two cherubims, of all things which I will give thee
" in commandment to the children of Ifrael *".

The emblem of the ferpent was marked yet more decidedly by
the exprefs direction of the Almighty. That animal had ever
been confidered as emblematic of the fupreme generating power
of intelligent life.   And was that idea difcouraged, fo far as it
went to be a fign or fymbol of life, when God faid to Mofes,
" make thee a brazen ferpent, and fet it upon a pole, and it fhall
" come to pafs that every one who is bitten, when he looketh
" upon it, fhall live? +".   If that emblem was continued in the
Jewifh difpenfation as an innocent fign of prefent life, was the
reference to it lefs diftinguifhed in the New Teftament, when
Jefus Chrift, placing himfelf in analogy to the exaltation of that
ferpent by Mofes, and therefore recognizing it's ufe, declared
" that thofe who fhould look up to him with faith fhould obtain
" the life which was eternal ? ‡".

In an enquiry which profeffes to follow the fine arts, we
fhall not fuffer ourfelves to be led too far into collateral views,
although as collateral they have a manifeft relation to the principal object.   We fhall therefore only mention another inftance
to the fame purpofe with thofe which have been adduced.   Fire
had ever been confidered as a primary emblem of the fupreme

---

* Exod. c. 25. v. 22.   Numb. c. 7. v. 89.   + Numb. c. 21. v. 8.
                        ‡ John, c. 3. v. 14, 15.

source of all things; an emblem, which was moft ftudioufly che-rifhed by thofe who had received and retained the moft ancient ideas of the Scythian theology, and which even they who were moft diftant from thofe original ideas never failed to cherifh.   In many countries it gave a facrednefs and an inviolable afylum to the building in which it was lighted up for religious ufes *.   When Zoroafter endeavoured to reform the corruptions of that theolo-gy, he left this ancient emblem undifturbed.   It was farther con-fidered as a fymbol of that great Being which always was exiftant; and therefore the habit became embraced very early, and at all times by thofe who adhered moft clofely to the primitive princi-ples of that theology, to keep up that fire perpetual on fome particular altars, or in fome particular temples.   A proof of this is given by Paufanias† among the Arcadians, who arc faid to have maintained the ancient Scythian theology more ftrictly than any others of the Greeks‡; that people kept up a fire perpetu-ally burning before the ftatue of Pan, in the interior part of a temple confecrated to him.   It was not in the fame fpirit of reli-gious ufe, but it was neverthclefs in a continuation of the fame religious emblem, that the Ifraelites were commanded to keep up on the altar of burnt-offering a fire which fhould be always burning, and fhould never go out§.   They were forbidden to fa-crifice by fire as the nations around them had done‖; yet it was unqueftionably retained as an emblem or fymbol of purifi-cation, when all the fpoils of the enemy, and all that was unclean, were made to pafs through it **.

The continuation of thofe ancient emblems of theology in a

* D'Ancarv. vol. 1. p. 190, note.
‡ D'Ancarv. vol. 1. p. 363, note.
‖ Levit. c. 18. v. 21.   Deut. c. 18. v. 10.

† Lib. 7. p. 677.
§ Levit. c. 6. v. 9, 12, 13.
** Numb. c. 31. v. 23.

degree of impreſſion, but not in that impreſſion which they had once obtained, induces no argument to impeach the divine wiſ-dom. It muſt be underſtood that thoſe emblems, when they were firſt employed in the patriarchal theology, and were firſt diſſeminated by the Scythians to other countries, were innocent in their purpoſe; they were intended as ſigns to lift the mind in various ways to the contemplation of the ſupreme original princi-ple of all things, but not as images to repreſent his attributes or his acts, and much leſs to intercept and abſorb his worſhip*. It was in the proceſs of time that mankind, ſuffering themſelves to loſe ſight of this diſtinction, began to ſubſtitute thoſe attributes and acts, ſo figured in thoſe images, in the place of that adorable principle which had produced the one, and to which the other appertained†. When therefore the Almighty recognized thoſe emblems, it was done to ſhew the world how groſsly the primi-tive ſenſe and uſe of them had been perverted, to ſtrip them of the idolatrous ſenſe to which ſuperſtition had brought them, and to teach mankind that while the ſign may be innocent, which ſerves merely to point the thoughts to a divine principle, they ſhould be cautious to keep it innocent, not to confound that ſign with the object which is ſignified by it, nor to let the mind entertain the conception of his divine likeneſs in any of his works, who will neither be reſembled by any thing, nor be worſhipped through any imaginary reſemblance. This inſtruc-tion he could more forcibly convey by the notice which he thought fit to take of thoſe emblems than if he had never noticed them at all. At the ſame time there was manifeſtly in that no-tice of them a degree of indulgence to thoſe partialities which had become rooted by length of ages, while they were properly

---

* D'Ancarv. vol. 1. p. 189, note.   † Ibid. p. 49, note.

chaſtiſed. But that indulgence was not greater than the wiſdom which moved with ſo much tenderneſs to bring his people round to the melioration of their principles which he had in view. Had he expreſsly cruſhed every riſing thought in their minds, which ſhould lift itſelf to religious views by the means of thoſe emblematic ideas to which they had been accuſtomed, he muſt have wrought a miracle on their minds at once, without which moſt probably they would never have been brought to better principles of religion. Proceeding as he did, inſtead of conflicting with their prejudices, and arming them againſt his reform, he gently led thoſe prejudices to his own purpoſes ; he ſuffered his people to borrow, if they pleaſed, thoſe helps to the mind, which had been ſanctioned by the pureſt of their patriarchal forefathers, ſo long as the mind was kept clear from any idolatrous corruption ; and ſo he led them, in fact, to conceive that in the embracing of his revelation no violence was done to their modes of thinking, they were not thrown into any new channel, or at leaſt they were not thrown completely out of an old one.

It is not needful to argue, nor will it follow as a conſequence, that thoſe helps to the mind may be equally proper to be encouraged in the religious progreſs of all people, in all ages, and under all degrees of revealed knowledge. It is ſufficient for the preſent queſtion, that the Iſraelites were accuſtomed ſo to move in their views of religion, and that divine wiſdom ſaw it fit to conſult thoſe habits in the extent which has been ſhewn. But another conſequence, univerſal in it's application, will follow from thoſe divine meaſures ; that in all important reforms there is great wiſdom in conſulting reaſonably the prejudices which have long ſubſiſted, in moving by degrees rather than by abrupt and unqualified ſeverity to the eſtabliſhment of the very beſt inſtitution, and in making the moſt prudent compromiſe not with the principles which are wrong, but with thoſe which may be hazardous in their exerciſe, rather than multiply difficulties to the ſuccefs of thoſe which are right and precious.

We ſhall now return to our principal enquiry, which has been ſomewhat interrupted by theſe circumſtances of the Jews. But they were ſo combined in their ſource with that which became a main-ſpring to the arts, that we could not do them juſtice by a more contracted diſcuſſion. If they do not immediately concern the progreſs of thoſe arts, yet they give ſtrength to all the relative circumſtances in which thoſe arts are intereſted.

BOOK II.

EGYPT.

CHAP. I.

All it's arts, and earlier knowledge, derived from Asia, and from Scythian principles—those arts very ancient, but difficult to be traced to their epochs, and scarce in their remains, from various causes—the palace or mausoleum of Oysmandes—paintings in the monuments of Upper Egypt—no reason to expect many progressive improvements in the arts of that country—the Israelites instructed there in the arts they afterwards executed—the ardour of Sesostris to improve Egypt—all his embellishments annihilated by progressive calamities after his reign—the loss of freedom followed by a complete depression of the spirit of art—that spirit not to be revived by Alexander the Great, sought in vain to be reanimated by the two first Ptolemies, and irrecoverably extinguished by the slavery to which the Egyptians have ever since been doomed.

THE Egyptians obtained their knowledge of the fine arts from Asia. The fables of their own chronicles*, and the language of some writers influenced by those fables, may have represented that people, and have caused them to be often considered, as settled, or at least as civilized, earlier than any others†, and consequently

---

* Auguſt. de Civit. dei, lib. 18. c. 40.

† Goguet's Orig. of Laws, vol. 1. p. 65.

as not likely to derive from Afia their firft advances in knowledge. And we will not fay that they were not fettled as foon as
any others, if they are confidered as brought into Egypt by Ham
the fon of Noah; although Juftin, fpeaking of their antiquity,
and meaning undoubtedly their fettlement as much as their civilization, fays, that they were never fo ancient as the Afiatic Scythians; " Ægyptiis antiquiores femper Scythæ vifi*". Neither
fhall we wait to enquire into the firft evidences of their knowledge, which muft have been pretty much on a level with the
firft knowledge of every other people, until they became by fome
means more improved. We fhall only obferve that the fame tradition, which gives them their defcent from Ham, brings them
with him as a colony from the plains of Shinar†; and that the
firft of their legiflators, who has ever been fpoken of as giving
them written laws, was Mneves‡, with whom their monarchy
properly began: but he was not earlier than Ninus on any chronological reckoning; and that period, we fhall recolleſt, was
1500 years after the Indians had received their Vedams from
Brouma.

It may alfo be conceived that the Egyptians were not likely to
derive their earlier knowledge from Afia, when it was one of
their firft maxims, never to leave their own country§, and one
of their firft political inftitutions, to exclude all ftrangers from
it‖; and that leaft of all were they likely to derive any know-

---

* Juftin, lib. 2. c. 1.   † Goguet, vol. 1. p. 48.

‡ Diod. Sic. lib. 1. p. 19, 105. Mneves pretended to receive his laws from Mercury; and from thence the Egyptians regarded Mercury as the inventor of hieroglyphic writing. Plato, p. 374. E. p. 1240. A. They had laws before from Vulcan,
Helius, and Ofiris, but not written. Diod. Sic. lib. 1. p. 17, 18.

§ Clem. Alexand. Strom. lib. 1. p. 354.

‖ Diod. Sic. lib. 1. p. 78. Strabo, lib. 17. p. 1174.

ledge from India, when the Indians went out of their own country no more than they. But thefe circumftances will throw
no great difficulty on the faét, that they derived their earlier
knowledge from Afia, and even from India. For as all popular
maxims and political inftitutions are apt to be invaded, fo
were thefe. It is an eftablifhed record of hiftory, that in very
ancient times individuals went from Egypt into Greece, and
formed colonies there *; and that in times more ancient ftill one
of the ports in Egypt was open to the veffels of Phœnicians
alone†. In thofe veffels undoubtedly all thofe were fhipped
that migrated from Egypt; and by the fame means an avenue was
always open to a communication with Afia, and India itfelf, although the Indians were more rigid in their maxim of ftaying
at home, and feeking no fettlements elfewhere, than the Egyptians.

But we muft come yet clofer to the faét. The Scythians,
whofe greater antiquity in civilization, if not in fettlement, we
have already feen attefted by Juftin, had made a defcent upon
Egypt, before ever they fet their feet in India. Diodorus Siculus fays, that they penetrated as far as to the Nile‡: but Juftin
fays, "ab Ægypto paludes prohibuere §"; fo that they muft have
been in the country, and have done it fome fervice. Both agree
that they afterwards turned their arms againft the nations of Afia,
and fubdued them. Whatever impreffions of another kind that
vifit might leave upon the Egyptians, there can be no doubt but
that people derived from thence, or from the general diffufion
of Scythian principles, that caft of fentiment which fixed their

* Goguet, vol. 1. p. 64, 65.　　† Herod. lib. 1. n. 1. lib. 2. n. 179.
‡ Diod. Sic. Biblioth. lib. 2.　　§ Juftin, lib. 2. cap. 3.

religion, and gave the firſt birth and direction to their arts. This is plain from the ſtrength in which thoſe principles were ever found eſtabliſhed there from the earlieſt times.   We mean not to ſay that thoſe principles abſorbed all previous ideas in the Egyptian mind, as they did in the Indian ; for the Egyptians were a great people from the firſt, and it was enough that even in their ruder ſituation they admitted other ideas to be engrafted on their own. Superſtition, wherever it is fed, is an eaſy avenue to ſuch effects ; and from thoſe effects the Egyptians certainly received the pre- dilection, which has never ſince left them, for emblematic know- ledge.   The main principles therefore of Scythiciſm became their own, and were mixed with the bent of their own primitive notions, under names which their own language gave, or which their previous reverence for characters had made habitual *.

If we were even to diſtruſt the idea of a Scythian influence on the minds of the Egyptians, we cannot ſee how an influence amounting to the ſame thing, and productive of the ſame noti- ons, may not be ſuppoſed conſiſtently to have followed from their own leader Ham or his immediate deſcendants.   For the princi- ples of religion, which Brouma derived from the deſcendants of Japhet, are aſſerted to have been pure and ſimple, directing the mind to one only, ſupreme, and eternal God†, to whom

---

* D'Ancarv. vol. 1. p. 308, note.

† D'Ancarv. vol. 1. p. 107.   The modern hiſtorians of India, taking their docu- ments from the ſacred books of that country, are ſufficient to aſſure us of this fact. Holwell, ſpeaking of Brouma, whom he happens to call " Brahmah", ſays that " he preached the exiſtence of one only eternal God," (Holwell's Hiſt. p. 72.)   Dow gives a more explicit account, recording part of a diſcourſe which Brouma, called by him " Brimha" is ſaid to have held with his ſon Narud, as it is found in one of the ſa- cred books of the Bramins, from which that author has literally tranſlated it.   In that

however the mind raifed itfelf by emblems : it was the corruptions of mythologies, and the mifchiefs which perhaps are naturally engendered by an emblematic religion, that broke in upon
the purity and fimplicity of thofe firft principles. The fame
principles therefore, confidered as authentic in their origin, would
naturally find their way to all the fons of Noah as well as to
one of them ; and under the fame idea of their being affifted by
emblems, they would certainly be cultivated by all in the fame
manner. If this fuftains at all events the probable influence of
principles, fimilar to thofe of the Scythians, in Egypt as well
as in the reft of the world on it's firft fettlement after the flood,
it cannot be urged to contradict exprefs authorities which have
bidden us to look to Scythian movements in particular fituations, for the production of that influence, fo congenial with
what is known to have been the ancient principles and habits
entertained in Scythia.

By thefe means it came that the Egyptians, as well as the
Indians and Perfians, had both the fexes in their divinity under
the names of Ofiris and Ifis* : thofe two fexes were often conjoined in one figure of that divinity, as the Indians had conjoined them in their Brouma, and the Perfians in their Mithras.
Ifis, the female part of that divinity, was confidered as the moon,
correfponding with the feminine emblem of the Indian's nocturnal fun ; her lighted Tyrfus, the fymbol of day, was reverfed as a
fymbol of night and darknefs, in the fame way as it was feen reverfed befide the nocturnal fun in Afia†. She was alfo confidered

paffage Brimha is fpeaking of the fupreme Being, and fays, " being immaterial, he
" is above all conception ; being invifible, he can have no form ; but from what we
" behold in his works, we may conclude that he is eternal, omnipotent, knowing
" all things, and prefent every where."

    * Plut. in Ifid. et Ofirid. D'Ancarv. vol. 3. p. 165.   † Ibid. vol. 3. p. 167.

as the mother of the world, and from thence there was put over her head that myſterious veil, to which the inſcription in the temple of Sais alluded*, ſimilar to the veil which in Aſiatic figures was generally thrown over a part of the male figure, a veil which they meant to ſay no mortal ſhould raiſe.   If the Venus Anaitis, which expreſſed the female ſex of the Perſian Mithras, had wings, theſe were alſo given to the Egyptian Iſis, and to the Circopithecus which was one of her emblems.   A diſk with a circle in the middle was made the ſymbol of Oſiris, as it had been given to the Perſian Mithras.   And in the worſhip of the former the ſame ceremonies were obſerved, which diſtinguiſhed the celebration of the death and reſurrection of the latter in Perſia†.   The Egyptian divinity was repreſented on the leaves of the tamara ‡, or of the lotus a ſpecies of the tamara, which was the great emblem of divine character originally brought from Scythia, and afterwards employed by the Indians, to whoſe deified Brouma it was peculiarly devoted §.   Pan was the deity firſt worſhipped in Egypt, as the principle of all things ‖ ; and Pan was found originally in Scythia, and by degrees in every part of the eaſt **.   That principle was variouſly perſonified by others, and as variouſly by the Egyptians.   When it was revered in the ox of the Scythians, and of all the Aſiatics after them, that ox was alſo embraced and worſhipped as a god in Heliopolis; and, what is very remarkable, they gave it in that city the name of their great legiſlator Mneves††; at other times it was diſtinguiſhed by the name of Apis, which was but a variation on the Scythian Papæus, or father‡‡.   When the Egyptians perſonified the ſame

* Plut. ibid.   † D'Ancarv. vol. 3. p. 164.   ‡ Ibid. vol. 1. p. 6.

§ Ibid. and p. 111, 133.   Vol. 3. p. 93.   ‖ Herod. lib. 2. p. 145.

** D'Ancarv. vol. 1. p. 309.   †† Strabo, lib. 17. p. 805.

‡‡ D'Ancarv. vol. 1. p. 310.   Vol. 3. p. 97.

primitive principle by the goat, and under the two fexes of that
animal, they only made choice of a different fymbol of fecundity from that which had been employed by the Afiatics in the
image of fire *. It is remarkable however, and cannot be paffed by when we are fpeaking of that goat, to what a pitch of extravagance, incredible if it were not unqueftionably attefted, the
veneration paid both to the male and female of that animal had
arrived, as a confequence of the worfhip of Pan, when in the
town of Mendes particularly females actually proftituted themfelves to the one fex, and men to the other. Herodotus afferts
this to have been done there in his own time, and to his own
knowledge†. Strabo confirms the fact‡. And a paffage in
Plutarch affures us that it was done in his time, which was in the
reigns of Trajan and Adrian§. They had the ferpent of the Afiatics, the fymbol of life, with which their Ifis and Ofiris, and their
Pan, was furrounded, and with the figures of which the diadems
of their princes, and the bonnets of their priefts, were adorn-
ed‖. And they had the egg, which makes a part of the cofmogony not only of the Japanefe but of all the nations of Afia**;
with this difference, that the creature contained in that egg was
fuppofed to be matured and produced by the breath of a ferpent,
inftead of the breath of an ox††. Their fphinxes, and all their
combined figures of animal-creation, took their origin from the
fable of the mother of the Scythians, who in her intercourfe with
Jove brought forth an offspring that was half female and half a fer-
pent‡‡. Their pyramids and their obelifks arofe§§ from the idea

---

* D'Ancarv. vol. 1. p. 304, 309, 310, 320. Vol. 3. p. 40.
† Herod. lib. 2. fec. 46. p. 108.   ‡ Strabo, Geog. lib. 17. p. 802, 812.
§ Plut. in Gryll. p. 989. A. See D'Ancarv. vol. 1. p. 320, 321, note.
‖ Ibid. vol. 1. p. 476. Vol. 2. p. 96, 104.   ** Ibid. vol. 1. p. 115.
†† D'Ancarv. vol. 1. p. 115.   ‡‡ Ibid. p. 55.   §§ Ibid. vol. 2. p. 90, 91.

of flame, or of the rays of light, the original emblems of the fupreme principle of all things, which were firft introduced by the
Scythians, were eftablifhed throughout the eaft, and were left in
all their force by the corrections of magifm itfelf, when it ftrove
to level every other emblem of divinity.

It is in vain to think of affembling, and it is not our bufinefs
to affemble, all the proofs of thofe impreffions which the Egyptians derived from Scythian principles eftablifhed over all the
continent of Afia. The reader, who wifhes to purfue that enquiry, will find thofe proofs difcuffed at large in the original
work of M. D'Ancarville. Having juft noticed, as briefly as we
could, in order to ftrengthen the Scythian influence over all the
eaft as a fact, and in order to fhew the true origin of things in
Egypt, we fhall now fall more immediately into our purpofe,
when we obferve that thofe principles, fo obtained by the Egyptians from Afia, gave the firft incentive and the firft caft to all
their arts.

A religion, which takes into it's plan the affiftance of emblematic reprefentation, cannot fubfift without painting and fculpture.
Words can never fill the idea which the figure brings home to the
fenfes. And therefore we might fafely conclude that both thofe
branches of the fine arts immediately followed an emblematic
theology, to which they were fo neceffary, if we had not abundant proofs of the fact. In all the points of that theology, which
have been noticed above, that fact fpeaks for itfelf, and warrants
it's own inference to every other circumftance in the fame theology. In Egypt, as it appeared in every other country which
drew from the fame fource of knowledge, the fpirit of the arts
muft move in conformity with the views of the people, and

would manifeft itfelf in every clafs of ingenuity which was deftined to be connected with thofe views. That fpirit would afterwards become enlarged, as it felt it's own views and it's own
powers expanded, to the reach of objects originating from general genius; although the firft views, to which it was excited,
would never perhaps be loft, when they came into contact with
others; they would remain, as they have done through all the nations of the eaft, more efpecially in the branches of fculpture,
the happy monuments to guide us with affurance to the origin
of thofe principles and habits which gave the earlier features
to the country.

In this view the arts of Egypt will mount to a high antiquity,
although we were to conclude that the Egyptians were without
the art of writing until the reign of Mneves, whofe age has already been remarked, or, as a paffage in Pliny would lead us to believe, 400 years later. For that author fays*, " Antoclides un-
" dertook to prove by monuments that letters were firft invented
" in Egypt by one Memnon fifteen years before the reign of
" Phoroneus in Greece, which goes back to the year 1788 be-
" fore the Chriftian æra." To this laft idea we fhould make a
great difficulty of fubfcribing, becaufe we can hardly be perfuaded
that the Egyptians were without the ufe of fome letters fo long as
to the time of Mneves, although it might be true, and it feems to
be authentic, that till then their laws had not been committed to
writing. They muft have been very unfortunate to be deftitute
of letters fo long, when fome very early intercourfe had paffed
between them and the Scythians, who firft gave writing to the
Indians, as the Vedams have always been allowed to teftify; and

* Lib. 7. p. 230.

when, before the time of their Mneves at leaſt, the Syriac character was common in Aſſyria, where it was inſcribed on ſome
monuments of Semiramis *, and either that or ſome other character well known to that princeſs, or eaſily interpreted by others,
was then employed in India by it's monarch, who wrote to her
the letters of reproach which are mentioned in hiſtory †. But
let that matter have ſtood as it might, it will not follow that the
arts of painting and ſculpture were not older in Egypt than letters ; the former might certainly have made a progreſs, how imperfect ſoever the people were in the advantages of writing. For,
in fact, thoſe arts were themſelves the firſt writing in the world,
and the language of nature.

When we would make our way to thoſe arts in the remoter periods of Egypt, we find many difficulties which impede our ſteps.
The ſingular fabulouſneſs of it's hiſtory, and the want of chronological certainty in all it's remoter progreſs, except what may
happen to be gathered from collateral circumſtances, darken our
views extremely, and deprive us wholly of preciſion.   Nor have
we leſs to lament in the various devaſtations which have added
ſcarcity to darkneſs in the proofs of the ancient arts of that country.   The ſeveral invaſions of the ſhepherds, who were animated
not merely by rapacity, but by deſperate ignorance, to the overthrow of great cities and of every thing that was cultivated and
elegant within them, put to flight all the firſt arts of Egypt, and
all that had grown up from Scythian or Aſiatic communications,
and drove them to ſeek ſhelter wherever there was wealth or any
portions of cultivation undiſturbed to receive them.   Moſt probably that ſhelter was given them on the other ſide of the Red

* Diod. Sic. lib. 2. p. 127.   † Ibid. p. 129.

Sea, in Arabia, at Edom which was then the richeſt city in the world*. When the country had long recovered from thoſe deſolations; when ſhe had ſeen her artiſts, with many others who were natives of Aſia, brought home by Seſoſtris after his ſuccessful expedition into the eaſt; and when ſhe had been raiſed in the courſe of many ages more, by the growing taſte of her princes and by her own proſperity, to the higheſt figure of art and magnificence which ſhe ever reached; then the leveling hand of Cambyſes, not more inimical as an invader, than hoſtile as one of the magi in principle to all painting and ſculpture, completed the overthrow of all that had been ſo long and ſo zealouſly accumulated, as far as hands could deſtroy. Few therefore are the veſtiges of Egyptian genius on which we can now look, and they are not many which are left recorded in the volumes of hiſtorians. The paintings of Egypt will of courſe be expected to have left fewer traces of their progreſs. In that branch of art our views of that country cannot be circumſtantial. There are not ſufficient materials to warrant diſcuſſion. We are enabled to be more diſtinct upon it's ſculptures.

The palace or mauſoleum of Oſymandes muſt give us a ſtriking aſſurance of the progreſs which had been made in the arts at that time; whether he lived, as ſome have thought+, the immediate ſucceſſor of the firſt Buſiris, which was ſomewhat later than the period of Semiramis; or, as others have conceived‡, ſubſequent to Seſoſtris, which would be 400 years later. Diodorus Siculus, who deſcribes that edifice, ſays nothing of the age in which Oſymandes lived; every opinion therefore on that point muſt

---

* Bruce's Trav. vol. 1. p. 428   + See Rollin's anc. Hiſt.

‡ Marſham, p. 403. Gouguet, vol. 2. p. 141.

be conjecture.   We shall only remark, that there is nothing in the works of art in that edifice, which should appear too much for , the earliest age in which that monarch has been placed, when we look back to what was done of those works in a period full as early by Semiramis in Assyria.   The genius of Egypt, which has ever been held forth as a pattern for general enterprize among the ancient people of the earth, must have been tardy indeed in it's progrefs, if with equal means of information, which it appears to have had, it could not accomplish as much as Assyria did in an equal procefs of time.

Ofymandes appears to have been a prince of great elegance and tafte in his day.   Diodorus Siculus defcribes many fumptuous edifices erected by him ; among thofe edifices his palace or maufoleum, whichfoever it was, has been eminently diftinguifhed for the paintings and fculptures with which it was adorned.   When we look to the fubjects of thofe works, we shall have reafon to think that no man in any age could difcover a fairer and more enlightened judgement than he did in the employment of the genius around him, which was not tamely devoted to dull or contracted objects, nor lavished on fcenes of favage life, nor wholly engrossed in allufions to himfelf, but fenfibly enlarged to a variety of contemplation which might become a great fovereign; and in each of thofe parts the fubject was characteriftically great.

* In one place was reprefented in a multitude of fculptures his expedition againft the Bactrians, a people of Afia, whom he had invaded with 400,000 foot, and 20,000 horfe.   In another

* Diod. Sic. lib. 1. p. 45. edit. Rhodom.

part was difplayed the variety of fruits and productions, with which PAN, the great fource of all things, had enriched the fertile land over which Ofymandes reigned. A third group of figures reprefented the monarch himfelf, as the high-prieft of the country, offering to the gods the gold and filver which he drew every year from the mines of Egypt. In another part of the edifice was exhibited in an infinite number of figures an affembly of judges, in the midft of a great audience attentive to their decifions ; the prefident or chief of thofe judges, furrounded by many books, wore on his breaft a picture of truth with her eyes fhut—thofe emphatic emblems, beyond which no age could go for the impreffion of that wifdom and impartiality which ought to prevail in adminiftrative juftice.

Where fhall we go for maturer thoughts than thefe? The firft fubject was perfectly fair in the monarch who had exploits to fhew, in which his country was interefted. The fecond was elegant, and gratefully refpectful to the country itfelf, as a land of plenty and felicity. The third was pious, and a high atteftation of the religious principles with which he felt and exercifed the fovereign truft repofed in him. And the laft fubject was every thing that can exalt fovereignty itfelf, that can dignify the human mind or human fociety, and that can enfure the love of a people. In the whole of thofe works he meant with great modefty to inform pofterity, that his country was the feat of many comforts, that his reign had not been deftitute of valour, and that both his reign and his life had been conducted with piety to the gods, and with juftice to men.

We cannot avoid a remark on the probability which has been held forth to us, that fome parts of that edifice, which was the feat of thofe works, are ftill left to be beheld. The defcriptions,

which modern travellers * have given of the ruins of one moſt
ſuperb edifice in Upper Egypt, correſpond ſo ſtrongly in the ſuite
of it's apartments and in ſome of their decorations with what
Diodorus Siculus has related of the palace or mauſoleum of Oſymandes, that one is apt to conclude it was one and the ſame
ſtruͤ ture which gave the ſubjeͤ t to the reports of both.

If in that edifice the works of ſculpture ſhould have predo-
minated over thoſe of painting, which neverthelefs are highly
ſpoken of; and if the paintings employed in the famous labyrinth,
eſpecially when it was re-ornamented by Pſammeticus, have ſha-
red the ſame fate with thoſe of Oſymandes, although they were
much later in time, ſo that we can only ſpeak of them in general
terms ; there are other paintings among the other monuments of
Upper Egypt, which modern travellers have ſeen, and of which
they have ſpoken in terms that cannot but raiſe attention. Thoſe
paintings are deſcribed as laid on the hardeſt plain ſurfaces, whether of marble or ſtucco, in ſuch peculiar ſtrength of colours
that they ſeem, as it were, cut in the ground, and their tints have
continued to the preſent age ſo immoveable and freſh, that one
would think, as the people of the country expreſs themſelves,
" the artiſt had not yet waſhed his hands ſince he had painted
them †".

Till very lately we have had no opportunity of judging ſpe-

* Lucas, vol. 3. p. 37. et ſeq.   Granger's Voy. p. 43. et ſeq.   Pocock's Eaſt,
vol. 1. p. 139, fol. edit.

† Relat. du Sayd. ap Thevenot, vol. 2. pt. 3. p. 4.   Sicard Mſs. du Levant, vol.
2. p. 209, 211, 221.   Vol. 7. p. 37, 160, 163.   Lucas's Voy. vol. 1. p. 99, 126.
Vol. 3. p. 38, 39, 69.   Granger, p. 35, 38, 46, 47, 61, 73.   Rec. d'Obſerv. Curi-
euſes, tom. 3. p. 79, 81, 133, 134, 164, 166.

cifically of the merit of thofe paintings, which have been reported as remaining in Upper Egypt, from any drawings of them by
travellers. A gentleman, who has lately gone through that country, has now given us engravings of two of thofe paintings in one
of the fepulchres near Thebes *. They are the reprefentations of
two different muficians playing on two different harps. He fays
that thefe were found on pannels of ftucco, hard as a ftone, and
fmooth as paper, in the entrance of one of the fepulchres, which
contains the prodigious farcophagus of Menes or Mneves, as fome
faid, or of Ofymandes, as it was faid by others: in the opinion of
that writer, formed as he fays on the defcription given by Diodorus
of the maufoleum of Ofymandes, it could not probably contain
the farcophagus of that monarch, and he thinks it equally improbable that it held the bones of the other. Admitting that opinion
to be rightly formed, we may obferve by the way, that the tradition of the country which gives that fculpture to Mneves or Ofymandes, and confequently fuppofes them not to be far afunder,
guides us very ftrongly to a preference of that idea which makes
the latter of thofe monarchs far more ancient than Sefoftris, and
places him next in fucceffion to Bufiris, who was the immediate
fucceffor of Mneves. Beyond this we have nothing to urge from
that tradition againft the fentiments of one who has been upon
the fpot, and who declares that the fepulchre from which thofe
two paintings were taken by him does not anfwer to Diodorus's
defcription of the maufoleum of Ofymandes ; although it would
have clofed our minds with more fatisfaction, if that writer had
told us whether he had found in that quarter any other remains
of buildings more fpacious than this fepulchre, or anfwering
more nearly to that defcription of Diodorus ; and more efpeci-

* See Bruce's Travels, vol. 1. p. 126, 134.

ally if he had informed us whether this sepulchre appeared, or
not, to be those remains which have been so minutely described
by Lucas, and Granger, and Pococke, who conceived that they
found in them the mausoleum of Osymandes.

The paintings now in question are supposed by that writer to
have been done in the time of Sesostris, who did not rebuild but
re-ornamented Thebes and it's adjacente difices, after the destruction brought upon them by the invasion of the shepherds. In that
opinion we will let the antiquity of those paintings rest, while we
bestow a reflection on their execution, which is more material to
our enquiry. Were we to take our judgement of that execution
merely through the medium of the engravings given to us, we
should be likely to flatter too much those ancient artists of
Egypt, and to draw conclusions of their powers which would
probably need to be corrected by further information. For in
those plates, we fear, the engraver has been more attentive to his
own reputation than to the satisfaction of that curiosity which
looks to the quality of the original execution. We are more
contented, however, when the author of those travels informs us,
" that we may consider those paintings as having the same de-
" gree of merit with the works of a good sign-painter in Europe
" at this day."

This account does not elevate the powers of the Egyptian
pencil; and we do not know that those powers should be expected in much elevation under any circumstances of that country. Therefore the precise merit of those paintings would become an imperfect guide to any particular age for their production; although there are reasons why they may be taken as a
general standard of painting in Egypt. Could their examples be

encreafed by many others, they would all moft probably coin-
cide with national circumftances to convince us, that there, as
well as in Affyria, and India, and the greateft part of Afia, the
arts in general went on in an equal ftate, they ebbed and flowed
very little in merit, they foon reached their point, and beyond
that they feldom advanced far. The fame caufes, wherever they
prevail, will always produce the fame effects, or nearly the fame.
In Egypt, as well as in Afia, profeffions were hereditary * : ingenuity of courfe became languid, or at leaft it never rofe to high
emulations, where the mind was doomed to it's line of purfuit ;
if the fon equalled the father, he had no reafons to exceed him,
and he never ftrove to do it. It is remarkable that with the fimilarity of thinking and of tafte in Egypt and in Afia, the refpective fates of thofe countries have ftrongly correfponded ; the
commencement and the duration, at leaft of the Affyrian and
Egyptian empires, have born pretty nearly an equal date.

With thefe difadvantages and fhackles, whofe weight indeed
they never felt, there was great ardour now and then in their
princes, which kept up a body of arts among the people. The
children of Ifrael gave in the wildernefs the fureft teftimonies of
the progrefs which the Egyptians had made, particularly in all
the branches of fculpture, before the reign of Sefoftris. While
they were captives in Egypt, "they had learned all manner
" of workmanfhip of the engraver, and the cunning workman,
" in gold, in filver, in brafs, and in the cutting of ftones, and
" in the carving of wood†." In confequence of thofe inftructions they were enabled to form the golden calf ; which fhews, by

* Plato in Tim. p. 1044. Ifocrat. in Bufirid. p. 328, 329. Diod. Sic. lib. 1.
p. 86. Lib. 2. p. 142. † Exod. c. 35.

the way, the train of Scythian theology running through Egypt, and taking poffeffion of the Ifraelitifh mind. Two of their own fculptors, Bezaleel and Aholiab, are particularly diftinguifhed in the important commiffion of making the golden images of cherubims and all the ornaments for the tabernacle and the ark of the covenant. The foundation of all that fkill was laid in the inftructions of Egypt.

The epoch of Sefoftris was a great epoch for the country, and we doubt not as great an epoch in the hiftory of it's arts to thofe who ftood near it, and were enabled to fee it diftinctly. He was born with all the qualities which can form a great monarch, and the education he received from his unfortunate father, who found his grave in the Red Sea when he purfued the Ifraelites acrofs it, was proper to give every effect to thofe qualities. He had conceived a high notion of eftablifhing the character of his nation in every magnificence which could befpeak an ingenious, enlightened, and great people. And he exemplified his views in every poffible way that was afforded him by the genius of his own country, or by the moft celebrated abilities of ftrangers. It is no wonder that almoft all the remains of fine art, which have been found in Egypt, fhould at once be afcribed to that prince by moderns, who were affured of his extenfive munificence, his fumptuous works, and his zeal to carry every fpecies of tafte to it's perfection, but who had never confidered thoroughly the great antiquity of the fine arts in the world, and confequently had not attained that conclufion which will follow from the knowledge of that antiquity, that thofe who were older by many ages than Sefoftris on the throne of Egypt were abfolutely young in the hiftory of thofe arts. It was referved, however, for him, whatever had been the real glory of others, to lift Egypt to very

great celebrity, and to improvements which were new in many
refpects to her experience.   But, unhappily, it was not referved
for him to enfure more to pofterity, or for a longer time, than
other princes had done who had gone before him.   A kind of
fatality feems to have hung over Egypt, which no fooner faw
itfelf in an elevated period, high in reputation, and diftinguifhed
by it's elegance, than it was vifited by new depreffions.   We
read in general terms of paintings, fculptures, and magnificent
ftructures executed under the patronage of Sefoftris ; but fuch
was the complexion of fubfequent events, that we know as little
of the fpirit and purpofe of the works, with which thofe ftructures were ornamented, as we do of thofe ftructures themfelves.
We muft therefore be contented to look at that fplendid reign
with a general admiration, fubject neverthelefs to the mortifying
reflection that between us and the fcenes it had to offer a cruel
veil is drawn, which no induftry or management can put afide.

No fooner had that monarch difappeared from the earth than
the throne was filled with infignificance in his fon and fucceffor,
which was encreafed in every fucceffion for many generations.
In fuch a fituation of things it was impoffible for Egypt to
efcape the invafion of troubles, if it were only from the ambition
of others.   An Æthiopian prince firft held her in fubjection,
returning to Anyfis the meafure which had before been dealt to
Æthiopia by Sefoftris.   And what could Egypt or the arts gain
from Æthiopia?   We will ftop for a moment, as it is convenient, to fee what good could flow to either from that connection.   We will not fpeak with contempt of the ancient Meroe,
her literature, her fcience, and her gymnofophifts.   But Meroe
had nothing to fay in the fine arts, any more than the reft of
Æthiopia.   The laft traveller in that country, far more inti-

mately acquainted with thofe parts of Africa than any of the
few that went before him, has told us enough of the wretched
and regular poverty of thofe arts in Abyffinia at all periods,
and of the ideas with which they were there purfued even in
Chriftian æras, where religion itfelf became the impulfe, and fcripture afforded the field*. Nothing emboffed, nor in relief, ever appeared in their churches, becaufe it would be reckoned idolatry.
They would not admit a crofs even at the top of the ball of their
military ftandards, becaufe it caft a fhade. Yet their temples,
fuch as they were, had always abounded in religious pictures :
there had always been a fort of painting known among their
fcribes, a painting on parchment nailed upon the walls, hardly
lefs flovenly than paltry prints in a country ale-houfe, inferior to
the daubing of our worft fign-painters. And what was their beft
tafte ? " St. Pontius Pilate and his wife :" " St. Balaam and his
" afs :" " Sampfon and his jaw-bone :" and, to name no more,
" Pharoah on a white horfe plunging in the Red Sea, *with*
" *many guns and piftols fwimming on the furface of it around*
" *him ;*" this laft fubject feemed to be the chef d'oeuvre of their
ingenuity, as it graced in miniature the front of the prieft's mitre
at Adowa. About the middle of the fifteenth century Nicholas
Branca Leon, a Venetian painter, went into that kingdom ; he
gave the Abyffinians fome fpecimens of his art in holy families ;
but placing the child, as he would moft naturally do, on the left
arm of his mother, it fo outraged their ideas of things, that an
infurrection enfued †.

We have gone a little out of our way to introduce this epifode,
not improperly connected with our narrative. Such was at all

* See Bruce's Trav. vol. 3. p. 315, 316.   † Ibid. vol. 2.

moments the extreme ignorance and obſtinacy of the Æthiopi-
ans, whoſe dominion of Egypt could only entail miſery upon it,
while they themſelves were incapable of being improved by that
connection.

The depreſſion of the arts of Egypt was accelerated in the
next change of her ſituation, when ſhe was divided among twelve
principal lords in her own land ; and although the ſurvivor of
theſe for the firſt time gave ſtrangers a ſettlement in the country,
and many of thoſe ſtrangers were Greeks, ſome of whom might
probably be employed in the decorations then given to the labyrinth, yet Greece was but then young in the arts, if we are to
ſpeak of them in fame, and the ſun of Egypt was haſtening to
ſet. The purpoſes of divine providence, pronounced by divine
prophecy, made other deſolations neceſſary for a length of years
under Nebuchodonozor the Second. And when the deſolations
ariſing from that cauſe ceaſed, a new turn was given to her miſery
by the invaſion of the Perſian, who made the meaſure of it full
both to her arts and to her freedom. From that time ſhe has been
governed by foreigners, whom ſhe has uniformly deſpiſed. And
although the next of thoſe foreigners was the great Macedonian, who carried the arts to their higheſt ſummit in Greece ;
yet that circumſtance, with all the ſtimulus which might be ſuppoſed to ariſe from an acquaintance with Grecian artiſts, could
but have little effect on the genius of the Egyptians, who never
could forget that they were ſlaves, and that their maſter was an
alien.

If that maſter could not re-kindle the arts among them, in vain
ſhould we look for that effect in the race of the Ptolemies who
helped themſelves to this part of Alexander's dominions. Under
ſome of the Ptolemies indeed the Egyptians ſaw themſelves once

more an independent empire ; they faw themfelves again brilliant in inftitutions for the encreafe of knowledge ; they might
fancy themfelves once more at home, and in poffeffion of character. Let juftice be done to the firft and fecond Ptolemies, who
were lovers of arts and fciences, and univerfal literature, and who
ftudied to approve themfelves in thofe refpects as fincere fathers
of the country as if the blood of Egypt had flowed in the veins
of their anceftors for ever. The latter of thefe efpecially, who
was diftinguifhed by the addition of Philadelphus, was never exceeded by any in his love for the arts of elegance : Greece was
then at it's meridian in thofe arts ; and the immortal Aratus *
affifted that fovereign of Egypt to re-embellifh that country
with the moft precious works that could be obtained from the
pencils of Greece. But Ptolemy was not an Egyptian, and his
people were. He might collect indeed, and he might even flatter himfelf that his patronage could tranfplant anew the fpirit of
the fine arts into the land over which he reigned, making thofe
who had been the preceptors of his own countrymen to become
their difciples in turn, and to learn greater excellencies than they
had ever been able to teach. But that day was paft ; the fpirit
of that people was broken ; and even if the prejudices of their
original principles and habits were at all loofened, there was nothing to which emulation could adhere ; the profperity they felt
under thofe princes was but a tranfitory gleam, which was followed through twelve uninterrupted fucceffions by fcenes of
anarchy, rebellion, bloodfhed, and ruin, that terminated in a new
change of fervitude to the Romans.

If thefe were, or affected to be, too fond of the arts to make

* Plut. in vita Arati.

destruction upon them, yet they stripped Egypt of it's best works
to enrich their own metropolis. Since their days the Saracens,
the Mamalukes, and last of all the Turks their present masters,
have never suffered the Egyptians to know the change from a
province to a kingdom. Some of those masters committed de-
solations no less cruel to learning and genius than those which
had been committed by their Persian predecessors : and all of them
have been so radically averse to images and paintings, that in a
country which was once a great nursery of ingenious arts, there
appears almost a total dearth of every thing which could shew
that the pencil more especially, whose works are more easily sus-
ceptible of ruin, had ever found one who could handle it there.
In such a country is it not grievous to find the concatenation of
events so adverse, that in all the length of time through which we
have gone, comprising from it's first settlement to the commencement of the Roman power in it 3000 years, there is not left to
us the name of a single Egyptian sculptor, nor the name of a
painter except Philocles, whom Pliny would vainly conceive to
have first shewn the art both to that country and to Greece [*].
Names indeed may be lost, and nothing but curiosity suffers
when they are no longer known. It is a more sensible regret,
that when we have excepted a few paintings which may remain
in the monuments of Upper Egypt, we are not enabled to speak
precisely of another production of the pencil but the portrait of
Amasis alone[†], which was bestowed by that monarch to the
inhabitants of Cyrene, and which was so late in time that it
preceded but a few years the subversion of the empire. That
portrait shews that the art was there; and it is for us to consider
it, if we please, as a last relic of that ancient kingdom, deposited
in better security from the storm which was gathering around it.

[*] Plin. lib. 35. [†] Herod. lib. 2. n. 182.

What evidences of the pencil have fince exifted there, or may ftill exift, muft chiefly be fought at Cairo. And of thefe we are enabled pretty well to judge from thofe pictures of faints on fkins of parchment, in a ftyle very little fuperior to what has already been mentioned as executed in Abyffinia, for which the monarchs of that kingdom have recourfe to the artifts of Cairo, when they would adorn a church in a better manner *.

CHAP. II.

The fculptures of Egypt diftinctly confidered.

The firft advances of the Egyptians in that art—their predilec-
tion for coloffal figures—the general ftyle of their fculptures
very defective in defign and elegance—that ftyle very foon
fpurned by the Greeks—the collection of Egyptian fculptures
by the Romans no proof of their tafte.

As the fculptures of Egypt are the moft confiderable of it's remains, we are enabled to view them fomewhat more diftinctly. The reader has already been apprifed, that we can hardly go too far back in antiquity, to precede the exercife of fculpture in that country. There is nothing wrong in the idea that the Egyptians might engrave on wood and ftone, and cut them into figures, before they knew the art of working metals : for the example of many favage nations makes that fuppofition extremely proba-ble †. But their knowledge of metallurgy, which has always ap-

---

* Bruce's Trav. vol. 3. p. 315
† Acad. des Infcrip. tom. 19. p. 252.   Relat. de la Riviere des Amazones par
D'Acugna, tom. 3. p. 104, 105.

appeared moſt early among thoſe who were moſt attentive to agriculture, and eſpecially in the working of gold, ſilver, and copper, was among their firſt diſcoveries, and may be found there in a few ages after the flood *.   Their gold and ſilver was employed in the moſt ordinary uſes †, as it was done among other nations with whom thoſe metals abounded ‡.   By throwing any of thoſe metals into fuſion, they knew how to make them take the form of ſtatues.   Nothing can denote more aſſuredly the knowledge which the Egyptians had in the working of metals than what is related in the ſcripture of the formation of the golden calf by the Iſraelites, and more eſpecially of the deſtruction of it by Moſes, in the deſert §.   The firſt ſuppoſes great ſkill and intelligence ; but the laſt involves an operation, which to thoſe who work in metals, and are verſed in chymiſtry, is known to be extremely difficult.   That ſecret, by which Moſes made the golden calf, when burnt and reduced to powder, ‖potable by the Iſraelites, and, as chymiſts know, moſt nauſeous in it's taſte approaching to the magiſtery of ſulphur **, we muſt conclude that he had learned from the Egyptians, among whom he was born and brought up, and in whoſe wiſdom and ſcience the ſcripture tells us that he was deeply inſtructed ††.

With this knowledge of the means of ſculpture in their hands, what was the taſte or quality of deſign in which the Egyptians

---

* Agatarchid. ap. Phot. c. 11. p. 1341. Diod. Sic. lib. 3. p. 184. Lib. 5. p. 19.

† Herodot. lib. 3. n. 23.   Diod. Sic. lib. 1. p. 19.

‡ Strabo, lib. 3. p. 224.   Voy. de Coreal. tom. 1. p. 250.   Conq. du Perou, tom. 1. p. 76.   § Exod. c. 32. v. 20.

‖ Stahll, vitul. aur. in opuſc. chym. phyſ. med. p. 585.

** Senac. n. cours de Chym. tom. 2. p. 39, 40.

†† Acts, c. 7. v. 22.

employed it ?   Through the whole courfe of their hiftory, as far
as any proofs are left by which we can judge, that tafte was devoted to the coloffal and gigantic figure.   They feemed intent only
to ftrike the beholder with furprize and awe, or they conceived
that nothing was excellent which was not hugely majeftic.   This
obfervation does not reft on the fphynx, from the dimenfions of
whofe head we can judge of the full fize of that enormous figure,
nor on any works particularly felected ; all the ftatues erected by
Sefoftris, and whatever remains of fculpture are ftill to be feen
in Upper Egypt, are fo many monuments of that coloffal tafte*.

If that hugenefs of defign were brought into any meafures of
elegance, or if in any of their other fculptures taken on a more
moderate fcale there appeared any advances to a precifion and
correctnefs in tafte, then was the coloffus a beauty ftill, and thofe
other fculptures were patterns of emulation.   But the fact is,
that all thefe were equally deftitute of the elegant and the agree-
able†.   They difcovered neither genius, nor talents, nor juftnefs.
They were aukward as well as incorrect.   In their affemblages
there appeared as little meaning as variety.   The Egyptians indeed knew not how to defign fimple figures, nor to give them in
groups.   In their common fculptures they took the method of
drawing them, which was moft eafy, and that was generally in profile ; for bodies feen in full, or in a fourth inclined, require more
fkilfulnefs in their reprefentation ; and yet, notwithftanding the
greater facility of the former choice, the heads, hands, and feet
had neither motion nor expreffion.   They difguft by their heavi-
nefs, their monotony and incorrectnefs.   And the variation which

* Herodot. lib. 2. n. 107.   Diod. Sic. lib. 1. p. 67.
† Goguet's Orig. of Laws, &c. vol. 3. p. 75.

length of time might be suppofed to produce was nothing. When we fpeak of any one period, we may be underftood to fpeak of all. Plato fays that the ftatues made in his time by the Egyptians differed in no refpect from thofe which had been made a thoufand years before*.

Of the general ftyle of Egyptian fculpture we may judge with no lefs fatisfaction from inferences afforded by the Greeks than from pofitive authorities furnifhed by Egypt itfelf. From the time of Cecrops to Dædalus, containing a period of more than 300 years, the Greeks knowing no better followed the Egyptian models †. When Dædalus came forward, the age was fo ftruck with the improvements he introduced, that his ftatues were faid to be animated, and to move of themfelves ‡. Thofe expreffions were merely comparative. Their meaning was, that his ftatues were more natural, and had lefs clumfinefs and inaction, than the Egyptian. The fact is, he detached the legs and arms from the body, and gave them an attitude §. But what were his ftatues after all ? Plato, coming a long time afterwards, faid that the fculptors of his age would be ridiculous, if they made ftatues in the tafte of thofe which were executed by Dædalus ‖. Paufanias, who had feen many of them, confeffes that they were fhocking**. What then muft have been the ftatues of Egypt ?

It is only left for us to obferve concerning the fculptures of

* Plato de Legib. lib. 2. p. 656.
† Strabo. lib. 17. p. 1159.   Paufan. lib. 30. c. 19. p. 257.
‡ Plato in Mænone, p. 426. Arift. de Anima, lib. 1. c. 3. De Repub. lib. 1. c. 4.
§ Diod. Sic. lib. 4. p. 319.   Eufeb. Chron. lib. 2. p. 88.
‖ Plato in Hipp. maj. p. 1245.   ** Paufan. lib. 2. c. 4.   Lib. 3. c. 19.

that country, that after the moſt laborious endeavours of the
Egyptians to render their memory immortal in this branch of the
arts, they failed of attaining a charaćter to which any genius
could be annexed.   The Greeks, who drew from thoſe ſources,
made little account of the ſculptures that were Egyptian, from
the time when they came to have any knowledge in the arts*.
The Romans indeed in later periods collećted ſculptures from
Egypt, even when they were full of Grecian works.   But that
was no proof of their judgement, if it was not a proof that they
had none in theſe things.   Thoſe collećtions were indiſcriminate,
and were purſued by pride, as the ſpoils and monuments of conqueſt, rather than as the reſearches of real taſte.

* Strabo, ubi ſup.   Pauſan. lib. 7. c. 5.

CHAP. III.

*The architecture of Egypt devoted to the raising of enormous
masses—that taste of building naturally prompted and kept up
by the abundance of stone, marble, and granite in that country,
and by the facility with which those immense blocks were separated and employed—some of the most convenient principles of
building unknown to the Egyptians, and the cause of great
clumsiness in the whole of their designs—the detail of parts no
less disorderly and uncouth—the tabernacle set up by the Israelites in the desert not to be considered as an expression of the
Egyptian manner of building—the famous labyrinth worthy
enough of being visited by strangers for the immensity of it's
plan, without inducing any conclusion in favour of it's taste
—the Egyptian style hardly ever followed by Greeks or Romans
out of Egypt—all ages nevertheless indebted to the Egyptians
for the cultivation of geometry, important to a radical skill
in architecture—how much it is to be lamented that so much
labour and treasure was wasted in such immense edifices to no
purpose.*

L ET us now turn our reflections to the state of architecture in
Egypt. We shall not trouble the reader with repetitions of that
unvaried devotion, with which the Egyptians were attached to
enormous masses in their edifices as well as in their sculptures.
It is nevertheless proper to observe, that those enormous masses
were necessary to the purposes of duration, which was the first
object they sought to ensure in all their public works. They
aimed, if it were possible, to render those works immortal, and

to enable all their monuments to brave all the injuries of time.
The ſtrength and immenſity, which promiſed ſecurity to that
purpoſe, gave alſo whatever in their ideas conſtituted the grand
and the aſtoniſhing.   From thence it was, as well as from the
ſcarcity of wood, which they had not even for fuel*, that hardly
any of that material was employed, or is now found, in their public buildings.   And thoſe amazing blocks of ſtone, marble, and
granite which they piled upon one another, in the conſtruction
of thoſe buildings, were ſo abundantly ſupplied by quarries which
lined, and ſtill line, Egypt on the weſt, as to render all conſiderations of œconomy in the uſe of them unneceſſary : thoſe blocks
were ſeparated from their beds, without digging for them through
the earth as we do in Europe ; they were removed to their place
of deſtination with the greateſt dexterity by water; and they
were lifted into their places either by rollers, or by other machines worked by the ſtrength of numbers, with greater facility
than will eaſily be conceived by thoſe who are accuſtomed to
more improved principles of mechanics†.

Theſe circumſtances may explain the cauſe of their being devoted to thoſe enormous maſſes in their buildings.   Where thoſe
maſſes of materials could be had with ſo much facility, they became a bias on the public taſte, abſorbing perhaps other nicer
conſiderations.   The ſituation of a people, and the nature of the
materials within their reach, have always influenced the architecture of the country.   When the Gothic taſte aroſe, as it will hereafter be ſhewn, if it was not originally led, it was at leaſt aſſiſted
very eſſentially, by the general ſupply of ſtone in ſmaller blocks

* Granger's Voy. p. 13, 152, 153.   Lucas's third Voy. vol. 3. p. 211, 212, 286.
† Pliny, lib. 36. ſec. 14. p. 735.   Herodot. lib. 2. n. 125.

throughout thofe parts of Europe in which that tafte prevailed, and by the power of executing it's grandeft defigns with materials of any dimenfions whatever. It might be e fy to fhew that in the general fpirit of every other fpecies of tafte, or in fubordinate modifications of it, the like caufe has uniformly produced the like effect. But of this enough is faid, when the principle is mentioned.

Thofe enormous piles became more clumfy fill, and more aukward to the fight, as the Egyptians knew not fome of the moft convenient principles of building. They were entirely ignorant of the art of throwing an arch, or making a vault. We do not find that they even knew how to cut arch-wife the blocks of ftone which formed the heads of their doors. Thefe were all terminated by a lintel ftraight and even; or they were cut out of one huge block*. It will eafily be conceived how fhockingly rude and hideous all the openings of their edifices muft appear, when thus managed; how completely deftitute of every thing that could lighten or break the dulnefs of uniformity muft be the face of every elevation. But that ignorance fubjected the Egyptians to further proofs of clumfinefs. Every beam was formed by large ftones refting at each end upon the walls; and the roofs were alfo conftructed in that manner †. But as thefe might have given way in any confiderable length, columns became neceffary to fupport them ‡. Thus one immenfe mafs laid the foundation for another; and piles within piles became needful.

* See Pococke's Trav. vol. 1. Norden's Trav. vol. 2.

† Thevenot, vol. 1. p. 419. Lucas's third Voy. vol. 3. p. 38, 264, 265, 275. Voy. to the Levant, vol. 1. p. 42.

‡ Lucas, ubi fup. Granger, p. 38, 47, 68, 69, 73.

If their buildings were thus flovenly and difagreeable in the
grofs, they were not lefs fo in detail. No rules of proportion, no
advantageous difpofition, no decided plan, nothing that looked
like defign, or meaning, or principle in the execution, were ever
prefented to view. All was dull and fpiritlefs. They knew nothing of the refources furnifhed by the arts of elegance. They
were abfolutely ignorant of what belonged to the decoration of
an edifice. Columns they had, and capitals ; but in a moft poor
and wretched tafte, and whimfical enough. Thofe capitals were
often compofed of womens' heads, frequently four, dreffed very
fingularly, and put back to back : thofe heads were moreover
crowned with a cube a few feet long, which formed a cornice,
and fupported the cieling. Entablatures we find, but of great
clumfinefs. They affected ornaments, but moft ridiculous in
their execution, their defign, and diftribution. On this head indeed their ignorance was extravagant. They were utterly uninformed of what conflituted ornament, and of it's proper adjuftment. Truth was inceffantly tortured in it *. A tirefome and
unvaried monotony ran through it. It was fcattered everywhere
alike, and with profufion. They had no idea of a juft and fuitable union of fculpture and architecture. In the whole œconomy of their moft fuperb edifices a barbarous confufion was
vifible.

The tabernacle fet up by the Ifraelites in the defert has been
confidered as participating of the manner in which the Egyptian
temples were conftructed †. We know not why that idea fhould
be entertained, when the plan of it, and all the feveral propor-

* Lucas, p. 33. et ubi fup.   Pococke & Norden, ubi fup.
† Calmet, vol. 2. p. 391.

tions of it's parts, were minutely directed by the Almighty himfelf to Mofes *. If it's plan were Egyptian, ftill it was not the
plan of the Ifraelites, nor the refult of their experience obtained
in Egypt; but it muft be faid, that God chofe to purfue the Egyptian ftyle: and why the divine wifdom fhould be fo limited in it's
exercife, it will not be eafy to illuftrate. Surely we may as readily admit the conftruction of the whole to flow from his original
directions, as the formation of the feveral inftruments and garments to be employed in his fervice, which we muft be fatisfied
had no relation to any thing that had ever been ufed in the
world for the offices of religion. If the general model of that
tabernacle, and all it's proportions, be confidered as a regular
and perfect whole, for the ufes to which it was defigned, they
could not but be perfect, when they were fuggefted by divine
wifdom; but we do not fee what induction can arife from thence
to elevate the judgement and fcientific exactnefs of the Egyptians,
unlefs it could be fhewn that thofe principles of proportion were
generally maintained in their ftructures. If the employment of
columns with bafes and chapiters in the tabernacle, and the en-
richments beftowed on thofe columns, fhould be confidered as
exemplifications of what was practifed in Egypt; we muft recollect that the Egyptians were not the firft to give thofe examples;
they were found in Perfia above 1700 years before the tabernacle
was built; and, in truth, they were coeval with the firft ideas of
architecture, they were natural to every ftructure which had parts
to be fupported, and they became more enriched in proportion
to the dignity of the ftructure.

The famous labyrinth has been fpoken of as a wonder in architectural fkill†; and in fome refpects perhaps very reafonably,

---

*. Exod. c. 25. v. 9. Cap. 31. v. 3, 6.   † Rollins's anc. Hift. vol. 1. p. 8.

without becoming an evidence of cultivated taste. There was
enough in the immensity and singularity of it's plan to excite
admiration, and to attract the visits and the study of the earlier
Greeks. Nothing like the stupendous pile employed in that labyrinth, nothing like the wonderful disposition of it's interior
parts, had been known to the world; or if there had, it was natural for men who were fond of architectural studies to enquire
what the human mind had been able to accomplish in the formation of so peculiar a design. * Fifteen hundred rooms
upon a floor, with as many under ground, interspersed with ter-
races, and ranging around twelve halls (if those were not rather
twelve palaces, as they have been called + :) all these so regularly disposed, and communicating with each other, as to form
a perfect maze inextricable to strangers; innumerable sculptures
filling every part; and this immense pile, constructed wholly both
in it's walls and roofs with white marble, terminating above in a
pyramid forty fathoms high; gave surely invitation enough to
the curiosity and study of the world, without taking account of
the taste that was displayed in the elevation and finishing of the
whole. That taste, and the genius which was competent to such
a plan, are different things. The last depends chiefly on the
strength of native invention: the first must be raised by the progress to which the age has been trained.

From the construction therefore of that labyrinth no proofs can
be drawn of an excellent architectural taste in the Egyptians. The
style of their buildings never gave a precedent either to the Greeks
or the Romans out of Egypt, unless it were from mere whim, as

* Herodot. lib. 2. n. 148. Strabo, lib. 17. p. 1165. Plin. lib. 36. sec. 18. p. 739.
† Pomp. Mela, lib. 1. c. 9

emperor Adrian once thought fit to adopt it; and unlefs it be true, which we may very much doubt*, notwithftanding what has been current in ancient tradition, that Dædalus, who certainly faw this Egyptian labyrinth, built another of confiderable magnitude in Crete, upon the fame model. The Greeks and Romans indeed not only repaired many ancient edifices in Egypt, but adorned that country with new and magnificent monuments: in thofe works they blended an adherence to the Egyptian ftyle with fome portions of better tafte that were introduced. And from thence it is that travellers fpeak of having feen in fome of the Egyptian remains Corinthian columns, and even columns of the compofite order†, forming with the reft of the building a mixture of Egyptian, Greek, and Roman architecture together. But thofe things were only done in Egypt; and if the Egyptian ftyle was ever followed there in new works by thofe new mafters of the country, it was evidently done in compliment to the peo ple. There was nothing in that ftyle itfelf to induce a union with any other; it had no relation or refemblance to that which was tranfmitted by Greece or Italy ‡. It had nothing to do with any principles of the orders. It's columns were like none of thofe eftablifhed by later tafte. To characterife rightly the works to which it gave exiftence, they were enormous piles without much ingenuity, the labour of infinite patience, and poor defign.

Neverthelefs, if it was not the fortune of the Egyptians to lead fubfequent ages in an excellent tafte of architecture, they

* See the reafons for this doubt ably ftated, Goguet's Orig. of Laws, vol. 2. p. 208, 211.   † Granger's Trav. p. 38, 39, 58.

‡ Athen. lib. 5. c. 9. p. 206. Lucas's third Voy. vol. 3. p. 17, 39, 264. Sicard Mem. du Levant, tom. 2. p. 209.

gave all who came after them the important example of founding
that art on the science of geometry. Of that science they have
ever been considered in antiquity as the people who laid the first
foundation *. Some moderns indeed, affecting a nicer criticism,
have insinuated the contrary, grounding their oubts on this circumstance, that the discovery of two very simple geometrical
theories was first made by Thales and Pythagoras in Greece †.
The proposition attributed to Thales was, that a triangle, which
has the diameter of a circle for it's base, and whose sides meet in
the circumference, is necessarily rectangular. The other proposition attributed to Pythagoras demonstrated that the square of
the hypothenuse is equal to the squares of both the other sides.
Of these propositions it has been hastily concluded by those
moderns that the Egyptians were ignorant, and consequently,
that they could have no great skill in geometry. But that is beg-
ging the question. For the fact is, by the most direct and respectable testimony of antiquity ‡, that both those Grecian philoso-
phers derived from the Egyptians, among whom both of them
lived many years in the most intimate friendship with the priests
of the country, all their scientific knowledge, and particularly
that of geometry. So that, in truth, they did not originally discover, but only first published in Greece, the theorems which we
have mentioned, and the credit of which seems without reasonable
dispute to be due to the Egyptians.

That people was moved to the cultivation of that science, not

---

* Jamblic de vita Pythag. c. 29. p. 134, 135. Porphyr. Pythag. p. 8, 9. Julian
ap Cyrill. lib. 5.

† Weidler's Hist. Astron. p. 64. Anc. Univ. Hist. vol. 1. p. 396, 397.

‡ Plato Plut. vol. 2. p. 875. E. Jamblic. sup. segm. 7, 8. Minut. Felix, p. 111.
Clem. Alex. Strom. lib. 1. p. 354. Diog. Laert. lib. 1. segm. 24, 27.

merely becaufe it was a ftudy which fuited their fpeculative and philofophical genius*, but becaufe neceffity compelled them to underftand it. No nation was ever called to a more early or more conftant attention than Egypt to the divifion and menfuration of land, which gives the firft idea and the ftrict definition of geometry: they were called to that knowledge not fo much in confequence of the changes occafioned by the inundations of the Nile†, as by the neceffity of adjufting continually the tribute impofed upon the lands‡, which could not be equitably levied without a menfuration of their feveral quantities. The two primary branches, therefore, of geometry, known by the name of longimetry and planimetry, or the meafuring of ftraight lines and of furfaces, unavoidably forced their way very early to the knowledge and cultivation of a people fo peculiarly circumftanced. And the more profound branch of ftereometry, or the menfuration of folids, could not be long hidden from thofe who were led to fome of it's firft and fimpleft principles by the practice of leveling, and who had need of it's beft improvements in the conftruction of thofe great works to which they were early devoted, and which muft have called for the union of theory with practice. What could they have done in thofe prodigious operations, without the aid of a comprehenfive geometrical fcience? Without that aid how could they have tranfported from the mountains, and reared upon their bafes, thofe numerous obelifks and coloffal ftatues which they erected? How could they have provided for that duration, for which their works were projected, without a due calculation of the proportions given to every part, and of the bearings for which every part was fitted? It is

---

* Diod. Sic. lib. 1. p. 91. var. lib. 3. epift. 52.

† Strabo, lib. 17. p. 1136. Caffiodor.

‡ Herodot. lib. 2. n. 109.

by the application of the theories of geometry to the different
queftions which concern motion and the equilibrium, in which
confift mechanics properly fo called : and mechanics they
certainly had very early in fome branches *, although it be probable that thefe were the laft parts of mathematics that were
brought into a regular fyftem. But what would have been thofe
mechanics in their hands, if left to random-guefs, or no better
afcertained than by the habits of practice, uncorrected by the
lights and affurances of fixed-and permanent principles.

Thefe are confiderations everlaftingly important to architectural profeffion, and they are left by the example of the Egyptians
as leffons infeparable from a radical purfuit of that profeffion.
Whatever additions may have been fince ingrafted by the progrefs of architectural tafte on thofe demonftrative fciences, not a
tittle of their importance has been fuperfeded or weakened ;
they muft ever remain at the foundation of architecture, if it be
calculated for duration. We will not fay that the Greeks, with
lefs maffes of ftrength than were employed by the Egyptians, and
with far more tafte and elegance of defign, did not render their
edifices equally capable of duration : but that takes nothing from
the importance of geometrical fcience, which will hereafter be
found to have been as ftudioufly cultivated by the Greeks as by
any others ; it only fhews that they were more improved in the
knowledge of proportions, and that they knew how to relieve
their buildings from thofe dead maffes of folidity promifcuoufly
employed, with an equal prefervation of ftrength and of duration.
But that ftrength and duration was not accomplifhed by their
tafte and elegance in defign, and they were too wife to look for

* See Goguet's Orig. of Laws, vol. 1. p. 262.

it from thence. How far regard has been paid to thefe confider-, ations and principles by modern architects, this is not the proper place to obferve. Our intention is, to mark thefe for the pre- fent, as the primary culture of the Egyptians ; leaving to future ftages of our inquiry the evidences or the neglects of that cul- ture, as they fhall be found to arife.

There is an obfervation, however, which the contemplation of Egyptian works hardly ever fails to excite. A reflecting mind naturally enquires, for what purpofes were thofe aftonifhing edi- fices raifed ? If they had been palaces, if they had been temples; the pride of kings, or the pride of a people to do them honour on a great and enlarged fcale, fhould have found it's vindication in the good fenfe of ages, as well as the piety whofe venerable or fumptuous dedications to the Divinity have never failed to carry the acquiefcence of every mind, enlightened or not. If they had been only thofe obelifcal monuments*, which were raifed to immortalize a fovereign, by fhewing the extent of his power, and the nations brought under it; we would not crufh the ambition of which a whole people muft participate, nor pro- nounce as an abufe that expenditure of public labour and public treafure, which records what may be claimed by a nation as a fame, perhaps juftifiably and honourably won. If they had been thofe tombs of greatnefs, which might pafs for tombs, al- though they had exceeded moderation, and had exhibited all that fuperior art could employ to make us honour the royal afhes depofited there ; no tongue fhould fpeak but with applaufe of the reverence, which ftrove to guard from common prophana- tion, or to diftinguifh from common mortals, thofe remains which

* Herodot. lib. 2. p. 111. Diod. Sic. lib. 1. p. 67, 69.

once did conftitute to every civilized mind the firft reverence and the firft diftinction upon earth.

But thofe edifices, which were moft diftinguifhable for their extravagance, particularly the pyramids*, and alfo many of thofe vaft erections in Upper Egypt†, and that of Ofymandes beyond the reft, were tombs which outftripped the fcale, the labour, and the expence of palaces, temples, and public monuments. When in one of thofe pyramids we fee the unremitting labours of no lefs than 100,000 men for thirty years‡; and when we learn by an infcription upon it, that the garlic, leeks, and onions furnifhed to the workmen coft 220,000l. fterling: when in fome of thofe *maufolea* near Thebes we are carried by the defcriptions of travellers, ancient and modern§, through long fucceffions of veftibules, periftyles, halls, and other apartments immenfe in their height and fpace, aftonifhing in their grandeur and in the choice of marble or ftone, awful in the coloffal magnitude of the figures within them, which often fupported the roofs in the place of columns, and thofe roofs forming a terrace of fuch extent that the Arabians are faid to have built a village upon fome of them ||: when we are informed that of thefe magnificent *maufolea* there were no lefs than forty-feven in the neighbourhood of Thebes : and when we find that the deftination of all thefe works, and of the pyramids, was to receive perhaps only one human body, and to affure to the fovereigns that raifed them the poor and fcanty poffeffion of fix feet by three : we ftand

---

* Goguet's Orig. of Laws, vol. 3. p. 64.   † Ibid. vol. 2. p. 140, 149.

‡ Herodot. lib. 2. n. 124, 125.   Diod. Sic. lib. 1. p. 72, 73.

§ Ibid. p. 56.   Lucas's third Voy. vol. 3. p. 37. et feq.   Granger's Voy. p. 43, et feq.   Pococke, vol. 1. p. 139.   Sicard Mem. du Levant, tom. 7. p. 161.

|| Lucas, ubi fup.

aghaft at the improvident fpirit which could fo lavifhly and un-
neceffarily wafte the labours of millions, although it were true
that thofe labours were tafks, that thofe who underwent them
were flaves and prifoners of war, and that no more treafure was
employed than in the ordinary rates of the moft ordinary provi-
fions ; we are difgufted with the mind, which could feel fo little
for the people over whom it prefided, and with the ideas which
could fo miferably proftitute the nature of patronage in the arts,
if in any moment it were conceived to be patronage; we lament the nation and the government, where the profecution of
public magnificence is not conducted on better principles, where
the monarch will be content to grind the people down for the
furtherance of his vanity, and where the people cannot refift
the ruinous diffipation of their fubftance. If works of public
magnificence are ever beheld with fatisfaction, if the indulgence
of an elegant and munificent fpirit in monarchs is ever honourable to themfelves or their country, if the patronage of the fine
arts is ever what it fhould be, it is when it brings no public hard-
fhip in it's train; when the purpofes for which it is difpenfed,
although they be not ftrictly commenfurate perhaps with the expenditure beftowed, will bear the approbation of the judicious,
and are worthy to be nourifhed at much expence ; when a wife
œconomy, meafuring itfelf by public and private circumftances,
fets proper limits to an otherwife unbounded munificence of mind.

This is a character of patronage, which, wherever it is realized on a throne, makes the fine arts to be precious, and the
cultivation of them to be general, becaufe the people have nothing to rue in the higheft elevation of thofe arts. But that was
unknown in Egypt: all her monuments rofe upon the open
facrifice of fuch a principle of patronage. Yet the people,

tame as they were by habit, fhewed now and then that they were
not abfolutely infenfible of what was hard, and what was wrong.
Indignation and difguft very often took poffeffion of their hearts;
the fecret murmurs of oppreffion grouled upon the tongue; and
when the monarchs, who had fo oppreffed them, dropped, they
were often followed by execration and uproar to their interment,
not always in thofe fecret repofitories which they had prepared
for themfelves, guarded by an immenfe compafs and fecurity of
edifice.   Thus all the efforts of their ambition were frequently
ineffectual in the end.   When thofe edifices were bereft of the
manes, to the reception of which they were devoted, all memory of their founders perifhed, and not a record of their
origin was left but in the exactions by which they had been
raifed.   So juft is the reflection of Pliny, when he calls thofe
edifices " regum pecuniæ otiofa ac ftulta oftentatio"; and fo
literally true is the account he gives of their end, when he adds,
" inter eos non conftat a quibus factæ fint, juftiffimo cafu obli-
" teratis tantæ vanitatis auctoribus*".

* Plin. lib. 36. c. 12.

BOOK III.

GREECE.

CHAP. I.

Preliminary obfervations on the general turn of mind, and fome national policy, of the Greeks, which were favourable to per- fection in the arts—the means by which they obtained the firft knowledge of thofe arts from Afia and Egypt—the Greeks themfelves not improbably a people of Afiatic defcent—the Pe- lafgi from Caucafus fettled in Greece—the principles of Scythian theology introduced by the Pelafgi, and not loft in Greece un- der all the variations of their own fubfequent mythologies, and the multiplicity of deities that fprung from thence—thofe prin- ciples of Scythicifm the fource of the earlieft Grecian fculp- ture, which was all emblematic, and fo continued to the age of Dædalus—coins and other fculptures, and characters of wri- ting too, capable of being afcertained in Greece before the ar- rival of Cadmus—fculpture pufhed in thofe early ages by many circumftances not fo immediately felt by painting—the heroic ages, however, not favourable to much advancement in tafte— Grecian fculpture refcued from the point at which it flood in Afia and Egypt, when beauty was given to it, which was firft learnt from Homer—the acquirement of that beauty in the gene- ral forms of the Greeks the foundation of various fettled re- gulations, and of a regular policy—the prefervation of that

beauty, and the characteristic perfection of their sculptures,
studied in the correctness of contour, which was not lost even
under their drapery—how far the principles of beauty were re-
conciled with the study of Nature—the peculiar style of their
drapery assistant to the perfection of their figures—the peculiar
sublimity of their expression derived from philosophy, and
tending to strengthen it's principles—that sublimity of expres-
sion not confined to the countenance, but governing the whole
attitude—that sublimity of expression the best model to the first
studies of artists—some qualification nevertheless necessary to
the painter in the study of antique sculptures.

WE are now brought to Greece, that illustrious land of art,
into which were conveyed from Asia and Egypt those seeds of
taste and genius, which were carried to a cultivation that left the
countries, from whence they came, in the aspect of rudeness and
barbarism compared with that into which they were removed.
Never on earth was it more conspicuously seen than in this instance, that the disciples were greater than their masters in every
branch which had constituted the relation of discipleship.   Perhaps it was not in a brilliant originality of invention that the
Grecian character stood most conspicuous ; if indeed the difference be great between the ingenuity which strikes out an original device, and that which carries the principles discovered by
others to stages of perfection which the first discoverers never
knew.   However that be, in the latter quality of invention,
genius, and taste the Greeks unquestionably had no rivals.   The
rudiments which they received became perfections in their hands :
those arts, which had been admired elsewhere, acquired with
them a new species of elegance, which left all their former excellencies in shade.   Thus, whatever they owed to others for the

communication of inventions, they compenfated amply by the rich improvements to which they carried all difcoveries.

They were moft happily calculated to do this both by the turn of their minds and by fome parts of their policy. Naturally fond of novelty, they were not only open to the introduction of whatever was rare and ingenious, but they fought and courted it ; while the quicknefs of their apprehenfion prefently made all principles their own. Thefe difpofitions gathered ftrength and eftablifhment from their civil regulations. From the time when they had overcome the difficulties and alarms confequent on thofe inteftine hoftilities with which they were plagued for many ages, it was a leading feature of their character to open their country to all that would vifit it ; not for the fake of looking at ftrangers, but of acquiring what they knew. Their encouragement of ingenuity in every branch was moft decided, and fomewhat extraordinary too, when we confider from what countries they derived the whole train of their arts. It might naturally have been expected, that as they were rude and barbarous at firft, fo they would have fallen into the trammels of their preceptors, who were in poffeffion of all the fame and character which then exifted on the earth, and that they would have made the profeffion of arts hereditary as in Afia and Egypt, if they had not made them fubordinate to other purfuits, and at leaft to other profeffions. It certainly befpoke a very enlarged freedom of mind not to be feduced by thofe examples, and more efpecially to difcern a better fource of perfection in the very reverfe to the principles of their mafters. Accordingly they left Afia and Egypt to their own contracted and miftaken policy. The cultivation of all the arts, and of the more elegant ones efpecially, was either a primary object with them, or it was fecond to nothing.

A city valued itfelf as much on having produced a citizen famous
for fome liberal talent, as for having given birth to a philofopher, a law-giver, or a hero of the firft character.   Painters, architects, and fculptors enjoyed the moft flattering diftinctions.
Pofterity celebrated their names in feftivals.   And as if the elegant arts could not be purfued but in concert with the moft liberal turn and the beft education of mind, it became in procefs of
time an univerfal decree of the country, that none but perfons of
genteel birth fhould be admitted to ftudy and purfue them.   If
that regulation fhould be thought to have carried the matter too
far, or whatever opinions may be formed concerning it in a broad
view, it certainly produced two excellent advantages.   In the
firft place, it threw into the arts all that refined and fuperior intellect, all that philofophic dignity, which ftamped their character in Greece ; and in the next place, it caufed them to be profecuted with an independent and difinterefted fpirit ; the emulation of fame more than of lucre became the bias to their ftudies;
every artift looked only to the perfection of his art ; the artift
and the patron became as it were combined in the fame perfon ;
their fpirit was alive to make their arts the records of the country.   Thus that aftonifhing perfection, which no other people
were ever able to reach, became accomplifhed in every branch;
and thus the country became filled with thofe works of elegance,
whofe amount muft appear incredible on any other fyftem, if we
are to reckon for all as we are authorifed to affert of Rhodes,
which, befides innumerable paintings, poffeffed at one time no
lefs than 6000 of the choiceft ftatues *.

Thefe advantages, however, were the refult of time, and ftudy,

* Plin. lib. 35.

and experience. It will be proper to fee how the means, which led to them, opened; and what direction they took. As this will carry us firft to the contemplation of fculpture, which appears to have taken the lead in the public works of the Greeks, as well as of moft other people, and from the influence of the fame caufes, (although the more private ufes of painting, at leaft in it's fimpler defign, muft have exifted in all periods) we have thought proper to call the reader's attention to the former branch of art in the firft inftance.

The communication which the Greeks had with Egypt in the firft periods of their hiftory, or rather the means by which they became acquainted with what was known and done there, were afforded them by the Phœnicians, who traded conftantly with the coafts of Greece *, and who were the only people (as we have already obferved) to whofe veffels the confined policy of Egypt permitted a port to be opened in thofe times. But their communication with the continent of Afia was more eafy and direct. The Phœnicians alone were an excellent avenue to that communication. But they were not the only or the principal avenue. The Pelafgi, inhabiting the country adjacent to the mountain Caucafus, came into Greece, next after it's firft inhabitants†. They came there, confequently, before the arrival of the Titan princes by whom they were ultimately driven at leaft from a part of Greece, and whofe arrival is fixed to the age of Abraham, full 1900 years before the Chriftian æra. The firft inhabitants, with whom the Pelafgi thus mixed, fhould appear from fome circumftances to have fprung from the fame origin, and to have come from the fame country, with the Pelafgi themfelves; at leaft the reafons,

* Herodot. lib. 1. n. 1.   † Strabo, Geog. lib. 6. p. 327.

which M. D'Ancarville has brought to fupport that fuppofition originally his own, have confiderable weight*. We fhall abftract them in few words. Pliny fays † that the firft name of that mountain was Graucafus, i. e. nive candidum. That name is compounded of *grau*, and *cap*, or *kop*. The firft of thefe we have embraced in our language by the word *gray;* the French exprefs it by *gris;* but the Danes have preferved *grau*, and in it's original fenfe as well as form, meaning *a white* colour. *Cap* or *kop*, changed for eafier termination into *cafe*, meant, as it ftill means with us, and was employed by all the Celtic nations to mean, *a top* or *fummit*. Keeping to the firft branch of this definition, all that chain of the Alps which ftretches from thofe that are called *Cottian* to thofe which are known by the name of *Penine*, was diftinguifhed by the general appellation of *graian*, i. e. the white or grey Alps. If that abridged name was given to that ftretch of mountains, how eafy was it for the people inhabiting the neighbourhood of Graucafus to be called *Graian, Graii, Greeks*, inftead of *Graucafians?* The idea of Eufebius in his chronicle, and of the geographer Stevens, that Greece took it's name from a prince called Græcus, the father or fon of a king of the Pelafgi in Theffaly, needs a great deal of matter to make it out, and is too abrupt a foundation for the name of fuch a country; yet in one view it is capable of ftrengthening the probability of the conjecture here made, if it be fuppofed that Græcus, fhould there ever have been fuch a prince, derived his own name from the country from whence the Pelafgi came. If the Titans be looked upon as the anceftors of the Greeks ‡, or as the founders of their government, ftill thofe Ti-

---

* D'Ancarv. vol. 1. p. 250, 251, 252, note.　　　† Lib. 6. p. 181.

‡. Orph. Hymn 36. v. 2.　　D'Ancarv. vol. 1. p. 52.

tans themfelves came from the neighbourhood of the fame Caucafus.

But the Pelafgi originated from that country, and became fixed
in Greece. The veftiges of their migration thither, and of the
influences of that migration, are very general. They gave their
name to many communities and diftricts of Greece. Herodotus
fays, that the Ionians, the Æolians, and the Lacedemonians, who
were originally Dorians, were all known in remote antiquity by
the general name of Pelafgi *. To the people of Argos, a town
in Theffaly, Homer has given the firname of Pelafgian. The
name of the town itfelf fignifies, as Strabo affures us, *a camp* †;
and fo it carried in it's name the habits of the Pelafgi to dwell in
tents on their arrival in Greece : the name of Argos was therefore Pelafgian, and the Theffalian language preferving that name
fhews itfelf to have been a dialect of the other ‡. Thefe people
continued to rule the country, or a great part of it, for feveral
ages, until thofe who were in Theffaly were driven from thence
by Deucalion the fon of Prometheus §.

The mention of thefe people opens upon us a very important
view in the hiftory of the Grecian arts. To their fettlement in
that country we muft look for the foundation of thofe arts, and
for the firft genius with which they were taken up. The Pelafgi were defcended immediately from the Scythians, in whofe
country the Caucafus ftood ‖. They became therefore the im-

---

* Herodot. lib. 1. fec. 56. p. 21.   Lib. 7. fec. 95. p. 413.
† Strabo Geog. lib. 8. p. 372.   ‡ D'Ancarv. vol. 1. p. 254, note.
§ Dionyf. Halicar. Antiq. Rom. lib. 1. c. 9.
‖ Plin. lib. 6. p. 181.   Apoll. Bibl. l. 1. c. 7.   D'Ancarv. vol. 1. p. 251, 254,

mediate inftruments of conveying into Greece thofe principles of
theology, which their Scythian anceftors had fpread through
Afia, and which of courfe infufed the fame fpirit into the arts of
the former country, and gave them the fame original direction by
which thofe of the latter had been uniformly controuled.   Some
variations will naturally appear in the denomination of characters, which the influence of fubfequent mythologies in Greece
had introduced to a fhare in thofe principles : the fame thing
happened, as we have feen, in Egypt ; and in the fame fhades of
difference we have found the fame original principles of theology diverfified through the feveral nations of the eaft.

That theology, which thus found it's way into Greece was Scythicifm ; and it only gave way to Hellenifm, when the Pelafgi loft
their footing in the country by the fuperior prevalence of the
Titan intereft, from whofe deified princes iffued all the new gods of
Hellenifm, at a period which acccording to the Arundelian marbles anfwers to the year 1521 before our æra *.   All that multiplicity of new deities, commonly called heathen, but more precifely Hellenian or Grecian, into which the religion of that country then branched, was in truth only fo many variations or fubdi-
vifions of the fupreme and primitive principle of Scythicifm,
and fo many exemplifications of the attributes and powers of that
primitive principle, all referable ultimately to it's fuperior fource
and fway†. The Zeus, or Jupiter, who ftepped into the place of
that primitive principle, was eafily derived, by the change of a
letter or two, from the *Tho* or *Theo* which the Pelafgi carried into
Greece as the name, and the only name, by which they fpoke of

* Marm. Oxon. Epoch. 6.   D'Ancarv. vol. 1. p. 252, 255, 256, note.
† Ibid. p. 271, 273, note.

God or the primitive principle *, and which the Greek language completely embraced when it called all it's divinities Θεω. The Greek word Ζέω, which fignifies to burn, was the fame variation with the fame original reference, which it bore very naturally at leaft in the habits of the Pelafgi, and of the Scythians before them, and of the Greeks after them, with whom fire was the firft emblem of that primitive principle. We are led to conceive that the variation, by which the word Ζευς was formed, was fubfequent in time to the idea which had produced the word Ζέω; for in Olympia the Greeks facrificed to fire, under the name of Vefta, before they facrificed to Jupiter†. That Jupiter, and Tellus the goddefs of the earth, whom Herodotus‡ exprefsly couples together in the adoration of the Greeks, and alfo the figures of the Bacchus Myfes male and female in one §, not excluding all the other divinities of Greece which were united, and as one may fay married, in both fexes ‖; all thefe were manifeftly a continuation of the theological principle which gave the *two in one*, which had eftablifhed the Papæus and the Apia of the Scythians, the Ofiris and Ifis of the Egyptians, the Brouma and Saraffouadi of the Indians, and had been purfued by the laft-mentioned people in all the combined male and female figures that are found in their pagodas. Bacchus and Apollo, by whom, as Macrobius affures us **, the Greeks meant only to exprefs different provinces of one and the fame divinity, were new figures of their own, correfpondent to the fame views which

* D'Ancarv. vol. 1. p. 217, 227, 249, 270.

† Paufan. lib. 5. p. 411. Herodot. lib. 4. fec. 59. p. 243. D'Ancarv. vol. 1. p. 111, 138, 139, 218, 219. ‡ Ubi fup.

§ Orph. Hymn 41. v. 3. D'Ancarv. vol. 1. p. 76, 92, 100.

‖ Ibid. vol. 1. p. 235, 236. ** Macrob. Sat. lib. 1. p. 141.

had eſtabliſhed in Aſia the ox and the lion as the emblems of
the nocturnal and diurnal ſun*: ſo they were meant to be conſidered in the tomb of Bacchus, which was ſhewn at Delphi, cloſe
by the golden ſtatue of Apollo.　Theſe and many other peculia-
rites in the caſt of their divinities, created by their mythology,
but founded in a reference to a better and more ſolid principle,
were properly explained† to the initiated in the ſacred myſteries
inſtituted by Orpheus, who was himſelf of Scythian origin, and
therefore was likely to explain them aright; and from whoſe
time we muſt not fail to obſerve that the ox, which had
been as much received in Greece as elſewhere, and had once
in Eubæa a cave which was called his palace, ceaſed to be
worſhipped as a part of the ancient coſmogony ‡.

But the ſtrongeſt feature of the Scythian theology, or of
variations upon it, in Greece was found in the worſhip of
Bacchus; whoſe worſhip, and whoſe every repreſentation,
was filled in the courſe of time with all thoſe circumſtances §
which were employed in the worſhip, and in all the repreſentations, of the deified character that really conquered and civilized
India.　The Greeks had forgotten how thoſe circumſtances had
been introduced among them, and they were ignorant of their
real deſtination, even while they were uſing them ‖.　When in
proceſs of time they came to find, by their own migrations into
India, all thoſe circumſtances ſubſiſting and employed there in all

---

* D'Ancarv. vol. 1. p. 64, 233, 271, 273, 275.

† Macrob. ubi. ſup.　Euſeb. præp. Evang. lib. 3.　D'Ancarv. vol. 1. p. 64, 271,
364.　　　　　‡ Ibid. p. 115, 140, 141.　Strabo Geog. lib. 10. p. 445.

§ See thoſe circumſtances as they occur in D'Ancarv. vol. 1. p. 97. et ſeq. 111,
112, 116, 117, 127, 132, 134, 135, 143, 198, 203, 215, 223, 228, 230, 261, 278.

‖ Ibid. p. 64.

their force, they vainly imagined that their Bacchus had been the perfon who conquered that country, and that thofe rites, and cuf: toms, and ideas had been tranfplanted thither from Greece it-felf*; confequently they fubftituted the name of Bacchus for that of Brouma ; and probably it was not long before they be-lieved, whatever others might do, that Bacchus was born in In-dia †, and that they could find the record of his name in the de-nomination of many towns, that were even built by him, in that that country ‡. Thus the foundation was laid for that miftaken fuperftructure, with which the Grecian hiftories were filled, erected on a mythological phantom, whofe fabulous and empty tale Eratofthenes had difcernment enough to difcover §.

Thefe things are neceffary to be ftated in a refearch after the origin and progrefs of the Grecian arts, becaufe from thefe prin-ciples fo growing in that country thofe arts took their beginning. The firft efforts of their fpirit rofe on emblematic ideas ; which had no force, at leaft to the fenfes, until it was given them by the aids of art. Thofe emblematic ideas, widening as they advanced, afforded to the ingenuity which was fo needful to them a field that was hardly to be bounded. They mixed themfelves in every circumftance, whether of convenience or ornament, of private value or public ufe, to which the aid of ingenuity could be called. The mind, that once feels thofe ideas as the impreffions of religion, feels them in every thing ; and when they come to take poffeffion of a people, their features will be found in all that paffes from hand to hand, as well as in the more ftated and folemn repre-fentations which concern religion itfelf. There is an anxiety

* Diod. Sic. Bibl. lib. 2. p. 151.   † Ibid. et lib. 3. p. 232.
‡ D'Ancarv. vol. 1. p. 98, 99, 100.   § Strabo Geog. lib. 15. p. 687.

alfo that will rife from thofe impreffions, and will ever be pufhing the efforts of art from one ftage of ability to another. Fame itfelf will pufh thofe efforts forward, but never fo warmly as when the emulation is engaged with what concerns the fupreme Being; when it feeks to give a fort of fenfible form to the ideas which are difficult to be grafped, and more difficult ftill to be reduced into fhape; when it dares to make us fee what is invifible, and to bring to our very fenfes what is hardly capable of being concei- ved. In this peculiar emulation the feelings of the ruder artift would make up fomething for the deficiency of his powers. The impoffibility of reaching the end to which his mind would afpire, far from difcouraging his views, would only urge him continually to new efforts, and to attain what perfection he could in thofe ftages that lay within his compafs. He could never think to fuc- ceed in the reprefentation of the divine Nature, becaufe it cannot refemble any thing that ever was made; but he might hope, in the progrefs of thofe emblematical ftudies, to give to the human nature a beauty capable of recalling at leaft the idea of that perfection, which our feeble apprehenfions attribute to Him whofe divine qualities are beyond the reach of every com- parifon.

Thefe views gave the firft difcovery of arts to the Greeks, as they had done to other people; and thefe continual efforts led thofe arts from ftrength to ftrength. That ftrength became gra- dually more encreafed in Greece, even while it's arts were all em- blematic, becaufe thofe efforts were greater and more conftant than any where elfe; and they were helped forward by a more thriving and progreffive genius in that people than they had found in any others. Neverthelefs, the ftages through which they paffed to any degree of ftrength in art, and firft in fculp-

ture as we have faid, were but flow. As fuch, they carry the
furer marks of a very high antiquity among a people who were
naturally brilliant in mind. And as their fculpture opened with
an emblematic theology, fo we fhall find the principles of that
theology, only modified by the peculiarity of their own fables,
keeping poffeffion of their fculpture until an attention to Nature,
both in character and execution, ftepped into the place of the
other in the age of Dædalus, but never to root it out entirely.

It was not the firft impreffions of that theology, which the
fculpture of the Greeks was enabled to meet. It muft therefore
have been in remote ages indeed, when the objects of that theology, to which fculpture was fo important, were fatisfied by large
and tall ftones fet up as ftatues of the divinity, in thofe places which
were meant to be confidered as the fcite of a temple, but which
had no other mark of fuch a defign than the enclofure made by
a circular fofs *. Sometimes thofe ftones were fingle and detached : fometimes they were connected by others thrown acrofs:
fometimes, again, they were arranged three together : and at
other times the only diftinction they had was the conical, pyramidical, or obelifcal form which was given them. Under all
thefe circumftances they were confidered as emblematic images,
expreffing by their largenefs the majefty of that Being, to whom
devotion was there offered ; by their ternary arrangement that
three-fold power of the Divinity, which creates, preferves, and
deftroys all things ; and by their myftical forms that active, vivifying, and enlightening fpirit in the divine nature, of which fire
and the fun are the moft natural emblems—the firft, refembled in
it's afcending and pointed flame by the conical and pyramidical

* D'Ancarv. vol. 1. p. 459.

form, the latter imitated in it's rays by the obelifcal ftructure *.   Thefe theological ideas, thus burfting from the mind of
rudenefs and imperfection, and fo inertly expreffed in huge, and
one may fay in fhapelefs, ftones, ftood neverthelefs the teft of
every refinement attained in emblematic ftudies : they were not
loft when the fculpture of the Greeks was enabled to convey
them by a more active, decided, and improved expreffion in gems
and medals, and coins, and ftatues.   It is by the information afforded in thefe, far more than by any remains of thofe facred
ftones, of which there are neverthelefs fome in many parts of
the earth, that we are enabled to know what were thofe firft
fanctuaries of religion, and thofe firft religious images, which
engaged the attempts of mankind.   With fo great veneration
were thefe refpected by the Greeks, that when they were in the
power of fubftituting the fineft coloffal ftatues in their place, they
preferred the others, and left them undifturbed; they recorded
the memorial of them on their coins and medals, when the elegance of their fculpture might have been feen in a thoufand
more exquifite forms.

The firft efforts of their fculpture were moft probably
found in thofe engravings which were made on agates and other
ftones of a harder nature†.   If this fhould appear extraordinary, or too much for thofe firft efforts, let it be remembered
that although the fkill of engraving on thofe ftones was equal
to any that could be wanted for the production of an impreffion on coins, yet that of moulding and throwing the material into fufion was not neceffary.   Many of thofe ftones, engraved in remote antiquity, have been preferved to the prefent
times; although there are not more than three or four of thofe

engravers, whofe names have come down to us in ancient authors.

Coins were indifpenfible to their neceffities in very early times,
and the Greeks had them in all the progreffion of art from fimple moulding to the more finifhed impreffion, on gold, and filver,
and brafs *. But thofe coins were in every ftage of that progreffion the emanation of Scythian practice: Ericthonius brought
immediately from Scythia thofe which he firft introduced into
Athens 1463 years before our æra †; and there were other coin-
ages in Greece long before that period‡, fome of which were unqueftionably brought there by the Pelafgian fettlers. All thofe
coins, however, bore in their form and their expreffion, whether
ruder or more improved, the recorded principles of the prevailing theology; and in the more ancient ones there was the moft
decided fimilitude to thofe that were fabricated in the eaft, and
are ftill feen there, both in the various forms of the monies,
and in the treatment of their reverfe, and in the whole operation by which they were finifhed§. The obelifcal monies, which
feem to have been at leaft as early as any others in Greece, and
were actually derived from Afia, were an exprefs record of the
firft devotion ‖. The coins in form of the *Teffera* had the fame
eaftern origin, and ftill fubfift in Tartary, although they have
been difcontinued in Greece for more than 2700 years **.

The fymbolic characters expreffed on their coins, and afterwards on their medals as they came into ufe, were all drawn

---

* D'Ancarv. vol. 1. pref. p. 1.   † Ibid p. 23.   ‡ Ibid. p. 30, 31.
§ See ibid. p. 57, 60, 410, 416.   ‖ Ibid. p. 1, 9, 10, 21, 22, 57, 409,
411, 443.   ** Ibid. p. 58, 410.

from the fame eaftern fource, and were referable to the fame theological principles. The emblematic ox was as old as the people
who firft inhabited the country, and was revered by the Greeks in
the living animal, as it had been revered in Afia and in Egypt, before ever their arts were enabled to give it's figure on their coins
and medals *. When it appeared on thofe of Thefeus, it was
late in time ; and in that inftance we fee how little Plutarch had
gained the proper clue of things, when he gives as a reafon for
that impreffion of the ox, that it was the intention of Thefeus
either to immortalize the Marathonian bull, and the general
Taurus of Minos, or to encourage the citizens in the cultivation
of their lands†. The intention of Thefeus was that fame intention, which was long cherifhed by the Greeks, of preferving in
their fculptures, and particularly in their coins and medals, the
ideas which had marked them early, and with which their firft
growth had begun, whether thofe ideas then continued to be
purfued in their firft fimplicity, or were retained in all their firft
influence, or not. For at that period we muft recollect that
Orpheus had difcontinued in the facred myfteries the reverence of the ox, as a part of the ancient cofmogony.

The ferpent, whofe influence in the emblematic fyftem was
equal to that of the ox, and whofe origin was equally Scythian ‡,
became equally diftinguifhed in the fculptures of the Greeks.
The fable of Echidne, the mother of the Scythians, gave her
figure terminating as a ferpent to all the founders of ftates in
Greece; from whence their earlieft fculptures reprefented in that

---

* D'Ancarv. vol. 1. p. 140, note.　　　　　† Plut. vita Thefei.

‡ D'Ancarv. vol. 1. p. 483.

form the Titan-princes, Cecrops, Draco the firſt king of Athens, and even Erichonius *. In alluſion to the ſame ſource the ſer-pent was ſymbolized in many of their ancient baſs-reliefs as the leader of armies and colonies: gryphons, in Scythian habits, are found fighting for particular people †. It was a relic of the ſame original idea, when prieſteſſes were repreſented offering meats to that animal‡; and when Phidias placed a ſerpent beſide the ſpear of Minerva in the image which he made for the citadel of Athens, which was abſolutely conſidered as guarded by that creature §. It's combinations with other figures in the Grecian coins and medals were all referable to the ancient coſmogony or theology derived from the Scythian creed ; whether the ſerpent was ſeen infolding an egg, as in the medals of Phœnicia ‖; or twiſted round a trident, the type of the ſea, to ſhew it's imagined rule over humid nature, as in the images of Tartary ** ; or en-circling a flambeau, the known Thyrſus of Bacchus, to beſpeak it's emblematic reference to that deity, who ſtood as the god of life and death †† ; or with a ſtar under it, and a creſcent over it, to denote it's ſymbolic relation to the primitive principle which drew the world from night and chaos ‡‡. The variations in which it was repreſented were almoſt infinite : and we cannot wonder at any expreſſions of importance given to that emblem by the Greeks, when we recollect that through the medium of it's ſuppoſed inſpiration, under the name of Python, the firſt ora-cles of Delphi and Dodona were conducted, before ever the name

* D'Ancarv. vol. 1. p. 52, 54, 453.

† Ibid. p. 454, 489. ‡ Ibid. p. 473, 483.

§ Ibid. p. 48, 485. Herodot. lib. 8. ſec. 41.

‖ Ibid. p. 480. See pl. 23. No. 5.

** Ibid. p. 482. See pl. 22. No. 10.

†† Ibid. p. 463, 464. ‡‡ Ibid. p. 481. See pl. 23. No. 3.

of Apollo was known in Greece*. When that deity was fubftituted by the Grecian mythology as the vifible oracle, ftill he
was called the Pythian Apollo, and his priefteffes Pythians ; from
thence it was alfo faid that Apollo had killed the ferpent Python,
whofe place he had taken†. Yet, as if the Greeks were afraid to
lofe the popular influence, as well as the popular name, of the
ferpent, thofe oracles were ftill confidered as originating from
him, and on that account he was often reprefented alive on tri-
pods in the reverfe of Grecian medals ‡.

The vaft variety of types given by the Greeks to all their divinities, and particularly to Bacchus, does not more abound with
the proofs of ingenuity, than with thofe of Scythian principles ;
and more efpecially when thofe types were the very fame that
were employed by many of the Afiatic nations to mark the attributes of their divinity. In thofe types or fymbols there was
certainly a ftage of advancement in genius beyond the idea of
expreffing the fuperiority of divine power, or divine wifdom, or
divine forefight, by many hands, or many heads, or three eyes
given to their figures §. And yet that feems to have been a primary idea ; for the Greeks purfued the fame method for a confiderable time‖. A whimfical, and poor, and vicious mode of fymbolical expreffion it certainly was ** ; although the difficulty be
acknowledged, and efpecially in lefs polifhed ages, of coming
in a better way to the object at which they aimed, and which was
to exprefs ideas not eafy to be comprehended by forms concor-
dant to the natural order of things, and to give the exhibition of
imaginary powers and acts as foreign to the common order of

* D'Ancarv. vol. 1. p. 454, 482.
† Ibid. p. 483, note.
‡ Ibid.
§ Ibid. p. 51, 56, 464.
‖ Ibid. p. 50, 54.
** Ibid. p. 54, 56.

events as that arbitrary alliance of forms was to the order of Nature. That difficulty, however, was in part overcome by many of the eastern nations themselves. The activity of Grecian genius was never likely to be shackled by it long, unless from a voluntary respect for antiquity, and for the first traits of their favourite theology. If in the pursuit of this new spirit of allegory a language was opened in sculpture very different from that which had been originally spoken, the freedom and the novelty of the change decided presently the Grecian choice ; and the superior elegance of design, which was consulted in that change, turned every argument in it's favour. Instead of the ungracious multiplication of parts, or the equally ungracious combination of different species of beings, the various attributes and powers of the Divinity were expressed by types or emblems, whose forms or properties were conceived most apposite to the illustration of those attributes and powers ; while the reference to that original source, from whence the first ideas of those qualities had flowed, was maintained as far as it was possible.

The horns of a young ox given to the figures of Bacchus, from whence he was called by the poets *corniger*, was equal in expression, and much more than equal in elegance of design, to all the representations which had been given of him by the face of the ox put upon the human frame, or by the human countenance added to the frame of the ox *.

The mitre put upon the head of Bacchus by the Greeks, as it was put upon that of Brouma by the Indians, spoke with more elegance and concisenefs, although with more emblematic pro-

* D'Ancarv. vol. 1. p. 352, 461.

fundity, that ancient cofmogony which to this hour is told at Japan by the figure of a real ox butting againſt a real egg, in order to aſſiſt the birth of creation from it's enclofure; for that egg, when divided in halves, became the very form of thofe mitres or bonnets. The Greeks made fo much of that idea, and were fo well pleafed with it, that both in their paintings and fculptures they gave thofe mitres or bonnets to the brows of Caſtor and Pollux ; and in that application they found an egg for their own origin, while they allowed one for the birth of the world; for they wiſhed it to be underſtood, that they came forth from the egg of Leda formed by her conneſtion with Jupiter, and they were vain enough to ſhew fuch an egg fufpended from the cieling of a temple at Lacedæmon *.

To mount their deities on birds or animals was common with the Greeks. When Bacchus, either as Liber Pater or as Libera, was reprefented on their medals and bafs-reliefs feated on a fwan that rode on the waters, with fiſhes around it; the idea was a plain one, that in their creed that deity ruled over humid nature, as his emblem the aquatic ferpent was of courfe confidered to rule over it. That creed they borrowed from the ancient theology, which looked up to the fupreme generator of all things as drawing forth the world from the bofom of the waters, and as prefiding over their influence, without whofe moiſture they knew that neither the earth could be habitable, nor could any of it's creatures fubſſ, nor any of it's produſtions vegetate †. They alfo borrowed from the eaſt the very emblem which they applied thus to their Bacchus ; for Brouma was often reprefented by the

---

* Paufan. lib. 3. c. 16. p. 246.   D'Ancarv. vol. 1. p. 132.
† Ibid. p. 134, 354.

Indians as borne upon the *Annon*, which Sonnerat tells us is a
fpecies of the fwan, and is the fame bird that was given by the
Greeks to Bacchus *. If we would know why that fpecial province of prefiding over all humid nature was given to Bacchus,
and was expreffed with fuch various attention by the Greeks,
an hymn of Orpheus will explain the reafon†. Bacchus is there
celebrated for having extinguifhed by water a fire which was originally confuming this earthly globe. That notion found it's
way to the Greeks from a fimilar tradition among the Scythians‡;
although they knew nothing of Bacchus, and confequently never
meant to apply it to him. That application was the fruit of
Grecian mythology. It was the fource, however, of all the liba-
tions on the earth which Bacchus is ever reprefented as making in
any of the Grecian paintings, or fculptures, or engravings.

When dolphins, and other fymbols of waters, are feen on their
medals with the ox, the emblem of Bacchus, it is evidently a
part of the fame mythology, grafted on the fame Afiatic principles §.

The ivy, with which the figures of Bacchus were crowned,
arofe alfo from the fame principles, and was intended to illuftrate
the fame purpofe. That plant grows fpontaneous in moift and
fhady places : it was therefore chofen as well as the tamara for
an aquatic emblem. If the latter announced alfo a divinifation
of charaƈer, the former befpoke the god of waters. And Plutarch's authority is full to the point, that "Bacchus was confi-
" dered by the Greeks as the lord and mafter of all humid na-

---

* Sonnerat's Voy. vol. 1. p. 143, note C.   † Orph. Hymn 46. v. 2. et feq.
‡ Juftin, lib. 2. c. 1.   D'Ancarv. vol. 1. p. 283—288.
§ D'Ancarv. vol. 1. p. 224.

" ture *." That deity was therefore crowned with ivy, not as the god of wine, but as the god of waters. † From thence the mufes came to be crowned with ivy, becaufe mythology had faid that the mufes accompanied Bacchus into India, grounding itfelf on the hiftory that many women accompanied Brouma thither. Thofe women were characterifed, at leaft in fable, as great proficients in fcience, and from them were felected many who were confecrated to the worfhip of the emblematic principle of all generation.   They were therefore naturally crowned with that ivy, which the Scythians carried in all the feafts and orgies for which thofe women were confecrated.   When the mufes had thus gained the crown of ivy, we fhall no longer be at a lofs for the reafon why it was given to poets, and became in the expreffion of Horace " doctarum hederæ præmia frontium." When it was mixed with the laurel in the crowns given to Apollo on fome of the Grecian medals, it befpoke with great eafe the union of that deity with Bacchus, as exhibiting together only different exemplifications or attributes of one and the fame primitive principle, and the adherence of the Greeks to the ancient theology, which had uniformly tranfmitted the idea of two in one ‡.

But vine-leaves were alfo an emblem appropriated to Bacchus —an emblem, originating from the Greeks themfelves, when they confidered him as the god of wine.   If thefe formed a crown to the figure of the fun in fome of the Grecian medals, the language and intent was in fact the fame as if they had crowned the head of Bacchus himfelf, who was fubftituted by the Greeks for the nocturnal fun which had been given by the Indians to Brouma §.

* Plut. in Ifid. et Ofirid. p. 365.   † D'Ancarv. vol. 1. p. 222, 223.
‡ Ibid. p. 275, note.   § Ibid.

In fome bafs-reliefs Bacchus as an infant is feen crowned with thefe leaves of the vine in a cradle, which takes the form of the half of an egg cut in two from end to end : and there we fee the creed, which reprefents his birth, connected ingenioufly with the ancient creed of cofmogony, and illuftrating the title of ωγενής, " born of an egg," which was given him by Orpheus * : the Greeks meant to fay that his birth was the birth of the world from the egg of chaos †.

In fome of the Grecian medals ringlets detached from the reft of the hair, and rifing up like little flames of fire, are feen on the heads both of Apollo and Bacchus, but lefs numerous on thofe of the latter than they appear on the former. By that ingenuity the artifts of Greece recorded in thofe two deities the fun of the world, confidered by the ancient theology as the firft defcendant or fon of the primitive principle of fire, and only diverfified into the diurnal and nocturnal fun, the latter of whom was of courfe lefs illumined than the former ‡. When thofe ringlets or fparks were feen on the heads of other gods or goddeffes, they marked equally the divine filiation which was afcribed to thofe deities as defcendants of the Titans, who were concluded to be defcended from heaven.   And when the fame fymbols were given as a diadem to the heads of Grecian kings, it was done in profecution of the like claim affumed by them, after the example of many eaftern princes, to be the fons of a god, which the kings of Macedon particularly afferted to themfelves §.

But the diftinction of the diurnal and nocturnal fun was ne-

---

* Orph. Hymn 5. v. 2.　　　　　† D'Ancarv. vol. 1. p. 276, 277.
‡ Ibid. p. 273, 274.　　§ Ibid.

ver feen more ftrongly or more ingenioufly conducted in the
fculptures of Greece than under the fymbols of the lion and ox,
when feen together.   Thefe were refpectively the types of either
fun.   In fome bafs-reliefs they were reprefented as iffuing, both
of them, from the fame leaves of the acanthus, which was itfelf
an emblem of fire, like the fruit of the pine on the top of the
thyrfus.   As they rufh forth from thofe leaves, they take an oppofite courfe from each other, defcriptive enough of the oppofi-
tion between day and night ; while the equal ardour of both to
be gone fhewed very expreffively the flight of time*.

We have juft mentioned the thyrfus, but it affords more abundant notice.   It was attached almoft conftantly as a kind of fcep-
ter to the figures of Bacchus ; and it was a very fignificant fymbol, although the Greeks derived it entirely from the Scythians.
It carried in it's name the fource which it obtained from the Aga-
thyrfes, the eldeft branch of that people : it carried alfo in it's
name another reference which it bore to the *Thyr* or *Theo* of the
Scythians, and confequently it became an emblem of the fupreme
principle defcribed by that name : it became that emblem from a
part of it's form; for the apple of the pine or fir put upon the top
of it's rod, refembling by it's conical or pyramidical fhape a rifing
flame, eafily fixed it for the fymbol of fire, in which the fupreme
principle was firft emblematically viewed.   To that principle,
by the progrefs of mythology, Bacchus became fubftituted in
Greece†.

When Diana of Ephefus was reprefented in a car drawn by two

---

* D'Ancarv. vol. 1. p. 271—273.   † Ibid. p. 261—265.

oxen, from whence fhe gained the name of "boum agitatrix," the affurance we have that fhe was confidered as the moon, and the clofenefs of thofe fymbols to the noɛturnal fun, give us that part of the eaftern theology again. And when her figure was taken in a male as well as a female form, making good the words of Arnobius, who fays that fhe was addreffed in prayers as equi-vocal in fex *; we know that the Greeks were led to that choice by a principle which never arofe firft in their country †.

The deity, to whom the Greeks gave the name of Pan, *the All*, and whom they reprefented with the face and legs of the goat‡, becaufe that animal had been an original emblem of the *Theo* or primitive principle revered by the Scythians, was a fubjeɛt replete with emblematic fymbols in the hands of the Greek ar-tifts. When he was feen with a diadem on his head, his general authority over all that exifted in nature and creation was clearly and concifely expreffed §. When he was reprefented playing on a flute, they meant to fhew, that he was the principle of harmo-ny to the univerfe ‖. When they gave him hairs refembling fea-weeds, which are caft upon the fhore, from whence ftatues of Pan fo dreffed were frequently erected there, and from whence alfo he gained the name of *Littoral* **, it was an eafy mode of expref-fing that fupremacy which he had over the waters, as well as over all the earth ††. When, inftead of being reprefented naked, as he generally was, the fkin of a leopard, called *nebrides*, was thrown over his fhoulders; the variety of colours and afpeɛts,

---

* Arnob. adv. gent. lib. 3.   † D'Ancarv. vol. 1. p. 237.
‡ Herodot. lib. 2. fec. 46. p. 108.   § D'Ancarv. vol. 1. p. 332.
‖ Orph. Hymn 10. v. 7.   D'Ancarv. vol. 1. p. 333, 334.
** Theocrit. Idyll. 5.   †† D'Ancarv. vol. 1. p. 331, 332.

as well as of things themfelves, difperfed through all Nature over which he prefided, was meant to be announced *. When he was defcribed with a fhepherd's crook, his guardianfhip of flocks was diftinftly given †.

But how came the Greeks by that idea of Pan, on which this laft fymbol was grounded? It's paffage to them from the Scythians can eafily be traced. That people, a paftoral people, whofe wealth confifted in their flocks, naturally looked up to their *Theo* or primitive principle for the protcftion of their fubftance as well as of themfelves‡. When the power of that primitive principle, in the multiplication of all creatures, came to be revered under an emblem prefent to the fight, the nature of the goat decided that choice§. It was therefore by an eafy procefs of idea, that the Greeks, having received the old emblem of the fupreme generating principle, and which was to the Scythians the emblem of it's paftoral protcftion, gave the fame charafter of paftoral protcftion to their Pan, whom they fubftituted for that generating principle.

The fame folution will alfo explain at once the origin of all thofe figures of Sileni, fatyrs, tityri, and fauns, confiderably diverfified from each other, but all retaining more or lefs the marks and charafters of the goat, which mythology had introduced and attached to the reprefentations of Pan, and afterwards to thofe of Bacchus, when he came to be fubftituted for that deity ‖. All thofe emblematic figures were only fo many various expreffions of that fupreme vivifying aftion, which animates all things, and

---

* D'Ancarv. vol. 1. p. 337.   † Ibid. p. 327, note.   ‡ Ibid.
§ Ibid. p. 320.   ‖ Ibid. p. 330.

spreads itself over all kinds, and species, and individuals in creation, however diverfified by names, or forms, or ages, or fexes,
or employments *.

What we have juft intimated concerning the fhare which Bacchus came to have in thofe fubjects, will pave the way to an explanation of many other circumftances or fymbols attached to the
reprefentation of that god of the Greeks. It may naturally be
fuppofed that many of thofe fymbols originally appropriated to
Pan, and others peculiarly calculated for Bacchus, would in time
be fo confounded by artifts, that they would be applied in fome
inftances indifcriminately to either, though not without the purpofe of preferving a myfterious fenfe†, in which they were refpectively concerned : this was the cafe, when the goat's beard of
Pan was given to Bacchus ; and, on the other hand, when the
long robe of Bacchus, called *Baffarides*, was put upon the figures
of Pan ‡.

What we have faid will alfo explain at once the origin and
purpofe of all thofe figures of Bacchus which go by the names
of *Satyr*, *Dafyllius*, or *Lafius ;* in all of which is expreffed,
under fome little difference of defcription, the quality of hairy-
nefs peculiar to the goat §. When we recollect that the immediate character of Bacchus was that of the ox, which was his
firft emblem, it muft appear furprifing how the Greeks fhould
ever think of uniting to that character another fo extremely different from it as that of the goat ; and more furprifing ftill, how
they fhould have found the powers of art to effect that combi-

---

* D'Ancarv. vol. 1. p. 325.   † Ibid. p. 335, 336.
‡ Ibid. p. 337.   § Ibid. p. 338, 339.

nation, fo correctly adjufted as to make itfelf plain and diftinct, without fuffering from the predominance of either character over that of the other; and, again, without lofing any of that nice adjuftment by the injury done to the human figure through the exceffive prevalence of either of thofe characters over it's peculiar traits*. This was certainly a phænomenon of art, for which it is next to impoffible for lefs capacities than theirs to account diftinctly; and yet there can be no doubt of the fact. A ftronger inftance can hardly be adduced of the perfection to which their genius had arrived.

Previous, however, to the reach of fo much fpirit in art, the emblematic fymbols on their coins and medals had derived a new fpirit, not merely from the endeavour to give more beauty to their compofition, but from deeper reafons connected with mythology itfelf. In the forms of thofe fymbols the Greeks effayed to illuftrate more than the mere truth of the figure which conftituted the fymbol; they ftrove to fhew the caufes and foundation of it's fymbolical reference and ufe. While they were not wantonly carelefs of the laws of Nature, by departing from the general forms which fhe had prefcribed; they conceived themfelves at liberty in the treatment of the fymbol to compofe it in fome degree as they pleafed, to ennoble it by new proportions, and to bring within it's outline fuch a defcription of it's parts as appeared moft perfect, with the alliance too of other parts which would beft complete it as a myftical figure for the object propofed, whether that outline was precifely fuch as was found in Nature or not. Thus in the quadrilateral monies of Athens, which

---

* D'Ancarv. vol. 1. p. 339, note. The obfervations of M. D'Ancarville, tending to explain in fome degree the procefs of thofe aftonifhing compofitions of figures, are deeply founded in philofophic art, and worthy of the reader's attention.

bore the impreſſion of an ox, the horns there deſcribed were by
no means the common horns of that animal; they had a round-
neſs and a largeneſs which were not ſeen in any horns whatever;
and they terminated in the form of obeliſks, whoſe form was in-
geniouſly bent and adapted to the contour of horns. Now the
obeliſk was a known ſymbol of the rays of the ſun. The Greeks,
therefore, in that alliance of parts given to thoſe horns of the
ox, and in the peculiar management of their form, plainly dreſſed
them ſo as to ſhew their ſymbolic relation to Bacchus as the
noſturnal ſun *.

In the formation of thoſe myſtic figures which engrafted a new
and more enlarged ſpirit on the ancient ſtyle, the Greek artiſts
were juſtified, as Ammonius tells us †, by Ariſtotle on the common diſtinſtion between a natural and a ſymbolic repreſentation; for Ariſtotle was too indifferent about the fine arts to have
reached, in all probability, the ſource and the elements from
whence thoſe myſtic figures were drawn: but he ſays, "there is
" this difference between the repreſentation and the ſymbol of
" an objeſt, that while the former adheres faithfully to the na-
" ture of the objeſt repreſented, the latter is entirely depen-
" dent on the imagination of him who compoſes it, and who
" may give it that variation or compoſition which he ſhall
" think beſt calculated to convey the idea which his own mind
" has entertained, and which he does not mean to repreſent mi-
" nutely, but to ſignify by an appoſite ſymbol." In the treatment of thoſe ſymbolic forms the Greek artiſts aſted as the poets
of Greece had done, who by the mode of expreſſion, by the
combination of many words or ideas in one, were enabled to

* D'Ancarv. vol. i. p. 424—426.   † Ammon. in Lib. de Interpret.

throw into that one the precife impreffion at which they aimed, the collective impreffion of all the aggregate parts, which could never have been conveyed by any of thofe parts themfelves in their feparate ftate*.

In thefe emblematic works were the fculptural arts of Greece employed in the earlier ages, until Dædalus made his appearance†. If in the purfuit of the emblematic figure Nature had been violated, if to the conftitution of that figure more parts had been given than were natural, he ftrove to recover thofe laws which were warranted in Nature, he brought the artifts of Greece to an exact imitation of her forms, and thofe at leaft who followed his principles abandoned from thenceforth the ftyle which Greece had received from Afia, and to which Afia never ceafed to adhere‡. Neverthelefs, fome ancient figures of that emblematic fpecies, adopted by fuperftition, or by the habits which are equal to it, or by the neceffity of maintaining the figures employed of old in the fervice of religion, were facredly preferved, and even frequently repeated in later times by the moft celebrated mafters§.

That attention to Nature, for the introduction of which, as a melioration of the Grecian fculptures, Dædalus was credited, muft not be fet down as very improved beyond the interruption it gave to emblematic defigns. As an expreffion of the natural figure, if we combine with the mere figure any ideas of it's fpirit, certainly much more than was done in his fculptures, and in thofe of his fchool, was wanted to conftitute any con-

* D'Ancarv. vol. 1. p. 426, note.　　† Ibid. p. 55, 425.

‡ Ibid. vol. 2. p. 395, note.　　§ Ibid. vol. 1. p. 55, 425.

fiderable melioration of defign, if there were in that age any
fculptures at all, affecting the plain and diftinct natural figure,
with which they might be compared; for, as we have already
had occafion to remark, on the authority of Plato, Paufanias,
and others, nothing could have advanced much lefs beyond the
mere block, or beyond the fculptures of Egypt, than his figures.
They did indeed manifeft an attention to Nature, fo far as that
was proved by a regular difplay of the feveral parts of the figure,
by the feparation of the arms and legs, or at leaft of the latter*,
and by fome little communication of attitude: but, beyond thefe,
their pretenfions to the expreffion of Nature were very hum-
ble†; although in thefe circumftances fome ftep was undoubtedly
gained in art, and it was to the credit of Dædalus that he was
able to go beyond the rudenefs and deformity of fuch fculptures
as the palladium, and the ftatue of Amyclas, and that of the
Ephefian Diana, all of them made before his time, and only diftinguifhed from columns by the head, and the hands, and the
extremity of the feet‡. The ftatues on the tomb of Choræbus
at Megara, we doubt not, were in that rude ftyle; for they were
made 250 years before the age of Dædalus, and about 1540
years before our æra §. It was certainly to the credit of Dædalus that he was able to give the Greeks fome rules in the practice
of their fculpture ||. In his fchool, which produced many re-
fpectable difciples, among whom Endius was eminently marked,
they faw for the firft time the arts of defign purfued on fome regularity of principles**. Perhaps it is true, that he carried the

* D'Ancarv. vol. 2. p. 423.   † Paufan. lib. 2. cap. 4. p. 121.
‡ D'Ancarv. vol. 2. p. 261, 262, 423.   § Ibid. vol. 2. p. 343.
|| Diod. Sic. Bibl. lib. 4. c. 31.   D'Ancarv. vol. 1. p. 55.   Vol. 2. p. 284, 285.
** Paufan. lib. 8. cap. 53. p. 708.

imitation of Nature fo far as to have made portraits of his ſtatues; which, although it were a conſiderable ſtep in the firſt endeavours to follow Nature, might yet be done by thoſe who had
a talent for it, without much merit in the general figure.   It is
on the language of Apollodorus that this idea is grounded, who
ſpeaks of ſome ſtatues of Hercules, done by Dædalus, which
were very like the original*.

Dædalus had ſome cotemporaries in art, whoſe names are
tranſmitted by authors, but not with equal fame that is
given to him†.   The age in which he lived, how late ſoever
it came in the antiquity of Grecian ſculpture, ſeems to have
given the firſt opening to freedom and truth in that art.   The
family of Dædalus was very ingenious, and an important acqui-
ſition to that age.   They ſeem to have been born for the fine arts.
Whether or no it be true, as Pliny has aſſerted‡, that Euchir the
father of Dædalus firſt introduced, or, as it is ſaid, invented painting in Greece; we may reaſonably conclude from the mention of
him in that way, that he had made himſelf noticed in that art.
We are aſſured, however, by Diodorus Siculus that Talus the
nephew of Dædalus invented the potter's wheel, by means of
which the Greeks began to execute thoſe fine vaſes, in which
they afterwards ſo much excelled §.   Whether Dædalus himſelf
invented the plaſtic art, or that of moulding figures, and alſo the
art of caſting them in metals, is not quite decided; but he was
at leaſt maſter of thoſe arts, if Ariſtotle ſays rightly, that two
ſtatues repreſenting himſelf and his ſon Icarus were caſt by him,

---

* Apollod. lib. 2. c. 6. p. 126.   D'Ancarv. vol. 2. p. 292, note.
† Pauſan. lib. 7. c. 4. p. 531.   D'Ancarv. vol. 2. p. 285.
‡ Plin. lib. 7. c. 56.   § Diod. Sic. Bibl. lib. 4. c. 29.

the one in lead and the other in brafs[*]. In this circumftance, therefore, Pliny muft have been miftaken, when he gave the invention of the plaftic art to Theodorus and Rhæcus of the ifle of Samos[+], who did not come upon the ftage of life till the firft olympiad at fooneft[‡]: probably that author was mifled by confounding that Theodorus with another artift of the fame name, but a native of Miletus, who appears to have been cotemporary with Dædalus[§]. The genius of this laft artift feems to have been of a general kind in fculpture, to fay nothing of him as an architect; for among the many ftatues dif-perfed over different parts of Greece, which he made of his friend and cotemporary Hercules from various materials, one was made of pitch, which fo deceived Hercules himfelf, that miftaking it for a man in the night, he flung a ftone at the figure[||]. It was not merely in fingle figures that his art was feen. Paufanias tells us, that the Gnoffians had a bafs-relief in white marble by his hand, which reprefented the dance of Ariadne, defcribed after-wards by Homer in the Iliad[**]. The age itfelf appears to have been emulous of ingenuity: for Plutarch fays, that the Meropi-des, who lived in the fame period with Hercules, and confe-quently with Dædalus, firft conceived the idea of reprefenting the graces in the hands of the god of mufic[††]. And Endius did not fall fhort of that fpirit, when he executed at Erythræ th figure of the graces and the hours in marble[‡‡]. Hercules en-couraged that progrefs in genius; for he confecrated many figures in different parts of Greece, as well as the lion in ftone

---

* Ariftot. de Mirab. Aufcult.

‡ D'Ancarv. vol. 2. p. 292, note.

|| Apollod. lib. 2. c. 6. p. 126.

†† Plut. de Mufica, p. 1136.

† Plin. lib. 35. c. 12.

§ Athenag. Athen. regat.

** Paufan. lib. 9. c. 40. p. 793.

‡‡ Paufan. lib. 7. c. 5. p. 534.

at the temple of Diana Euclea in Thebes *. It was not long after that period, when Helen was carried off to Troy : and the curiofity of antiquarian refearch has difcovered that fhe then took with her a ring formed of an afterite ftone, or a ftone in the form of a ftar, which fhe ufed for a feal, and on which was engraved the figure of a fifh.+. Ulyffes alfo, who went to the war which followed that event, carried with him a ring, on which was engraved the figure of a dolphin : it is remarkable that Stefi-chorus fays, the fame figure was engraved on his ring and on his fhield ‡.

When it is faid by many authors §, that the Greeks had not arrived to the ufe of marble and ftone in ftatues until the time of Dipænus and Scyllis, that is, about the 50th olympiad; the inftan-ces which we have juft mentioned will be fufficient to evince the error of fuch an idea ‖, without adducing many others which may be drawn from antiquity. It is plain that thofe writers, who have reprefented the movements of Grecian fculpture as fo tardy, have been led by that progrefs of fkill which has appear-ed moft probable to their own minds, rather than by any atten-tive refearch into real facts. Or if an authority was reforted to, the filence of Homer concerning ftatues of marble and ftone is taken as a fufficient proof that no fuch works had exifted in Greece at the time of the Trojan war ; as if that poet was com-pelled to mention every thing that was then known and practifed in his country. The fact is, that hardly any materials can be named, in which ftatues have been formed, and which were not

---

* Paufan. lib. 9. c. 17. p. 743.
† Photii Biblioth. cod. 190. ex Ptol. Hephæft. lib. 7. p. 494.
‡ Plut. de folert. animal. p. 985. § Plin. lib. 36. fec. 4. Goguet, vol. 2.
‖ D'Ancarv. vol. 2. p. 286, 287. p. 227. Vol. 3. p. 87.

employed for that purpofe by Dædalus and his difciples*. Endius, we are affured, wrought many ftatues in ivory† : and there can be no doubt that his mafter had done the fame. Paufanias, de-fcribing the ftatues of Jupiter and Juno, which were in the tem-ple of that goddefs built at Olympia by Oxilus in the next cen-tury after Dædalus, and which were quite in the fimple ftyle of Dædalus himfelf, fays exprefsly that they were made not only of ivory but of gold ‡. It is improbable, that when the art of cafting ftatues in metal was known in the age of Dædalus, as we have already obferved, that age fhould be incompetent to the ufe of any metals whatever in which ftatues were caft at a time fo little diftant from it, and by artifts who had advanced nothing upon the execution of Dædalus himfelf. We fhall think lefs of the employment of gold and filver even in coloffal fculpture, when we recollect what was done in that way at Babylon, and in the temple of the ox at Japan, in ages far more remote, and perhaps lefs informed in many parts of art, than that of which we are fpeaking in Greece. And therefore when Homer, fpeaking of the Trojan war, which happened according to the Arundelian marbles 1209 years before the Chriftian æra, and within fifty years after the time of Dædalus, defcribes not only ftatues of gold §, but various other fculptures of extraordinary workman-fhip in gold, and filver, and ivory, and tin ‖ ; we have a reafon-able affurance from all the circumftances which have already been mentioned, and that affurance is capable of being ftrength-ened by many other collateral evidences of real works in fculp-

* D'Ancarv. vol. 2. p. 291, note.
† Paufan. lib. 2. c. 47. Lib. 8. c. 46. p. 694. D'Ancarv. vol. 2. p. 260, 285.
‡ Paufan. lib. 5. c. 27. p. 418.   § Iliad, lib. 18. v. 516.
‖ Iliad, lib. 18. v. 561. Lib. 28. v. 548. D'Ancarv. vol. 2. p. 290, 291.

ture which might be adduced, that neither in thofe particular details, nor on the fubject of the fhield of Achilles, he has merely indulged poetic fictions, but has defcribed what at leaft was in the capacity of the arts to accomplifh at the time of which he wrote *.

The truth is, whatever was moft rare and coftly in the materials of ftatuary, it was moft ardently coveted in thofe ages. of Greece; as if the confcioufnefs of what they wanted in tafte and execution fuggefted to them the probability of it's being made up by the luxury that was afforded in the materials themfelves†. The fame thing took place in the nations of Afia‡; with this dif- ference, that while they were intent on the coftlinefs of the mate- rials which they employed in the ftatues of their divinities, they were negligent from firft to laft of that which fhould have been their primary ftudy, the advancing towards perfection in the art; for they hardly ever rofe beyond a certain point of ability; whereas the Greeks, although deficient in tafte and fkill, did not fuffer their pride in materials to interrupt their progrefs in art. Neverthelefs fome ages elapfed before that pride ceafed to be a ruling paffion; they had not loft it even when they firft reached the high perfections of fculpture§.

When it is faid, that ftatuary itfelf was invented by Dædalus, or by him and Theodorus the Milefian together ‖, if by ftatuary be underftood the formation of the diftinct human figure, perhaps the idea is a juft one. Statues, which partook of the column

---

* D'Ancarv. vol. 2. p. 288.　　† Ibid. vol. 2. p. 296, 297.
‡ Ibid. vol. 2. p. 299—303.　　§ Ibid. vol. 2. p. 306, 307.
‖ Athenag. ubi fupra.

as well as of portions of the human frame, were certainly the oldeſt with which the Greeks were acquainted. Their great antiquity is marked in the examples, which have already been mentioned, of the Amyclean Apollo, and the Epheſian Diana ; and in others ſtill earlier by a century at leaſt, which might be adduced under Danaus *; but more eſpecially in thoſe on the tomb of Chorǣbus, which were earlier than all the others, and were the oldeſt ſtatues in ſtone which Pauſanias had ſeen in Greece †. Theſe were at once columns and ſtatues, not figures placed upon baſes, as the Latin interpreters have wrongly under-ſtood them to be ‡. Thoſe ſtatues, which more properly deſer-ved the name, by giving the parts of the human figure diſtinct, were certainly not older than Dædalus. The progreſs, by which ſtatuary advanced to the condition which it obtained under him, may be traced in antiquity, and will be properly related in this place.

Stones or columns of the obeliſkal form ſerved at firſt, as we have already remarked, to repreſent the divinity. In the mean time the influence of emblematic theology had eſtabliſhed living forms, and that of the ox in an early inſtance, as exemplificati-ons of the attributes and acts of the divinity, or at leaſt as a me-dium through which thoſe attributes and acts were contemplated. It was not long before new ſuperſtitions engrafted their growth on thoſe ancient emblems. It was conceived that the attributes of the divinity would be more diviniſed, if we may ſo ſpeak, and be lifted more ſublimely to the contemplation and the worſhip of man-kind, if they were not left to be viewed in the baſer animal alone,

---

* Pauſan. lib. 2. p. 154.   D'Ancarv. vol. 2. p. 281, 282.

† Pauſan. lib. 1. c. 43. p. 106:   ‡ D'Ancarv. vol. 2. p. 281, note.

if the ftamp of the human countenance at leaft, beyond which
the mind could raife itfelf to no created form, were added as the
mirror of thofe attributes.   In confequence of this, the ox affumed the human head, or it became united more or lefs in it's
parts to the human frame* ; for, not to have gone hand in hand
with the authority of primitive emblems, and with the fanction of
the ancient theology, was a meafure againft which that new theology itfelf would have revolted.   In that meafure, however, by
which the human head was feen affociated with a religious emblem, and of courfe connected with fome ideas of the divinity,
we are to confider the foundation laid for all the other ftatues of
divinities in human form, and for all the progrefs which was given
to fculpture in that way†.   That confequence became gradually
manifefted with the growth of national mythologies.   When
thefe took a ftrong poffeffion of the human mind, although the
fame reverence was ftill retained for the emblems of primitive
inftitution, neceffity feemed to dictate the reprefentation of that
new order of divinities by fome fpecific form, and that of courfe
was human.   The old timidity, which durft not feparate the
human head from the emblematic animal, was ftill unable to
go this new length without confulting at leaft popular feelings,
if not it's own private reftraints.   Therefore it only changed the
fhelter to it's movements ; it embraced one object of ancient reverence inftead of another ; the human head, and perhaps fomething more of the human form, was combined with thofe obe-
lifkal columns, whofe religious ufe had obtained the early attachment of the people‡.   Thefe were the firft ftatues of deities in
Greece : and if Eufebius and others be right in their authorities,

─────────

* D'Ancarv. vol. 1. pref. p. 15, 16.   † Ibid. vol. 1. p. 177.   Vol. 3. p. 137.
‡ Ibid. vol. 2. p. 281.

thefe were as old as Cecrops, who was fixty-three years older than Cadmus in Greece, and whofe arrival there is determined by the Arundelian marbles* to the year 1582 before our æra : thofe authorities tell us, that Cecrops firft introduced into the temples of Greece the ufe of images†, which could not have been any others than thofe columnal images of which we have fpoken. We muft recollect that the images on the tomb of Choræbus were placed there only forty years after Cecrops. If images, then, in that form were as old as that king of Athens, how much older muft have been thofe emblematic coins and medals with the ox and the human head ? We muft confider them as going back to the moft ancient times of the Greeks, to the times of the Pelafgi, who brought to Greece it's firft arts, it's firft emblematic theology, and it's firft letters too, long before Cadmus came into the country‡. However thefe things might be, refpectively, in point of antiquity, fo ftood the progrefs of ftatuary in the columnal image, when Dædalus came to refcue it from all it's confinements, and fhewed the way by which it might become more worthy of it's name.

It muft neverthelefs be confeffed, that however unworthy an emblematic theology was to detain fculpture always in it's trammels, and to fhut out the elegant views of Nature, it was owing to the influence of that theology, among other circumftances, that fculpture was pufhed in Greece not only fooner than painting, but more vigoroufly for many ages. The variety of ways; in which fculpture was enabled to meet the objects of fuch a the-

* Epoch, 1.
† Eufeb. Chron. lib. 2. p. 55. Præp. Evang. lib. 10. c. 9. p. 486.
‡ D'Ancarv. vol. 2. p. 366, 371, 372. Ifidor, Orig. lib. 8. c. 11. p. 69.

ology in coins, and medals, and ftatues, and bafs-reliefs; the facility with which thefe were made to enter into all the fituations and tranfactions of fociety, and to keep alive the principles of which they were the records, gave it a great advantage which could not equally be felt by painting. Befides thefe, fuperfti-tion as a paffion could not readily find in painting that force and effect of gratification, which no reprefentation can ordinarily bring fo home to fuch a mind as the image that is formed by the fculptor's hand. Perhaps the fublime and the beautiful, which we fhall find were not long before they took poffeffion of Grecian zeal, were gratified moft completely by that art which gave the human figure in it's fine proportions, and in all it's fineft expref-fions of character, to their full contemplation. Where nothing of that kind was concerned, the fpirit with which architecture was purfued took along with it the purfuit of fculpture as accef-fary at leaft to the other, and encreafed the demand for ftatues, and bafs-reliefs, and all the ornaments of the chiffel, which give dignity or grace to ftructures. Under thefe impreffions we can-not wonder to find the predilections for fculpture fo ftrong, and the perfections of it fo highly ftudied and advanced, as they were in a progrefs of time among the Greeks. Every city was a fchool emulous of it's exercife: every ifle, and every town in that ifle, ftrove to rival every other in the accomplifhment of that art. Nor was that zeal confined to any one age of Greece. We do not refer particularly to thofe periods in which fculpture feemed moft proud of it's powers, and felt the moft cherifhing encouragements. The fculptors who followed the age of Peri-cles, and that of Alexander, feem to have been no lefs anxious for their art than any that went before them.

It was well for the growth of fculpture, as an elegant tafte, that this love of it's perfections was fo warm in the Grecian breaft. For, without going back to times of which there may be no regular record, a thoufand years muft have elapfed in the hiftory of that people, in the courfe of which they muft have felt little elfe but thofe domeftic difcouragements, which are ever moft hoftile to ingenuity, and under which nothing fhort of a decided paffion for the fine arts could have fuftained any branch that is fo called. The times, to which we refer, were truly called heroic ; for then military atchievements and the fhedding of blood were the whole employment of the Greeks as a people. Public tranquility was not to be enjoyed, and then that which is private will rarely be known, or only with much imperfection. We fhall pafs by the numberlefs petty divifions which took place among themfelves, and reckon only the more eminent caufes of general commotion—the two wars of Thebes, which put all Greece into a flame, and the laft of which ended with the ruin of that city—the expedition of the Argonauts, which eventually brought on the ever-ruinous meafure of employing the flower of the country in a diftant land—the league next formed for the deftruction of Troy, which became the fource of the moft unhappy diforders in Greece—and, laft of all, the revolution which the return of the Heraclidæ caufed in Peloponefus, and which re-plunged Greece almoft into the fame barbarifm, from which the colonies formed by migrations from Afia and Egypt had drawn it. Let thefe events be reviewed, and then let it be faid, if amidft fuch circumftances the .Greeks had time to breathe. But in all thofe events another confequence was ripened, that every ftate was rendered poor, and weak, and inconfiderable, the neceffary care of individual prefervation precluding the power of cultivating the means of general welfare. Let that confequence be confidered, and then let it be faid, if it were eafy for the Greeks to cultivate the arts.

Thofe fcenes of turbulence undoubtedly kept back the Grecian genius extremely, and contributed to lengthen thofe fuccef-fions of time in which thofe arts were moving to any eminent advantage from the principles laid down by Dædalus. Some greater refpite indeed was given to thofe colonies which were pufhed out into Afia Minor within a century after Dædalus, in confequence of the general crufh which was felt by Greece in the conflicts brought on by the return of the Heraclidæ into Peloponefus; and in thofe colonies was undoubtedly laid the foundation of new ftrength to the general advantages of arts, and fciences, and literature too. They came prefently to enjoy a greater quietude, and they lay fomewhat nearer to a communication with the original fources of art in Afia and Egypt. But no diftinction muft be made between the degrees of cultivation in the colonies and the mother-country; however feparated nominally, and yet hardly feparated in fact, they were all equally Greeks, their communication with each other was conftant, and the progrefs of one was the progrefs of both. This obfervation, whofe truth is unqueftionable, will fettle at once all the fancied pretenfions to an originality of genius, or a priority of cultivation in the arts, which are fometimes fet up in favour of the former to the difadvantage of the latter. In both fituations, however diverfified by fome circumftances, we find the fame participation of general caufes, the fame retardation to the arts operating with an equal effect for the fame length of time; as if it were equally true in the political, as in the natural body, that the head and the members fhall all feel alike for the better or the worfe. If in any inftance thofe arts feemed to be more forward in the colonies than in the mother-country, it was in architecture only, for which a plain reafon may be given, that in the neceffity of founding new cities it's principles became more immediately important to new colonies. Whether they were original in thofe principles, a better opportunity than the prefent will hereafter be afforded to our difcuffion.

It will not appear furprifing, when we look back on thofe public events, affecting every part of Grecian fociety, that the principles of natural expreffion in fculpture, fuggefted by Dædalus, fhould have employed near 500 years before they were carried into any ftrong acquirements of tafte. At leaft, it was nearly that length of time before any monument of tafte appeared, concerning which we are enabled to fpeak from any records that have come down to us. We muft go for that monument to the period which faw the commencement of the Olympiads; but it is found at Corinth, and not in the Grecian colonies. The monument, to which we allude is the Coffer of Cypfelus, of which Paufanias has left fo fine and fo minute a defcription, to whofe account of it we fhall refer the reader*. That coffer was made of cedar, and the figures upon it were partly of gold and ivory, and partly formed in the wood itfelf. The report which Paufanias has given of that piece of art abundantly juftifies the judgement which M. D'Ancarville has paffed upon it's defign and execution. In the former, it was fuperior beyond all comparifon to the compofition of the bafs-reliefs on the fhield of Achilles: and in the latter, it may be confidered as equal to the ftate of fculpture in Italy in the 15th century†. This will be thought a high encomium indeed; and that monument deferves to be highly fpoken of for it's age: but this does not

* Paufan. lib. 5. c. 37, and 38.　　　† D'Ancarv. vol. 2. p. 329.

mean to fay that it's execution was in the firft tafte of Greece; for we muft be reminded that the fummit which was reached by fculpture in Italy in the 15th century was never equal to the perfection which it obtained in Greece.   In that ancient monument we find the firft openings, which antiquity has left to us, of that ideal beauty and that expreffion of character, which is certainly the moft important point in the art, and which the age of Dædalus could not convey.   To make that capacity peculiarly their own, and to carry it as far as it was capable of being carried, was the glory of the Grecian artifts.   And what muft we think of that genius, which amidft all the depreffions and tumults of the heroic ages, was enabled to raife itfelf up to that idea, and to carry on the progrefs of art to fuch a fpecimen as that monument afforded, near 800 years before the Chriftian æra, and near thirty years before the foundation of Rome.

It was that ideal beauty, and that expreffion of character, fo wonderfully perfected by the Greeks, without which all the arts, and particularly fculpture, muft have ftood for ever at the point in which they were left in Afia and Egypt, notwithftanding the degree of advancement which was gained by Dædalus.   The Greeks had been working their way to that ideal beauty, and that expreffion of character, through all the ftages of emblematic art; and the ftep that was taken by Dædalus was a happy movement towards it.   They began to perceive, that beauty could not be expreffed but by a harmony of proportions, and a regularity of forms, and that character muft be the refult of foul, or of foul combined with peculiar traits of figure.   It was neceffary therefore not only to get rid of every thing that was not confonant to Nature, but to affemble whatever was found moft perfect in that nature itfelf.   If power and ftrength were to be

difplayed, they would be exprefled with far more elegance, and
a more harmonious effect, by the amplitude and vigour of the
mufcles, and by the relative grandeur of the whole frame to all
it's parts, than by the multiplication of heads and arms. When
that beauty and character were applied to divine figures, and to
exprefs the attributes of Divine Nature, all emblematic forms
were gone; or, at leaft, the only emblem that remained (if fo it
can be called) was in that harmonious conftitution of fublimity
given to the figure, and diverfified according to the fuppofed
traits of the divinity to be reprefented, which made the human
frame to become the mirror of a divine beauty and a divine character, fuch as never could belong to itfelf. By means of thofe
ftudies the fpirit of art accomplifhed, in time, thofe divine ftatues
in Greece, which were never to be refembled by thofe of any
other country in the world, and whofe foundation in ideal beauty
and character became regularly conveyed into all the other fculptures that came from the hands of the Grecian mafters. They
were indebted for their firft and beft impulfe to thofe views of
art, and for fome rules of reaching them too, to the poems of
Homer, who had firft fhewn the capacity of forming divine
figures by his pen, and in whofe works they had found fuch animated defcriptions of beauty, and fuch continual eulogies of it
too, that the impreffion on tafte and genius became impoffible to
be refifted *.

The Greek artift did not draw altogether from the ftores of his
own mind that ideal beauty, whofe name may poffibly fuggeft
fuch an apprehenfion. It was fitly called ideal, when it was employed to conftitute the character of divinities : and it was alfo

* D'Ancarv. vol. 2. p. 311—314

ideal in a proper fenfe, when it was made up from the felection
of various exifting perfections in real Nature; becaufe in that
cafe the mind of the artift muft lead to that general determination of character, which not only precedes all choice of particular forms, but conducts the affemblage of all, and makes up
in the iffue what may ftill be left imperfect by any poffible combinations to conftitute the character intended.   The reader will
perceive from hence what were the means of which the Greeks
availed themfelves, to accomplifh that high perfection of beauty,
in divine figures.   They felected from many of the fineft human
forms thofe different traits of perfection, which beft fuited the
age and character given by mythology to that particular divinity; thefe they combined with fuch admirable artifice, that
the whole feemed to be either the copy of the mind itfelf, or the
copy of one only perfect form*.   Thus Zeuxis formed his He-
len†.   On thofe principles Polycletus completed his ftatue called
" the Rule."   The fame means were extended, and with the
fame good fenfe, to all greater fubjects by the pencil as well as by
the chiffel : Polygnotus led the way to it as a painter, making it
his maxim in the difplay of greater characters to give that refemblance which beautiful Nature afforded, but which he endeavoured to render ftill more handfome by the fupply of his own
mind.

That ftudy of ideal beauty never fuffered the Greeks to reft
till they had brought the general forms of their men and women
to be that beautiful Nature, which might be taken as a moft
finifhed model in their perfons for any fubject of character be-

---

* Maximus Tyrius Differt. 7.   Cicero de Invent. lib. 2. c. 1.
† Dionyf. Halicarn.   Plin. lib. 35. c. 9.

low divinity. Hence came that aftonifhing elegance of figure, with which all the Grecian fculptures, and we doubt not their paintings too, were marked ; and which were only tranfcripts of living Nature to be feen among them every hour of the day. The reply, which was made by Eupompus the painter to Lyfippus the fculptor, might have been made with truth by every artift in the country : when the latter was furveying a fine figure in a painting of the former, he afked, from what fculptor the model had been obtained ; to which Eupompus anfwered, pointing to crouds in the ftreets, "there are my models, 'tis Nature I follow, " we need not the models of a workman *". There is no doubt that Greece afforded more models of beautiful Nature in the hu- man frame than any country that ever was known. We will not contradiĉt the idea, that fo general an accomplifhment of figure might have been affifted by the influence of a moft mild and temperate climate. Hippocrates and Galen have both laid down that idea as a principle †. The truth of it is faid by travellers to be manifeft in Georgia, which they call "that country of beauty, " where a pure and ferene fky pours fertility‡" Yet we fhall not take the oracle's word for it, which gave to one element only, and that was to the lymph Arethufa, the power of forming beauty §.

Thofe peculiar advantages of Greece will ftand on better ground, when the ftudy to obtain and make them general was fupported by many regulations of policy, and bent to itfelf a va- riety of cuftoms and habits. They were the refult of the gym-

---

* Plin. lib. 34. fec. 19.   † Hippocr. περι τοπων, p. 288. Galen, p. 171. B. I. 43
‡ Chardin's Voy. Perf. vol. 2. p. 127, et feq.
§ Eufeb. præp. Evang. lib. 5. c. 29. p 226.

naſtic exerciſes of the Greeks ; of their diet, which was calculated to counteract corpulency ; of their dreſs, which never im-
peded the freeſt uſe of the limbs ; of their happy ignorance of
thoſe diſorders, which are moſt deſtructive to beauty ; and of
their various rules to avoid every deforming cuſtom. The caution of Alcibiades, when he was a boy, and refuſed to learn the
muſic of the flute, left it ſhould diſcompoſe his features, was
not peculiar to himſelf alone above all the other youths of
Athens. To theſe circumſtances we may add that univerſal eaſe
and freedom of manners, unreſtrained by the rigour of forma-
lity, which gave Nature to be ſeen in all her freeſt movements.
Thus the Greeks became models of the beautiful in either ſex.
And the opportunities of ſtudying thoſe models were as familiar
as poſſible : they were afforded by every ſolemnity, every feſti-
val, almoſt every public occaſion ; without fixing upon the people
an extravagant charge of indecency, or at leaſt without fixing thoſe
ſtrong impreſſions which might be ſuppoſed to ariſe from ſuch
opportunities, and which were conſiderably diminiſhed by the
force of habit. In conſequence of thoſe habits, the eye became
diſtinctly acquainted with the conſtitution and turn of beauty in
all it's attitudes ; the elaſticity of the muſcles, and the ever varying motions of the human frame in all it's ſituations were made
familiar to the artiſt in a far more perfect manner than can ordinarily be obtained from any hired models in modern academies *.
From thence they were enabled to digeſt into principles what
was thus familiar to their obſervations. They were enabled to
form certain general ideas of beauty, and certain rules of proportion as well for the inferior parts as for the whole. Theſe
came in time to be ſo perfectly eſtabliſhed, that if an individual

---

* Winckelm. Reflect. on Paint. and Sculp 8vo. p. 10.

appeared more beautiful than the generality, the standard by
which the comparison of that beauty was made was their sculptures—" he was as beautiful as a statue ;" reversing the language
which in modern sculpture would be used in such a case—" it is
the beauty of perfect Nature itself."

To follow that beauty of Nature, so acquired by the Greeks,
through all the concomitant circumstances in which it was mani-
fested in their sculptures, is to take up those sculptures in all their
characteristic perfections : it is to unfold those excellencies of
their art, which have gained the never-ceasing celebration of
ages. It is our duty to pay this debt to the memory of those
immortal artists ; and it is our happiness, that we are enabled·
from existing monuments to ascertain those characters of their
sculptures, which time has not suffered us to give of their paintings, unless by authority derived from others.

Yet we cannot take so wide a compass as is embraced by painting, when we speak of the powers of sculpture in a general view.
As a fine exhibition of Nature, undoubtedly she meets the eye,
and strikes the mind, with an advantage which is not always
derived from flat surfaces. Yet that advantage is narrowed
again by the scale of subjects to which it is confined, perhaps in
some measure by the nature of things, which does not easily give
it the capacity of addressing to our contemplations, with an equal
effect, multitudinous figures in a combined subject. This has
been attempted in bass-reliefs, but not with complete success,
especially by the ancients, whose imperfect knowledge in that
branch of perspective necessary to it became a considerable addition to all the other natural difficulties of the undertaking.
Nor have the moderns, with a more perfect knowledge of that

perfpective, been able to exhibit in the bafs-relief of fculpture the fame compafs and variety of fubject, which can be given by the pencil. Neverthelefs, the capacities of fculpture in all it's branches are admirable, and in the hands of the Greeks they muft demand an eulogium, which will need no enthufiafm of tafte to exalt and inflame it.

In all the Greek figures the precifion of contour was a ftrong characteriftic diftinction. By this contour we are to underftand not merely the delicacy of the extreme outline, but the correct proportions of parts which that outline contains. This was ad-jufted, in general, by the Greeks, with the niceft hand even in their moft tedious works, on gems ; although it is evident that the line by which Nature divides completenefs from fuperfluity is the fineft imaginable, and moft difficult to be hit : if ever it was miffed by them, it was in running into leannefs*, to avoid corpu-lency which of all things fhocked them moft. Perhaps there was another qualification to their correctnefs in this circumftance, that they exhibited the bony and cartilaginous parts of the body, fuch as the clavicles, the knees, the arms, &c. nearly as fmooth and even as thofe parts that were more flefhy. And yet we muft not carry this obfervation fo far as to forget, that the wrift-bones were often drawn with a degree of angular fmartnefs. The fact is, the delicate was their ftudy, in the purfuit of which they over-looked leffer niceties, although founded ftrictly in general Na-ture, which they thought it right to improve by the more beauti-ful, or to felect that more beautiful if it were found only in a fingle inftance of Nature. But, as we have already obferved, that more beautiful and harmonious regularity of frame was no un-common appearance in the figures, and efpecially in the youthful

* Plin. lib. 35. c. 10.

figures, of the country; fo that in felecting it they needed not
to depart from an exactnefs in copying Nature. The celebrated
gladiator of Agafias in the Borghefe may be taken as a ftandard
both of that fmoothnefs of parts, or want of bony prominence,
which we meet with in all the other Greek ftatues, and of Nature
as it commonly appeared among them. For the fculptor was
compelled by the Amphictyones, who were judges of his per-
formance, to take the victor at the public games in a ftrict refemblance of Nature, and in the very form and attitude of body,
in which he overcame his antagonift*. And that ftatue was in
all probability one of thofe that were erected in the places where
the games were held, to the memory of the feveral victors†.

The remark we have juft made on their attention to Nature,
amidft their decided attention to beauty, will require to be extended further. If that attention to Nature fhould be confidered
by us as moft judicioufly maintained by a fcrupulous attention to
minuter parts, the Greeks acted on a very different principle in
their ftatues. Their difcrimination of parts was marked very
fparingly; if thofe parts were beauties, they were touched more
with reference to a harmony in the whole than for their own fake;
if they were the particular expreffions of particular geflure, rifing
on the body, they were foftened down from wrinkles, or plaits, or
humid expanfions of the fkin, into eafy and regular undulations
embraced by the flefh, which harmonioufly followed their direc-
tion‡. Shall it be faid, that this is not ftrictly Nature? At leaft, it
is the moft graceful and moft healthy Nature, as well as it was more
eminently the Nature of the Greeks; and if it had been lefs emi-

---

* Lucian, pro Imagin. p. 490.   † Winckelm. ubi fup. p. 169.
§ Winckelm. ubi fup. p. 15.

nently fo, the Greek fculptor was not afraid to felect for the eye
what was moft graceful and moft healthy. If any moderns have
conceived that more truth and more ability are difcovered in the
purfuit of Nature under it's individual circumftances, abftracted
from the confervation of an harmonious beauty in the whole, their
claim to admiration will fucceed with thofe who have juft difcernment enough to applaud the moles or dimples of a portrait, but
furely their own minds muft be as devoid of fublimity as the age that
fhould embrace their principles would become devoid of it. The
mind of the fculptor, which is able to foar above the fenfes, and
to form a complete whole by combining perfections which his
mind fhall affemble, ennobles thofe perfections which he fo com-
bines, leads the general mind to great contemplations, and lifts
his own art into the dignity of inftruction, which otherwife may
be levelled to humble imitation. He rifes on the luftre of talents,
inftead of creeping in the tamenefs of induftry.

The Grecian drapery, under which the correctnefs of contour
was rarely loft to the eye, forms another object of confideration,
and of particular excellence. It took a ftyle of it's own, which
has never been mended, and never can, if grace and freedom and
harmony are permanent principles. It was grand, and elegant,
and natural. The fmaller foldings fprung gradually from the
larger, and were loft in them again with perfect eafe, each relieving the other, and the whole difplaying an uniformity of truth
and fkill. There was nothing ftiff, nor abrupt, nor heavy; nothing huddled indifcreetly together; all was eafy, undulating,
and harmonioufly graceful. Thefe principles were maintained
in all their draperies, whether of a coarfer or finer kind; for
in fome of their reliefs, in their bufts, and in their pictures, draperies of a coarfer kind were admitted. But, in general, thefe

were of peculiar finenefs, and efpecially thofe of the Greek ladies, whofe robes took from thence the name of *peplon*. The thin floating texture was their prevailing tafte. In the difpofition of this, more or lefs licence was ufed according to the nature of the character. Bacchanals and dancing figures, even if they were ftatues, had garments more waved, and playing more upon the air. So the draperies appear for the moft part on their gems. Yet in all thefe the Greeks were extremely cautious not to exceed the nature of the materials. In gods and heroes, whom the mind reveres as the inhabitants of facred and awful dwellings, that wafted airy fyftem of drapery gave way to another more fimple, chafte, and modeft, and more fuitable to the gravity of their characters. Still the thin floating texture continued to form their general drapery. It miniftered to more ufes than fancy. It was a part of their predominant defire to difplay the correctnefs and precifion of their contour. Thofe thin draperies clafped the body, and difcovered the fhape. Thus their favourite contour was not loft, perhaps it was helped in the proportion wherein it might cafually or purpofely be hid. How far, and whether for the better, thofe thin draperies fo elegantly and fo advantageoufly employed by the Greeks have been abandoned by the moderns, will more properly be enquired under thofe periods in which the arts of the moderns fhall be reviewed.

The expreffion attained by the Greeks is the laft obfervation we fhall need to employ on their fculptures. And fomething more is neceffary to be faid on this circumftance, in addition to what has already been fcantily advanced. Many ages elapfed before they became mafters of this expreffion, even after their fculptures had acquired confiderable tafte in other refpects; and their philofophers had contributed greatly to fix this power.

Their paintings acquired it ; and it was their philofophers who affifted their paintings. Indeed their great painters were philofophers themfelves ; and therefore when Paulus Emilius defired the Athenians to give him a painter and philofopher to inftruct his children, they fent him Metrodorus*. In the Areopagetic fchools, and in the council-houfe at Athens, to name no other inftances, was collected a moft copious affemblage of expreffion in the portraits of all the great philofophers of Greece, drawn with that ftrength and accuracy of character peculiar to each, which gave their fouls to the eye†, and which has been ever fince affumed in every reprefentation of them which is moft legitimate. There was a language too, and a fentiment, in the writings of thofe philofophers, from which fame could never be withheld, and which therefore naturally found their way into the kindred writings of the fculptor and the painter. The ftudies of thofe philofophers were directed to the inveftigation of characters and manners : it was their zeal to explore, and their glory that they did well explore, all the latent receffes of the human heart, and all the fubtle difcriminations of human paffions : they followed virtue and vice through all their diftinct fhapes : and how much foever their theory of morals may appear to more enlighted minds to have been mixed with error and imperfections, moft certainly the pictures which they have drawn of thefe are as highly finifhed as could be done within the fcale of their principles ; and all their delineations of life and characters, of fentiments and meafures, are drawn with an energy which could not eafily be exceeded by any pen in the hands of genius.

Here therefore were examples of expreffion, naturally extending their influence to every part of tafte—examples, to

* Plin. lib. 35. c. 11.   † Sidonius Apollinaris, lib. 9. epift. 9.

which the hand that held the pencil or the chiffel was as competent as that which directed the pen—examples, which would have left us indeed to wonder if they had not been univerfally emulated by that active fentiment which diftinguifhed the Greeks. It was juft as reafonable to expect that their fculptors would breathe into all their ftatues and figures that force of expreffion in which they had feen the philofophers to fucceed fo well, as that Phidias fhould mould his Jupiter after the traits afforded by Homer. Plato, living in an age when that vigour of fentiment and expreffion was at the higheft, and helping not a little to kindle the fire of emulation which naturally fprung from it, might well fay of the fculptors then exifting, that "it "would be a fhame indeed if their ftatues were as tame as thofe "that were done in the age of Dædalus."

In the beft age of their philofophy, in the Socratic and Platonic fchools, the human mind was feen in a peculiar elevation. A dignity of fentiment was highly maintained, which fhewed the influence of philofophy, or, as they meant it, of virtue in an afpect which was certainly worthy to be admired, and the more fo becaufe it was of all things the moft difficult to be reached. Philofophy then looked down with neglect on every thing in the human mind that was not fuperior to every other thing which could invade, or at leaft overfet, it. It was marked by a fimplicity, which fought within itfelf alone what can beft ennoble the human character—a ferenity, fed by the confcioufnefs of that fimplicity—a fteadinefs, which would not be defpoiled of the principles which had become it's anchor—a grandeur conftituted by the habits of fuperior contemplation, and by that heroifm of feeling, which in the confcioufnefs of tried virtue mounts no higher than the calmnefs of fatisfaction; in the hurry of joy, exhibits no more than an inward pleafure; in the experience of great mifery, temperates anguiſh by fortitude; and in the tumul- tuouſneſs of thickening misfortunes, rides majeſtic in the whirl- wind, and unfubdued in the ſtorm.　This fedateneſs, this con- templative dignity of character, became the foul of fculpture, and marked with it's geſture and expreſſion the moſt approved Greek figures.　Hence they never failed to carry in their aſpect the impreſſions of a cultivated wiſdom, of a foul becalmed and ſtrengthened by reflection.　Look upon the Niobe, and all theſe principles of Grecian expreſſion are illuſtrated: in the utmoſt pangs of Nature ſhe continued ſtill the heroine, difdaining to yield to Latona.　Among other features, the clofed lip has ever been the index of the thoughtful mind.　How varied foever this fe- dateneſs might be under the preſſure of incumbent circumſtances, you never fee any of the Greek figures, unleſs in the expreſſion of contempt or great pain, with an open mouth.　The mouth of the Laocoon is open, and it is a ſtrong confirmation of our re- marks that under all his excruciating agony it is only fo much open as pain compelled.　That fedateneſs and ſtrength of foul, ſtruggling againſt the ſtrife of torture, is the more confpicuous when it fubmitted only to afford a proper vent to the groan that would be difcharged.　Had he not afforded that vent, had not the anguiſh within broken through all the refiſtance of firmneſs, and combined itſelf with that firmneſs in the countenance, all would have been outrageouſly unnatural, and inſtead of a fedate fortitude we ſhould have beheld a compofition of ſtill-life, of ſtrange quietude which might poſſibly not difguſt in the Spartan boy, who was the creature of cogent difcipline, or which might pleafe in the ſtoic, who was the hardy bigot to opinionated pride, but certainly would not do juſtice to that free and rational energy of fpirit in philofophy at large, which counts it a fufficient triumph that it can balance fufferings by fortitude, and maintain a portion of tranquility combined with the inevitable traits of affliction, but greatly fmoothing their furrows.

The tranquility, which was the fruit of the Grecian philofophy, affected no more than this; and this it could and did accomplifh. In this, therefore, fculpture was dignified as well as the fchool of the philofopher.

And it was not merely the expreffion of the countenance, but the whole attitude was governed by this principle of fedate and eafy dignity. The Greeks conceived that the pureft reprefentation of character was when it was feen in private, and as little as poffible impreffed by external circumftances. Their figures therefore muft be beheld as the images of thofe who thought themfelves alone and unobferved, who are looking only into themfelves, and whofe deportment is fuch as would naturally arife if they appeared before men of fenfe. No matter what is their pofture, whether they ftand, or fit, or lie down, it is with perfect eafe. Their fituation is always quiet, and the direction of every limb and member fpeaks that natural and eafy pofture which unites with a quiet fituation. The attitudes of Bacchanals only are violent, although in Bacchanals that violence does not reach the countenance, through which it is only a dawn of luxury that peeps. The Greeks confidered what was violent in gefture or feature, however urged by incumbent paffion, to be vulgar, to be natural indeed with common minds, and likely to ftrike a common eye with applaufe, but greatly below the true propriety of expreffion, becaufe it was below what could ever be found in a great man poffeffed of elegant and improved conceptions. Their ideas alfo, and their emulations, of grace, which cannot exist where the passions are violent, would not suffer them to select the expression which was excessive.

That circumstance was so much avoided, that they avoided even what was accumulated in expression. Their sublime was conveyed in great simplicity; they studied to express much in little, and they were complete masters in that superior management of *a little*, which not only distinguishes artist from artist, but draws the best line between the more and the less able in all parts of learning. Thus Homer, making all the gods to rise from their seats when Apollo enters, leaves far behind him in the true sublime all the ostentation of heathen theology,. So in the Laocoon, again, the pain and indignation which twist the nose, and the paternal sympathy which dims the eye-balls, are strokes of the highest expression, which produce a multiplicity and refinement of feelings to be reached by no complex attempts, and to be discovered only by those who are able to understand them *.

The only question which remains to be asked is, whether this sage dignity, and this energetic concisenefs, of expression in the sculptures of Greece, unquestionably involving the sublime of character, may be committed without prejudice to the young artist, whether sculptor or historic painter, as the model by which his first studies should be formed. It may be said, and it has been said †, that this purity of style, being stript of all that is excrescent, redundant, or very strong in expression, would narrow

* Winckelm. ubi sup. p. 255. 8vo.
† Objections to Winckelm. Reflect. p. 114. 8vo.

the genius of the youthful artift, and caufe him to neglect the
purfuit of Nature and character through all the variety of their
plainer and more common difcriminations—that in the youthful
efforts of genius there fhould be fome fuperfluity, fomething to
be taken off—and that it is eafier to amputate what is fuperfluous
than to communicate what is ufeful, as it is eafier to lop the
young rank branches of a vine than to give it vigour. The figure,
in which this argument is put, being grounded on the elegance of
Cicero*, may poffibly give it fome advantage. But the analogy
is not correct; nor is the conclufion juftly drawn from the excrefcencies which it may be proper to indulge and to nurfe in the
general vigour of talents, to a fimilar encouragement of fuperfluity in the fublime of tafte. The fire of genius will, in proportion to it's intenfenefs, become in time a more genial glow, as
the juices of the grape, when mellowed by age, become in proportion to their original ftrength a more rich and generous cor-
dial. But the fublime of tafte can never become more pure or
more mellowed than it is at once; there is nothing fuperfluous in
it, nothing to be lopped; it is the perfection of truth and Nature; nothing that is common or ordinary can enter it's compofition; and when attained, the artift that is capable of it is under
no temptation to employ in it's ftead, in thofe works which are
worthy of it, whatever may fall fhort of it's fpirit and it's ftandard. Yet, how does it narrow the genius, or the views of natural character? The mind, which can felect from the various
groups of expreffion that which is moft finifhed, muft be mafter
of all: the mind, which can comprefs a powerful fentiment or
feeling, muft be equal to the fkill which would fpeak them more
at large: the mind, which can combine what is thus felected and

* De Oratore, lib. 2. c. 21.

compreffed, muft have powers commenfurate to the fineft expreffion of art.

But the queftion may be reverfed, and it may be afked, if there
is not more danger to the perfection of art in the latitude of the
fuperfluity which is to be lopped than in the more corrected
compafs of the true fublime. In the firft there is much to be
unlearned ; in the laft there is nothing. To unlearn is the moft
difficult part of fcience, becaufe the mind naturally clings to
what it has purfued and made it's own. But to unlearn in fpeculative fcience is far lefs difficult than to unlearn in practical
tafte ; becaufe in tafte, whatever it be that is embraced, the mind
is in a manner made up, and derives from it's talent not only a
fatisfaction but a pride which it will not eafily furrender. In the
queftion before us, the ftudies which have purfued paffions and
feelings in their more ordinary appearances, from the perfuafion
that nothing is feen in fo much truth as when it is expreffed moft
at large, are moft likely to retain the habits of their bias in moft
frequent inftances, becaufe the bulk of mankind are attracted
moft by that which is moft commonly before their eyes ; to this
a far greater portion of artifts will be competent than to the
rarer beauties of the fublime, which requires a peculiar ftrength
and conftitution of mind to difcern it, and for which an artift
muft look inwardly into himfelf, in a confiderable degree. With
the greater part, therefore, the ftyle of expreffion which participates leaft of the fpirit and perfection of the Greeks, will be retained longeft, notwithftanding the more refined purity to which
they may afterwards be introduced ; becaufe that ftyle of expreffion firft occupied their ftudies, and formed their minds ; and
with the remaining few, if ever it yields to that more refined purity of Grecian expreffion, it is from a peculiar elevation of

fpirit and ftrength of judgement capable of difcerning the difference, and ftudioufly cherifhing the perfections which they have
difcerned. The firft fort, even fuppofing them lefs elevated in
fpirit and lefs ftrong in judgement, if they had been earlier impreffed with that fublimity of expreffion, might have rifen to
thofe capacities in it, of which the paft train and influence of
their ftudies will not fuffer them to be fenfible : and the latter,
under the fame early advantages, would become Greeks themfelves. How fhould it be otherwife? There is no more labour
to the mind, free and difengaged, allowing for the difference of
natural capacities, in the cultivation of a finer direction than in
the purfuit of one more humble. It may as well be trained to a
fenfe of the moft exquifite perfection as of that which is fubordinate. It is not neceffary that its refinement fhould advance
through the ftages of vulgarity ; nor that it fhould find it's way
to the fublime, which it cultivates, through any other principles
than thofe which conftitute the fublime. The foundations of art
laid in thofe principles promife the fureft prevention of mediocrity, they give the happieft earneft of elevation, and therefore
they muft certainly be laid in the greateft wifdom. Let the mind
be ftored with thofe principles before it has become engaged by
others lefs perfect, and they will be confirmed by habit, they
will become rooted by maturing judgement, the tafte and ftyle
that are acquired will affimilate to themfelves all the ftudies and
all the powers that fhall follow, not in the way in which principles lefs perfect would fo affimilate by the mere force of prejudice, but by that full fatisfaction of fentiment, which invariably
in polite art, however variably it may act in moral virtue, being
once impreffed with a confcioufnefs of dignity and elevation,
will never ftoop to embrace what is of a lower character, but

will make all things neceffarily pure to the purity of which itfelf is poffeffed.

The man of art, therefore, like the man of literature, cannot
too foon become familiar with thofe ftudies which open the views
of elegance, and with thofe examples which rivet them on the
mind.   It is by this method that any moderns have reached the
fublime of expreffion, and have maintained it as a feature of
their own character in art.   It was by this method that Raphael
made it his own.   He carefully ftudied all the antiques within his
reach, and of the perfections of fuch as were not within his own
reach he fpared no pains to become poffeffed by means of the
beft copies which others were employed to make for him. In him
therefore we fee all the fuperior felection of Grecian expreffion
revived, the dignity, the fedatenefs, the chaftity, the contem-
plative force, and energetic concifenefs of character; not borrowed, but original; moving indeed on the fpirit of the ancients,
but exercifing that fpirit in the free contemplation of Nature
through all the varied ftrength of fuperior character, and therefore making that fpirit his own ; difplaying the fruits of it in all
that natural variety from the original ftock which it will acquire
when lodged in a new breaft, as the bloffoms of a tranfplanted
tree differ from thofe that fprung in it's native foil.   Thefe indeed were not Raphael's firft views of art ; he faw nothing of
thefe in the fchool of Perrugino, nor in the fchools of Urbin :
but he no fooner became apprized of them at Rome, than the
foundnefs of his underftanding, and the maturity of his genius
grafped them all ; leaving to all that came after him this important leffon from his example, that the ftudy of Nature and of the
human mind in all it's higher feelings is the confummation of art ;

that the works of thofe ancients, who uniformly purfued and happily reached this confummation, muft be the eternal ftandards of inftruction from whence it muft be drawn ; that the fooner we become imbibed with it's principles, the fooner we move in the right path to greatnefs ; that without it we may be juft, we may be natural, we may be excellent in various ways, but we can never be fublime.

To the Greeks therefore let the young artift, whether fculptor or painter, go for fublimity of expreffion. I fay, for fublimity of expreffion; not meaning to urge to the painter that unqualified idea which has mifled fome, and to which thofe fculptures muft obvioufly be incompetent, of being univerfally profitted by them in his art. But in the fublimity of expreffion unqueftionably the difcovery of antique fculptures afforded a very important advantage to modern art in the painter's hand. Thofe fculptures difplayed the mind : they aimed at a character rather than an individual expreffion, even where there was a neceffity to preferve refemblance, and where they did preferve it : they foared from the humbler to the more elevated difplay, from the perfonal to the moral, from the private object to the public inftruction. So far they become models of ftudy to the hiftoric painter ; thefe are the emulations of his pencil; in thefe we expect to find the fuperiority of his talents. His judgement difcreetly exercifed will readily difcriminate the circumftances, in which thofe fculptures may become proper models to his pencil. To them the firft abilities in his art have been indebted for their beft perfection in modern ages : the fpirit of defign, which they have infufed, has given celebrity to many who have been vifibly deficient in other powers: and where the advantages of them has not been enjoyed, the want of that advantage has been the grand *defideratum* which the moft original abilities have not been able to fupply.

<hr>

CHAP. II.

The climate of Greece favourable to painting—whether Pliny be
right in the latenefs which he has given to it's firft effays in
that country—the fteps by which it's firft progrefs was marked
—the picture of Bularchus—the farther progrefs of the pen-
cil, and of the arts in general, obfcured by the adverfity of
public circumftances for 272 years till the retreat of Xerxes—
that retreat the firft epoch of vigour to all the Grecian arts—
the progrefs of painting in the hands of all the more celebra-
ted artifts from that period to the death of Alexander the
Great—it's higheft fame clofed with that age.

THE art of the pencil added in it's progrefs no lefs than that of the chiffel to the glory of Grecian genius. Whether or no it was true, that the climate of Greece was propitious to the production of beautiful forms in it's people, there feems to be no doubt that the painter derived many advantages from thence to the exercife of his art. He enjoyed a clear and vivid fky, fo needful for the beft lights; and a temperate, dry, and healthy air, fo convenient for the prefervation of his works. The country was verdant, and mellowed in all it's natural productions, which affifted the artift in his imagery and fcenes. Can there be a queftion that thofe caufes contributed to the lively and active turn of mind, by which the Greeks were marked? And why may not the feeds of genius, like thofe of animal and vegetable nature, depend on the influences of fky, and be capable of nutrition, advancement, or repreffion by the operations of the atmofphere?* We know how the Greeks would have anfwered that queftion, by their cenfure of Bæotia. And although the cenfure might poffibly originate in prejudice, and certainly was gainfayed by a few fplendid exceptions, yet if the principle laid down in fome codes of jurifprudence be true, " the exception " proves the rule†".

Illuftrious as the Greeks became in painting, it was but late in ages when any evidences of it, which we can call by that name, appeared among them. If Pliny had any authority for his affertion, that Euchir the father of Dædalus firft made it known to them, then what he has faid in another paffage muft alfo be true, that it was not underftood in Greece at the Trojon war‡. If we could believe that Pliny meant there to fpeak of it as a regular art, in any ftages of colouring, we might perhaps fubfcribe to his opinion, having no evidences to the contrary. But if it be underftood in it's fimpler ftages of mere defign, we can fee no reafon why the Greeks fhould not have been capable in their earlieft periods of thofe traits, which have appeared coeval with the earlieft periods of all the people of the earth. The fact is, that Pliny has ftudioufly endeavoured to modernize as much as poffible the introduction of this art in Greece, even in thofe cruder traits of defign from which it did probably firft advance among every people, to whom it was not brought at once in

* See Cumberl. Anecd. vol. 1. p. 198.   † Coke on Littleton, fæpe.
‡ Plin. lib. 35. c. 9.

VOL. I.   R r

better flages of progrefs.   For in the account which he has given
of thofe cruder traits of defign, while he has mentioned no periods to which they might refpectively be referred, he has advanced the names of particular men as the authors of every new
ftep, moft of whom appear from fome collateral circumftances
not to have been older than the war of Troy.   In this part of
his relation we have reafon to apprehend that he was biaffed by
a defire of making the Romans appear in this inftance of art
more forward than the Greeks.   For, having carried down thofe
fimpler traits of defign in Greece to the very fimpleft ftate of
colouring in a period coeval with Romulus, he adds this fingular
declaration, that "*even then* painting was perfect in Italy;" of
which he gives as proofs fome paintings in a temple at Ardea,
and others at Lanuvium in Tufcany*.   With refpect to the intereft which Rome may have in this queftion, we fhall pafs that
by for the prefent ; obferving only, that time has certainly left
Pliny in the poffeffion of his affertions, as to Greece, having
left us in the poffeffion of no pofitive evidences to contradict
him : the firft evidence of any regular picture in that country,
which antiquity has fuffered to come down to us, is undoubtedly
coeval with the age of Romulus.   We fhall neverthelefs judge
for ourfelves in this matter from that natural courfe of things
which has fhewn itfelf in other countries, and from which the
great antiquity of the Greeks fhould give us no caufe to conclude
that they were excepted.

The fteps, however, by which that author has reprefented
painting as rifing into power among the Greeks are natural, and
may properly be embraced.   It's firft effays were content with

* Plin. ubi fup.

the external lines of objects formed by the shade of the figure in the sun, and therefore called *shiography*. The name of Saurias is mentioned by Pliny as the first who drew a horse in that manner[*].

Within those external lines the internal parts of the figure, as the limbs, shoulders, hips, &c. were next attempted, but still in simple lines[†]; and therefore this stage of design was called *monography*. Sometimes Philocles the Egyptian or Cleanthes the Corinthian, at other times Ardices of Corinth and Telephanes of Sicyon, are referred to by Pliny for the first idea of this improvement[‡]. This monography, or lineal drawing, although it be found among the infant movements of design, must not be considered as of despicable capacity. Without supposing those ancients, by whom it was first practised, to have carried it's powers of expression to that developement of character and passion, which we have seen accomplished by it in modern days, yet we are assured by Philostratus[§], that those ancients could give it not only a degree of relief in particular parts, but such an expression as distinguished the general cast of the character, and such an approximation to colour in the general figure as shewed whether the individual were white or tawny.

In those stages of picture there was no colour employed[||]. The next step therefore was from simple design to simple colour, called the *monocromatic*[**]. We are not to conclude that any one colour only was known or used, for the Greeks embraced four primi-

---

[*] Plin. lib. 35. c. 3.
[‡] Plin. ubi sup.
[||] Plin. ubi sup.

[†] Quint. Inst. Orat. lib. 11. c. 6.
[§] De Vita Apollonii, lib. 2. c. 10.
[**] Ibid. & cap. 8.

tive colours from the firſt*; but only one colour was uſed at one time, and in one objeƈt, under the monocromatic. Pliny therefore, ſpeaking of thoſe works, very accurately ſays, and moſt conſiſtently with what the Greeks knew of colour, *ſingulis coloribus*, not *ſingulo colore*. Hygiemon, Dinias, and Charmas are mentioned by that author in one paſſage, and in another Cleophantus of Corinth, as the inventors or firſt praƈtiſers of that ſingle colouring. Under this head he has come much cloſer to the point of time, and it is produƈtive of ſome conſequence; for he ſays that Hygicmon, Dinias, and Charmas were *aliquanto ante Bularchum*, " ſome little time before the painter Bularchus," who was much better known in his period at leaſt than all the reſt.

Before we get to that painter it will be proper to remark, on the authority of Pliny himſelf, that in the uſe of the monocromatic there were two other artiſts who appeared very eminent, and gave a conſiderable extenſion to the powers of that ſimplicity of painting. Theſe were Eumarus the Athenian, and Cimon of Cleonæa†. Till theſe men appeared we muſt conclude that the monocromatic was vilely dull and infenſible, and that inſtead of mending, it had only prejudiced, the more diſtinƈt expreſſion of lineal drawings. For the praƈtice had been to repreſent alike all figures of the ſame kind, without diſtinƈtion of ſexes; and the uſe of it had not been carried to all kinds of figures. Both thoſe defeƈts were remedied by Eumarus. Yet much more was left to be done by Cimon his pupil, who was deſtined to riſe greatly upon the ſteps by which his maſter had advanced‡. For there was ſtill much ſtiffneſs and barbarity left

* Plin. ubi ſup. & cap. 7.   † Ibid. lib. 35. c. 8.

‡ Felib. vol. 1. p. 53, 54.

in every figure, and a great want of action and variety. Thefe
were referved for the genius of Cimon to do away, even with
the fimplicity of the monocromatic pencil. He threw his figures
into different attitudes, by which means he ftarted the firft ideas
and fpecimens of forefhortening*. For fo much is certainly im-
plied in the word *catagrapha*, along with the varieties of attitude
adduced by Pliny as illuftrations of his meaning, which could
not be done without forefhortening. The improvements of Cimon were not confined to the general frame. He gave diftinctly the joints of the limbs, and the veins of the body, in all his
nude figures ; and in his draperies he difcriminated the folds and
wrinkles. On thofe accounts it is no wonder that Cimon, more
than all the painters who lived before him, has been the fubject
of celebration by the pens of the learned from Ælian† to Gro-
tius‡. He was the firft great man that held the pencil in Greece ;
and he was the more extraordinary for his capacity of making
it productive of fo much expreffion in fo confined a compafs of
action.

We do not mean to urge thofe improvements of Cimon as
contradictions to Pliny's affertion, that the monocromatic was
firft brought into ufe " a little while before Bularchus," who was
coeval with the age of Romulus ; although, if we had not taken
that author's report, who has exprefsly ranked Cimon among
the monocromatic painters, we might have been led to infer
from fome circumftances in his improvements, either that he had
been earlier in time, and had fhewn his great and original powers in lineal drawings, or that he had been ftill later, and had

* Plin. ubi fup.   † Hift. Div. lib. 8. c. 8.
‡ Tranflat. Epigram. Anthologia.

arrived to the ufe of more colours than one. But an obfervation of Quintilian averts every dfficulty on this head. He
obferves, that "the ancient painters in the monocromatic could
" fo manage the fingle colour which they ufed, as to give every
" appearance of relief to parts, by making fome things to rife,
" and others to fall*". Let it pafs then, for any thing in the
example of Cimon, that the Greeks had gotten no further than
to the monocromatic painting a little before Bularchus.

If that were the cafe, the picture which has faved the name of
that artift from oblivion, muft have been either a monocromatic
execution, or but very little advanced beyond it. That picture
is undoubtedly the oldeft of which we can fpeak in Greece. It
reprefented, on fome confiderable fcale†, a battle of the Magne-
fians, a people of Afia Minor, fought in defence of the Jonians
and Eolians‡; and it was bought for it's weight in gold by Candaules king of Lydia, cotemporary with Romulus§. This laft
circumftance has generally impreffed thofe, to whofe knowledge
it has reached, with the idea that the pencil muft have been in
great power at that time in Greece. And yet it is poffible that
the language, reprefenting the purchafe, may fuggeft a more
enormous price than that which was paid, in fact, for the picture, whofe materials might not be heavy. Be that as it may,
there is no arguing on that ground to the merit of any work of
art in ages fo very remote, and fo little acquainted with the
perfections of which it was capable, where the purchafer too was
a prince for whom a Pactolus flowed, and turned up it's fands in
gold. If Bularchus, coming after Cimon, had the fortune to

---

* Quint. lib. 11. c. 3.   † Haud mediocris Spatii.   Budæus, lib. 7. c. 38.
‡ Bibl. Photii Art. 186.   § Plin. lib. 35. c. 8.

profit by the difcoveries which that artift had made, and if his picture exhibited the powers which Cimon could have exempli- fied, then there was juftly an eftimation due to it in that age, whatever was the ftate of it's colouring ; and all fubfequent ages have reafon to look with much refpect on the capacities then reached by the Grecian painters, how fhort or how long foever had been the time in which they had moved to thofe capacities. What the pencil had gained under Cimon amounted to this : it had at- tained the difcrimination of corporeal parts, with fome of the finer textures of the corporeal frame, as the joints, and the veins : it had reached the difcriminations of natural character ; action, and gefture in great variety ; and what was far more difficult than all the reft, forefhortening : it was mafter of much truth and neat- nefs in drapery. Thefe no doubt are all capable of various ftages of perfection ; and much more than thefe is neceffary to the full perfection of the art : we muft confider them here in a mediocrity of pretenfion. But if thofe talents fo qualified were fhewn in the picture of Bularchus, then let it have been bought for it's weight in gold, Candaules did not beftow his money for nothing. Whether or no Quintilian had that picture in view, he evidently fpeaks of paintings in the character of thofe times, and his obfervations feem to fettle the point of general merit on the one hand, and of general eftimation on the other, on a reafona- ble ground, although it be indeed fomewhat lower than one fhould expect from an eftimate which had paid a proper attention to the improvements of Cimon. He fays, " the firft works of the " pencil, recommendable in fact for their antiquity more than " for any thing elfe, perfectly fimple and without variety in " their colouring, yet as being the early productions of a grow- " ing art, or, if you will, the prefages of future brilliancy, na-

" turally pleafed and charmed all by their imperfect fketches,
" not to fay by their very groffnefs and barbarity *".

There can be no doubt but the genius and induftry, which had
carried the pencil thus far, would not ceafe their exertions to improve it's gifts.   And yet we muft lofe fight of thofe exertions for
a period of 272 years from the age of Bularchus. It is not painting alone, but the whole chain of the arts, that we lofe for that
period, unlefs in a few inftances hardly worthy of obfervation.
It is not neceffary to fuppofe, nor is it true, that they were all
ftagnate for that length of time. They kept themfelves alive,
they enjoyed vegetation, they crept on infenfibly, or there could
have been no foundation for the burft with which they came forth
at the end of that period ; but they were kept down by a concatenation of circumftances from becoming either potent in themfelves, or confpicuous to the world.   Thofe circumftances were
the iffue of the public government, partly conducted upon
ftrange and capricious principles, partly converted into a general
fcourge by feverity, partly difturbed, and partly overthrown by
revolutions : they were thofe public caufes, under which the fine
arts have ever fhrunk, and ever muft fhrink, if they do not ex-
pire, in every country upon earth.   It is our bufinefs to detail
thofe circumftances, which we fhall do with all poffible brevity.

At the commencement of that period, in which we left Bularchus, 720 years before the Chriftian æra, Athens, the moft
favourable of all the Grecian governments to the prefervation
of the arts, was governed by Archons, whofe power was limited
to ten years. However fatisfactory that fyftem might be to the

---

* Quint. Inft. Orat. lib. 12. c. 10.

people in the view of liberty, it was by no means equally pro-
mifing to the arts with that plan of government, which had left
the Archons in rule for life. For where the chief magiftrate
was to refign his fituation at a determinate time, and to account
for the whole of his adminiftration to a people who were perhaps
capricious, and perhaps rendered averfe to him, his patronage
was very unlikely to be fpirited, and the emulation of artifts
would confequently be tame. We fhall find in all the ages of
Greece, that notwithftanding the fine arts had a tenure of countenance there which they knew not in any other fituation, yet the
patronage which bore them up flowed principally from thofe
who held the reins of government. The truth and the importance of that fact was fully illuftrated under the Archons. While
they were continued for life, the arts had gained every progrefs
which we have hitherto related ; and upon the acceffion of de-
cennial Archons thofe arts began to retire from our view.

A revolution of nine Olympiads produced another revolution
in the government, more inimical ftill to thofe arts, by limiting
the Archons to one year, and inftead of one, appointing nine to
fhare the authority. That more decided overthrow of regular
patronage, which took place 680 years before our æra, proved
equally the overthrow of all civil reform, and of all order itfelf,
beyond the worft effects by which regal power had ever been
marked in any times. And from that hour, if we except the
diforders and exceffes naturally arifing from a fyftem which left
no fettled authority, nor any fettled plans of adminiftration, a
dead and lifelefs inaction took place, a ftillnefs both of intellect
and induftry, which left nothing of importance to mark the
country to other nations and other times, until it faw the adminiftration of Draco in the year 624 before Jefus Chrift.

His fevere adminiftration befpoke the univerfal diforders and exceffes which had preceded it. But laws written in blood are never likely to mend the wayward and vicious contradictions in human nature. After the experience of their inefficacy for near half a century, a Solon became neceffary to foften and heal by humanity, and by the confiderations of juft feelings, the irritations which had more nearly extinguifhed than reformed the people.

Solon was poffeffed of many elegancies of mind and talents : his philofophy was neverthelefs fupreme over all. If that philofophy would have led him to any cultivation of the finer arts, yet unfortunately he had not time to indulge the attention. His care could go no further than to the common mechanical employments*. Nor could the faint infpection of the Areopagus into every man's diligent employment of his time become a fufficient fpur to artifts, where there was no generous patronage to call forth an emulation. The fituation of the country afforded no fuch encouragement. Athens was rent by feuds and diffentions, in confequence of difafters abroad, as well as vexations at home. The code of laws, formed by Solon for the correction of abufes, fhews that all regular education, and all proper cultivation of talents, were grofsly neglected. In his time therefore the fine arts could gain no ground. When he was gone, the Athenians fhewed that they had thofe arts in their hands, if they had been called for : they erected a ftatue of brafs to his memory. But Pififtratus revoked many of his laws.

This man had affumed, and muft maintain, the tyranny. If all ingenuity was funk in diffolutenefs before, it was now become

---

* Plut. in vita Solonis.

torpid by flavery: at beft, it flumbered beneath the afhes with which liberty and itfelf were covered together. The firft talents in Athens bound upon their limbs the chains which Pififtratus had provided for them. This new revolution happened in the year 566 before the Chriftian æra. Yet does Pififtratus prefently become the epoch of the literary age of Greece. He founded in the latter days of his reign one of the fineft libraries that ever was collected. So far his ambition took an honourable turn. He was himfelf accomplifhed in all the learning of his age. His court became the refort of genius. Athens became lifted up anew. From that time fhe took the lead of all the other ftates in literature and fignificance: fhe became the fchool of philofophy, the theatre of poets, and the capital of tafte and elegance.

Amidft all thefe advantages, continued under the fons of Pififtratus to the conclufion of their reigns in the year 514 before our æra; the fine arts, although participating fomewhat in them all, could not call the days arrived which were capable of lifting them from their paft depreffion. Attica itfelf, with all it's endeavours to fhine again, was ftill too much in defolation to recover at once it's wealth and profperity. It had never ceafed indeed to feel, during the whole reigns of the Pififtratidæ, a very fenfible depreffion of fpirits from the confcioufnefs, ever grievous in a Grecian breaft, that it was governed by tyrants; for fo thofe were called, who had feized the reins of government, which they were not conftitutionally entitled to hold. That confcioufnefs, for which enlightened minds were never formed, was not to be erafed from the Athenians by the moft attractive accomplifhments of the tyrant himfelf; elfe, furely Pififtratus would have erafed it; and that people fhewed by the manner in which they met the elegancies of his reign, that they ftrove to erafe it from their breafts. But the victory over that confcioufnefs could not be completely gained to genius, till it was firft gained over the Pififtratidæ themfelves by their final expulfion. The general mind, completely fet free by the recovery of liberty, began then to expand itfelf in the pleafurable indulgence of elegant and ingenuous ideas. Yet was that indulgence a fhort one ; it was prefently reverfed by another check from another quarter to abfolute defpair. The event, to which we now refer, was the formidable invafion of Xerxes, which took place 480 years before Jefus Chrift. When that invader was overthrown in the fpace of a year in the battles of Salamin and Platææ, and was compelled to make his retreat into Perfia, then we come to the epoch in which every Grecian depreffion ceafed ; when the people felt themfelves alive from the dead ; when the country gained a new exiftence in that new fecurity, which brought wealth to her poffeffion, and made all her refources to flourifh ; when courage refumed it's feat and it's influence in the general breaft ; and when genius of courfe awoke from it's flumber, rubbed off the ruft with which it had been covered, and began to think of the fame which was referved for it's attainment in arts, no lefs than that which had been glorioufly atchieved by the Grecian courage in arms againft the enemies of the country. It is on the authority of Diodorus Siculus that we fpeak of that event in this manner. Thefe are his own words. " The expedition of Xerxes into " Greece, fupported by the wonderful extent of his forces, fo " terrified that people, that they counted affuredly on flavery " and ruin. But when beyond all expectations the war termi- " nated in their favour, the Greeks freed from the danger rofe " prefently into glory. Every one of their cities grew fo weal- " thy from the influx of riches, that the whole world had but to

" wonder at the sudden change of their fortune. For Greece
" prospered so exceedingly in the next fifty years after that event,
" that all the fine arts sprung forward, and became highly advan-
" ced by the wealth which flowed into her country, and which
" raised many famous artists, among whom was Phidias, the or-
" nament of the times *".

It was the brother of that Phidias, Panænus by name, whom
the Grecian records next bring forward 448 years before the
birth of Christ, to continue that thread in the progress of painting, which was broken by the chasm whose history we have endeavoured to supply. He carried to extent and advantage the
attempts in colouring, at which the art had long rested. The
remark, which Pliny has coupled with the character of that artist,
is striking, *adeo jam colorum usus increbuerat*†. It seems to
connect us immediately with the two centuries and more which
we have left behind in the hands of Bularchus, as if the interval
had been engaged to supply what was then left deficient in the
first advances of colour. The battle of Marathon, in the Pæcile
at Athens, is adduced by that author as a proof of the improvements which Panænus had given to that branch of the art.
In that painting the artist had portrayed from the life all the principal generals both on the Grecian and Persian side, which unquestionably required a great variety of colouring. To shew the points
of his art, was not the only important circumstance in that
thought : it was a most delicious advantage to a subject, which
came within 30 years after the event, to hand down to posterity
the very portraits of those men who had served their country so

* Diod. Sic. lib. 12. Hor. Epist. ad August. v. 93.
† Plin. lib. 35. c. 8.

well; they who were ftill living, and who had taken a part in
that fcene, would feed, while they viewed it on the remembrance
of what was fo dear to them, and they would fhed the luxurious
tear of affection over the portraits of thofe who were gone.
But we cannot help remarking further, that the invention of Panænus appears to have been wonderfully happy in that piece.
For it is faid that he there reprefented the faithful dog of Cynæ-
girus, from whofe fide, when he had loft both his hands in the action, that conftant animal would never depart, but fought in his
mafter's place when he was dead, and had then feized by the
throat a Perfian, who was expiring under the grafp of his fangs,
when he was killed at his mafter's feet.—Let the reader feel this,
and regret that he cannot review with his own eyes that rarity of
fcene, more beautiful than half the feats of heroes.

We have not yet done with Panænus. To him Greece was
indebted for the endeavour to kindle a general zeal in the arts by
committing himfelf to the firft public challenge in painting, and
to a generous exhibition of works for the trial of public opinion. That exhibition was made at Delphi, during the feaft of
Apollo, by that artift on one fide, and by Timagoras of Chalcis
on the other. The latter indeed carried the prize by the fuffra-
ges of Greece, and that is all the record which has been left to
us concerning him ; but the former was immortal in the portico
of Athens.

If the pencil was indebted to Panænus for fome improvement
in colour, it was much more indebted both in colouring and defign to Polygnotus. That artift, if he was not cotemporary with
the firft days of Panænus, came into fame very fhortly after.
Pliny fays that he was prior to the 90th Olympiad. It is agreed

that in his painting of the Trojan captives in the Pœcile, he gave the portrait of Elpinice, Cimon's fister, and a notorious courtezan, for the figure of Laodice. Elpinice therefore must have been then in some degree of youth ; and we know that her brother died in the 83d Olympiad, in middle age. His fister must have been considerably younger than he, or she would have been too old a portrait for Laodice ; and Polygnotus must have done that painting not long after Panænus in the 83d Olympiad, or still she would have been too old. From this circumstance we should be inclined to think that Polygnotus must have been quite as early as Panænus, whom the reader will recollect to have flourished 448 years before Christ. And we have said this much on a point of more curiosity than actual use, chiefly because Monsieur Rollin in his Chronological Table annexed to his Ancient History has put Polygnotus so late as the year 424 before the Christian æra. At that period, supposing Elpinice's brother to have died no older than forty, and that she was fifteen years younger than he, she must have been fifty years old, when Polygnotus selected her for the young and beautiful Laodice.

So much for the point of time when this artist came forward with those originalities, compared with which all that had been admired for painting before were as nothing. * He started at once from the old manner in attitude and figure, which with all the improvements of Cimon had yet much stiffness to lose. His figures were quite unshackled, and obtained in all situations an enlarged freedom, easiness, and indeed gaiety of air. The countenance was no longer a blank surface, or piece of paste. He shewed the world how to give it the expression of passion in

* Plin. lib. 35. c. 9.   Arist. de Arte Poetica.   Felib. vol. 1. p. 54.

every feature. The mouth itfelf fpoke, which hitherto had always been clofely fhut. His Ajax in the Pæcile gave at one look the brutal character of the man, whofe violence to the chafte Caffandra in the facred temple of Minerva was the fubject of council by the Grecian chiefs. In colouring he took a ground as new and original as were his traits of defign. To him we are indebted for the firft difcovery of light and fhade, of which he availed himfelf greatly in a new and agreeable appearance given to his draperies, particularly of women. Perhaps his fort was beft feen when he painted that fex, to whofe head-dreffes he had found a method of giving a moft elegant air, with a moft agreeable variety. Lucian, in the celebrated paffage *de imaginibus,* endeavouring to give the portrait of his perfect woman, felects the powers of this artift for that purpofe. He fays, " Polygnotus " fhall open and fpread her eye-brows, and give her that warm, " glowing, decent blufh, which fo inimitably beautifies his Caf- " fandra. He likewife fhall give her an eafy, genteel, flowing " drefs, with all it's tender and delicate wavings, partly clinging " to her body, and partly fluttering in the wind."

After this view of Polygnotus, what muft be the ftrength of that pencil which next appeared in the hands of Apollodorus, and caufed it to be faid of him, that before his time there was not a painting in Greece worthy to engage or detain the attention of the beholder * ? He entered on the theatre of arts a few years after Polygnotus, about the year 408 before the Chriftian æra. That high encomium of his pencil, which has come from the pen of Pliny, and we fhould naturally fuppofe was founded on the fentiments of former times, will probably be explained

* Plin. lib. 35. c. 9. Felib. vol. 1. p. 55.

without much difficulty by following the evidences which are ftill
left us of it's difcriminating perfections. We fhall firft conclude,
that the figures of Polygnotus, with all their life and expreffion,
went no further than a juft refemblance of Nature in it's ordinary
forms. Apollodorus was not content with that. We cannot fay
that he ftruck out the idea of that beautiful Nature, which became the delight of Greece, the ftudy of her internal policy, the
firft object of both painting and fculpture, and the teft of excellence in her fchools, becaufe we have already feen the marks
of that beautiful idea in the fculpture of Cypfelus 400 years
before: he was neverthelefs the firft painter who had exemplified it ably on the canvafs. · He gave it as the cloathing to all
his fubjects. It may feem ftrange, that this mafterly talent was
fo long in making it's appearance in painting, after it had
been feen in fculpture. Neverthelefs, the fact appears to have
been fuch. It has always been afcribed to Apollodorus, that he
was the firft painter who gave that advantage to his figures.
Does it not fhew the wider compafs, and the fuperior difficulties, embraced by the pencil? It's advances to perfection were
flower than thofe of fculpture, becaufe it had more powers to be
perfected. How ftrangely then muft Pliny have been miftaken,
when he afferted that "none of the fine arts was fo quickly car-
" ried to confummation as that of painting?*"

Colouring had not gained that advantage under Polygnotus,
which Apollodorus was enabled to give it. He rofe on the light
and fhade of his predeceffor by the more extraordinary difcovery
of the clair-obfcure. Befides that, he introduced a grace and
foftnefs into his colours, which left his predeceffor behind him.

* Plin. lib. 35. c. 3.

Yet it is faid that he was a mannerift in fome degree. Where every thing was fo new in the art, we fhall not wonder to meet fome things confined. The fervices he rendered were great, and it was not the leaft among the reft, that he formed the pencil of Zeuxis his difciple.

In the 95th Olympiad, or the year 400 before the Chriftian æra, this great artift was in the enjoyment of his fame*. Apollodorus his mafter faid of him, that "when the doors of the art "had been opened to him, he walked in and carried away all "that belonged to it." That only fhewed that Apollodorus did not fee completely all the perfections of the pencil; for in that penegyric he went too far. Zeuxis, however, determined not to leave the art where he found it, and he made his refolution good. In colouring it is not enough to fay that he was far greater than his mafter and all that went before him: the queftion feems only to be, whether he was not greater in that refpect than all who came after him, Apelles himfelf not excepted. He had the talent, peculiar to himfelf, of forming the clair-obfcure in the monocromatic or fingle colour, and in the more difficult manner of effecting it with white laid on a black ground, correfpondent in effect to our mezzo-tinto. This is what Pliny means, when he fays, "pinxit et monocromata ex albo." He pufhed his way to a further moft important exercife of the art in the infenfible tranfition of colours. In that talent the trial of fkill is well known, which he had with his cotemporary and rival Parrhafius, whofe fort that infenfible tranfition was, with all it's great effects in relief, and by whom it may be faid that thofe powers were eftablifhed in complete perfection†.

* Plin. lib. 35. c. 9.   Felib. vol. 1. p. 56.
† Ibid. lib. 35. c. 10.   Felib. vol. 3. p. 19.

The field was large, and ever will be large, in this art. It was not fo filled by thofe who had gone before, as to exclude Parr-hafius from new excellencies. The beautiful nature of Apollo-dorus was carried further by the perfect fymmetry of Parrhafius : that is, he formed his fymmetry not merely on what Nature had done in her moft beautiful exifting figures, but on what fhe might have done in the fulleft proportions of beauty. Thofe principles he illuftrated in a treatife, of which time has unfor-tunately left us no remains. To underfland this matter rightly, it muft be obferved that there were three ftages of procefs to this point of the art, and Parrhafius appears to have carried it to the furtheft extent of the three. The firft ftep was, to felect the moft beautiful forms in individuals. They next collected from many individuals what parts were moft beautiful in each, and out of thofe they compofed a whole, giving it thofe juft pro-portions which belonged to fuch a figure. But this was working upon Nature actually formed, which poffibly might never have exemplified the perfectly beautiful, or might not eafily afford it to be collected. Parrhafius therefore exhibited the perfect-ly beautiful in ftandard-proportions, or, to fpeak technically, in ftandard-fymmetry, and he exemplified it in his treatife ; a work, whofe object has never fince been fupplied.

In other refpects that artift improved confiderably on the ex-cellencies of Polygnotus, having carried to a more refined extent the life, and energy, and expreffion which the latter had given to his figures, and alfo the peculiar graces of the mouth, and the adjuftment of the hair, and the elegant dreffes of the head. It is no wonder that he took extraordinary pains in thefe orna-mental circumftances, when we know what is recorded of his attachment to the fair fex, and to fumptuoufnefs in female drefs *. It is to be regretted that this turn of mind fhould have carried his pencil into fubjects unfit for the virtuous eye.

Amidft thofe fteps, by which the art was rifing to it's fummit, it will naturally be thought that the zeal with which it's perfections were purfued, would cultivate the eftablifhment of fome public foundations, by which thofe perfections might be taught and maintained. There were at that time two public fchools of the arts in Greece, the one called the Grecian, and the other the Afiatic, fchool. Eupompus, of whom as an artift the lapfe of ages has left us little knowledge, flood neverthelefs fo high in character as to give extenfion to thofe foundations †. He prevailed that his native Sicyon, which had boafted to have firft introduced painting into Greece, and where it was then thought by many to be moft highly cultivated ‡, fhould fhare with Athens the honour of fupporting the art by a public fchool. From that time, what had been called the Grecian was divided into the Sicyonian and the Attic ; and that which had been the Afiatic took the name of the Ionian, in memory of the colony in Afia Minor, from whence the arts had gained an early affiftance. In confequence of thofe regulations, there became three fchools in Greece, differing fomewhat in manner, as all fchools do ; but proving, as they all do, the extenfion and improvement of the arts in the zeal with which thofe fchools are multiplied.

Pamphilus the Macedonian, who flourifhed in the reign of Philip the father of Alexander the Great, was the difciple of Eupompus ; and poffeffed, as we muft conclude, confiderable excellen-

---

* Junius de Pict. Vet. p. 49.   † Plin. lib. 35. c. 10.

‡ Plut. in Vita Arati.

cies, although we are not able minutely to ſtate them, becauſe the elegant and judicious Aratus ſelected all his pieces, which he was able to purchaſe, for Ptolemy Philadelphus *. He followed, however, his maſter's ſteps by ſeeking thoſe eſtabliſhments for the arts, which were conceived to dignify and raiſe them. From his influence aroſe that remarkable ordinance, firſt at Sicyon, and afterwards made univerſal in Greece, that the arts of deſign ſhould be practiſed by no ſlave, but that all other children ſhould be compelled to learn them. In his own character thoſe arts were undoubtedly ennobled, as he poſſeſſed all the *belles lettres* of the age, and exemplified that extent of education, for which he ſo ſtrenuouſly contended as an artiſt, and to which that ordinance was meant to lead the profeſſors of the arts. We have already touched on ſome advantages which were unqueſtionably given by that meaſure to the general ſpirit of thoſe arts, although perhaps it was not a meaſure which might fit any other country but it's own, in a general view. It was not the leaſt advancement which he gave to the pencil, when he brought up the man, after whom it might be needleſs to ſpeak of any advancement it received. The reader will anticipate the mention of Apelles.

† In the 112th Olympiad, or 332 years before the Chriſtian æra, this artiſt trained by all the improvements that went before him, and nouriſhed by the favour and patronage of Alexander the Great, carried his art perhaps to the higheſt pitch it could ever attain, at leaſt under thoſe advantages of colours which were then enjoyed by the ingenious world. The eulogium, which Pliny has given, is indeed unqualified : he ſays, "omnes prius " genitos, futuroſque poſtea, ſuperavit Apelles." Neverthelefs,

---

* Plin. lib. 35. c. 10.　　　　† Ibid. Felib. vol. 1. p. 63.

with all due enthufiafm, the limitation above-mentioned feems indifpenfible to be drawn, although it fhould be true in faƐt that no fucceeding ages, with the advantages of more materials in colour, have reached the whole excellencies of his pencil.   It is a very fenfible mortification, that when our minds are wound up by the reported wonders of this extraordinary artift, time fhould have bereft us of every trait by which we might have been ena- bled either to form a judgement for ourfelves, or to gratify on the moft fatisfaƐtory grounds that enthufiaftic applaufe, which has become irrefiftible from prefcription.   We have but to retail the general ftriƐtures, which have been left to us by thofe who were much nearer the fource of correƐt information.

When we review the advancements which Apelles gave to his art, the queftion feems only to be, whether he did not carry to the higheft conceivable point all the individual perfeƐtions which gave fame to any of his predeceffors, in defign, in colouring, in keeping, in the expreffion of charaƐter, in proportions, in con- tour, and in the moft perfeƐt beauty of Nature.   Be that as it may, if we are to take our fentiments from the decided fuffrage of antiquity, while he fhewed himfelf a mafter in all thofe gifts, he approved himfelf an original in another gift, which feemed as if it were vouchfafed immediately from heaven, and communi- cated by infpiration alone ; and that was, the grace which over- fpread every thing he did.   By means of that grace, the free- dom which he gave to his figures outftripped every improved idea of eafe ; his life was fuch as animation never poffeffed ; and the humanity of his forms partook of the celeftiality of Being. " Ideas," fays the well-informed Felibien, " can hardly conceive " thefe, and all language is too weak to exprefs them *."   With

. * Felib. ubi fup.

thofe enchanting powers as an artift, it is pleafing to know that as a man he united an equal modefty, that precious and never-failing proof not only of profeffional wifdom, but of wifdom in it's moft comprehenfive and accomplifhed ftate. Apelles would ingenuoufly declare that Amphion* furpaffed him in ordonance, and Afclepiodorus in proportions. Among the other attainments of his genius, the art was indebted to him for the difcovery of a varnifh, which contributed much to the mellowing of his colours, and ferved as a mirrour through which the eye might behold the brighteft tints without any offenfive glare, while at the fame time it fhielded his paintings from the foil of duft. Unfortunately that difcovery is loft to pofterity.

Confiftently with the voice of antiquity, we muft fuppofe, that he had no rival in his day in any one perfection of his art. And yet there was a cotemporary, concerning whom it might be concluded, from the expreffions of Pliny, that he contributed fome original improvements, which were not found in others. That artift was Ariftides, of whom Pliny fays, " is omnium pri- " mus animum pinxit, et fenfus humanos expreffit, quæ vocant " Græci ϊθη; idem perturbationes †". That author had faid before of Parrhafius, that he firft gave the expreffion of fentiment to the countenance, " primus argutias vultus dedit." And furely the pencil of Apelles after him could not be deficient in this, or it would ill be entitled to the eulogium which has been given it. How then could Ariftides be faid firft to paint the

---

* Quære, Are not almoft all the books wrong from Pliny to the prefent day in the name given to this artift ? Should it not be Echion ? See Durand's Notes on Pliny ad loc. Lucian in Herodot. Felib. vol. 1. p. 63. in margine.

† Plin. lib. 35. c. 9.

mind, to exprefs the fentiments or manners, taken in their beft
fenfe, and as the Greeks underftood them by the word ἦθη? It
is difficult to reconcile this nicety, at leaft with the prefervation
of confiftency to the author of it. A little reflection however
may carry us fome way towards it. There is certainly a difference between the painting of the mind, the foul, the internal
of the character, in it's fettled and calm conftitution, and the
painting of any particular affection prevalent on the countenance. If the merit of Parrhafius lay chiefly in the latter way,
then there was no inconfiftency with refpect to him in faying
that Ariftides was original in the former. But from a fair interpretation of the whole fentence we fhould rather conceive Pliny's
meaning to have been, that Ariftides was the firft painter who
could exprefs in the countenance and character all the various
fentiments and affections of the human mind, not only the more
regular manners, ἦθη, but the more violent paffions, *perturbationes :* a talent, which is rare indeed in the hands of one man,
and poffibly might not have been marked in any others before
him, although others might have admirably expreffed thofe fentiments or thofe paffions feparately. We know that the talent of
Zeuxis lay more eminently in painting the fofter and more regular manners, while that of Timomachus excelled in the more
vehement paffions. The Penelope gives the beft trait of the
former's pencil ; and the Ajax, or perhaps the Gorgon, as Pliny
fays *, beft exhibits that of the latter. If this ftricture be right,
it would feem that Ariftides could draw either a Penelope or an
Ajax, a Penelope or a Gorgon. Admitting this to be the cafe,
and that Ariftides was firft diftinguifhed by that talent, there is a
vaft field of art in which he might be left inferior to the powers,

* Plin. lib. 35. c. 11.

and confequently to the fame, of Apelles. But, after all, the confiftency of Pliny is not yet cleared. For how much lefs than that talent of Ariftides did Parrhafius exhibit in his δῆμον or genius of Athens? in which, according to Pliny's own account, he painted every different fentiment and manner, and every different paffion, that can be conceived to enter into the human breaft *.

Protogenes of Rhodes was another cotemporary of Apelles, and cannot be paffed unnoticed, when we recollect the very extraordinary admiration which his Jalyfus occafioned in Apelles himfelf †. Yet we are not fufficiently furnifhed by antiquity with the peculiarities of his pencil to fpeak of it with precifion ‡. Neither are we diftinctly informed of the feveral coats of colours, which Pliny fays he laid upon his paintings, in order to fhield them from the injuries of time and accident. On his Jalyfus he laid four of thofe coats, fo that if any one of them failed, a frefh picture rofe up underneath. We are yet to be informed how that is to be underftood; whether Protogenes painted the picture four feveral times in the ufual manner, without the intervention of any other medium ; or whether he ufed another medium, over every coat of which he painted the picture again. The latter idea has generally been embraced, more efpecially as the object propofed would not have been equally fecured by the former ; for it would not be quite eafy to take off a real coat of painting, immediately laid on another, without prejudice to that which lay underneath; and befides, thefe would form, in fact, only a thicker cruft, which would be more likely to crack than a thinner body.

---

* Plin. lib. 35. c. 10. † Plut. in vita Demetrii.
‡ See Plin. ibid. Felib. vol. 1. p. 65—67.

Perhaps the best paintings for keeping their texture are those, over which the pencil has never gone twice. Some of those are to be seen, particularly by Guido and Titian, which have stood a long test of time, and through which an accurate eye may partly perceive the canvas, not more naked now than it appears to have been at first. What that medium was, which Protogenes employed, we are nevertheless entirely unacquainted. A similar practice, if the practice were his, has been pursued in modern times. Some of the paintings in the collection of our unfortunate Charles I. particularly his portrait by Van-dyke now in fine preservation, were saved from the general wreck of his property by the ingenuity of an artist, who difguif-ed it by a coat of a gummy nature, as it is fuppofed, over which he painted the picture again more humbly, as will easily be conceived. The Diana of Titian, lately recovered by Mr. Weft, the prefident of our royal academy, from the lumber-rooms in which it had lain for many years, and which has many ftrong evidences of having been in the fame royal collection, was alfo covered with fuch a coat, over which it was painted again.

With the age of thefe artifts we are brought down very nearly to the overthrow of the liberties of Greece, which only furvived them a little more than 150 years. We have no need, however, to inveftigate the progrefs of the arts in that further period, be-caufe after the age of thofe artifts no further original progrefs was made, nor was there indeed room for it to be made. It is true that after Apelles many names arofe, to which celebrity was annexed, but not for any original perfections: fuch were Eu-phranor, Paufias, Nicias. Thefe and other names of their times bring us into the lift and the age of minor-painters; whofe age, like that of minor-poets, although it was not bereft of excellencies, yet as it was more fparingly illumined by the warming rays of admiration, feldom invites the fedulous inveftigation of inquirers. Such an age Nature muft have in all her greateft gifts. After the Cycle, which was made up full by the perfections of Apelles, there was no more room for another on the fame fcale ; Nature could go on no longer on the fame plan ; the fame ftretch of perfections could not be maintained ; fhe muft fink a little, and take new ground, in order to fhun the being quite exhaufted.

CHAP. III.

The prodigious progrefs of the Grecian arts from Pericles to Alexander the Great—that progrefs effected by the peculiar fpirit of patronage in thofe two characters—the fure advantages to the fine arts from every fuch patronage—no part of human talents fo dependent on patronage for fuccefs as thofe arts—the fupreme power in a country the only effectual fource of their nurture—the mechanical arts confiderably depreffed, where they are neglected by government—the principles and characters of Grecian patronage—the public fentiments of the Greeks highly favourable to elegant artifts—thofe artifts themfelves actuated by the moft liberal and ingenuous principles—the neceffity of fuch principles in the artifts of every country to give the fine arts perfection and a lafting celebrity.

It will now be proper that we confider more clofely the general caufes which carried the fine arts of Greece to that perfection and fuccefs, which they have been feen to reach. We find

that from the time when any date can be given to the painters in
the monocromatic to the age of Apelles, or, to fpeak more precifely, to the death of Alexander the Great, no lefs than 450
years were employed.   Out of that period we can only reckon
the laft 130 years, in which painting was at all in vigour and in
fame ; that is, from it's breaking forth with Panænus, and under
Pericles.   When at that time it broke forth from the cloud with
which Greece had long been obfcured, the reader will recollect
that it did but appear with imperfection.   The peculiar language
of Pliny on it's appearance at that time is a fufficient trait of it's
condition, " colorum ufus jam increbuerat :" he marks it as a
novelty, that the ufe of colours was then extended ; as if he
meant to tell us in better expreffions, that it had for fome time
fhaken off the monocromatic.   The fact is then, that in 130
years it rofe from it's infancy to full maturity ; it accomplifhed
all the vigour, perfection, and fame with which it has ever been
attended upon earth.

And what was the caufe, which gave it that extraordinary
growth ?   It was that, without which the fine arts are more im-
becil and weak than all the other gifts of man ; without which,
they are foon overfhaded by the coarfeft and humbleft of human
inventions ; but, with which, they beggar all the luftre that from
any other fource can ever encircle the human head.   It was patronage—fettled, fyftematic patronage—patronage that rifes not
merely to employ, but to improve—patronage fed by a genuine
fenfe of elegant improvements, as well as by views of glory—
the patronage of brilliant minds, poffeffed of fupreme rule, and
moving in the decided purfuit of what eternizes the applaufe of
power, and the beft glory of a people.   Till fuch a patronage
arofe, vain were all other admirations, applaufes, or encourage-

ments of the arts, although backed by the rich and great, or perhaps by the fhew of royal gold. Till fuch a patronage arofe, how did the arts ftruggle no lefs than three centuries for a faint exiftence, and fcarcely able to creep towards ftrength, although they wanted not occafionally the encouragements of individuals, and at all times the applaufe of all? What could they gain from the cafual favour of a Candaules, more than the weight of his money, and the contents of his purfe? The picture could make no more profelytes in Greece, let it's merit have been what it might: it was gone with the enraptured monarch into Lydia; where his zeal, once roufed fo high for the works of the pencil, had probably foon fubfided, being fatisfied with what it had obtained.

But when the dignity of the human mind, and the glory of giving full difplay to it's capacities, came to be rightly apprehended—when the fpirit of fine art began to be felt, with the advantages refulting from the beft cultivation of human ingenuity, not only by furnifhing the higheft delights to a polifhed tafte, but by perpetuating truth, virtue, fame, all the deareft events to a country, on which future generations may feed with happinefs and with a glorious emulation—when thefe principles and thefe views had made their way to a people, efpecially to thofe feats of power, which were beft enabled to give them their greateft force; then two individuals *, who held the reins of government, although at fome diftance from each other, were able to do in 130 years what from the beginning of the world could never be accomplifhed by the beft cultivations in the fame country. Nay, the former of them alone, Pericles I mean, was able in lefs than

* Pericles and Alexander the Great.

forty years to raife the arts to a fplendour, which left but few
perfections to be added to thofe which were then attained; for in
his time the pencils of Zeuxis and Parrhafius flourifhed; and
in fculpture Phidias, Myron, Glicon, Scopas, and Alcamenes; in
architecture Ictinus and Callicrates, Coræbus, Metagenes and
Xenocles; the feveral excellencies of thefe were difplayed in the
foundation or in the finifhing of the immenfe temple of Pallas,
and the Eleufinian Chapel. So much was done by one man,
determined to fland forth at the head of the fine arts, and to give
fcope to the ingenious talents of his country. And fuch was the
effect of his patronage, that not all the dark and wayward and
difaftrous events, affecting efpecially the Athenian ftate, which
filled the whole interval between his death and the rife of Alexander the Great, were able to crufh their growth.

Poffeffed of that fettled ftrength, how differently were they enabled to look in the face the fame, or fimilar, circumftances under
which they had funk before? When they were in their cradle,
the fluctuating inftitution of nine annual Archons had fmothered
their infant-progrefs, by leaving them no fettled nurture: but
after the days of Pericles they could behold thirty tyrants under
the name of Archons, and the four hundred too combined in
equally tyrannical government, and even the general evacuation
of the ftate for a time, without lofing any part of the ground
which they had gained. One reafon for this, added to their own
ftrength, undoubtedly was, that hardly more than one generation
had paffed in that interval. Some of thofe difciples, who were
laft brought up at the feet of the great mafters under Pericles,
might without improbability have continued on the ftage of life
till Alexander was born. Had his days been more remote, it is
hard to fay, what confequence would have followed. But feel-

ing as he did, in his exalted fituation, a fuperior love for the fine arts, and unaffected by any circumftances to fhackle or bound his patronage, what could refift it? What was there that muft not flourifh under it's favour? What could the coldnefs or the blank of near a century preceding oppofe to the warmth of his invigorating beams? Could more than he fupplied be needful to make human ingenuity generoufly afpire, to carry that afpiration to perfection, to lift that perfection into luftre?

It is yet too foon to lofe the leffons that will fpring from this fubject of patronage. What happened in Greece has been verified in every age and country of the world. The more elegant arts could never get forward by any poffible means without a pure and exalted patronage. To adduce the proofs of this in every period, and in every quarter where they have attempted to rear up their heads, would be to bring their whole hiftory together. The peculiarity of their fituation, as it refpects this point, is ftriking. There are none of the human talents fo critically circumftanced as thefe, and fo dependent on caufes or events over which they can have no controul. Eloquence will pufh it's way into fame and fituation, in fpite of all refifting circumftances. Military prowefs will atchieve for itfelf grandeur, renown, and wealth without the help of any other hand than it's own. And literature, in every branch, is fure to carry the world after it, which will contribute to all that it's talents can feek. Even the arts which concern only the loweft and moft ordinary utilities of mechanical fkill, can carve their own fortune and fuccefs with confiderable affurance.

Not fo thofe finer portions of art, which leave to all other inventions the more proper name of trades, and which by their exquifite combinations unite in their powers and in their ufe the effects of eloquence, literature, and atchievement, and alfo convey thefe by lafting monuments to the fervice of pofterity. It is not enough that the poffeffors of thofe arts are emulous or con- fpicuous : the people around them, at leaft in higher ranks, muft have a correfpondent tafte, although they have not an equality of fkill, before the tafte and fkill of profeffors can reach their proper value. It is not enough that they are patronized by the more wealthy, or the more fignificant, in fcattered fituations : what ftandard-tafte, what ftandard-perfections, or what ftandard- advantages can accrue to a country from the finer arts, fupported only in fo defultory a manner? It is not enough that thofe arts receive all the affiftance which can arife from the objects of com- merce : the country may be ferved at home, and honoured abroad, by thofe means; but the arts will never be brought to reach their higheft point, becaufe wherever gain is concerned, the encouragement which flows from it's views to the emulation of genius muft be limited. Nothing lefs than the protection and nourifhment afforded by the fovereign power of a country can give thofe arts a full eftablifhment and growth : it is when they are taken up by that public ftrength which can rear every thing ; when they are warmed by that fuperior countenance, in which the public attention is naturally concentered; and when they are called to thofe purpofes of elegance, and glory, and grand inftruction, which are the natural views of thofe who watch over the enlarged interefts of a nation ; it is then that thofe arts ex- pand, and emulate, and foar, and prove the rank which they hold in the gifts of the human mind.

The protection and encouragement of the fupreme government is alike important to the beft advancement of every thing that

confifts in talents. Thofe very mechanical arts, on which every
fociety depends for it's firft accommodations, are found to
droop, where there is no attention in the government to their progrefs, and no fyftem of encouragement is held forth to their
views. Read the hiftory of the prefent inhabitants of Cartha-
gena*. You find a people as bright, as ingenious, and as forward
in their talents as any people exifting. They arrive betimes to a
great maturity in all the arts which are known in their country,
as well as in every other part of their knowledge. But when
they fhould be met by the inviting hand of government; when
their importance fhould be felt, and their perfeverance encouraged
by thofe honourable views which ingenious merit may reafonably
contemplate, then they find their own zeal to be their only enjoyment, and their only profpect. Hence, inftead of endeavouring to improve on their mafters or themfelves, a natural indolence checks their progrefs; they fall back in chagrin, and droop
in defpair; leaving imperfect thofe effects of their capacities,
which were rather furprifing at an early age, and would have
been confummate if they had experienced the nurture of government. Such is the cafe of that people, as it is reported by thofe
who have vifited them, and who have witneffed in their examples
how ineffectual are all other incitements to ingenuity, if that
which flows from the fupreme power of a country be wanting.

What then was the fpirit and character of that patronage, by
which the arts were fo aftonifhingly raifed and matured in
Greece ?

In the ideas of what was virtuous and honourable among enlightened heathens, in their notions of what was excellent and

---

* See Ulloa's Voyages, vol. 1. p. 33, 34.

glorious in general, in their opinions of human events and of divine adminiſtration, we are not to expeƐt ſuch principles as would naturally diſtinguiſh minds enlightened by revelation. Conſequently, in their ſupport of the arts, and particularly of painting, as a cogent impreſſion of great and inſtruƐtive leſſons, we muſt not expeƐt them to be guided by thoſe chaſte and correƐt ideas, which would beſpeak them poſſeſſed of the pureſt truths, and aƐtuated by the beſt views of glory.

The aƐtions of gods who had no exiſtence, aƐtions perhaps which never found a human being to perform them—feats of heroes, which under the diſcipline of better knowledge would be deemed fitter to be buried in oblivion than to be recorded—events, which have had their foundation more in vain-glory than in faƐt, in the adulation which particular countries have been uſed to pay to a particular race of men more than in any real cauſe whatever— the immortalizing of deified men and women, whoſe pretenſions to divinity were not half ſo ſolid as ſome uſeful ſervices rendered by them to the people—theſe objeƐts will naturally be ſuppoſed to engage the attention of thoſe ancient Greeks, who were greatly attached to the heroic, and very open to fable and impoſition. And when to thoſe objeƐts we have added the real events which formed the better hiſtory of Greece, and were glorious in it's annals; when we have added the immortalizing of thoſe real and worthy heroes, who nobly ſtood by their country in it's greateſt dangers ; theſe ſubjeƐts, with occaſional ſcenes of ſubordinate virtue, or ſubordinate appeal to particular feelings, and now and then ſome harmleſs *jeux d'eſprits* upon the canvas, will be found to conſtitute the general purpoſes which the arts of Greece were called to aſſiſt.

When the Amphictionic council filled the temple at Delphi, when the senate of Athens filled the portico of that city,
when all the principal cities of Greece filled their galleries and
public buildings, with those scenes of martial ardor on which
the fate of their respective commonwealths depended ; with those
scenes in the Trojan war, which perhaps'existed only in the creation of the poet, but which were nevertheless attractive and
illustrious to the Greeks ; with the portraits of those philoso-
phers, who stood succeffively at the head of inftruction, and
were memorable for the peculiarities, if not always for the folidity, of their principles : was not that patronage as great and
judicious as could be planned by wifdom, or embraced by art,
looking each of them to the caufe of public or private virtue ?
When a tyrant* of Elatæa, or a king† of Pergamus, participating in the triumph of elegant arts, called forth from the celebrated pencils around them figures of deities‡, twelve in one
fubject, at 300 pounds weight of filver for every figure ; or
figures in war §, a hundred in one fubject, at ten pounds weight
of filver for every figure ; or the fingle figure of Bacchus‖, at the
value of 6000 festerces : we admire their rapture, but we cannot
impeach their judgement, which aimed to keep up the reverence
of what they held as religion, and their reverence of deeds which
crufhed the inveteracy of their Perfian enemies.   Their "high
" priefts at worfhip"** kept up the fame reverence of religion.
Their "Jupiter on his throne, furrounded by all the gods"††, carried that reverence as high as it could go.   Their " hell, or infer-
" nal fhades"‡‡, had it's foundation in their belief, and it's ufe

---

* Mnafon.   † Attalus.   ‡ By Afclepiodorus, for Mnafon.
§ By Ariftides, for Mnafon.   ‖ By Ariftides, and purchafed by Attalus.
** By Apollodorus, Zeuxis, Parrhafius, Apelles, and almoft all the celebrated artifts.
†† By Zeuxis.   ‡‡ By Nicias.

upon their minds. Their " wreftlers"*, and their " chariots in
" the race"†, kept up the hardinefs of their nature, and the activity of their policy. " Alexander holding thunder", or " tri-
" umphing, attended by the image of war whofe hands were tied
" behind"‡, were quite legitimate to the character and conduct
of that hero, concerning whom we do not wait to enquire whether his heroic deeds were always juft or neceffary. His immortalizing by thirty ftatues the memory of fo many valiant officers
who fell in the paffage through the Granicus, was natural and
juft in him who had fo many obligations to their valour.

To give in one word the character of Grecian patronage, it
aimed to maintain religion, to perpetuate valuable truth and inftruction, to immortalize illuftrious merit, to record glory preci-
oufly acquired, and along with thofe objects to affift the improvement of the arts themfelves.

Thofe objects were confiderably helped by the prevalence of
public fentiments in favour of arts and artifts. The latter were
called forth, as Pliny reprefents, by kings and ftates §. They
were confidered as public benefits‖, as citizens peculiarly gifted
to ferve their country, by recording to pofterity the fame or the
inftruction that was precious. They were looked upon as watch-
men**, appointed to mark the events that were paffing, and to
felect for public attention whatever was of public moment. Virtue, public and private, equally moved thofe who gave the call
and the artifts who obeyed it. The latter, feeling the important
truft committed to their hands, difcharged it like men of virtue;

* By Zeuxis, Parrhafius, and Eupompus.   † By Ariftides.
‡ By Apelles.   § Plin. lib. 35. c. 1.
‖ Plin. lib. 35. c. 10.   ** Ibid. lib. 35. c. 10.

they left all mean and felfifh confiderations behind them ; if they could afford it, and often if they could not, they gratuitoufly gave their labours as men who confidered themfelves employed for the public honour and the public good. The proofs of this fact are very exalted, and not a few. Hence Protogenes. amidft all his fame, was content with a fmallhut in a garden. Myron the fculptor did not leave enough behind him to be remembered by his heirs. And Lyfippus, who was followed by all the firft patronage of his age, felt the laft ftroke of want, while he was finifhing a ftatue *. Yet thefe were none of them marked for extravagant living. They fought, with numerous others in their profeffions, the more precious gain of honour. Their minds feem to have been impreffed by a common infpiration, that there was a glory arifing to the country from their profeffions, and that their own enthufiafm might lengthen the meridian of their arts, by ftimulating future generations to follow their difinterefted emulations. We fhall not wonder at thofe ideas, when we recollect the honourable ground on which the ftudy of the fine arts was placed by the decree of univerfal Greece. When that ftudy made a neceffary part of the education of all that were free-born, and no flave was permitted to purfue it, what but the moft honourable ideas of the arts could follow ? what could be fo ftrong in the cultivation of them as the emulation of fame ?

Leaving that object behind, the fine arts might probably have ferved the purpofe of telling a ftory, or preferving a character. But views fo humble never comported with the higher feelings of talents. The Greeks difdained them. In their whole fyftem both of nourifhing the arts as patrons, and of exercifing them as

* Petron. Satyric. p. 422. Ed. Burm.

artifts, they pufhed forward to the very reverfe of thofe views. They fcorned mediocrity, they grafped at perfection. It was the ambition of every man, as well as of Zeuxis, to add fomething to his art, and never to leave it at the point in which he found it. Thus they were always moving from ftrength to ftrength, and from lower degrees of excellence to higher. To employ, or to be employed, came by no means up to their views, which were to improve. By thefe examples they taught other ages and countries how boundlefs was the field for improvement afforded by the fine arts, and efpecially by the pencil, whofe fcope of excellence, rifing continually into more precious effects with every additional advantage, will never be exhaufted by any zeal.

Felibien, whofe fentiments are always juft, has confirmed thefe reflections with forcible expreffion. "At the time", fays he, " when virtue alone conftituted the pleafure of the fine arts, they " flourifhed furprifingly: a moft agreeable ftrife was exhibited " among the moft able, in the production of fome new excel- " lence ; that the arts might never reft where they were, nor the " means of improving them lie latent, but that the glory of " difcovering and communicating to pofterity whatever might be " fought in thofe arts, fhould be enjoyed by thofe virtuous ages"*.

If there be a truth which lies more immediately than any other at the foundation of that decline in the fine arts, which marked any fubfequent ages of Greece, or has been vifible in any other countries where they have once been poffeffed in vigour, it is the reverfe of that glorious ftrife which diftinguifhed thofe virtuous ages ; it is, when that love and purfuit of virtue, of fame, and of elegant improvement have not actuated the whole.

* Felib. vol. 1. p. 79.

CHAP. IV.

The general character of Grecian architecture, as superior to that which had ever been seen before—the Greeks original in that superior character—original also in the constitution of an order, although they might be led to it by observations of what had been done elsewhere—the antiquity of their first order, the Doric—the process of the orders on philosophic principles, according to which the Grecian mind decided every thing—every possible character proper for the variety of architectural structure provided for in those orders, whose principles no caprice of subsequent ages has been able to move or vary—the establishment of a distinct character, founded on a strict attention to the nature of things, the fixed object of the Greeks in each of their orders—the extent with which that distinct character was maintained by them in every part and portion of an edifice, so as to form a complete whole, a very important and curious speculation—the philosophy of engaging our most rational sensations aimed at and accomplished in a most striking manner by their architecture—that object greatly assisted by their studies and their powers to produce harmony—how that harmony was effected—the affinity which has been supposed by many to subsist between the measures of architecture and music—the great caution with which any arbitrary invasions of the Grecian examples, and especially of the principles of their orders, should be attempted—some licences nevertheless discoverable among the Greek architects themselves, but with no violation of principles—their knowledge of perspective—

their attentive ſtudy of geometry—the Cariatides, and Perſian
ſupporters—the ſtrange extenſion of theſe by moderns—the pecu-
liar manner in which the Greeks diſpoſed their private man-
ſions—the means by which they were enabled to raiſe ſuch
innumerable and coſtly edifices.

LET us now conſider the architecture of the Greeks.   In their
hands we ſhall ſee it come forward in a new aſpect, as an art of
elegance, poſſeſſed of all the proportions of beauty, and in it's
whole arrangement founded no longer upon chance, or at beſt
on the calculated ſolidity of great maſſes, but on the finer
principles of Nature, truth, and reaſon, deciding not only on
the needful meaſures of ſolidity, but on what ſhall conſtitute the
juſteſt ornaments.   From thoſe principles deeply ſtudied by the
Greeks we ſee delicacy united with ſtrength, elegance with grandeur, taſte and intelligence with the uſe of the plaineſt materials ;   the art, which in it's origin was merely uſeful, now became
charming in it's effects ;   if, before, it was it's beſt character that
it provided for the firſt conveniences and comforts of ſociety, it
was now rendered productive of the firſt leſſons in grace, and
regularity, and beauty ;   if, before, it was capable of aſtoniſhing
by the immenſity to which it's works were carried, it· was now
enabled by the wonders of it's ſymmetry to excite an admiration
that never could ceaſe.

   In theſe views the art may properly be ſaid to have been created
by the Greeks.   They owed to no other people on earth what
diſtinguiſhes architecture in theſe views, however they were
aſſiſted in it's plainer and more ordinary rudiments by thoſe who
had been their general maſters in all the arts.   It was their own
genius that brought forth this art in the genuine compoſition of

fublime. From their own invention proceeded all the beauties with which it was invefted, and which with very few exceptions may be pronounced to be all the beauties of which it is capable. They furnifhed the models, they prefcribed the rules, which, with very few variations, have governed and muft ever govern thofe who would execute in the beft tafte monuments worthy to defcend to pofterity. In the three orders of architecture formed by the Greeks are comprifed all the principles which have ever occurred to the ingenuity of man as moft natural and effential to the conftitution of folidity, elegance, delicacy, and richnefs, or of the ornaments beft befitting each of thofe claffes, as they may refpectively be employed to characterize the ftyle and fpirit of the edifice that is raifed.

To go fuch great lengths, with no better documents than they had before them, muft fet the inventive genius of the Greeks on a high ground indeed. Perhaps that inventive genius appeared more in architecture than in the other fine arts ; at leaft, it was fhewn forth here in a great abundance of parts, in things which are of the firft diftinction, and to which they were led by the feweft helps. The fpacious arch, the elegant portico, the finifhed column, the rich and regular entablature, the beautifully rifing and yet the lightened roof, the power of giving a different expreffion to all thefe, were difcoveries which either might claim to be new, or in which their fame could be but little diminifhed by any fteps that had been purfued before. Such extraordinary capacities advancing in times fo early to thofe lengths, beyond which perfection has never been conceived by the ages that have followed, have not afforded many examples in the hiftory of mankind. The Afiatics and the Egyptians, whether they be confidered as more rude or more enlightened, could not equally furprize us by the meafure of their difcoveries in architecture, fo far as that meafure can be afcertained, although it rofe upon much fcantier beginnings; becaufe thofe beginnings were natural to the human mind, when once it was turned to the fcience of building; and all their fubfequent difcoveries,. if they were more than the rudiments of maintaining ftrength, were thofe rudiments of decorous finifhing which the firft ideas of that fcience would fuggeft. But the Greeks were too ripe in genius to be contented with firft ideas; they were too mature in judgement, and too perfevering in ftudy, to reft on rudiments; or they ftruck out rudiments themfelves, on which no further improvements could be grafted.

To do juftice to the extent of Grecian genius, it is not neceffary to fuppofe that in the conftitution of the Doric order, which is generally confidered as their firft, they were perfectly new in every idea, and were led by nothing that had exifted before in the architecture of others. The invention was great and original enough, which decided on the principles and proportions that entered into fo new and elegant a conftitution as that of a regular order. But when we recollect the age that muft be given to the temple of Perfepolis, now in ruins, but in it's perfect condition when the Greeks were forming their fi ft order; when we look at the columns now ftanding there, and fee the other approaches there made by the mere force of natural idea to all thofe parts by which an order is embraced; and when we are affured that they derived from the fculptures in that temple fome of the emblematic ideas which appeared on their moft ancient coins and medals and feals, particularly the " ox with the " human head," of which that temple exhibited the oldeft example that we know of in the world, and the only example of it in marble : when we look back upon thofe circumftances, can it

be imagined that the Greeks did not find their way to that celebrated ſtructure, or that they did not compare with their own
minds whatever was preſented to their obſervations there, as well
as thoſe advancements in architecture which were found in Egypt?

What then was the antiquity of their firſt order? This queſtion has been anſwered, but apparently with more haſte than preciſion. There are few points in antiquity leſs capable of being
preciſely aſcertained. The origin of that order has been connected with the age of Dorus the ſon of Helenus, and grandſon
of Deucalion * ; which was about 1380 years before the Chriſtian æra. We make no queſtion, for it's name imports, that it
obtained it's conſummation in the hands of the Dorians. But
if that conſummation be referred to the Dorians ſettled in Peloponeſus along with the returning Heraclidæ, fourſcore years after
the taking of Troy, it will make a difference of above two centuries in it's age. And it ſo happens, that the oldeſt Doric ſtructure we find upon record, and of which we can ſpeak aſſuredly
as Doric, is the temple of Juno built by Oxilus at Olympia in
Peloponeſus in the eighth year after he had obtained the ſovereignty of Elis on the ſucceſs of the Heraclidæ, with whom
he came at the head of ſome Dorians into that country†. The
age of that temple then was 1121 years before our æra.

It does not follow that the origin of the order commenced with
that temple, for it muſt have been gradually brought to it's completion. And accordingly we find that 263 years before the
foundation of that temple, Œnomaus erected a palace at Piſa in
Elis, of which he was then ſovereign: ‡ one of the columns of

* Vitruv. lib. 4. c. 1.   † Pauſan. lib. 5. c. 16. p. 416.
‡ Pauſan. lib 5. c. 20. p. 428.   D'Ancarv. vol. 2. p. 289.

that palace, almoſt periſhed with age, and held together by iron-bands, was ſhewn to Pauſanias when he made his travels in Greece. Now Œnomaus was cotemporary with the ſons of Hele-nus [*], and the precife age of that palace was 1384 years before the Chriſtian æra. That palace exhibited an order; and that or-der appears at leaſt to have approached very much towards the Doric. M. D'Ancarville pronounces it to have been the fame with that which was afterwards called Tufcan [†]; for which his reaſons are that the Doric was not then formed, and that monu-ments of a ſimilar architecture, which have gone by the name of Tufcan, have been viſible at Piſa in Etruria, and at Croton and other towns in Magna Græcia, which were all founded by the fame Pelaſgi who built the Piſa in Elis.

We ſhall make no objection to thoſe reaſons, and leaſt of all to that which conveys from Greece the origin of the order called Tufcan, of which we ſhall ſay more in it's proper place. Yet great uncertainty has always attended the diſcriminations made between that order and the Doric, of which none can be igno-rant who have read the remarks that have been variouſly made upon the amphitheatre at Verona, and upon the Trajan column at Rome. From that cauſe aroſe the notion, that in Etruria the Doric was poſſeſſed as early as in Greece [‡]. That there is room for ſtrong diſcriminations to be pointed out is certain; and per-haps no man has ſucceeded better in that view than the Marquis Maffei in his treatife on the amphitheatre above-mentioned. But thoſe diſcriminations never affected main principles, nor do they prove that the Doric might not have grown out of the other,

[*] D'Ancarv. vol. 2. p. 273, 275, 282, 289.　　　　[†] Ibid. p. 282, 289, 367.
[‡] Leoni's Alberti, p. 141.

which we fhall here more properly call Pelafgian than Tufcan. It is well known that in the ftrict examples of Doric order, there is a vaft variety, but with the prefervation of the fame original principles; and the fame thing was done by the Greeks in all their other orders. In the Tufcan itfelf Vitruvius fpeaks of it's having been executed in various ways; in fome of which it might undoubtedly have paffed for the Doric*. Why therefore might not thofe earlier Pelafgian ftructures be confidered as the movements towards that maturer order which was eftablifhed by the Dorians? If we reafon in this manner, there is no knowing to what periods we muft go back for the real origin of the Doric. M. D'Ancarville obferves truly, that the architecture, or, as he calls it, the order purfued in the palace of Œnomaus muft have been of a date vaftly prior to the æra in which it appeared there †. Thofe, on the other hand, who will not reafon thus, muft at leaft relinquifh the opinion, if they have held it, that the Doric was the firft order known in Greece : the inference is then neceffary, from the palace of Œnomaus alone, that there was another order in ufe before it.

But when we fpeak of the palace of Œnomaus, we fpeak of the work of a modern age compared with thofe fragments which obtrude themfelves on our notice in ages infinitely more remote. What was that order, or that architecture, of which the ancient Samothracians, inhabiting an ifland in the Ægean fea now called Samandrachi, fo uniformly and conftantly fpoke ? Diodorus Siculus reports it as their regular tradition, recorded too by the hiftorians of that ifland, that " long before every other deluge " known in thofe parts of the world," (evidently meaning thofe

* Vitruv. lib. 4. c. 7. De Tufcanicis generibus.
† D'Ancarv. vol. 2. p. 367.

of Ogyges, Deucalion, &c.) " an immenſe inundation of the
" ſea broke forth, which covered ever after a conſiderable part
" of the lands of Samothrace, and alſo not a little of the neigh-
" bouring Aſiatic coaſt ; and that in after-times fiſhermen in
" thoſe parts very frequently brought up in their nets the chapi-
" ters of ſtone columns, which they had dragged from the bot-
" tom *." The deluge of Ogyges, much older than that of Deucalion, happened very near 1800 years before the Chriſtian æra.
We are loſt, when we would follow Diodorus beyond that
epoch to look for the chapiters of ſtone columns in Greece or on
it's coaſts. And yet aſſuredly thoſe were no viſionary or fanciful
diſcoveries, any more than the immenſe banks of human, and
other animal, bones, which have been found in thoſe parts, and
which could not have been thrown ſo partially together by the
univerſal deluge, nor by any other cauſe than ſo partial an inundation, inſtantaneouſly taking place †. Thoſe chapiters were the
works of thoſe people, whoſe bones are ſcattered in ſuch exceſſive heaps over that country. They ſhew that in the very remote times of that deluge, whatever was it's epoch, thoſe people
had towns, had arts, had architecture which made ſome pretenſions to order or to elegance ; and the inference would have been
reaſonable, if we had not an expreſs authority for it, that they
had alſo literary monuments, the loſs of which in that deluge,
and the long ignorance that enſued, cauſed it in after ages to
be ſaid that Cadmus firſt brought letters into Greece ‡. Down
to the time of Auguſtus the Samothracians ſhewed the various
altars raiſed in their iſland on the ſpots where the waters ſtopped,

* Diod. Sic. Bibl. lib. 5. p. 369.   D'Ancarv. vol. 2. p. 358, 361.
† D'Ancarv. vol. 2. p. 357, 360, 361.
‡ Diod. Sic. Bibl. lib. 5. p. 376.   D'Ancarv. vol. 2. p. 346, 347.

and their anceftors found a refuge from their fury *. But where is the hiftory that will conduct us to that ancient period in Greece, fo curious to be known?

These lights, fmall as they are, breaking out upon us, naturally enforce the apprehenfion of a much greater antiquity than has been commonly conceived in the architecture of Greece, and indeed in all it's arts: they alfo give confiderable ftrength, if it were wanted, to thofe evidences which prove both architecture and arts to have fubfifted in Afia for an antiquity amounting to more than a thoufand years beyond the ordinary calculation of chronologifts.

How fuperficial then muft be the views of thofe, who have formed their opinions concerning the antiquity of the Grecian orders from fuch circumftances as the filence of Homer on the fubject of regular architecture, and of architectural ornaments, and of many of thofe inftruments which are conceived to have been neceffary for architectural works? + We have already had occafion to remark on the weaknefs of fuch opinions from the ftate of Grecian fculpture demonftrated by facts. But it feems to be a prevalent idea with many, to make the world and every thing in it as young as poffible. And certainly in that idea the labour of refearch will be greatly faved, and the knowledge of the antiquarian and of the modern will be brought very much upon an equal footing.

Leaving here the difficulties which attend the antiquity of the firft Grecian orders, we fhall profit more by purfuing their philo-

* Diod. Sic. ubi fup.   D'Ancarv. ubi fup.
+ See Goguet's Orig. of Laws, &c. vol. 2. p. 205, 206, 216.

fophy, and learning what they teach. It is fufficient for us to take them up as wife and fixed principles of architecture, emanating from Grecian genius and ftudy, let the time in which they fo emanated at firft have been earlier or later, and whether it were under the names of Pelafgian or Doric.

It feems to have been implanted in the Grecian mind, from the moment it became ftrong, to do nothing but upon the principles of philofophic reafon. That people conceived that there was fuch a thing as truth in Nature, according to which they could adjuft correctly whatever was connected with proportion; and they rightly fought it in the human frame. In the conftruction of a great edifice nothing was either more ornamental in itfelf than the column, or might fo properly be embraced for the ftandard of particular tafte and ftyle, or for the index of that relative tafte and ftyle which ought to be purfued through the whole of any particular ftructure. The firft thing therefore which they ftudied to perfect was the column, according to thofe principles of proportion which the wife Creator of Nature had prefented to their obfervations in the nobleft living column to be feen in all his workmanfhip, the frame of man. In that frame the foot is properly the diameter, and therefore it was taken for the diameter or thicknefs of the column; and calculating at firft, though fomewhat lefs correctly, that the height of man was fix times the meafure of his foot, they made the diameter of their columns a fixth part of their height; or, in other words, they made the columns fix times higher than they were thick *. Afterwards correcting more properly their firft calculation by the idea that the foot of a man was a feventh part of his height, they added

* Vitruv. lib. 4. c. 1.

a feventh diameter, and made their columns feven times as high as they were thick*. It fhould neverthelefs be obferved, that the proportion of columns to their height was lefs in porticos, and other fuch buildings than in temples, of which we have a particular proof in a Doric portico at Athens†, where the columns are only fix diameters high.

Having thus gained the diameter, they proceeded in the ufe of it as they obferved the great Creator had proceeded in the human frame, all the parts of which they found concordantly regulated by numerical proportions, and that one part ferved for a common meafure to all the others. They therefore made the diameter a meafure, by which more or lefs multiplied, divided, or fubdivided, they arrived at the due proportion of all the other parts of their ftruĉure. By this medium, and by no other, are obtained all the meafures of the bafe, the fhaft, the neck, the capital, and the feveral members of the entablature above.

It is neverthelefs proper to obferve, which we fhall do with more connecĉion in this place than in any other, although it equally concerns all the other orders as well as the Doric, that when the Greeks had thus gained their diameter from the human foot, it was not their defign, nor was it neceffary in their way to perfecĉion, to conftruĉt the feveral component parts of their column in the fame analogy and proportion to the whole as the feveral component parts of the human frame bear to the whole body; for inftance, that the capital, or the neck, fhould poffefs the fame proportionable meafure of their whole column as the

* Vitruv. lib. 4. c. 1. Plin. lib. 36. c 56. p. 755.
† See Stuart's Athens, vol. 1. c. 1. p. 2.

human head or the human neck poſſeſs of their reſpective
bodies.   This, I ſay, was neither intended nor neceſſary, becauſe they were forming a column as the foundation of an
order, not a human image.   The ſeveral members of the column roſe, therefore, in proportion to the ſpecific height and
compaſs of that column, without deriving any further example from the human frame than concerned the general idea
of their being adopted as members.   And yet, varying as theſe
did from the rules of proportion obſerved in the members of the
human body, they were no leſs perfect in their place than the
others.   If the head of man in a ſtrong and maſculine form engages about an eighth part of his whole height, taken on an aver-
age of five feet eight inches, which if denominated in the Doric
order would amount to an eighth part leſs than a whole diameter;
the capital of that order, taken as the mere capital, and mea-
ſuring only, as it does, half the diameter of the column below,
which although it riſes to more height than man, is yet not of
man's bulk, nor formed in the faſhion of man, is juſt as much in
perfect proportion to it's own body as the head of man is to that
on which it is placed.   The Ionic column is a degree more ſlender
and more elevated than the other, and on the ſame principle it's
capital obtains a degree leſs in meaſurement.   The Corinthian
advances ſtill more into elevation, but takes a new ground of
meaſurement to it's capital, reverſing the rule that governed in
the other two, but retaining ſtill perfection to itſelf.   For it's capital engages a whole diameter of the column below, and ·one-
ſixth part more.   But that column was peculiarly dreſſed above
others, and that circumſtance alone required a more diſtinguiſhed
capital, if the richneſs and elevation of the capital had not fur-
·niſhed an original cauſe to the order itſelf.

Thus was at length perfected the order called Doric, with this further circumstance attending it, that no base was put to the column *. The reason for this is not easy to be assigned, whether it was omitted on purpose, or for want of that maturer consideration which has ever since invariably given a base to every column, whether of this or any other order. They might have been led to that omission by the example of the Egyptians, whose massy columns †, if we may judge from those numerous ones which now remain in the edifices of Upper Egypt, had no base. It has been supposed that the Doric column was formed in imitation of the naked man, and therefore that the base, answering to a shoe, was omitted ‡. But would not that supposition leave the difficulty greater? For the naked man has a foot to support his body; and then they departed with their eyes open from the principles of strength and stability which they had professed to follow. Perhaps a better reason may be urged for their omission of the base, and which might apologize in their minds for so material an omission, if we are disposed to think that it was purposely done. The Greeks of those times, as well as the Egyptians, ranged their columns very near to one another. The latter did this, because, not knowing how to construct an arch, they conceived it not prudent to leave too much to a flat stone covering the void space; and the former did it from their first notions

---

* Vitruv. lib. 4. c 1. Ware's Palladio, p 17. Chambray's Parallel, p. 15, 20, 38. Stuart's Athens, vol. 1. p. 1.

† See a sketch of these in Goguet's Orig. of Laws, &c. vol. 3. p. 74. Yet, the Israelites in the wilderness had learned to employ bases, as well as chapiters, to their pillars in the tabernacle. But when we read the 31st chapter of Exodus, particularly the 3d and 6th verses, we shall pause before we conclude that every portion of knowledge displayed in the workmanship of that tabernacle was merely of Egyptian instruction.   ‡ Chambray's Parallel.

of greater ſtrength.   Had they then applied baſes to their columns, the paſſages between each would have been rendered ſo
narrow and inconvenient by the angles and projectures of the
baſes, that people as they paſſed would have been apt to ſtumble
upon them.   It might therefore have been their deſign, by avoiding the baſe, to keep the pavement clear and unembarraſſed to
paſſengers.   They might chuſe to prefer conveniency to beauty,
preciſely for the ſame reaſon which afterwards occaſioned Vitruvius to direct that the plinth of the Tuſcan column ſhould be
rounded off; that order being adapted, like the Doric, to edifices of great buſineſs and reſort, and in which therefore a plain
but noble ſimplicity of ſtrength is required.

But on whatever reaſon they acted reſpecting the baſe, a capital
was inevitable, correſponding to the head of man, and without
which the column would have been an unfiniſhed trunk.   In
Egypt they had never ſeen a column without a capital, odd and
unmeaning as thoſe capitals were.   The mind of man ſeems never
to have entertained the notion of a ſhapeleſs block, abruptly
terminated.

With reſpect to ornament in the Doric order, whoſe firſt pro-
feſſion was ſtrength with ſober dignity, no acceſſions from ornament were ſought in the entablature, but ſuch as became the
manly dreſs, and ſuited the ſtrong and manly character.   It was
conceived that the nearer thoſe ornaments kept to the ſimilitude
of thoſe parts which were moſt material and ſtriking in the formation of a timber-building, the nearer they would be to Nature,
and the more congenial to the plainneſs of this order.   Triglyphs
and mutules beſpoke the greater timbers of the roof: the metopes repreſented the ſpace between thoſe timbers; and the orna-

ments on thofe metopes were generally taken from the ftrength of animal nature, particularly exemplified in the heads of oxen. Yet we fhould not reach the full contemplation of the Greeks in thofe felections, if we confidered them as embraced merely from their expreffions of ftrength. The reader has by this time become perfectly familiar with the rank in which the emblematic ox was received in the ancient theology of the Greeks, as well as of all other nations to whom the principles of Scythicifm had reached. What ornament therefore could fo confiftently be introduced into the conftruction of their temples, as that which gave the firft features of their emblematic religion, if it's natural character of ftrength had not particularly fuited the character of this order? And therefore it is remarkable that the patera, well known for it's eftablifhed ufe in religious rites, was often affociated with the head of the ox in thofe ornaments.

Sometimes, however, this fimplicity of ornament has yielded to one more rich and elegant, of which we have an exemplification by Mr. Stuart * in the metopes of one of the pediments in the Doric temple of Minerva Parthenon, which are filled with admirable fculptures of an uncommon kind; and fo is the frize quite round the temple. In another Doric ftructure, of which a fragment is given by the fame author †, the triglyphs, which in all other inftances appear to have been confidered as ornaments themfelves, are moft fingularly and richly decorated with fuperadded fculptures.

The guttæ or drops, reprefented in the foffits of the corona, and which feem invariably to have been employed as the efta-

---

* See vol. 2. c. 1. p. 10. pl. 3 and 4.   † Vol. 1. p. 1.

blished ornaments of thofe foffits in this order, were introduced
with perfect nature, becaufe the corona was the gutter in which
the rain water was received.

It is natural for mankind to rife upon their own difcoveries.
The Greeks fettled in Ionia wifhed to throw more delicacy into
their ftructures.   Confcious that they could not improve the method purfued in the compofition of the Doric, they needed only
to vary it, by taking the proportions in the frame of woman inftead of man.   In that frame the foot became, at firft, the diameter of a feventh part of the height ; and rifing afterwards in
proportion to the increafe at which it had been calculated in the
Doric order, it gave an eighth part to the thicknefs of the column.   To this order was alfo given a bafe, which not only
anfwered to the fhoes or fandals more decently guarding the
female foot, but ferved as a focket or cafe in which the column
more delicate in it's frame might repofe with more folidity ; it
was therefore made in the manner of twifted cords, or of a large
cable, fupplying that repofe.

In ornaments a greater indulgence was taken than in the Doric
order, and yet thefe were extremely fimple, conformable to the
matron-character, and intended to reprefent it's drefs.   The
channelings along the trunk were meant to imitate the folds in
in the robes of women.   Sometimes thofe channelings were fo
terminated as to give room for very elegant ornaments on the
upper part of the fhaft above them, an example of which is
afforded in the Erectheum at Athens*.   The volutes or leaf-work
of the chapiter reprefented the hair hanging in curls on each fide

* Stuart's Athens, vol. 2. c. 2. pl. 5.

of the neck : and the fruit or flower-work carved on the front refembled the hair on the fore-head. In the Ionic temple on the Ilyffus an example is afforded where the ornament called echinus, or eggs and anchors, is continued under the volutes, and quite round the building, contrary to the cuftom which has been much embraced by moderns *. In that temple other circumftances of fingular tafte were feen in this order. The mouldings differed much from all other Ionic examples, with which we have been acquainted ; their forms were extremely fimple, but very elegant, and fo well executed, that the temple of which we are now fpeaking may be reckoned among the firft works of antiquity in this order†. The dentil, which imitated the projeɛtion of leſſer joifts, was thought fuitable to an order profeffing lefs ftrength, and therefore it was felected for the Ionic, as the triglyphs and mutules reprefenting the projeɛtion of greater timbers were appropriated to the Doric.

Still there was wanting a charaɛter of richnefs, to which neither of thofe orders approached, and even a greater degree of delicacy than was reached by the Ionic. The attainment of thefe was referved for more diftant times, and appeared in the Corinthian order. Yet thofe times perhaps were not fo very diftant from the origin of the other two orders as they may generally have been fet down. We are far from being ready to agree that the Corinthian arofe with Callimachus, only 540 years before our æra. But this difcuffion we fhall waive for the prefent, as it would carry us too far from our attention to the conftitution of this order, referving it for the time when fome evidences refpeɛt-

---

* Stuart's Athens, vol. 1. c. 2. p. 7. pl. 7. fig. 1.
† Ibid. c. 2. p. 7.

ing it's antiquity will come before us in the architecture of **Regal Rome.**

It was not any change in the firſt principles of reference to the human frame, but merely an extenſion of thoſe principles which was wanted for the foundation of that order. The human frame muſt ever remain the moſt perfect ſtandard of proportion in all Nature. Yet that ſtandard, although uniform in it's conſtitution, is ſomewhat varied in it's qualities, which throw a different meaſure into the different claſſes of it's proportion. In the female form the proportions of the grown woman, and of the young virgin, are numerically different with reſpect to the whole frame of each, although ſyſtematically they are the ſame, and governed by the ſame analogy, both with reſpect to themſelves, and to each other, and to the form of the other ſex too. To the virgin-frame therefore the Greeks next reſorted for thoſe new characters which they wiſhed to attain. From thence their order roſe in a new delicacy drawn from the proportions which they had taken for it's rule. The diameter of the column became only the tenth part of it's whole height, which gave a nobler elevation, while equal ſtrength was maintained in greater elegance of ſtructure ; and that nobler elevation gave a proportionable encreaſe to the intercolumniations or openings between the columns, by which means greater lightneſs ran through the whole, and the delicacy that was every where maintained. became more diſtinct to the view.

The channelings along the ſhaft were in their purpoſe as applicable to this order as to the Ionic. Thoſe channelings were not always terminated in that preciſe form, in which they may generally have been obſerved. In the choragic monument of Lyſicrates, commonly called the lanthorn of Demofthenes, their lower extremities defcend below their ufual limits into the fcape of the fhaft, while their upper extremities terminate in the form of leaves, and make a firft row of foliage in the capital*.

The Attic bafe, appropriated to this order, gave a delicacy and beauty which was extremely well fuited to the peculiar frame of this column, and was by no means reached by the Ionic bafe, even when joined to it's own order. While the component parts of this Attic bafe were in thofe more delicate proportions, which diftinguifhed Corinthian from Ionic, the plinth taking a fomewhat larger fpace gives the appearance of greater folidity than is attained by the Ionic, with all it's increafed thicknefs of parts. In one inftance, perhaps among many, had they been equally refcued from the ruins of time, I mean, in the portico at Athens, commonly fuppofed to be the remains of the temple of Jupiter Olympius, pedeftals were carried from the bafes down to the ground†; and the plinths of the bafe projected there beyond the die of the pedeftals‡. In another inftance ftill more fingular, that is, in the octagonal tower of the winds, no bafes at all were given to the columns of this order§.

But richnefs along with delicacy, which no invention has fince been able to equal, was confpicuous in the capital. That capital, long eftablifhed in general knowledge, did in all probability fpring from Callimachus. Let the accident related by Vitruvius as having fuggefted that thought to Callimachus be true or fictitious, nothing could be more happily devifed to exprefs either a

---

* Stuart's Athens, vol. 1. c. 4. p. 32. † Ibid. c. 5. pl. 3.
‡ Ibid. p. 43. pl. 7. § Ibid. c. 3. p. 19. pl. 3.

general richnefs of object, or the particular elegance of a young
lady's head-drefs which it was meant to imitate, than the foliage
difplayed in waving fcrolls, and rifing in various rows like curls
judicioufly difpofed by art, and made to fwell in new embellifhment around the head which is by Nature ornament itfelf to
the fex. It is remarkable that the Greeks, felecting that foliage
from the bear's foot for the purpofe of that imitation, were fo
accurate as to adopt that fpecies of the plant which is more
fmooth and cultivated, abandoning the other which was wild
and rough.

But new beauties arofe from it in their hands, when they came
to difpofe it's ornaments for the crowning of the column.   The
fcroll which rofe in the uppermoft height they threw out and
fpread a little more on either fide, fo as to produce two admirable effects, which could not otherwife have been attained, and by
that means were moft naturally attained; the one for ornament,
and the other for real ufe.   As an ornament, thofe more vigorous
and fpreading fcrolls not only carry on the whole drefs to terminate in a becoming fwell, inftead of leaving it either formal or
ungraceful in a perpendicular compafs, or meagre by verging to
a narrower point, but they form an angle at each end, which
gives a moft pleafing contraft to the roundnefs of the column
below.   In point of real ufe, they afford a moft needful, and at
the fame time a moft natural, fupport to the abacus or flat covering above, which as a part of the entablature rifing from thence
muft neceffarily fpread itfelf beyond the mere compafs of the
column, and could not be left without a full fupport to it's whole
meafure.

Much pains have been taken by fome moderns, feduced by the

affectation of originality, to fubftitute for that upper fcroll or volute fomething elfe which might perform the fame fwell, and anfwer the fame purpofe of fupport to the abacus. And we will not fay that the characters of richnefs and elegance, or the refources of human invention for the difplay of thofe characters, in the capital of an order, are confined to the bear's foot, the bafket, and the tile; but we may venture to affirm, that with the prefervation of the fame foliage no natural combination will ever be made, and with the prefervation of the fame purpofe and effect no equal fubftitution will be found.

It muft neverthelefs be obferved, that the Greeks were no more tamely uniform in the employment of this capital, than they were in the rules by which they formed the channelings or the bafe of the column. In the octagonal tower of the winds the upper range of leaves was not divided like the bear's foot, or like any other of the foliages proper to the Corinthian capital, but they were fmooth, and refembling what we fhould call water-leaves*. Again, in the choragic monument of Lyficrates thofe water-leaves, rifing immediately out of the channelings, become a firft row of foliage in the capital below the bear's foot. The fame inftance will afford us other proofs of fingular variation, which the Greeks were not afraid to indulge, while it broke through no rule of reafon or propriety which they had laid down for the government of their tafte. In that choragic monument the cornice was fingularly crowned with a fort of a fcroll, which we fhall call Vitruvian, inftead of a Cimatium. How often that practice might have taken place, we know not; that being the only inftance of the kind in ancient ftructures which has come

---

* Stuart's Athens, vol. 1. c. 3.

down to us, although in fome ancient medals there are examples
of temples crowned in the fame manner*.

It was not always that they indulged that richnefs and elegance of drefs, which this order might naturally bear, and
which has generally been conceived to be juftified to any extent.
In the portico at Athens, which has already been mentioned,
this order was employed in the moft fingular fimplicity.   No
part of the mouldings were enriched ; only the foffit of the co-
rona† : three fides of the building were without ornaments of
any kind ; and the front was in a ftyle of fober magnificence,
without one ornament of fculpture, while not a trace of orna-
mental decoration appeared in all the infide. We muft recollect
that the building of which we now fpeak was a portico, if Mr.
Stuart has rightly conceived it ; and it is for no other reafon more
probable that it was a portico, than that fo much plainnefs and
fimplicity was maintained there in the ufe of the Corinthian order.   The Greeks were a modeft people, chafte in the exercife
of their genius, and reftricted in the pride and luxury of their
architecture to the occafions which were great, and in which the
dignity of the ftate or the fanctity of religion were concerned.
In all thofe buildings which were not devoted to either of thofe
purpofes, a characteriftic fimplicity was preferved and ftudied.
The portico was only a degree more public than their own dwellings.   In thefe laft they dared not, or they would not, as repub-
licans indulge a fplendid and decorative appearance.   That portico too, of which we are fpeaking, was deftined to be made
rich with other fplendors of art.   The ornaments therefore,
which it might have derived from architecture would either have

* Stuart's Athens, vol. 1. c. 4. p. 29.   † Ibid. vol. 1. c. 5. p. 43. pl. 8.

drawn the general attention from thofe other works of art, collected there for the immortalizing of their heroes and of their
country, or they would have been loft in the general affemblage.

Thefe then are the orders which fprung from the Greeks, and
in which their architecture was employed. Thofe which were
the invention or the employment of others will be found in their
refpective fituations and periods. Of the Grecian orders the
Corinthian being the lateft in time was of courfe not feen in their
moft ancient, nor indeed in their moft confiderable, edifices.
The temples of Jupiter and of Juno at Olympia, that of Diana
at Ephefus, that of Minerva at Athens, and that of Thefeus,
were either of the Doric or Ionic order *. In Ionia the latter
was moft reafonably to be expected, and accordingly it has been
found moft abundantly there †. It is rather fingular that in
Egypt is now remaining at the ancient Ptolemais, now called
Ptolemeta, perhaps the only temple exifting in the firft manner
of executing that order, the work of Ptolemy Philadelphus ‡. It
was natural that the Corinthian fhould make it's firft appearance
at Corinth. Yet in Athens was feen it's moft eminent difplay.
The Romans neverthelefs employed it far more frequently than
the Greeks.

In thofe three orders the Greeks conceived very rightly that
they had furnifhed every character which could be given to
architectural ftructure. All the diverfity, which Nature had expreffed in the great prototype of human ftructure, by which they
were guided, was purfued in thofe orders. The human frame is

---

* Vitruv. lib. 7. præfat.   Paufan. lib. 5. c. 10.   Spon's Voy. vol. 2 p. 420, 455.
† Chambray's Paral. p. 41.   ‡ Bruce's Trav. Introduc. p. 41.

feen in the three gradations of mafculine ftrength, of delicacy joined with a prevalent fimplicity, and of greater delicacy ftill united with an elegance of form and richnefs of drefs. What further charaĉter than thefe can architeĉture take? In all it's branches, whether for ornament or ufe ; for ftrength or gaiety ; for the elegant retreats of pleafure, or the rougher throng of bufinefs ; for the refidence of princes, or the abode of private individuals ; for the purpofes of religion, or thofe of ftate-concerns ; the fpirit that beft befits the edifice fhall be found in one or other of thofe orders : the fpirit that beft fuits the circum. ftances and condition of thofe, whether they be individuals or a public, by whom any of thofe edifices may be creĉted, fhall find it's convenient accommodation in the various degrees of ex- pence with which thofe feveral orders are purfued.

In fucceding times attempts have been made to enlarge their compafs ; but the unfuccefsfulnefs of thofe attempts have proved the fufficiency of the ftandards eftablifhed by the Greeks : they have terminated, at moft, in the creating of a nominal addition to the number of thofe ftandards, without introducing any vari- ation in their nature and their principles. The ingenuity of man has never yet been able to keep pace with his defires of adding a new ftandard in Nature to thofe which fatisfied the Greeks. If he has fought new ground, it has been more in ornament than in proportion that his refearches have been gratified ; and that gra- tification has been gained not fo much from an equal warranty in Nature as from the licence of his own choice. More frequently that licence has been direĉted to a combination of the Grecian orders themfelves, and to the formation of a new charaĉter from the compofition of the feveral properties of the old. Nothing can render more honour to the completenefs of the Greek invention than the idea of such a composition; but perhaps it disparages in an equal degree the pretensions to original genius in those that adopt it; it yields an easy compliment to vanity, without any expence to indolence; but, after all, it is the last idea which the Greeks would have indulged, with all the licence to which they were unquestionably entitled of making the freest use of their own discoveries.

In each of those orders it was a fixed object of the Greeks to establish a character. And that character was so distinctly relative to each, that it was maintained in it's place with the most cautious attention. The strength of the Doric was not confounded with that which was not characteristic of strength, or which was characteristic of less strength than belonged to the Doric species : the delicacy of the Ionic was never vitiated by that which contributed to the solidity of the other: and the greater delicacy still, the elegance, and richness of the Corinthian shewed nothing of those component parts which were peculiar to either of the others, and which in them became dignity, but in this would have been meretricious and absurd. On this principle Vitruvius observes, that the Greeks never suffered, because consistency forbad*, the Ionic dentil to be shewn on Doric chapiters, or the Doric triglyph on the Ionic columns. The dentil represented the lesser strength of small joists, and the triglyph denoted the greater solidity of tie-beams. Both therefore were improper to fill the place of the other. In every other circumstance they were equally careful to preserve the uniformity of design, and to put nothing out of it's place, because they were too philosophic to see any advantage in the violation of the nature of things.

* Vitruv. lib. 1. c. 2.

The nature of things held and directed them evermore ; it was facred to their minds. In all their conftructions of the parts of architecture, and in all the fymmetry and proportion of thofe parts, they proceeded on thofe principles which had their exiftence in the nature of things, and which were capable of being demonftrated as truths or proprieties in general argument. And therefore Vitruvius exprefsly remarks again, * that whenever the dentil was employed by the Greeks, it was never put under the mutules or modiglions, which reprefent the ends of the principal rafters, but above them, becaufe it would be a falfe principle of workmanfhip to put the leffer and the weaker under the heavier and the ftronger. For the fame reafon he alfo obferves †, that the Greeks never gave the example of either mutules or dentils on the pediments of their edifices in front, but a fimple cornice, becaufe neither the principal rafters nor the leffer joifts project towards the front, but form the eaves on the flank ; and this obfervation of Vitruvius is confirmed by the example of a Doric portico afforded by Mr. Stuart, where the mutules are omitted in the cornice over the pediment ‡. It concerns both thofe inftances of practice in the Greeks, when we fpeak of a deviation in modern ages from the principle maintained by them in the former of thofe inftances ; and the Roman temples feem to have introduced the deviation. In thofe temples dentils appear under modiglions. Count Galliani is perhaps the only modern who has fufficiently explained the reafon of that procedure. He fays, that when the dentils are above the modiglions, they cannot · be placed in the horizontal cornice under the tympanum. In order therefore to make the fronts of their edifices equally elegant

---

* Vitruv. lib. 4. c. 2.　　　　‡ Stuart's Athens, vol. i. c. i. pl. 6. fig. 3.
† Ibid.

with the other parts, the Romans were tempted to make this deviation from the practice of the Greeks. Thus, by departing from the Grecian principle in the one inftance, they made their way to that which the Greeks had ftudiously avoided to exemplify in the other. They were fure to be followed by thofe who were not fond of being reftricted to the natural order of things, or who conceived that elegance might be drawn with equal fuccefs from a freer fcope and leffer exactnefs. And if that be true, or if the Greeks were too narrow and formal in their attachment to the truth which is exemplified in the nature of things, then thofe moderns are right.

But the character eftablifhed by the Greeks in their feveral orders is worthy of attention for it's extent. In this view it has never been fufficiently confidered by writers in general. And yet in this view, beyond queftion, the high merit of thofe orders will beft be feen. It was not the contemplation of the Greeks merely to form a column in diftinct perfection. Their object went to afcertain the fpecies of character, which fhould mark every part and portion of the edifice, for which any one of thofe orders was adopted. In this there was good fenfe, and without this all their boafted ingenuity in the formation of the orders would have been but an empty flourifh, which would have left architecture itfelf a mere caprice, deftitute of any real ftandard by which it's fpirit in any cafe could be decided, and the only one of the fine arts humiliated to the condition of being without variety of fpirit and character, or without principles by which a diftinct fpirit and character in it might be fcientifically maintained.

In the works of the pencil, the infinite affemblage of colours and fhades of colours affords not more diftinct views than the vaft variety of character and execution in which thofe works are beheld under all the great mafters, who have only followed the principles inherent in the art, and moft congenial to their own fpirit. In fculpture the majeftic, the graceful, the foft and tender, the fevere, every diftinction of character, is decidedly maintained to pervade the whole execution, and to form a whole to the eye, on principles as fixed and juft as any fpecies of truth in Nature. In mufic, all thofe characters and difcriminations of fpirit and fentiment and tafte, which are found in the conftitution and procefs of the other arts, are beheld in equal ftrength, and become refpectively the foul of the compofition in whatever ftyle it may be caft; fo that the folemn, the lively, the pathetic, the tones of love, or the tones of war, fhall form and finifh the air by which our feelings are addreffed. Is the fpirit of architecture alone bereft of this compafs? No. The orders will lead us in any ftructure to form a whole under each, as ftrictly characteriftic of the tafte and ftyle prefcribed as would come from the hands of the moft accomplifhed painter, fculptor, or mufician, ftudying to give any theme all the perfection which comprehenfively belongs to it. The feveral members or portions of the column, which becomes the order of the edifice, may feem to fuperficial minds to have no farther reach, and to convey no farther inftruction, than to the fhare which they hold in that particular column to which they appertain. But the man who has deeply ftudied their principles, and purfued their more diftant relations and ufes, will be led to all the proportions that arife out of the order, and are demanded by any part of the edifice; to all the ornaments that become it; to every circumftance in the outline and in the finifhing too.

Is the ftructure to be Doric? The proportions every where

must be such as produce the appearance of manly strength and quiet dignity. Height must not predominate. The parts must be few: the breadths grand: the outlines distinct: the outlines producing movement both in length and height must be few in number, and decided in their character. All the mouldings of course will be Doric. The compartments will not be numerous: the piers will exhibit a suitably strong effect: the openings will be found both in number and dimension correspondent to the general face and rules of that strength which presides over the whole.

Take the contrast to this in the delicate beauty and richness of the Corinthian. The proportion of height to breadth must every where be greater: the breaks must be more numerous, and less bold: the parts must be delicate, without being paltry, or frittered away: the apertures more numerous, and of more slender proportions: the aid of sculpture may be called in to adorn the whole: the delicacy both of the materials and of the execution must keep pace with the elegance of the whole composition.

It is not our purpose to write for professional men, therefore we do not pretend to speak here in those figures which would make these things more plain. Whoever will take the pains to read Vitruvius with attention, will draw these things in great precision from their source; he will see not only the possibility, but the obligation, of carrying on the same character, whatever it be that is selected, through all the component parts, if I may so speak, of the same composition; and he will not fail to admire the clear and philosophic manner in which that wonderful man, who alone connects us with ancient Greece, has explained these principles so deeply rooted in science and so involved in figures. That it requires the hand of steady judgement, and cool comprehensive recollection, to design and fill up completely in character any great outlines drawn from these orders, is beyond question ; but that is the very genius of architecture, and it was the pride of the Greeks.

Emulating this establishment of character in all their works, architecture became in their hands the philosophy of engaging our most rational sensations. Those who have come after them, those at least who have looked no farther into this art than to it's mechanical attainment, may have no notion of the analogy of it's proportions to the finer sensations of the human mind ; but with the Greeks it absolutely became a philosophic study to produce a work, which should strike the intelligent as forcibly by it's principle and execution as any other art of design was known to be capable of doing. And why should this be impossible ? Why should it be thought a fanciful philosophy in the Greeks to produce in architecture a theme, which should speak to the genuine feelings of the human breast ? There are structures of a lesser kind, which can unquestionably do this. The well-designed monument, according to it's quality and purpose, can either strike us with admiration, lift us into gaiety of heart, or sink us in sadness. What do we say to the fictitious structures of the theatre, whose regular and forcible execution to the distant eye, although in fact but the rude and simple imitation of real structures, draws forth every sensation that it pleases to draw ? With the enchanted palace of Armida all becomes magnificent and voluptuous to our senses. Let the scene change, and let the hall of Pluto present itself, it is met by horror and affrightment. Do we behold the temple of the Sun ? the soul is enwrapt with admiration. Is it a prison that succeeds ? we know no feelings but those of distressed concern.

It was thus that the Greeks endeavoured to build. It was to excite fome powerful and ufeful fenfation that their genius in architecture was employed. They held in contempt the idea of placing ftone upon ftone without meaning, and of introducing ornaments without reference to a confiftent effect: they knew nothing of raifing a ftructure which fhould even ftrike by a general impreffion every eye that beheld it, but which fhould leave every judgement diffatisfied, and every mind undecided about it's object.

The means by which they made their architecture thus interefting may be comprifed in the general power which they confpicuoufly poffeffed of producing harmony. This is the true key to all our fenfations, the firft impulfe on the human mind, and the fure mover of great effects in it. Whatever is harmonious muft always be interefting. All men indeed have not the fame organs, or are not prepared by the fame ftudies, to receive it alike; but to pleafe it never fails; if it does not ftrike every man as completely as the man by whom it is created, it never fails to make that impreffion which fatisfies as much as if it were fcientifically underftood. Nature herfelf charms us evermore, only becaufe fhe is every where harmonious; fhe continues for ever the great rule of truth and perfection to art, only becaufe the moft perfect relation fubfifts between all the parts of every object, and between all the objects and fcenes upon the face of her creation to one another. The fine arts therefore can have no other fource of intellectual fatisfaction to the world, but as they are the vehicles of harmony, and exprefs it with new and variegated force not only upon the more refined and cultivated, but upon every fenfible, mind.

Architecture, in the conception of the Greeks, fhould be

ftrenuoufly raifed to the production of this engaging effect. The
field they took for this purpofe was a large one : every circumftance, at leaft in the external defign, was made contributory to
it's fuccefs. It was feen in the nice adjuftment of every edifice
to it's fituation, and to that pofition in the fituation which Nature and experience taught in fuch a cafe, or which it's peculiar
deftination required. It was feen in the judicious relation of all
the maffes to the fpot in which they flood ; in their proportionable relation to each other ; and in the fkilful divifion of all their
parts, fo effential to the prefervation of a clear and unembar-
raffed fimplicity ; in the exact correfpondence too of all thofe
parts to one another, fo effential to the prefervation of a needful
uniformity. It was feen in the whole fcope of the elevation,
which exhibited not fingle beauties in fingle places, but a confiftent participation of the fame beauty in it's whole detail. It was
feen in the happy diftribution of lights and fhadows mutually
relieving each other, and throwing out with more force the bolder features of the building. It was feen in the proper apporti-
onment of thofe lights and fhadows to the character intended, fo
that it fhould become all gay and chearful, or fhould take a ferious caft, or fhould participate of gloom. It was feen in their
chafte and fparing ufe of ornaments, confcious as they were that
thefe if not chafte, and perfectly analogous, and temperately
employed, do but moleft the harmony of defign, which like true
beauty needs but itfelf to pleafe all that behold it. It was feen
in the careful maintenance of a confiftent unity of purpofe thro'
the whole, which unity of purpofe was not yet fo rigid, nor neceffary fo to be, as to exclude a cautious ufe of variety, for inftance in the terminating lines, fome of which might be ftraight,
others curved, and others again mixed of both, provided that
variety moderately employed was brought to bear confiftently

with the general fyftem, and did not produce difcord. Variety is
without doubt a great beauty in every thing, when it becomes con-
gruity, when it brings together in a regular manner things different, but proportionable to each other ; and without that variety,
harmony will certainly be incomplete. It is by that variety fo
brought together and proportioned that mufic accomplifhes all
it's wonderful effects. When the bafe anfwers the treble, and the
tenor agrees with both, there arifes from that variety of founds
that harmonious union of proportions which properly conftitutes
the power and the perfection of mufic.

In this view, and probably in the famenefs of principle by
which the meafures and proportions of architecture and mufic
are conducted into harmony, there may be room for thofe who
feel an enthufiafm for the former to enlarge, as they have done,
on it's affinity with the latter. That Nature is fure to act with a
conftant analogy in all her operations is what may fafely be allowed ;—that thofe very numbers, by means of which the concord of founds affects our ears with delight, are the fame which
pleafe our eyes and our minds, may eafily be credited ;—that in
the formation of thofe great concords throughout Nature fhe
may have fo ordained it, that they fhall fall with a degree of regular conftancy on certain progreffive numbers, is what we fhall
not deny, when philofophers in all ages have taken fo much pains
to prove it ;—that the ternary principle, which Nature appears
in various ways to maintain more eminently, is one of thofe
progreffive numbers which fhe may have formed particularly fuccefsful in the production of thefe great concords, is more than
probable, becaufe it is abfolutely demonftrated in the harmony
of mufic, as well as in various harmonies of Nature ;—that
architects have availed themfelves of this ternary principle in a

diſtinguiſhed manner, along with other numerical principles, for the compoſition of the members of their edifices, and have made uſe of the ſeveral proportions ariſing out of the progreſs of that principle for the attainment of many proportions in their own art, is what we cannot diſpute, when it has been ſo ably urged by many of the firſt writers* in that claſs entitled to the firſt confidence for their ſolidity and good ſenſe.

It is ſufficient for us barely to mention theſe things, having no intention to dwell on them, however they might contribute to the profoundneſs of architectural ſcience; becauſe it is not quite ſo clear to us whether the Greeks, with whom we are at preſent engaged, actually formed their principles of architecture on the clear view and the decided purſuit of thoſe principles of harmony. Let Thebes have been built to the ſound of Amphion's lyre, it ſhall paſs with us for fable. Let the temple of Solomon have been raiſed exactly to the meaſures of muſic, it ſhall remain an embelliſhment to the "harmonic architecture" of Ouvrard a Frenchman, and to the commentary of the Jeſuit Villalpanda a Spaniard, who has ſet to muſic, if we may ſo ſpeak, but in reality has reduced to muſical meaſures, the ſcripture-proportions of that temple, as well as thoſe of other ancient buildings, and all the rules of Vitruvius. To thoſe writers we leave the honour of puſhing refinement as far as it will go, being contented for the preſent to know that the principles of Grecian architecture were laid on the moſt ſolid and rational foundation, for the pro-duction of a gracious harmony, whether that foundation and that harmony had more or leſs of the muſical ſyſtem in the con-templation of thoſe that framed them.

* Vitruvius, Alberti, &c.

By this time perhaps it will be conceded, that the Grecian orders were the refult of accurate and deliberate ftudy, and that the perfections in architecture poffeffed by that people were not ftumbled upon by chance. If this be allowed, a departure from the precife principles of any of thofe orders, a latitude in the employment of them which is not warranted by the example of the Greeks, fhould certainly be very cautioufly confidered, and requires to be vindicated on better grounds than the private caprice of architects, or the prefumption that beauty may be hit upon by the flight of unregulated genius. We are fenfible that this argument may go to reftrictions which good fenfe, and a veneration too for Greek examples, would never mean to impofe. It may be faid, that thofe orders, as the ftandard-language of architecture, no more exclude variations of expreffion than the Greek language in it's beft age forbad thofe varieties of ftyle, which, with equal correctnefs in all, diftinguifhed the pureft orators, hiftorians, and poets of Greece. It has been faid*, that any writer would deferve to be laughed at, who dared not to ufe one word which he could not find in Tully; and the obfervation has been equally carried to the architect, who fhould not dare to adopt one article that was not fanctioned by the ufe of the Greeks in the precifion of the order. Thefe fimilitudes are ingenious; but either the parallel does not hold completely, or it ftill leaves the Greek orders fecure from any arbitrary invafions. So far the parallel may agree, that as in all languages, fo in the orders of Greece, there is a ftandard-principle of correctnefs, which will readily determine what variations of ftyle are legitimate, and what are otherwife. But the variations of ftyle in writing will always be

* By Erafmus.

more abundant than thofe which can flow from the orders of architecture. Becaufe in writing what branches out as a variation of ftyle from the ftandard-principles of purity becomes in architecture thofe ftandard-principles themfelves. The ftrong and nervous, the chafte and delicate, the rich, luxuriant, and diffufive, which emanate with various fpirit of expreffion from a language whofe principles of truth and correctnefs are regulated over them, become in architecture not that emanating fpirit of various expreffion, but thofe very original rules of language, that very fource of principles, from which every variation muft flow. But the variations of ftyle muft neceffarily be more limited, where they are no longer branches from rules, but rules themfelves.

True, however, it is that the Greeks themfelves took fome liberties with their own orders. But this fhould be rightly underftood, left that which was principle in them fhould be made the caufe of fanctioning the want of principle in others. The liberties they took were fuch as. argued that they were perfect mafters of all that naturally grew out of the principles of their orders, not fuch as proved them to be unfteady in thofe principles themfelves. We know of no inftance in which they mangled their orders for the purpofe of intermixing them in the fame portions of defign. They fometimes employed two different orders in different portions of the fame edifice, keeping each diftinct in it's place. But the circumftances, in which that was done, always vindicated plainly it's propriety ; as in the Erectheum at Athens, which, according to the beft opinions formed on the different levels of the porticos leading into each end of that edifice, appears to have been one temple over another. Where reafons of fo ftrong a kind did not urge them, they were very fparing of that meafure, efpecially in thofe purer times when they were difengaged from the influence of the Romans, who were more inclined to indulge it without fuch reafons. In like manner, they were extremely cautious how they broke through the conftituting principles of any of their orders : they never increafed on any account the ftandard-diameters in the heighth of their columns ; nor did they ever decreafe the ftandard-meafures of their entablature, unlefs invited by the purpofes of perfpeftive. When moderns have enlarged the former to the height of 14 or 15 diameters, or have wantonly diminifhed the latter until they occupy no more than the proper meafure of the architrave, affuredly they never found an example of that conduft in the Greeks.

In addition to the inftances which have already been adduced, and in which a latitude or variation was taken for the purpofe of fhewing the richnefs of their invention, the moft frequent inftances in which that latitude appeared were in thofe circumftances which made it materially affiftant to the fituation of their defign. And fo far the latitude, which violated in no refpeft the wifdom of the orders, muft be allowed to be fair, fince they were made conducive to their proper purpofe, the effeft of defign; for the energy of defign would be deftroyed, if it were never to move out of exact trammels, while it did not abandon a proper and confiftent fymmetry. To thofe licences, however, the Greeks contrived to give a new principle, which, although it were created by neceffity, feemed to eftablifh itfelf as fatisfactorily as if had been regularly dictated by the order in queftion. For inftance, when in the infide of temples which had no roofs, but colonades for fhelter, they introduced two heights of the fame order one above another, for the purpofe of affording galleries, and of leffening the diameters above, they wifely made the entablature of the lower order to confift of the architrave alone, at once giving greater ftability to the ftrufture, and avoiding the

abfurdity of reprefenting there a gutter over the lower order.
If ever they departed from rule in dimenfion, it was, where the
effects of vifion were to be confulted, as will prefently appear
when we come to fpeak of their perfpective. Perhaps the greateft
deviation from general fyftem was exemplified by Hermogenes,
when he contrived the Pfeudodipteron, or, in other words, when
he took away a whole range of columns to enlarge the portico;
and for that liberty he has been commended by Vitruvius, becaufe it was ufeful.

After all, thofe examples of licence in the Greeks will never
be capable of furnifhing an argument to the fuperficial architect
for the feeking of new beauties from the excurfions of his own
imagination. For in all thofe licences the Greeks kept fteadily
to the principle of a confiftent order, never incumbering it with
that which did not belong to the purity of it's idea. If they bereft it of fome of it's members, if they increafed others, if they
altered proportions, they never introduced confufion.

It will naturally be fuppofed that in the management of defign
with fo much care and thought as the Greeks have manifefted
and particularly in the production of thofe harmonious effects of
which we have fpoken, the knowledge of perfpective muft have
been accurately underftood, and ftudioufly cultivated by them.

We have hitherto avoided to enter on this fubject, even when
we were fpeaking of their paintings, becaufe, however difcriminated may be that procefs of perfpective, which reprefents bodies
on a flat furface, and throws them at various diftances, from that
which gives the view of objects, whether round or angular, rifing
in the horizon and terminating there in certain lines, all the prin-

ciples branching from one and the same science must necessarily be intimately connected ; and therefore we thought it best to reserve the whole, both as to painting and architecture, for one general discussion. And that discussion was left to be taken in this place, because the perspective of the Grecian architecture stands on decided evidences; whereas that of their paintings is brought home to us by more slender facts, the depredations of time having left us, there, as we might naturally expect, more to infer than to know by positive proofs. In these last their powers of perspective has been made a question among moderns. Hamilton has not scrupled to assert *, that perspective is to be reckoned entirely among the improvements of modern times, that the mathematics of the ancients did not involve the principles of that science, and that wherever it appeared among them. it was pursued more by the judgement of the eye than by any certain rules. It is true, that we have none of their books on that subject, by which we can judge of their principles in it, except a treatise of Euclid, which was too late in time under the Ptolemies to be applied to the flourishing days of the arts in Greece: that others more ancient had written upon it, we learn from Vitruvius ; but to what extent of system their principles went, we know not, as those treatises are lost. Yet it is not from the want of those evidences that we ought to conclude any thing on this subject, and especially to the prejudice of their knowledge. That conclusion seems to have been chiefly led by the style of their bals-reliefs ; from whence an inference has grown, that all their figures in their paintings were very much disposed in the same manner, that is, whole, and on the same ground, and either not much in groups, or those groups afforded very little of the

* See the preface to his Treatise on Perspective.

perfpective of a graduating diftance. Whatever foundation there may be, in fact, for thefe fpecifications of their want of perfpective in painting, yet when they are drawn as inferences from bafs-reliefs, they can never be regular. We have already had occafion to remark on the very confined capacity of per-fpective, which either belongs to works in bafs-relief, or has been exemplified in them at any time. How that comes to pafs is not material to the queftion, what was the fkill of the Grecian pain-ters in perfpective, and therefore it ought not to prejudge that queftion.

There are other evidences which will affift us more clofely in the progrefs of that queftion. It appears that in early days thofe Grecian painters, who applied themfelves to fcenery, had acqui-red fo much of perfpective as enabled them to give all the effects of it to thofe objects which they introduced into their fcenes. The authority for this is quite fufficient, as it refts on the invetigation of Vitruvius, who tells us in the preface to his 7th book, that when Æfchylus wrote his tragedies, which was about the time when Xerxes invaded Greece, " Agatharcus made fcenes, and left a " treatife upon them ; and that after him Democritus and Anax- " agoras went ftill further in that way, fhewing the power of " imitating Nature by making all the lines to vanifh to one " point as to a centre, when viewed at a fixed diftance : by which " means they were enabled to reprefent in their fcenes the images " of real buildings, as they ufually appear to the eye ; whether " they were painted on horizontal or upright furfaces, they " exhibited objects near and at a diftance." This authority, al-though it fpecifies the reprefentations of buildings among other objects, yet comes very home to the point of our enquiry ; and much nearer to that point we conceive, than many of the argu-

ments advanced by an ingenious modern advocate* for the powers of the Grecian painters in perfpective. When the authority
we have quoted exprefsly defcribes thofe powers to be " the
" making all the lines to vanifh to one point as to a centre, when
" viewed at a fixed diftance ;" what more can befpeak the fyftematic principles of perfpective?

And yet none of thofe Grecian paintings, which time has left
to modern ages, appear to have reached that character of perfpective, which is given by Vitruvius to the two fcenifts above-
mentioned. The drinking pigeons, now preferved at Rome,
are unqueftionably proved to be thofe " wonderful pigeons" of
which Pliny has fpoken†, and confequently they were the work
of that Sofus of Pergamus, who was the moft celebrated artift in
Greece for works in mofaic, of which thofe pigeons are a moft
charming example. Works in mofaic have always been confidered as a clafs of painting, no matter whether properly or not ;
but fo far as perfpective may be concerned in them, there can be
no objection to their being fo confidered. Thofe pigeons are
perched on the edge of a bowl filled with water, which bowl is
placed upon a table. One of them is drinking, the fhade of
whofe head and neck beautifully dyes the water : two others
have drunk, and are feen in the various action either of fwallow-
ing the water, or of picking themfelves, while they are bafk-
ing in the fun. Nothing can be more admirable and complete
than the whole action and expreffion of the birds themfelves.
But the vanifhing point of view in the bowl and in the table is
by no means one and the fame, although they are prefented in
the fame direction. It is true, that mofaics have never been

* Webb, on Ancient Painting.   † Lib. 36. c. 60.

rated equally high with the works of the pencil, and confequently the talents difplayed by artifts in that way may be confidered as no fair criterion of thofe which are poffeffed by celebrated painters. But the talents, which could execute fo admirably the pofition and attitudes of thofe birds themfelves, together with the deceptions of the bowl and of the table, and which evidently aimed at a perfpective in all, could as eafily have furnifhed that perfpective on fcientific principles, as in an irregular manner, if the former had been underftood. And it muft be recollected that Sofus was no inferior artift, but at the head of all others in his own line of profeffion.

It is the want of that one vanifhing point, and oftentimes of a vanifhing or degradation at all in the affemblage of objects, which meet us in thofe otherwife delightful fubjects of painting drawn from Herculaneum, and Pompeii, and Stabia, which are now in the mufeum of Portici *. We confider thofe paintings as the works of Greek artifts, becaufe the names of many of thofe artifts appear there, and we have no doubt from abundance of collateral circumftances, that all thofe paintings, or at leaft the beft of them, were executed by artifts called from Greece †. There are among them numerous groups; but they all appear to be very much on the fame ground, and to exhibit but imperfectly that degradation which is produced by diftance. Where fome of thofe fcenes are filled up by architecture, with figures appearing in the openings, there feems to be more of perfpective; and that looks as if the practice of it were eafier to them in lines and angles than in the figures of bodies. In all thofe fub-

---

* See Le Antichita di Ercolano, 4to. Roma, 1789, Tomaffo Piroli; a fmaller edition correfpondent to the grander one in the library of the king of Naples.

† See D'Ancarv. vol. 2. p. 16.

jects we cannot pronounce that there are any, which appear to have only one point of fixed view. In landscapes, one should certainly expect to find that point; and an intelligent traveller *, who has lately gone through the Two Sicilies with very attentive observation, remarks expressly on some paintings of that kind which had been found in the ruins of Pompeii, that he was not able to discover in them any systematical knowledge of perspective. Let it be said, and taken for granted, as that writer has candidly suggested, that those paintings must not be set down as the works of the first Grecian masters, who cannot be supposed to have been employed there on works so ordinarily met with, as those paintings were, in houses of all ranks and denominations: yet if the principles of true perspective had been commonly understood by the painters of those times, we should naturally suppose that they would not have been found wanting in those of a subordinate class; for among the artists of our own country at this day, where those principles are perfectly and currently understood, there is hardly an ordinary painter, who will not finish in true perspective whatever scene he undertakes. And if it be added, that those paintings were probably done under the Roman power, when the brilliancy of the Grecian arts was greatly gone by; yet it is plain from the excellency of design in those works, which is most admirable in general, that all the marks of brilliancy in the best artists of that country were not lost, and that the authors of those works were not incompetent to those talents which had become universal in Greece.

Thefe things we state, as it is fair to do, on both sides of the question. Yet there remains an inference which will force itself upon our minds, or at least will raise a new question for our de-

* See Swinburne's Travels in Two Sicilies, vol. 3. p. 151.

cifion. It is this. That the Greeks were complete mafters of perfpective in architecture, there can be no doubt ; we fhall prefently find that affertion confirmed by the moft abundant proofs. It may then naturally be afked, can it be poffible to fuppofe that the Greek painters were deficient in that which was fo thoroughly underftood by the architects of their country, and which was quite as important to the perfection of their art as to that of the others? We muft allow that there is great force in this queftion. And as we cannot difpute the authority of Vitruvius, founded on his well-known accuracy of inveftigation, which has recorded their power of perfpective fo early as the time of Æfchylus, " by making all their fcenes to vanifh to " one point as to a centre, when viewed at a fixed diftance ;" it becomes very difficult to fuppofe that they, who in every other inftance moved with rapid fteps to all the perfections of the arts, fhould lofe in that particular inftance what they feem no fooner to have thought of than to have gained, and what was fo indifpenfible to their characters as artifts, that without it, or with an imperfect knowledge of it only, we have no idea how they could acquire any character at all among thofe who were judges of what was Nature. So accurately has Vitruvius expreffed himfelf in the paffage above referred to, when he defcribed the progrefs which Democritus and Anaxagoras had made in perfpective, by faying that " they fhewed the power of imitating Nature."

Leaving therefore this point to the judgement of the reader, or to the more fuccefsful inquiry of others who may obtain better evidences to decide it, we fhall pafs to the confideration of thofe powers in perfpective which their architects had attained.

It was a primary ftage, which, as far as it went, opened a

great paſſage to their architectural perfpective, to know the effects of vifion as they were produced by diftance. And thefe were gained by the fculptors as well as the architects of Greece, for the fame reafon that where great diftances intervened between the objects and the eye, thofe effects were equally important to be afcertained by both. This is proved in the well known conteft between Phidias and Alcamenes, to produce a Minerva which was to be elevated on a high column *. The work of the former, while it was beheld on the ground, had nearly caufed the author of it to be ftoned, as if he had meant to infult the Athenians by the extravagant and caricature expreffion which he had given to the whole figure of that goddefs, and to every fea- ture in it; but it became foftened into natural proportion and perfect grace, when it was lifted up into it's deftined fituation; while that of Alcamenes, whofe delicacy of execution and per- fect fymmetry had before decided every voice in it's favor, be- came totally loft to all difcriminate obfervation, and confequently difregarded, at it's full height. Yet it is plain from this inftance, that thofe effects of vifion as produced by diftance were not uni- verfally underftood by artifts in the time of Phidias, becaufe they were miffed by Alcamenes a very celebrated man, and they were not apprehended by the general body of the Athenians. Whe- ther or no this circumftance may ferve to acount for that want of a thorough perfpective which has been remarked in thofe artifts who painted at Herculaneum and Pompeii, without involving the firft Grecian mafters in the fame conclufion, muft be left to the confideration of the reader. The like circumftance hap- pened, from which the reader may draw the fame ufes, if he pleafes, in the head of Diana fet up on high at Chios†; which

---

* Tzetzes Chiliad. xi. hift. 381. & Chiliad. viii. hift. 193.

† Plin. lib. 36. c. 5.

shewed indeed the science of the artist, but the want of a scientific perception in others. He had made the goddess to look severe on those who came into the temple, but mild on those who went out of it; that is, the figure, like the Minerva of Phidias, appeared rougher as you approached it, but more softened as you moved to a greater distance : and when the people considered that effect as a kind of prodigy, they only shewed that they were not familiar with the laws of vision.

But let the Grecian architecture speak for it's own perspective. It will be sufficient if we adduce those evidences of it, which are of an obvious and striking impression. In the outside of temples, the columns which stood at the angles were of a greater diameter than the rest, because they were more in the open air ; which, without the aid of a back ground or shade to throw out the true dimensions to the eye, naturally diminishes those dimensions, and consequently gives to superior grossness the effect of apparent equality. For the same reason, when the portico of a temple had two rows of columns, the inward row was smaller than the outward. And further to aid the deception, in fluted columns those smaller ones had a greater number of flutes than the larger, because they had a new ground of comparison to combat in the larger ; for in flutes a greater number of angles meeting the eye expofes of course a greater surface by their girt ; if therefore the smaller columns did not avail themselves of an increased surface by an increased number of angles beyond the larger columns, they could never appear of equal diameters with them. But we find the Greeks actually altering the true proportions of columns and entablatures at certain distances, that so they might counteract the effects of vision. We find them actually omitting the perpendicular parts of cornices elevated at a

great height; becaufe by the laws of perfpective thofe perpendicular parts are not diftinctly vifible to the eye at great heights ;
and they are made lefs vifible, in confequence of another effect
which thofe laws have ordained, that while the projecting parts
gain in bulk by their heighth, the perpendicular parts muft lofe.

It is curious to follow the various proofs of their ingenuity in
the management of many parts of the entablature, for the purpofe of confulting perfpective. Some of their cornices project
aftonifhingly, efpecially in the Doric order, of which there are
the greateft examples from their hands at Pœftum. We may alfo
felect another example, although it were at Rome, in the theatre
of Marcellus, which was affuredly the ftructure of a Grecian
architect ; for neither were the Romans then fo ripe in tafte as to
produce fo perfectly pure and chafte a model of Grecian art, nor
did fuch a model ever come from their hands, nor did they build
at that time with ftone, as far as we can trace, but with bricks ;
whereas that theatre was conftructed of ftones prodigioufly large,
which were intended to reprefent an immenfely ftrong rock, to
be dreffed with all the poffible fimplicity of art. In that drefs
two orders were employed, in each of which the fame foundation
is afforded to the obfervations we would make. The immenfe
projections of the crown in the Doric cornice below, and alfo in
the Ionic above, were perfectly right in that great mafs of edifice, and in the ftages of their refpective elevations ; they were
wonderfully grand in their effect. In the former of thofe cornices the architect fhewed a very accurate knowledge of the effects
of diftance upon vifion, by exerting a very fingular example ;
for inftead of forming the drops which compofe the ornament of
the foffite, and fall upon the triglyphs, all equal in fize, he flo-
ped them gradually towards the outfide ; knowing, that to the

eye which looked up at them from beneath they would appear all alike, and would moreover affift in fome meafure the projection which he wifhed to maintain in all it's ftrength. In the latter of thofe cornices he manifeftly confulted perfpective at the expence of rule. For, knowing at the immenfe height in which it ftood from the eye, that the ufual diminution of it's proportion as an upper order would caufe it to appear as nothing, inftead of lef-fening it a fourth *, he gave it hardly any diminution at all†. In thefe circumftances, which will afford fufficient examples of their attention to perfpective, is evidently demonftrated their know-ledge of it's principles.

It was not merely to draw finely that this knowledge affifted them ; they employed it as architects in their whole practice. It gave them the moft fublime and precious gift, with which the mind of the architect can be filled, and without which he can never be original, nor advance beyond a poverty or tamenefs of defign. Where fhall the fpirit of architecture be found, but in a full and clear preconception of effect ? And where fhall that pre-conception of effect obtain it's radical capacity, but in the accurate knowledge of perfpective ? It is by perfpective that we know before-hand effects according to height, and according to the po-fition in which a building is viewed, whether angularly, or in a fide-elevation ; for it has very different proportions in all thefe cafes. It is by perfpective that we afcertain the different effects of cornices according to their different elevations, and of all projections on high both as to themfelves and as to what comes above them, a great part of which they will always cut off. It

---

* See Vitruvius, lib. 5. c. 15.

† See a profile of thefe cornices in Chambray's Paral. p. 21, 45

is by perfpective that we are affured of the effects of columns
from their various fituations, and are enabled to counteract the
deceptions that will arife from thence; for inftance, in an upper
row of columns placed over a lower order, which will ever appear lefs than their due proportion. In fhort, it is by the education of perfpective, that the architect brings at once to the eye
of his mind the future effects of every proportion and pofition
which he gives to the edifice, and how far beauty, convenience,
and propriety will be attained, and will imprefs themfelves on
every obferver. To the obferving eye thefe things, and every
part of his fkill, muft be accommodated, or there is no longer
beauty, convenience, and propriety in his ftructure, which will
oftentimes be loft in the error of Alcamenes.

It was then in thefe great powers of preconception that the
Greek architects came forth from the ftudy of perfpective, and
fhewed themfelves accomplifhed in all the finer language of defign. They did not move by tame rules and turgid precepts, or at
leaft they did not wait for fuch directions. They left thofe rules
and precepts to the idiots, as Vitruvius calls them *, the dull
and fhallow defigners, who know not how any thing will appear,
unlefs they firft fee it executed ; or who have gotten perhaps at
moft a notion of picturefque effect, and value themfelves upon
that moft delufive poffeffion, which is productive only of weaknefs, flutter, and falfehood, if it be not combined with a found
knowledge of perfpective.

The fact is, the Greeks were poffeffed of all the genuine
fources of beauty, which were fo intimate to their minds, that

* B. 6. laft chapter.

beauty came regularly from their hands without the tedioufnefs of purfuing it through experiments.   He that has the foul of a poet will take his flight with affurance, and will carry after him every imagination pleafed with thofe images of Nature, and that beauty of ideas, which flow fpontaneoufly from his mind, and which every man fees and knows to be natural and beautiful, and to be immutably true and immutably forcible in their reach ; and yet they muft not be attempted with the fame fuccefs by the man, who meafures his movements, and trammels his conceptions. A great mufician will carry captive every heart with thofe juft, and delicate, and infinitely varied touches of expreffion, which although correct to the laws of mufic, yet carry the features of ftrong originality ;—features far more affecting, becaufe they are original, and more fublime too than will ever be reached by him, whofe foul cannot move without labour and ftudy to all that harmony can give.   That fpirit of poetry, that fpirit of harmony, the Grecian architects had tranfplanted into their fcience; all the fources of ftrong and elegant impreffion were the natural pur-fuits of their minds, and the happy fruits of their ftudies; and thefe they knew, as great mafters, how to felect and combine in a moment with the greateft effect of which they were capable.

But the ftudy of geometry, diftinctly confidered, formed a very important part of their character as architects, and contri-buted in a very effential manner to the perfections which they reached. This is a point of view, on which every man muft keep his eyes intently fixed, who would trace correctly the abilities of the Greeks in architecture, or who would emulate thofe abilities in himfelf.   In this ftudy are laid the elements of that art, without which all is fuperficial, fanciful, and unprincipled. We have feen how early and deeply it took poffeffion of the Egyptians,

how powerfully it fhewed it's ufes amidft the defects of much tech-
nical fkill, how happily it fupplied to a certain degree the want
of tafte, and what prodigies of ftructure it enabled them to raife,
almoft fuperior in many inftances to all the ravages of time.
The Greeks had perhaps more reafon than the Egyptians to know
the importance of that ftudy, becaufe they had feen that importance in a greater fcope of experience accumulated by preceding
ages, and confirmed to them by their own induftrious and celebrated refearches into the theory of architecture ; and befides they had
been intent on the acquirement of tafte, which they had acquired, and which might be dangerous to the progrefs of architectural perfection, if it were not regulated and controuled by thofe
principles of fcience, which will forbid tafte to be fubftituted for
ftrength, or will teach it to be fo combined as to grow out of a
juft diftribution of proportions in ftrength, which effentially
conftitutes architectural fkill, and is the firft thing demanded in
every edifice.

The ftudy of geometry was therefore deeply purfued by the
Greeks, efpecially after the heroic ages. They availed themfelves of all that their geometrical mafters, the Egyptians, had
attained in that fcience, long before Euclid a native of Alexan-
dria had deduced his profound and fyftematic demonftrations.
The theorems, which we have already mentioned to have been
made known to them by their own countrymen Thales and Pythagoras, are fufficiently indicative of further inveftigations purfued by thofe philofophers in that fcience. They fhew us that
mathematics were then confidered as a valuable part of philofophy, in whatever fhape it was embraced. But to the architect
they became the primary philofophy. And the Greeks were too
wife and profound in all things to take up the philofophy of

architecture without it's elements and fundamental principles. They would have been mad to have attempted such edifices as they conftructed, without a radical preparation in geometrical ftudies, more efpecially as they ufed no cement, which in fact is but of little ufe where larger blocks are employed. It was therefore of the firft confequence, not only that all their materials fhould be prepared with exactnefs, but that they fhould alfo be difpofed with juftnefs, and with a relative proportion to what they were intended to bear. An indifcriminate folidity is abfurdity itfelf, inafmuch as it becomes wafte if it be more than is wanted, and ruin if it be lefs ; and where it is difcriminated, but not judicioufly, the parts that are to bear moft may fuffer prejudice from an overcharge of weight on thofe which are to bear leaft. Had the Greeks therefore been lefs perfect in geometry than they were, and lefs attentive to it's principles, the remains by which we are enabled to judge of their fkill would not have endured any thing like the ages which they have furvived ; they would have been long ago, without a fingle exception, bafelefs fabrics leaving not a wreck behind. That wife people in all their architecture calculated every thing on geometrical precifion. The neceffity of that knowledge was carried even to their painters, to whom it was prefcribed as a very important ftudy in all the lectures of Pamphilus*. All the parts of their edifices, however, were fo nicely proportioned and balanced, that what was faid in humour might hold well enough in the principle, although it were not true in the comment, that *let a bird perch upon one end of a wall conftructed by them, it's weight would be felt by the other.*

Having now difcuffed the moft material objects which prefent

* Alberti on Painting, B. 3. p. 264.

themfelves to our confideration in the architeÄural fcience of the Greeks, and in their ufe of their own orders, it may be proper to make fome obfervations on thofe devices, which they were induced to combine with fome of thofe orders, under the names of Cariatides, and Perfian fupporters ; which are by no means to be confidered as an order of themfelves, but (as Chambray * obferves) a metamorphofe of other regular orders by fubflituting women or men for columns. The firft of thefe, exhibiting the female figure, were put under an Ionic entablature ; to the laft, as reprefenting men, the Doric was applied. But no alteration was made by thefe in the regular proportions of either of thofe orders, and therefore they mufl be looked upon as a fpecies or modification of either. How the Greeks came to embrace this thought of fubflituting human figures for columns, is fo well known, and is fo commonly found in all the books upon architeÄure, that we fhall not take up time to relate it. Suffice it to fay, that to eternize the treachery of Grecian women, or the overthrow of Perfian foes—to perpetuate the memory of thofe captives, whom Greece was moft proud of reducing to flavery, and whofe captivity might otherwife be foon forgotten, they were brought forward in the drefs of their refpeÄive countries, to the conftant view of the public, and of future generations, in the ignominious fituation of bearing cumbrous weights, like infenfible blocks of ftone. The Greeks might poffibly be led to that idea by the Egyptians, in whofe edifices we have already feen immenfe ftatues, and very often of women, employed inftead of columns to fupport a maffy cornice. Whether the like reafons, which introduced it into Greece, led the way to it in Egypt, or whether it was taken up there from whim and a de-

* Paral. p. 58.

fire of producing a more ſtupendous extravagance, we know not;
but in the Greeks it became a perpetuity of triumph.   They
were cautious neverthelefs in the uſe of that triumph, that the
diſplay and the record of their reſentment might not prejudice
the reputation of their wiſdom.   It was not therefore in all ſorts
of buildings that thoſe figures were introduced, the occaſions of
employing them judiciouſly muſt be choſen, and doubtleſs were
choſen by the Greeks*.   To have employed them indiſcrimi-
nately would have been a departure from that genuine reaſon
and nature of things, which was their ſtudy and their pride.
The nature of things, indeed, was out of the queſtion here, as
much as when the ſame thing was done by the Egyptians, who
conſulted extravagance more than Nature ; and it was in this only inſtance that the Greeks were induced to take ſo large a ſtride
from the ſettled purity of their principles.   They had indeed a
reaſon for it, although it was no reaſon inherent in architectural
ſcience, but a mere reaſon of policy, which for once they ſuffered
to connect itſelf with their taſte; and that reaſon muſt become
their apology.

But what apology ſhall be found for others, whether ancients
or moderns, who have followed the Greeks in that reaſon ſo peculiar to themſelves ; who have followed them indeed in the only
circumſtance which was leaſt defenſible in their architecture ;
and have followed them too with infinite extenſions of that circumſtance, which loſt ſight of every thing that could be borrowed from Greece ?   It is ſaid that the Romans very ſeldom made

---

* The temple Pandroſium is one of thoſe ancient edifices, and the only one that
has come down to our knowledge, whoſe entablature and roof are ſupported by
Cariatides.   See Stuart's Athens, vol. 2. c. 2. p. 17.

ufe of the Cariatides*, although they often employed the Perfian
fupporters. For the laft they had a reafon of their own to give,
as good as that which was affumed by the Greeks, efpecially in
the days of the latter emperors, when thofe Perfian fupporters
were feen on the arch of Conftantine, more with reference to
what had been gained from the Perfians by other emperors, and
particularly by Galerius who had wrefted five provinces from
Narfes their fovereign, than by Conftantine himfelf who had
made indeed a fuccefsful expedition into Afia againft Sapor II.
but that was at the clofe of his life which he terminated in that
country. The Perfian had been a conftant thorn in the fide of
Rome, as well as of Greece, efpecially after the acceffion of
Artaxerxes, who having broken up the kingdom of Parthia,
which had lafted near 500 years, only renewed with more violence the contefts which the Parthians had entailed on the Romans. We cannot therefore be furprifed that the Romans fhould
embrace the example fuggefted to them by the Greeks of ftigma-
tizing the Perfians, whatever they might do with the Cariatides.
It has fo happened that no remains of the latter in their architecture have come down to us; yet Pliny† mentions thofe of the
Pantheon; we muft therefore take it for granted that Cariatides
were employed there, although no diligence of modern obfervers has been able to find in that temple, which remains fo entire
to this day, any fituation that feems likely to have admitted
them. It would have been a mark of fingular good fenfe in the
Romans, if they had never employed them at all. When time or
circumftances have refcued from modern ages the proofs of their
having been employed, the event has not been unfavourable to
the character of the Romans, becaufe they had no reafons of

* Chambray's Paral. p. 60.   † Lib. 35. c. 5.

policy or flate for the indulgence of fo unnatural an idea as the putting of women to do the office of columns; which muft ever be attended with an inherent defect, even if it be fo managed that the eye can be deceived in the burthen with which they are charged, as when they are joined to a wall, and a confole is put over them, which fhall appear to bear all the weight of the entablature. But to employ them in temples, where under every fyftem of religion men have affembled to look for mercy, and fhould come with hearts of peace, muft be improper, if the original idea be retained, that they were captives, and are expofed as captives.

Whether the moderns have been aware of any reafons why the Cariatides fhould not be employed without diftinction or reftraint, we know not; but while they have attempted infinite variations, as it were to obviate particular objections, they feem difpofed to lofe no hint which was furnifhed by the Greeks. If the whole female figure was thought inconvenient, as interrupting too much the intercolumniation by it's flowing veftments, the head alone has been introduced inftead of a capital to the column, and the head-drefs has been adjufted to the refemblance of volutes or fcrolls, fo as to fall in with the Ionic column. If the whole figure has been thought too difproportionate for the other columns, the arms have been cut off to make them appear more light and delicate; and fometimes half the figure has been feen to proceed out of a vagina or fheath. If human figures, efpecially when expofed as flaves, have been thought objectionable, particularly in fome fituations; they have only furrendered up their places to ideal ones, as mufes, graces, virtues, and angels. We will not condemn the emblematic figure, when the primary objection does not continue, and it is not overcharged with

weight.   Freed from this difficulty, we will confider it as taking
a new ground to itfelf, whatever might have been it's origin in
fact, and as not improperly filling fome fituations with advantage
to moral fentiment.   When virtues are put to fupport the crowning of a throne, and are judicioufly chofen, they are an exercife
of genius which brings more forcibly to the mind the contemplations naturally attached to the object.   We will not fay that
the fabled characters of hilarity and gladnefs, properly employed
in the hall of banquet, may not be introduced there with advantage to the feftivity, which while it is innocent is honourable.   It
is a more awful idea, although it hardly concerns architecture
unlefs as a defign, and although it paffes from the human to the
mere animal figure, when the eagle is put to fupport the facred
book of revelation : but furely the emblem, whether naturally
or mythologically viewed, affifts the reflections of fublimity and
infpiration.

There is but one point more on which we fhall fpeak to the
architecture of the Greeks, and that is, the difpofition of their
private manfions.   In this circumftance, if we pay no attention
to their habits of living, they will appear inferior to themfelves
in the other ufes of their architectural fkill, and to the moderns
in many countries.   For they occupied a very great, and what
fhould feem a very needlefs, fpace in their houfes ; they appear
to have been at the pains of very little contrivance in the diftribution of the whole according to art or the beft convenience;
thofe offices, which one fhould think moft properly difpofed at fome
diftance and out of fight, were brought the neareft and forward-
eft to view, and crowded clofely together.   It cannot be denied
that architecture muft not found it's fame merely in the perfection
of external defign ; the interior difpofition of the edifice to the

purpofes for which it is raifed conflitutes an important part of
that fame, although it has not been fufficiently ftudied, but has
indeed been too much overlooked by the beft architects in every
age, either becaufe it has been thought lefs converfant with genius, or becaufe it is not the firft thing to diffufe their character
through the obferving world.   But it is that part of their fkill,
which contributes in fact to our firft and laft fatisfactions ; and
among the qualifications of that fkill certainly it is not one, to
wafte an immenfe area in offices which a mature invention would
difpofe with equal or greater elegance, and with more utility, in
a more compacted compafs.   If the Greeks appear not to have
cultivated this invention, we muft refort to their manner of living for the reafon.   The men and women did not live together
in habitual fociety, they had their feparate parts of the building,
in which they refided ; fo had the ftrangers, who dined with
the mafter of the houfe only the firft and laft days of their vifit ;
fo had the flaves, and the other fervants that received wages.
With thefe cuftoms a man's family took up in their ordinary ufe
three times the extent of building which would have been fufficient
on any other plan. Great room was likewife required for walking,
wreftling, converfations, and all the various exercifes in which
that active people were continually engaged.   The manner, in
which the houfes of their better citizens were generally difpofed
for the reception of a family living under thefe regulations, may
be found defcribed by Vitruvius, inveftigated more clofely by
Scamozzi, and more precifely reduced into a ground-plan by
Palladio.

It may be afked, how the Greeks were enabled to raife fo
commonly not only thofe fpacious manfions, but the immenfe and
coftly edifices for public ufe or public pride, and indeed all the

works of expenfive art, which filled every part of their country. In this queftion we are apt to be led by general conceptions of their fituation as not being poffeffed of thofe refources of wealth, which have diftinguifhed other countries and governments in modern times: we are apt to be ftrengthened in thofe conceptions by the recollection that the foil of Greece was by no means fertile, without great induftry and cultivation: we recollect fome leffons of their moft efteemed philofophers, which were very difparaging to trade, and contemptuous of all the profeffions devoted to the gaining of money; thefe are pronounced by Xenophon, Plato, and Ariftotle as unworthy of a free man [*]: Ariftotle[†] maintains, that in a well-ordered ftate the right of citizens fhould never be given to artifans; Plato[‡] will have a citizen punifhed who fhould enter into commerce; and both agree in prefcribing that agriculture fhould be purfued only by flaves[§]. But thefe were the reveries of theorifts in their ftudies, which, however they might be imbibed by fome, certainly did not exprefs the principles on which the Greeks acted, nor the habits of any one ftate, unlefs it were Lacedæmon, whofe military conftitution was a fingular exception from the reft. Hefiod and Plutarch have more truly defcribed the principles and habits in which the Grecian ftates were conducted, at a time when none of them, and Athens leaft of all, did make that figure in trade and commerce which they afterwards fuftained: thofe writers tell us that no labour was accounted fhameful; that no art, no trade made any difference among men; and that traffic was efteemed

---

[*] Xenoph. Æcon. p. 482. Plato de rep. lib. 2. de leg. lib. 8. p. 907. Arift. de rep. lib. 7. c. 9. lib. 8. c. 2. lib. 3. c. 4.

[†] De rep. lib. 3. c. 5. p. 344. A.

[‡] De leg. lib. 2. p. 799.

[§] Plato de leg. lib. 7. p. 891. Arift. de rep. lib. 7. c. 10. p. 437. D.

honourable by the Greeks*. Thefe affertions have reference even to the time of Solon, who went fo far in the encouragement of arts and manufactures as to make a law by which a fon was exempted from the obligation of maintaining his father, if he had been taught no trade†. It required indeed more than another age to fee Athens in a condition to profit effectually by the wifdom of his regulations. But the fpirit of traffic was then begun in Attica, although it's beginnings were fmall; and it was much older in other parts of Greece. It had been carried by other ftates to a very great extent both by land and fea, before the Athenians came to abforb in a manner it's advantages and it's glory.

The fact is then, that commerce and navigation gave the Greeks the abilities of accomplifhing all their various and expenfive works of art. That commerce and navigation had long been gathering ftrength, and by the time the country was become high in the arts, wealth and confideration had flowed in through the channel of maritime traffic and maritime power, fufficient to accumulate all that it poffeffed of the arts of elegance. The Corinthians, fituated moft conveniently for commerce, and indeed for the univerfal controul of all the Greeks, by the power of hindering one part of the country from communicating with the other, were fo far more commercial than military, that they were content to overlook all the other advantages attendant on their fituation for thofe which commerce afforded. This they pufhed to fo great an extent, that while the trade of Greece was carried on only by land, the whole of it neceffarily paffed through their hands ‡; and when navigation came to be more generally under-

---

* Hefiod Op. et dies, v. 311. Plut. in Solon, p. 79. D.
† Plut. ibid. p. 90. ‡ Thucid. lib. 1. p. 12. Strabo, lib. 8. p. 580.

flood, which they had begun to cultivate foon after the Trojan war *, it was not long before they became the ftaple of all the merchandifes confumed in Greece †. By thefe means they amaffed great wealth, infomuch that their city was called by the poets " the opulent" ‡. She was without contradiction the richeft and moft voluptuous city in Greece; and her people, fatisfied with the amaffing of great wealth, thought of nothing but the means of getting and enjoying it. It was certainly the moft honourable part of the luxury which their commerce afforded, that they fpared nothing to render their city one of the moft beautiful and magnificent in Greece.

The people of Ægina had gone before them in thofe enterprizes of commerce. Thefe may be regarded as the firft people of Greece in Europe, who became confiderable for their intelligence in maritime traffic, and who held in fact the empire of the fea for fome time by their naval forces §. They had great commerce in Greece foon after the return of the Heraclidæ into Peloponefus. They difembarked at Cyllene, from whence they made ufe of mules to tranfport their merchandife to the interior parts of the country ||. They were the firft among their countrymen who brought coined money into ufe as the medium of trade **. The opulence and profperity which followed them, the brilliancy of thofe fcenes in which they were engaged, are well known; but the Athenians did not permit thefe to have a long duration. When they were driven from their ifland by that people in the time of Pericles, we muft look to their conquerors for that com-

---

* Thucid. ibid..   † Ibid.   ‡ Hom. Iliad, lib. 2. v. 77.
§ Strabo, lib. 8. p. 576. Ælian. Var. Hift. lib. 12. c. 10. Eufeb. Chron. lib. 2. n. 1514. p. 129. || Paufan. lib. 8. c. 5.
** Marm. Oxon. Epoch. 29. Ælian, ubi fupra, et Strabo.

merce and that naval power which was wrefted from their hands.

In many other of the iflands, as well as in many cities of the continent, the advantages of commerce and navigation were fteadily purfued and felt.   The Rhodians rendered their name illuftrious by their naval laws, which firft reduced into a code the reafonable ufages of maritime traffic, and in fact the police of the fea.

Thefe then were the fources and the foundations of that immenfe wealth which flowed into every part of Greece, and rendered it's people competent to thofe immenfe expenditures which were employed on the arts of elegance. We fhall barely mention the mines of the country, although the hiftory of Athens in particular mentions very often the filver mines of Laurium, a mountain between the Piræum and Cape Sunium, and alfo thofe of Thrace from whence many individuals drew immenfe riches: we fhall barely mention thefe, becaufe they were a partial wealth, fo far as they were the property of private perfons; and if they were the property of the public, they have been found by fure experience never to enrich a whole people, at leaft in any degree equal to the opulence which flows from commerce.   Neverthelefs, as far as thefe went, they were additional means of making many rich, and of affifting and encouraging too their expenditures in the arts.

Thofe expenditures will appear to be a kind of neceffary ufe and enjoyment of their wealth, efpecially in fome fituations, as in that of Athens, where a prevalent frugality, modefty, and plainnefs through the whole of private life gave the diftinguifhing character of the people. In that city a man of wealth could not be diftinguifhed from a flave by his drefs*. The richeft citizens, and the moft famous generals, were not afhamed to go to market themfelves. Where thefe habits of living are eftab_lifhed, and wealth flows in at every avenue, what indulgence of tafte is there, to which that people cannot go without difficulty? Tafte indeed, if extenfively indulged, is a moft expenfive circumftance to the largeft fortunes; but without that indulgence, where thofe are the meafures of private life, great wealth muft become either an overflowing ftream, which muft deluge fome-where, and annoy the country around, or a ftagnated water equally unprofitable to it's poffeffor and the reft of the world. It was therefore no cenfurable part of their character, that this decided frugality and plainnefs in private life was combined with great public pride, and elegance, and fplendour. It was no wafte of their opulence, that the leaft neceffary, but moft polite, arts were fed by it's current, or fed in a meafure beyond what might be pronounced moderate. It was a bleffing, even if Ariftotle were prefent to hear it pronounced, that the riches which in any other direction could have miniftered only to the excefs of perifh-able and animal enjoyments, were made contributory to the rational delights of enlightened ingenuity, giving to their poffeffors a pofthumous fame, and fplendour to the country, when it's records were no longer to be traced.

The public treafure was fwelled by the fame means which made the people rich, and by many others befides. If the mines of Greece were a fource of private wealth, they equally helped to fill the exchequer of the ftate. In a treatife by Xenophon†, which

* Xenoph. de repub. Athen. p. 693.   † De ration. redituum.

enters at large into this topic, that writer demonſtrates the immenſe profits which might be made of thoſe mines by the public,
from the example of ſo many perſons whom they had enriched.

But we ſhall take a better view of their reſources in the regular revenues of their governments, which were great in other
reſpects, and ſo wide in their ſources that one ſhould think we
were inſpecting the revenues of modern empires. Thoſe of
Athens aroſe, and in no weak or ſcanty production, not only from
the working of mines, but from the ſale of woods ; from agriculture ; from duties laid on the import and export of merchandiſe ;
from contributions paid by allies, which were often wound up
high on various pretences ; from contributions annually paid into
the treaſury · by the · three firſt claſſes of citizens ; from general
taxes, which although moderate and even neceſſary at firſt, became after a while exceſſive and exorbitant ; from extraordinary
taxes of capitation on extraordinary emergencies ; and from
fines impoſed by the judges for various miſdemeanors. A national treaſure, fed and ſuſtained by theſe ſources, was capable of
doing wonders in the works of art, if the directors of that treaſure were ſo diſpoſed.

It was a main accuſation againſt Pericles, that he expended on
the patronage of the fine arts thoſe funds which were deſtined for
the public defence, or for public uſes. That queſtion will turn
very much on the fact, whether the public defence and thoſe public
uſes were neglected by Pericles. At the ſame time it muſt not be
advanced, that a prudent œconomy of the public finances, which
either may render leſs burthenſome the contributions of allies and
of the ſubjects themſelves, or without reducing thoſe contributions
may lay up the whole to accumulate againſt a great and ſudden

emergency, is not an important character in a great and good minister. The difficulty is, to afcertain the line that fhould be drawn between that ufe of the public revenues which calculates to render a country ftrong at all events, and thofe expenditures which give it luftre and celebrity among the polifhed nations of the earth. If the Athenian ftate was fo ftrong in the admi-niftration of Pericles, the Athenians themfelves had lefs caufe for complaint againft his patronage of the fine arts : for thofe among them, who probably could not have gained bread from any other application of the public monies, found themfelves refpectably fuftained, which perhaps they had a good right to find, as well as others who ferved their country in other ways. And what is the refult, in fact, of fuch a fyftem as that which was purfued by Pericles, fo far I mean, as ingenious merit, uncon-nected with what was diffolute or vicious, was patronized and reared ? It was but a circular rotation of treafure, which when it had run through ever fo many hands came back by one means or another to the public account, without tainting the public in it's courfe. If the ocean feeds from it's great plenitude the leffer rivulets, they all run back to pay their tribute to the fea again.

Thofe works of art were all accomplifhed by thofe who were members of the fame ftate. And they will naturally be thought to derive a greater and more rapid extenfion, when we reflect that every man was brought up to fome profeffion of a more active or more fedate kind. Socrates himfelf was bred a fculp-tor[*]. No man was permitted in Athens to be idle ; there was, befides, a high zeal of ingenious profeffion, which was more allured by the love of fame than by the thirft of gain. Under

[*] Paufan. lib. 9. p. 596.

such circumstances what effects of art can be considered as surprising? We shall cease to wonder that so many works of architecture, painting, and sculpture in all it's classes came forth from the patronage and the hands of such a people, and were carried with great rapidity to the greatest perfection.

CHAP. V.

The origin and general history of the Grecian colonies in Italy and Sicily, with reference to their culture—the principles of Scythian theology carried with them from Greece, and prevalent in the spirit of their arts—the evidences of their paintings, in the best periods, not very distinct; although circumstances encourage the presumption that they must have been eminent in that branch—their architecture most consummate, particularly in the Doric order, of which the noblest examples that are to be found in the world are yet remaining there—many of their larger works in sculpture carried off by conquerors, or devastated by convulsions of Nature—their coins and medals the great monuments of their celebrity—their admirable discretion in the impressions selected for many of their coins, or in their manner of treating them, in order to shew their origin, or character, or the local circumstances of their situation—Tarentum and Syracuse the two great repositories of exquisite and sublime genius in coins—the question discussed, whether that exquisite and sublime genius, exhibited in either of those two states, or in Magna Græcia in general, is to be set down as an original source of art, independent of Greece.

ANCIENT Sicily, and the sea-coasts of Italy, must next engage our attention, before we go to ancient Rome; because, notwith-

ftanding their vicinity to that city, their connections with Greece
were among the firft which they made, their obligations to Greece
for enlightened knowledge were of courfe very early in their hiftory, at leaft in what is known of their hiftory; and fo decided
were thofe connections and thofe obligations, that the fettlements
which were formed there, no longer following the divifions or
names of the countries in which they were refpectively fituated,
obtained from their native Greece one general denomination,
which fhewed their collective relation to it, by the name of
" Magna Græcia." *

It was the policy of the Greeks to relieve their own exceffive
population at home, or it was the fpirit of adventuring individuals among them to feek new fources of wealth, by new colonies formed along the countries now under our confideration.
They were not the firft ftrangers who came there, unlefs the Si-
cani were indigenous in Sicily, and unlefs the Cretans be confidered as Greeks, who founded the colony of Oria in the Terra
di Otranto of Naples an hundred years before the Trojan war †.
But they fixed themfelves, as fome of the Trojans alfo did, in
thofe countries immediately after the expiration of that war.
Were we to name the fettlements founded there about that time
by Diomed and others, it would be to relate the firft hiftory of
Argyripæ, Sipontum, Metapontum‡, Petelia, Canufium, Beneventum, Cuma, and Old Girgentum; befides many other cities

---

* Strabo, lib. 6. p. 253. Cluver. Geograph. vol. 3. c. 30.

† Swinb. Two Sicilies, vol. 2. p. 93.

‡ This was built by the architect who conftructed the Trojan horfe, Epeus Di-
crateus; in veneration of whofe memory it is faid that the Metapontin.s kept the
iron tools with which he made that horfe, as precious relics in the temple of Minerva. Plin. lib. 7. c. 56. Juftin, lib. 20. c. 2.

which are fpoken of as exifting, and flourifhing too, before either Rome or Carthage were heard of.

No fooner had thefe countries begun to fhew the free and independent ftates which rofe up in thofe colonies, all of which were formed on the fame freedom and independence of conftitution which they had left in the ftate from whence they came, but the natives of Italy flocked in great numbers to participate of their advantages, or to imitate their conduct by forming fettlements of their own ; and thefe were followed by Phœnicians allured by the profpect of commerce. However, we muft not yet confider Magna Græcia as formed by thofe free and independant colonies. It was between two and three centuries more, after the heroic ages were paft, and when Greece was becoming more meliorated and enlightened, that her citizens, urged on by a more general fpirit of migration, and perhaps encouraged by the parent ftate, gave the Grecian name, the Grecian language, the Grecian manners, and all the circle of Grecian improvements to be feen in more extended and thriving eftablifhments throughout thofe countries. It is in vain to name them all, which would be to go through the whole coafts of fouthern Italy and it's neighbouring ifland, at leaft to collect all the oldeft, the moft flourifhing, and moft celebrated cities in each, of which hiftory has fpoken. Suffice it for the object of our prefent inquiry to fpecify fome of the more confpicuous ftations, which reached a more than ordinary celebrity of character, and derived that celebrity from the Greeks in the periods of this more general migration.

In the territory of Naples, Tarentum ftood high ; the offfpring and model of Sparta at firft, but afterwards meliorated, polifhed, and enlarged by the philofophy of Pythagoras ; fo that it came to unite with it's natural fpirit of military prowefs the cultivation of arts, and fciences, and traffic, and the habits of all polite literature, which made it's fchools no lefs famous for the learning that was raifed in them, than the ftate itfelf was famous for the policy with which it was governed, the armies which it fent into the field, the fleets with which it covered the feas, and the profperity which attended it for ages, till by luxury and corruption all it's earlier good principles of govern-ment and morals and found knowledge became perverted and loft.

The republic of Sybaris had a character of it's own, in fome refpects a great one, in others a character which has been cen-fured. If the poet or the orator, the philofopher or the fatyrift, lafhes the foft voluptuary, the unfortunate Sybarite becomes the eftablifhed figure to his mind. And yet we are not affured beyond reafonable diftruft, that the indulgences of that people, fo highly pictured by thofe who were fure to draw a ftrong picture when they attempted to draw any, were more than what might be ob-ferved in a thoufand cities, which have been lucky enough to efcape that cenfure, when enriched by wealth flowing copioufly upon them through the channels of commerce. It is not true that the Sybaritans were univerfally effeminate, and facrificed every thing to the pleafure of the prefent moment ; becaufe, without great induftry, great ingenuity, and infinite attention, the two rivers which enclofed their low peninfula could never have been controuled in their courfe, and made falubrious to the people, fertile to the lands, and regular vehicles of riches to the ftate ; without an equal devotion to bufinefs, the warehoufes, and ftores, and immenfe accommodations for traffic, which adorned the

banks of thofe rivers, would neither have been raifed nor conftantly maintained. But indeed they had elegancies and tafte,
which in fome inftances were remarkable in their influence; they
fet the fafhion, in point of drefs, throughout Greece; their cooks,
embroiderers, and confectioners were famous over all the polite
world*. But they had alfo military glory, before the hafty
hour of their misfortune, equal to the wifdom for which their
councils were admired, and greater than the dominion which
they exercifed refpectably over a confiderable country.

They founded, or they reftored and augmented, Pæftum; but
certainly not for the extraordinary perfume of it's double-blow-
ing rofes † fo fingularly contrafted to the natural pernicioufnefs‡
of it's air from the quantity of fulphureous and ftagnated waters
around it. The derivative colony rofe up into extenfive importance, and fhews by it's prefent ruins how much the fpirit of
Greece was cherifhed within it, although by it's great diftance
it's people were wont to confider themfelves as banifhed from
their native Grecian fhores§.

The commonwealth of Locri, which was founded by Locrians
in Greece, and on the fcite of whofe city the prefent Gerace is
fuppofed to ftand, not only became confiderable by it's territory
and it's force, but was beheld with admiring eyes by the furrounding people, and even by the mother-country, for the code of
laws which was given it by Zaleucus, and which was pronounced
to be a mafter-piece of legiflation.

* Swinburn's Two Sicilies, vol. 2. p. 154.
† Biferique rofaria Pæfti. Virg.   Odorati rofaria Pæfti. Propert.
‡ Strabo and Martial take notice of this circumftance.
§ Swinb. Two Sicilies, vol. 3. p. 197.

In Sicily we might fpeak of Naxus, the oldeft colony in point of time, if Strabo's opinion be right, that Zancle was founded by thofe Naxians* ; which feems to be difputed by others, who give the Zancleans from Eubæa an antiquity as old as the age of Ogyges †. We might fpeak of Leontium, now called Lentini, which maintained to the laft it's correfpondence with the mother-country, and it's fidelity to her interefts ; and Catania, the fcene of fo much various fortune, and of fuch repeated devaftation from the neighbouring volcano. All thefe had the fame founders in the Chalcidians of Eubæa. We might diftinguifh Meffina, whofe fertility of country and advantage of fituation have fo often made it the object of invafion by commercial and enter-prifing adventurers, fince the time when it received from it's ear-lier mafters the citizens of Samos, and afterwards thofe of Mef-fina. But it will be fufficient to bring before the notice of the reader the republic of Syracufe, the emanation of Corinthian fpirit, which fooner or later abforbed in a manner the other co-lonies which have been juft mentioned ; that illuftrious Syracufe, whofe annals were, in fact, thofe of the whole ifland in which it flood ; and whofe celebrity in all thofe atchievements of genius and valour, which give fplendour to flates, could only be equalled by the mother-country from whence it had derived them all. With refpect to the improvements of genius, it is not of Syracufe alone, nor of the flates in Sicily alone, that we are enabled to fpeak in this manner. The greateft part of the colonies from Greece attained to fuch excellence in arts and fciences as em-boldened them frequently to vie with the ingenious and learned in the country from whence they fprang ‡.

* Strabo Geog. lib. 6.

† Eufeb. Chron. lib. 2. See D'Ancarv. vol. 2. p. 443, 444, 451.

‡ Swinb. Two Sicilies, vol. 3. p. 264.

But before we proceed to the difcuffion of thofe improvements
in arts which were made by thofe colonies, it will be proper to
fhew their participation in thofe fources of art, which gave the
firft direction to it's fpirit in Greece, and which are only to be
found in the principles of that emblematic theology which
fprang from the Scythians.

The ox with the human head, or the human head with fome
parts of the ox, which muft be confidered as the firft germ and
ftep of fculpture in the world, was common in the medals of all
thofe Grecian colonies *.   Over that head, deftined to Bacchus,
the trident is often feen in Sicilian medals, as it is feen over the
head of the Tartarian Erlick-Han†.   If the head of that emblematic ox was reprefented by fome defcendants of the Scythians
upon a battle-ax, he was reprefented in thofe Greek colonies
upon a fpear, both having taken that idea from the Scythians,
who carried that emblem before them in all their expeditions,
and regarded it as the emblem of the god of armies‡.

The worfhip of the ferpent was as current in all thofe Grecian
colonies as at Athens §.

Figures of Pan in bronze, of that kind which meets the character given him by the Scythians, or by the Pelafgi, have been
dug up from the ruins of Herculaneum‖, and clearly demonftrate
how ftrongly the principles of Scythian theology, in all it's various afpects, had become combined with the arts of Magna
Græcia**.

* D'Ancarv. vol. 1. p. 144, 173, 193, 431, 432.   Vol. 2. p. 113.
† Ibid. vol. 1. p. 463.   ‡ Ibid. p. 266, note.   § Ibid. p. 485.
‖ Bronzi di Ercolano, vol. 2. p. 383, 385.
** D'Ancarv. vol. 1. p. 303, 312, 327.

Figures refembling thofe of Indian and Chinefe idols have been dug up from the fame ruins. And nothing can be more certain than that thefe were never obtained by immediate communication with either of thofe nations, but by the diffufion of thofe common principles of theology, which had made their way to Greece, and from thence to her colonies *.

The reader will recollect what has already been faid concerning the flower or the leaf of the tamara or lotus, as the fymbol of divinifation employed by the Afiatic nations, and alfo by the Greeks, after the example of the Scythians. It is remarkable that in many religious monuments of Greece the facred fire is feen fupported by that leaf†, although that union of flame with an aquatic plant may appear quite unnatural, without the folution afforded by it's fymbolic meaning. The fame plant was alfo employed in Greece, as it had been in fome of the Afiatic nations, and particularly in Tartary‡, as an ornament to pedeftals of metal on which were placed the ftatues of divinities. Thefe things had all found their way into Magna Græcia. Among the bronzes difcovered at Herculaneum were fome of thofe pedeftals adorned with that plant§.

In the firft coins of thofe colonies wrought in thofe humble periods when they were caft in lead, the obolary or obelifcal monies, which derived their name and their figure, as we have already feen, from a primary principle in the Scythian theology, were in eftablifhed ufe ; and when in procefs of time monies came to be caft in more precious metals at Syracufe, fuch was the prejudice for the retention of thofe primitive forms, and for the

---

* D'Ancarv. vol. 1. p. 135, 136. † Ibid. p. 111, note.
‡ Voy. to Siberia, vol. 1. pl. 21. § D'Ancarv. vol. 1. p. 111.

principles connected with them, that thofe obelifcal coins were occafionally employed there fo late as the year 413 before the Chriftian æra*.

It is curious to fee the origin of a cuftom, which prevailed as much in thofe colonies as in Greece itfelf, and to which there is no doubt that we muft affign the lofs of an infinite quantity of thofe colonial coins and medals, important to the elucidation of their hiftory and their arts. The cuftom we mean was that of interring coins in the tombs of the dead, and fometimes of putting them in the mouths of the deceafed †, as a payment to Charon; which was a continuation of the principles, and only a fmall variation on the practice, eftablifhed among the Indians, who buried pieces of money near the ftone on which they had burned their dead ; for they did not inter them unburnt. That ftone, called by them " Aritchandren," anfwered to the Charon of the Greeks both in the mother-country and in the colonies‡.

Thefe facts are fufficient to connect with all thofe colonies the progrefs of thofe Scythian principles, which we have feen prevalent in the fpirit of the arts in every quarter of the world thro' which we have paffed. We fhall now inquire more clofely into the progrefs which thofe arts, or any of them, appear to have made in the moft brilliant of thofe colonies.

Much darknefs is undoubtedly thrown over this inquiry by the almoft univerfal ruin which has covered the greateft part of thofe

* D'Ancarv. vol. 1. p. 14, 15, 19, 20, 21.

† Lucian de Luct. p. 430.   Swinb. Two Sicilies, vol. 4. p. 93.

‡ Sonnerat's Voy. vol. 1. p. 90.   D'Ancarv. vol. 1. p. 443.   Vol. 2. p. 41, 46, 47, 94, 175.

Grecian fettlements ; fo that we muft be content to form our views on thofe fcattered hints which are fupplied by cafual circumftances, or by the remains of more durable art which time has left to us. The works of the pencil muft have met a feverer fate than any others. In the earlier ages of thofe ftates it cannot be thought that any fuch works were produced among them with confiderable merit. The epoch, which hiftory has given for the general eftablifhment of thofe ftates, is between 700 and 800 years before the Chriftian æra ; much about the time which produced the picture of Bularchus in Greece. If the reader recollects the obfervations which have been made on that picture, and on the ftate of painting at that time in Greece ; and if he calls to mind the affertion of Pliny, that "before the time " of Apollodorus there was no painting in that country worthy " to detain the eye;" it will fhorten at once any difcuffion on the ftate of the pencil within the fame periods in Magna Græcia, even if we could fuppofe that in the earlier days of their new fituation they had leifure, and inclination, and encouragement to ftudy it's improvements. But certainly the difficulties, with which thofe adventurers muft contend for a confiderable time, were equal to all the public difficulties and depreffions which retarded the exertions of the arts in the mother-country for more than 200 years from the age of that Bularchus to their revival after the defeat of Xerxes.

In procefs of time it is natural to conclude, that when the colonies of Magna Græcia became eafy, and eftablifhed, and profperous, their painters would rife with thofe public advantages. It is faid, but with what truth we know not, that Zeuxis was a native of Heraclea in Magna Græcia ; and it is certain that many of his capital works were placed in the cities of that country.*   But no evidences have arifen to fhew that he formed his pencil there, or that he painted there in the days of his fame. Thofe capital works might be done for fome of thofe cities, or they might be given as prefents, when he would no longer fell his pictures, as we know that he gave his Alcmena to the people of Agrigentum †, and fome other pictures to other ftates. It cannot, however, be doubted, that the emulation of the pencil which was diftinguifhed in him, and the encouragement of it which was fhewn in thofe cities, had formed other painters in Magna Græcia to confiderable powers in their art, although not equal to thofe which were reached by him, and although their names have been loft to the world.

In the triumph of Marcellus at Rome paintings were exhibited among the exquifite treafures of art which he had brought from Sicily ‡.   It is quite as reafonable to prefume that, at leaft, many of thofe paintings were the works of mafters in Magna Græcia, as that they had been collected from the mother-country.   And if it be faid, that the Romans were then no judges of good paintings, and that they were fure to admire thofe performances as the fpoils of a conquered enemy, without any reference to their real merit ; yet the mind of the mature, the refined, the accomplifhed Marcellus, muft not be fet down as fo deficient in elegant difcernment ; nor does either the felection which he made of thofe fpoils, or his boaft to the Greeks that he had given to his countrymen the firft impreffions of tafte, by prefenting thofe works to their view §, look as if he himfelf was quite devoid of that tafte ; at any rate, it is not likely that the paintings he

---

* Swinb. vol. 2. 130.   ‡ Plut. vita Marcelli.
† Plin. lib. 35. c. 9.   § Plut. ibid.

brought were not the choiceſt in Magna Græcia, as nothing could be more eaſy for him, whatever was the meaſure of his own taſte and judgement, to find his way to thoſe which were moſt approved.

The freſco-paintings, which have been cut out from the walls of Herculaneum, and Pompeii, and Stabia, and which are now preſerved at Portici, are no proofs of what was done by the pencil in thoſe days when Magna Græcia was more independent, and the arts more brilliant through all the ſtates connected with Greece. Thoſe paintings were all, moſt probably, done under the Roman power, although by Greek artiſts either reſident there, or called from Greece, as we have already obſerved. At the two former of thoſe places we may almoſt be certain, that thoſe paintings were not many years old when they were buried by that dreadful eruption of Veſuvius in the 79th year of our æra ; becauſe ſixteen years preceding that event thoſe cities were almoſt equally deſtroyed by an earthquake*. Yet from thoſe paintings we may reaſon in ſome degree to the point now before us. We have already ſpoken of the great accuracy and correctneſs of deſign diſplayed in their figures. If ſo much capacity was retained in a period, when both Pliny and Petronius ſay " the powers of " the pencil were gone †", what muſt thoſe ſtates have afforded in the art, in their more ſhining days ? But the colouring of thoſe works, and alſo of the ornaments traced by the pencil on the walls and cielings, has been conſidered as inferior, as gaudy, glaring, and too ſtrong‡. To thoſe who have been accuſtomed to oil-

* Tacitus Ann. lib. 15. c. 22. Senec. Nat. Quæſt. lib. 6. c. 1.
† Plin. lib. 35. c. 1. Petron. Arbit. Satyric. p. 320.
‡ Swinb. Two Sicilies, vol. 1. p. 129. Vol. 3. p. 151, 154.

paintings, which will always expofe more of muddinefs, perhaps in the moft accomplifhed hands, than the clearer colours
employed by the ancients in works of frefco, thefe laft may very
probably appear too glaring and fhowy. If they were not ftrong
in one fenfe, they would ill befit the ground that was to imbibe
them, and would have infured to themfelves a very perifhable
effect.   Admitting thofe ftrictures on their colouring to be right,
that colouring leads us perhaps more directly to the circle in
which many of thofe artifts were found, and certainly to the
conclufion that thofe, who were many ages before them, muft
have been more accomplifhed. The management of colouring
is a circumftance, which, if it does not always difcriminate between provincial works and thofe which are done in the great
meridian of a country, yet fhews as much as any thing the difference between a meridian age and one that has long fince
paffed it.

Architecture was fure to engage their earlieft attention, becaufe
it's ufes were indifpenfible both to their convenience and magnificence ; and time has not robbed us of all the knowledge which
we fhould naturally be curious to obtain concerning this part of
their tafte.   No where within the influence or the connections of
Greece was the fpirit of architecture more completely Grecian
than in thofe colonies. They appear to have been extremely
attentive in this matter, moft chafte in their principles, moft decidedly juft to the fpirit of the order, and moft happy in the
production of a magnificence radically genuine, being conftituted
on fimplicity of plan, folidity in proportions, and greatnefs of
component parts. Purfuing thefe principles of original grandeur, which were undoubtedly the firft that were purfued by the
Greeks, they raifed in the Doric order thofe monuments, which

even in their ruins are fuperb; but where they remain confiderably entire, they imprefs the mind, which is accuftomed to reflect on the true fources of majeftic dignity, with a veneration which cannot be drawn forth, or made lafting, where the fimple and the folid are loft in richnefs, and where a luxuriance of drefs engages the imagination at the expence of the judgement.

At Pæftum is difplayed the true Grecian folidity, and majefty of tafte, in that order. Few cities have left fuch noble proofs of their magnificence, fuch monuments of their architecture*. There, befides another edifice in the nobleft ftyle of the Doric order, is a moft illuftrious example of the Pfeudodipteros in a temple whofe parts are almoft entire, and which may be fet down as one of the grandeft monuments of antiquity now left, and the rareft in it's kind. Metapontum indeed, out of all the great works which diftinguifhed it's opulence when a colony of the Pylians, has but two rows of columns, and part of an architrave left. But no where does the original fimplicity of the Doric order appear more genuine than in thofe fcanty remains †.

At Agrigentum, whofe people were faid to have built for eternity ‡, and whofe ftate was only crufhed by the general fall of Grecian liberty, other majeftic remains of priftine opulence and Doric architecture are to be feen, although much in ruins, except in the temple which is commonly called that of Concord, and which undoubtedly was of priftine conftruction, exhibiting to this day it's columns, entablature, pediments, and walls entire,

---

* Swinb. Two Sicilies, vol. 3. p. 198.

† Ibid. vol. 2. p. 118.

‡ This was the faying of the philofopher Empedocles a native of Agrigentum.

with the lofs only of part of the roof*. Of the tomb of Thero,
as it is there called, we know not what to fpeak, but that it
feems impoffible to have been the work of ancient Greeks, from
whofe hands a confufion of ornaments and proportions, a Doric
entablature crowning Ionic pilafters, never came unlefs it were
in that one inftance, whofe general elegance in it's form and
ftyle is hardly fufficient to give it a Grecian origin.

It is to be lamented that the temple, which of all others among
the edifices of antiquity in that part of the world was moft interefting to the curiofity of modern ages, I mean that of the
Olympian Jupiter, is ftill to be looked for, as to it's minuter
defcription, in the pages of Diodorus Siculus. Of thofe gigantic remains hardly one ftone is left upon another, although with
fome inveftigation the general tafte of the edifice has been pretty
well afcertained, and fome proportions of it's columns, which
lead in fome meafure by their analogy to reafonable conjectures
on the proportions of the whole†.

Syracufe, if we are to reafon from that univerfal magnificence
which left no equal to itfelf in Sicily, fhould have furnifhed to
fubfequent ages by far the moft numerous monuments of ancient
architecture and opulence, and certainly would have done fo, if
the meafure of devaftation through all the fucceffions of it's fate
keeping pace with the meafure of it's greatnefs had not overwhelmed thofe monuments, and left the greateft part of that moft
fplendid city at one time to become the habitation of wild beafts
and birds of the night. At prefent, the ancient Temple of Minerva, a Doric conftruction, on the fummit of which her ftatue

* Swinb. Two Sicilies, vol. 4. p. 19.   † Ibid. p. 24.

was fixed holding a broad refulgent fhield, is become the cathedral of the city, after it had been much curtailed by dilapidations, again reduced by an earthquake, and laft of all marred by new and incongruous fupplements of modern architecture. Some remains there are, but few, of another ancient temple to Diana. And thefe are all which appear to have been left from the ftupendous erections of their Grecian forefathers in that once celebrated city.

In all thofe ancient remains the diligent and educated obferver will find many things to excite his admiration, and inftruct his mind. He will find more abundant proofs, and more curious ones too, than are afforded elfewhere, of that order in it's original circumftances: he will find the true principles of architecture in general on an enlarged fcale, that it owes it's grandeur to fimplicity, and to a fyftem of few parts. He will find, in confequence, that prevalent fimplicity of ftyle every where cherifhed; and yet without a tamenefs of fimilarity in all things, and without thofe conftant fhackles of rule, which if invariably followed would lead to littlenefs, and deftroy great compofitions; or at leaft would deftroy the effect of differing defigns. While the great principles of the order are maintained, he will find ingenious variations in fome of the parts, as in the fhape of the capital, the fhape of the column, and the fhape of the plinth; in fome inftances he will find a reafonable and ufeful latitude taken, as in the Pfeudodipteros at Pæftum, where the architect extended his metopes in breadth, in order to place the triglpyhs at the corner; and in other inftances he will meet with novelties, as in the temple of Olympian Jupiter at Agrigentum, where the columns on the outfide were let half into the walls, the infide exhibiting a plain furface. At the fame time he will generally find a fyftem of proportion purfued throughout the country, and what may be called without difrefpeƐt a kind of provincial adherence to ftyle in fome things, as in the giving a cella and a peryftile to all the temples, except that of the Olympian Jupiter, which being erected to the fupreme deity of Paganifm might be fuppofed to differ effentially in it's defign from the reft *.

Great and noble as the difplay of architeƐture was in thofe colonies, we fhall fee them attaining a ftill higher celebrity in the branches of fculpture. Nor let this be thought extraordinary, on the fuppofition that their paintings were inferior. The advances of fculpture will ever be found to have been earlier than thofe of painting, to have frequently led the way to the latter, and often to have lafted for fome time when the latter has been loft to a country. And the reafon is not more difficult to be affigned than the faƐt. The ufes of fculpture, or at leaft the elegancies of it, meet our inclinations in various ways; it has therefore more candidates to encourage it, and confequently more to become mafters of it's art.

In thofe colonies the greater and the more bulky works of fculpture, which were not carried off by the Roman conquerors, nor devaftated by the Saracens, were moft likely to be buried along with the buildings in which they ftood, and the ground itfelf which fuftained them, by the convulfions to which that part of the globe has always been fubjeƐt. And fuch has been the cafe, in faƐt. A more complete defolation than was experienced by thofe colonies, in all that the zeal and perfeverance of fculptural ingenuity had been accumulating for ages, never happened

* Swinb. Two Sicilies, vol. 4. p. 25.

on the face of the earth. At Beneventum indeed the fragments of ancient sculpture are many *, exceeding what any other Italian city except Rome can boast of; and when we have seen those, and what other sculptures have been refcued from ancient ruins, and are now preferved at Portici and in the Studii at Naples, we have no more to expect, unlefs in those works which are handed down to us in the coins of those respective states.

Thofe coins indeed have met a happier fate; infomuch that we are able to afcertain, with great exactnefs, perhaps every different fpecies, with all their refpective characters, which belonged to any of thofe ftates. And it was not in any other parts of fculpture that a higher celebrity was attained than in thofe coins. Many of them carry as exquifite proofs of genius and fkill as were ever fhewn in that clafs of art on the face of the earth. In them the beautiful forms, the fine contour, the elegant attitude, the wonderful expreffion, which were fo peculiarly emulated and reached by the Greeks, were as highly confpicuous as in any of the larger fculptures which came from their hands. There were diftinctions indeed in their merit, as it would be ftrange if there were not among fo many ftates; and for thofe diftinctions it is not always eafy to account, as the leaft meritorious are not always found where the feweft proofs of the fine arts have exifted. At Pæftum the medals were exceedingly inferior to thofe of many other ftates in Magna Græcia, and greatly degenerated in fact from Grecian fkill; while their architecture, as we have feen, was Grecian perfection itfelf†. In fome of thofe ftates the coins alfo bear the marks of greater antiquity than in others; and among thofe marks the being incufi, that is, convex one fide,

---

* Swinb. Two Sicilies, vol. 2. p. 336. † Ibid. vol. 3. p. 198.

and concave on the reverfe, is confidered as one to be depended
on; fuch are the coins of Sybaris, and Caulon, and fome of
thofe of Croton and of Metapontum, which were among the firft
colonies formed by the Greeks in Italy*.

In all thofe colonies one decided adherence to propriety and
good fenfe was retained, amidft all the variety of images which
fuperftition, or accident, or fancy gave for impreffions on their
coins. By their general adherence to the emblem peculiarly appropriated to themfelves, or by their manner of treating it, they
delivered to pofterity the primary features of their own character, or thofe of their fituation, the origin from which they arofe,
or the ftages of antiquity which they wifhed to mark. Thus in
the early monies of Catana, fome of which are ftill exifting, and
reprefent the double oboli united by their bafes, and fo forming
the figure of an acorn lengthened at it's extremities, that people
engraved their name lengthway on the oboli, intending by that
practice to give the reference of their origin to the Athenians
who had done the fame†. The horfe and the rider, fo frequent
on the coins of the Tarentines, tell thofe, whom other records
might never reach, the characteriftic dexterity of that people in
horfemanfhip, and efpecially in battle, to which every cavalier
went with two horfes‡. The Metapontines gloried in hufbandry,
and in the fruitfulnefs of their foil; and they told it to all the
world in the ear of corn, or in the head of Ceres, on their coins§.
The Sybarites owed all their profperity (what a pity that they
fhould at laft owe their deftruction alfo!) to their river which

---

* Swinb, Two Sicilies, vol. 2 p. 121, 151, 189, 221.

† Jul. Polluc. Onomaft. lib. 9. c. 6. D'Ancarv. vol. 1. p. 14, 15, 19.

‡ Swinb. Two Sicilies, vol. 2. p. 97, 99.

§ Ibid. p. 120.

they had with great pains fubdued, and which they very well recorded by the bull with his head turned back upon his fhoulder[*]. The people of Croton immortalized their relation, or their fuppofed relation, to Hercules by his figure ftrangling the lion[†]. Thofe of Leontium recorded the truth or the fable, that wheat grew wild in their country, by the ears or grains of that corn[‡]. And thofe of Agrigentum marked the towering fpirit which left them for fome time no fuperior throughout Sicily, Syracufe excepted, by the eagle devouring all things within it's reach and within it's power in the elements around it, fometimes the fowls of the air, fometimes leffer animals that creep or run on the earth, and fometimes the fifhes of the feas[§]. The objects of the Syracufans were too high and multifarious to be expreffed by any one emblem, and therefore their coins abound with all that is grand in idea to a martial, a naval, and an exalted people[‖]. Meffina took it's name long after the reft, being fo called by Anaxilas the tyrant of Rhegium, who was a native of Meffene in Peloponnefus, and feized upon this colony. Before that event it was called Zancle; and there appear to be coins incufi, while it went by that name. On the change of it's denomination, it's coins of courfe took a new title, and a new device, undoubtedly to record it's firft connection with Anaxilas. But what was that device? It will appear a very fingular one, and yet it difcovers great dexterity to evade the direct acknowledgement of their own fubjection. Anaxilas is faid to have brought the firft hares into Sicily, and to have favoured the Meffinians in the firft inftance with that breed: that animal ac-

---

* Swinb. Two Sicilies, vol. 2. p. 151.   † Ibid. p. 189.
‡ Ibid. vol. 4. p. 66, 67.   § Ibid. p. 4.   ‖ Ibid. p. 74—86.

cordingly obtained a place in their fubfequent coins, almoft without an exception*.

At Tarentum the moft brilliant fituation in the Italian part of Magna Græcia, and at Syracufe the predominant power of Sicily, our inquiries will be fufficiently fatisfied of that exquifite tafte and fkill which the Grecian genius was capable of bringing forth upon coins. Thofe were the two great repofitories of art which created the greateft notice of the Romans, and firft opened their eyes upon thofe elegant works. If there has been any general fuperiority in the coins of either, it has been thought to preponderate in favour of the latter. " Beyond thofe of Syra-'' cufe," fays the Abbé Winkelman, " no mortal idea can got". Whether Raphael, in the forming of his mind to the fublime from the ftudy of the ancients, ever faw thofe coins, or not, it is im- poffible to fay : if he had not feen them, certainly there was but a fcarcity of beauty before him in that ftudy, as the beft ftatues, Laocoon excepted, were not then difcovered ; and fo much the greater muft have been the ftrength of his own mind, fo much the more muft it have been endowed by Nature with a fenfe of beauty, in it's fublimeft views, when he was capable of rifing fo near to a level with the Greeks from fo little of their works which was afforded to his contemplation. He complained indeed of that fcar- city of beauty : but that complaint would have been needlefs on an enlarged acquaintance with the coins of Syracufe, or of Taren- tum, or of the other free-ftates in general. In thofe coins the forms are above Nature, or they are fuch as Nature muft be peculiarly affembled to create. In faſt, they flowed from the Grecian mind, matured and elevated to that creation, as fpontaneoufly and na-

* Swinb. Two Sic. vol. 4. p. 155, 196, 197.   † Inftruſt. for the Connoiffeur.

turally as every elegance, which the clay receives, proceeds
from the hands of the potter.

Were the Syracufans then, or the Tarentines, or any other
of thofe free-ftates, original in thefe powers of art? Are we to
confider them as a new and independent fource, from which the
fine arts have flowed, or only as contributing to extend and enlarge the great fource of thofe arts which refted in Greece?
When we are doing juftice to the claims of any people for a
fhare in the progrefs of thofe arts, this queftion is entitled to
fome difcuffion. It cannot be advanced that colonifts muft for
ever be indebted to their mother-country for every progrefs in
knowledge which they fhall make, and that they can never be
confidered as original in any of thofe cultivations which may be
fhared by the country from which they came. Still the determination of this point will reft very much on the nature of the
knowledge or fcience in which they have become confpicuous,
and on the circumftances around them which may be fairly
conceived to effe\ct their progrefs in that knowledge or fcience.
To fpeak more clofely. · It is true, that in a part of thofe Grecian colonies great originality was manifefted in the fcience of
phyfic and furgery. Democides was the firft who dared to amputate a limb, in order to fave a life*. And this might very
well happen, without being indebted to the mother-country,
becaufe it was to be acquired by ftudy, rightly direct\ed, and
accurately confirmed by anatomical refearches, which in any
part of the earth would have been attended with the fame fuccefs. If Pythagoras was not a native of Croton, at leaft that
was his fixed place of refidence after his travels, and there was

* Swinb. Two Sicilies, vol. 2. p. 188.   † Ibid.

his fchool. It is faid,* that from him came the difcovery of that difpofition in the folar fyftem, which with fome modifications has been revived by Copernicus, and is now univerfally received as moft agreeable to Nature and experiment. And in this he certainly might be perfectly original without the help of Greece, becaufe it was to be gathered from ftudy, and from that comprehenfive and clofe inveftigation of philofophic principles, to which not Greece could lead him, but the mundane fyftem. In many other circumftances of virtuous and of valorous enterprize, if fuch in any ftage of perfection can at any time be called original, fome of thofe colonifts went far beyond the general race of Greeks in the mother-country. They carried the Olympic prizes before others, and it was a common proverb, that the firft of the Greeks was the laft of the Crotoniates†.

But there is no parallel between thefe cafes, or any others that depend on ftudy and refearch, and that of the elegant arts. No man can throw himfelf into a corner of the earth, or into a public part of it where thofe arts are not familiarly feen, and become a great mafter of their perfections, although there fhould happen to be fome well qualified to inftruct him. He muft have thofe arts before his eyes, he muft converfe with the firft mafters, and muft have time to contemplate the various circumftances which entered into the compofition and perfections of individual works, and which nothing but a perfonal infpection can give him. By thofe means he may indeed go beyond the men whofe works he contemplates, and may become another Corregio in new powers. But without thofe means and opportunities he can do nothing. Without thofe means and oppor-

* Swinb. Two Sicilies, vol. 2. p. 188.   † Ibid.

tunities the fine arts have never been diffused nor acquired in the world, since the time when by human institution or divine suggestion their first principles were caught. The Egyptians were trained by the progress which the Asiatics had made before them; the Greeks were led on to greater skill by the Egyptians, and their works; and every nation, which has since cultivated those arts, has been formed more or less by the works of the Greeks.

But it may be said, that Greece itself was confessedly original in the powers to which it carried the fine arts, although it had been trained by the Egyptians: and why then, it may be asked, should not the free-states of Magna Græcia be considered as original too, although we suppose them to have been trained at first by their native Greece, since they afterwards carried those arts to the most exquisite refinement in some of their branches, at a great distance from those to whom they were originally allied?

This argument will best be separated by the following question: what powers of originality, say particularly in sculpture, did those free-states or any of them exhibit?

So far as they were able to produce what was never produced in Greece, nay, so far as they were able in style to go beyond what the Greeks have reached, let them be set down as acting on original genius. But there was no power displayed in their coins, which was not to be seen in the sculptures of Greece. All that exquisite combination of genius and skill displayed in those coins, " beyond which no mortal idea can go," was found equally great in the best sculptures of their native country.

It is important in this case to know, that in the first process of their coinage for the obtaining of an impreffion by engraving formed in a mould, neither Italy nor Sicily knew any thing of that matter until it was communicated to them from Greece by Janus, who brought a colony into Italy 1363 years before our æra [*]. Not one of the Grecian colonies in thofe countries, except it were Zancle, was founded within 500 years after that period : and fome time before they were founded, the art of ftriking gold and filver coins was difcovered in Greece by Phidon of Argos, 895 years before Jefus Chrift, and 137 years before the fettlement of Syracufe [†]. Zancle, being much older than the reft in it's foundations, was more forward than all of them in that method of ftriking it's coins after the difcovery of Phidon; for it appears to have ftruck them in 32 years after that difcovery, that is, 863 years before our æra [‡]. Sicily therefore may be acknowledged to have obtained that art before Italy, but certainly not before Greece. And in the more comprehenfive execution of their fculpture, whether on thofe coins or otherwife, it fhould be remembered that fifty years before Syracufe was founded, the coffer of Cypfelus had been wrought at Corinth ;—that coffer, which had reached the exemplification of ideal beauty, and was equal to any of the fculptures of Italy in the 15th century. We are therefore to confider the progrefs of art in Corinth, of which Syracufe was an emanation, as carried into Sicily by thofe who founded that colony, and as forming it's tafte in the very firft inftance.

If any of the exquifite coins of Tarentum or Syracufe can be proved to be the productions of ages in which the Grecian fculpture was known to be inferior, then let thofe ftates by all means

---

* D'Aancarv. vol. 1. p. 33, 34, 439, 440.

† Ibid. vol. 2. p. 397, 435, 437, 441, 448, 449.

‡ Ibid. p. 443.

be fet down as acting on original genius, and let us at once reverfe our ideas, and no longer confider thofe ftates as helped and
trained by Greece in the elegancies of polite art, but Greece
herfelf as meliorated by thofe ftates, and deriving confiderable
elegance from them. If, for inftance, it could be proved that
any of the accomplifhed coins of Syracufe were done long before the time of Gelo, it would change very much the fhape of
our argument, although we fhould not forget that the very firft
principles of fculpture, which were given to Sicily, were brought
there by Dædalus, who did many works both as a fculptor and
an architect for Cocalus then king of that ifland. But the hiftory of Syracufe is univerfally obfcure for the two firft ages that
elapfed between it's foundation and the time of Gelo. Thofe
ages feem to have been employed in the cultivation of domeftic
ftrength, fecurity, and profperity, rather than in fcenes of external
policy or ambition, till that great defender arofe, who firft gave
the Syracufans to know their real power and importance by de-
feating the Carthaginians, the allies of that Perfian monarch who
was then gone forth to overthrow their mother-country. Here
therefore was the epoch, from which Syracufe began to be acquainted with great events. The ingenuity of a people, fuccefsful in great events, naturally rifes with the advantages that
follow. It is not improbable, that whatever proofs that ingenuity might have given of itfelf in the earlier periods of their
hiftory, it became winged with new fpirit to exert itfelf in the
growing renown of the country. But then mark the connection
of things : chronology will often throw the beft light on caufes
and events. Gelo was cotemporary with Phidias, or, there were
not ten years at moft between the period of fame to each. The
deliverance of Syracufe from the Carthaginians was on the fame
day with the battle of Thermopylæ, in Greece, which preceded

only by a few months the total defeat of the Perfians. If the artifts of Greece, on it's deliverance from Xerxes, felt the encouragements (as we have already fhewn they did) which pufhed them forward to every energy of which they were capable ; why might not the fimilar fortune of Syracufe, at the fame moment of time, and fpringing from the fame caufe, produce the fame effects there, and become the æra of life to the arts of that city ?

But did the arts then in either country become fo great at once ? No. That was impoffible. The Jupiter of Phidias was the production of efforts which the Greeks had been making (as we have already fhewn) for 200 years from the time when fculpture had begun to affume fome portions of merit. Thofe artifts therefore had been working their way to perfection from the period (to go no further back) in which Syracufe was founded.

Whatever was the precife progrefs of fculpture among the Greeks at that period, fhall it be fuppofed that the emigrants, who founded that city, were then more perfect in fculpture than their brethren whom they left in Greece ? If in the long interval of time between that period and the age of Gelo, it be faid that the Syracufans had acquired very confiderable merit in that art; fo had the Greeks too, for the principles and the efforts of tafte had then been working powerfully to the production of the Jupiter of Phidias. If it be advanced, that in any ftage of that interval, too early for the confummation of that fkill which appeared in Greece under Phidias, the Syracufans had completed all that exquifite perfection which is given to their coins ; then muft it be fhewn from what other theatre of the arts they had it, or one of thefe confequences muft follow ; they either had it by watching the progrefs of Greece, or they wrought a miracle, not having within themfelves equally eftablifhed refources with Greece for carrying on it's improvements.

But they acquired it undoubtedly from their communication with Greece. All the circumftances attending thofe colonies plainly fhew that, however feparated by diftance, they were one with the mother-country in all things. The Greeks fettled in Magna Græcia became neither Italians nor Sicilians, but remained Greeks for ever. Their habits and manners were all Greek: to this hour all the modes of drefling the hair, which are feen on the Grecian coins, are kept up among the lower order of females in Naples*. The very form and model of the Greek character is not yet loft: in the fifhermen of Santa Lucia is feen the true old Grecian feature, and elegance of perfon, which might ftill ferve as a fubject in an academy of defign†.

Their language was Greek, and continued to be fo when nothing elfe of their original country was left. It was fpoken without mixture, till it became fomewhat corrupted in fome places by the Latin, in confequence of new colonies formed by Auguftus in Sicily‡; and it was fpoken by the inhabitants of Roffano fo late as in the fixteenth century§.

In the earlier days of their ftruggles againft the common enemies of the mother-country and of themfelves, the rendezvous of the whole Greek confederacy was generally kept at Heraclea in Magna Græcia‖. Their refort to ancient Greece was perpetual: their philofophers and men of learning often fought the great meridian of the mother-country, for the purpofe of en-

* Swinb. Two Sicilies, vol. 1. p. 95.   † Ibid. p. 102.
‡ Ibid. vol. 3. p. 396-7.   ‡ Ibid. vol. 2. p. 164.   ‖ Ibid. p. 130.

lightening or of being enlightened: their citizens, who were ambitious of excelling in the public games of Greece, or who had the curiosity of feeing the great feats performed there, attended them like the inhabitants of the country. Nothing paffed in the Grecian councils, to which they fuffered themfelves to be indifferent; nothing new arofe, of which they did not feek to participate. Some of them were fometimes backward, and generally for preffing reafons, to affift Greece againft her foes; but none of them were backward, in their own exigencies, to feek her affiftance to themfelves. So univerfally attached were they to every thing that was connected with the great origin from whence they fprang, that at length when the Roman empire, which had gathered them all under it's dominion, came to be divided, Magna Græcia was affigned to the eaftern monarch, although it was fo nearly fituated to the weftern.

Can we doubt then, that as in every thing elfe, fo in the fine arts, fuch an intimate communication fubfifted always between thofe ftates and Greece, that the powers of the former muft be blended with thofe of the latter? Affuredly in Syracufe itfelf they muft have undergone the fame revolutions as the arts of Peloponefus; the whole hiftory as well as the medals of that celebrated ftate demonftrate, that it's correfpondence with the mother-Corinth, and with Sparta from whence it fometimes obtained generals, muft have been conftant, and it's participation in all the caufes, which concerned the progrefs of elegance among the Greeks, inevitable*.

* D'Ancarv vol. 2. p. 279, note.

END OF THE FIRST VOLUME.

www.ingramcontent.com/pod-product-compliance
Lightning Source LLC
Chambersburg PA
CBHW020857130726
47900CB00014B/907